Around the Grounds

Chris Nelson

About the author

From the moment he first stood on the cramped concrete terraces of the latter half of the 1970s, Chris Nelson has been hooked on the beautiful game. He has followed his hometown team through a landscape of dizzying highs and crushing lows, seen them slay mighty giants and watched them vanquished by plucky minnows. His journey has taken him from title wins through to relegations and from heady European adventures to the depths of administration. It has not always been easy following a team with a propensity for snatching defeat from the jaws of victory, but as any long suffering fan knows, when you pick a team, it's for life – not just for Christmas.

Chris Nelson is an adventure travel and sports writer. For *Around the Grounds* he has brought together the experience, knowledge and passion of club members, forum moderators, bloggers, fanzine editors and fans from the length and breadth of the UK to make this a true fan's guide to English football.

Acknowledgements

Additional editorial and research by Tim Nunn (Ipswich Town) and Demi Taylor (Leeds United). Also Pete Green (Grimsby Town), Mark Kennedy (Northampton Town), Matt Lawson (Scarborough Athletic), John Devlin (football strip maestro) for their Terrace Tales. I'd also like to thank all those who contributed their time, knowledge, wisdom, words and images to the project. Huge appreciation goes to the whole Footprint team, the Barcelona of publishers, who always give 110%, even when faced with extra time and penalty shoot-outs. Special thanks to the Golden Boot-winning Alan Murphy (Dundee), Angus Dawson (Bristol Rovers), Jen Haddington (West Ham), Pat Dawson (Leyton Orient), Ren Sibal (Liverpool) and Liz Harper (Aston Villa).

Rob Russell, Martyn Robinson (Accrington Stanley); Pat Llanwarne, Ian Morsman (Aldershot Town); Mike Francis, Andrew-Arseblog, Editor-CulturedLeftFoot (Arsenal); Derek Wilson, Richard Whitfield (Aston Villa); Jeffrey Benge (Barnet); Wilky OnThePontyEnd (Barnsley); Graham Hughes, Ben Tucker (Birmingham City); Peter Anslow (Blackburn Rovers); Jack Gaughan (Blackpool); Chris Deary, Chris Mann (Bolton Wanderers); Dave Jennings, Mick Cunningham, Ben Claxton, Steve Brown (AFC Bournemouth); Michael Wood, Mike Harrison, Jon Pollard (Bradford City); Jon Restall, Larry Signy (Brentford); Nick Jackson, Carl Richards, Laura Collins, Paul Camillin (Brighton and Hove Albion); Simon Rosher, Mark Knighton (Bristol City); Geoff Sayer, Ben Smithe (Bristol Rovers); Tony Scholes, Richie Crossley (Burnley); Chris McNeill, Aaron James (Burton Albion); Dave Giffard (Bury); Mike Slocombe, Clive Stanton (Cardiff City); Simon Clarkson, Tim Graham (Carlisle Utd); Clive Pearson, Simon Lawrence (Charlton Athletic); David Johnstone, Michael Baker (Chelsea); Pidge (Cheltenham Town); Richard Stacey, Stuart Basson (Chesterfield); Dan Humphries (Colchester Utd); Kevin Adams, Malcolm Wright, Lara Thorns (Coventry City); Gareth Gurney, Martin Shaw (Crystal Palace); Paul Middlemiss, David Simpson (Daggers); Daniel List, Simon Hawkins (Darlington); Martin Broadhurst (Derby County); Nathan Batchelor, Daz King (Doncaster Rovers); Steve 'Kipper' Jones, Simon Paul (Everton); Raymond Carter, Stuart Biggs (Exeter City); Stuart Mackie, Mike Blewitt, David Harris, Michael Simpson (Fulham); John Phipps (Gillingham); Pat Bell, Chris Smith, Rob Sedgwick (Grimsby Town); Adam Vital Hartlepool, John Cooper, Mark Simpson (Hartlepool Utd); Keith Hall, Martin Watson (Hereford Utd); Sean Makin, Jamie White (Huddersfield Twn); Les Motherby, Editor Boyhood Dreams (Hull City); Richard Meadows, Jake Parks (Ipswich Town); Kevin Markey, Dave Tomlinson, Maisie and Milo Tate (Leeds Utd); David Bevan, James Ireland, Scott Renshaw (Leicester City); Mat Roper, Jamie Stripe (Leyton Orient); Nathan Jackson (Lincoln City); John Maguire, John Pearman, Gerry Ormonde (Liverpool); Matt Beresford, Richard Stanton (Macclesfield Twn); Jack Pitt-Brooke, Dave Wallace, Ric Turner (Man City); Scott the Red, Barney Chilton (Man Utd); Robert Nichols (Middlesbrough); Paul Casella (Millwall); Brando, Anthony Herlihy (MK Dons); Michael Martin, Stuart Green (Newcastle Utd); Danny Brothers, Mark Kennedy (Northampton Twn) Ricky Bilverstone, Richard Short (Norwich City); Kevin Finnegan, Editor NFFC Blog (Nottingham Forest); Jacob Daniel (Notts County); Dave Moore (Oldham Athletic); Martin Brodetsky (Oxford Utd); Brian Seaton (Peterborough Utd); Gerald Taylor, Richard Wilson, Dave Rowntree (Plymouth Argyll); Colin Farmery, Tom Clayton (Portsmouth); David Griffiths, Robert Fielding (Port Vale); Simon Ostiadel, Stephen Cowell (PNE); Scott Jones, Clive Whittingham, Adam Bower (QPR); Graham Loader (Reading); Ryan Tomlinson (Rochdale); Richard Gaynor, Caz Neale, Sy (Rotherham Utd); Jim Balderson, Trevor Hannan (Scunthorpe Utd); Paul Holland, Happyhippy, Shorehamview, Sheepdip Blade (Sheffield Utd); Terry Hibberd, Chris Morris (Sheffield Wed); Adrian Plimmer (Shrewsbury Twn); Peter Gibson, Stephen Patterson (Southampton); Dom Clarke, Stuart Ridge (Southend Utd); Matthew Kett, Pete Hayman (Stevenage); Sam Byrne, Chris Larkin, Des Hinks (Stockport County); Alec Vjestica, Dave Knapper (Stoke City); Graham Saunders (Sunderland); Adam Griffiths, Alan Wessel (Swansea City); The professor, Mark Merriman, summerof69 (Swindon Twn); Chris Cox, Yellow Murphy, Chris Larkin (Torquay Utd); Richard Banks, Gareth Anderson (Tottenham Hotspur); Paul Harper, Mike Jackson (Tranmere Rovers); Steve Roy, Andrew Poole (Walsall); Andrew Worthington, Sam Franklin, Alan Cozzi (Watford); Paul WBAFansonline (WBA); Iain Dale, Graeme Howlett (West Ham Utd); Martin Tarbuck, Bernard Ramsdale (Wigan Ath); David Instone, Shaun M, Paul Berry (Wolves); Phil Slatter, Chris Holnes (Wycombe Wanderers); Simon Hodge (Yeovil Town).

Introduction

I still remember my first game at nine years old – the smell of hot dogs outside the turnstile's jaws, squeezing through a dark cramped terrace to the halfway line and emerging to view the huge packed ground. Queens Park Rangers were the opposition in this First Division tie. I quite liked their blue and white hooped strip. The stands were awash with a sea of scarves held aloft and the singing resonated like a throbbing pulse from the huge stand away behind the goal. The air was thick with cigarette smoke, swearing and the aroma of cheap beer in plastic glasses. QPR scored first, the ground went silent. I could pick out voices cursing players from way across the field of play. Then we scored. I say we, they weren't actually my team yet. I supported them in the detached kind of satellite way in which a nine year-old also thinks the Boomtown Rats are kind of cool. Suddenly I was swept off my feet, not in a poetic or philosophical way, but literally picked up by a surging crowd, lunging down the terrace in an avalanche of noise and bodies, deposited about five steps down from my original vantage point. The ground was buzzing with excited chatter, grown men hugging and patting each other on their backs. It was a wall of smiles. As the game unfolded QPR took the lead three times, and three times the score was levelled. It was an emotional and physical rollercoaster, alarming and exhilarating. Then, with the game ebbing away, we smashed home a winner – I could say 'we' for by now I was hooked: the suspense; the drama; the excitement. I went home elated and thumbed through my Panini football stickers, searching out players I had seen that very day. Was it like this every week? That year we finished in the top five, and I made nearly every home game. A couple of seasons later we were relegated. But they have been 'my' team ever since that fourth goal went in, through good times and bad, through promotions and relegations, through stunning highs and crashing lows. The names and faces of The Boomtown Rats are nothing but a blur to me now, but I can still remember the starting line-up from that very first game.

To me that's what being a fan is all about. Some people remember important years and dates in terms of world events; for football fans they're framed in seasons, games, distilled into mercurial moments of genius on the pitch or blown chances of head-in-hands frustration that bring on the well-worn mantra "if only". 1990? World Cup in Italy. We all have our heroes whose names we can recount in a heartbeat, those who've delivered for our team, and those losers who've left us reeling, cursing and cold. And that's why in writing *Around the Grounds* we worked hard to get the input of fans from each club across the country, capturing the real spirit of the stands, the real heart and soul of the teams. We've spoken to terrace hounds from the Anfield Kop to the Findus Stand, from the Stretford End to the Broadhall Way End to get the lowdown from the game's most important people; not the club itself – the fans. The support and feedback we've had has been fantastic, whether classic moments or personal memories, facts, stats and little-known nuggets or details about the best watering holes – home and away. Many thanks to all of you who took the time to get involved. The aim of the project was always to create something by fans for fans.

Good luck this season; I just hope you finish below us.

If having read the book you want to have your say, visit aroundthegrounds.co.uk or email chris@aroundthegrounds.co.uk.

CLASSIFIED CONTENTS

FIRST HALF

HOME COLOURS

- **Nicknames** The Reds, Stanley, The Accies
- **Founded** 1968
- **Ground** Fraser Eagle Stadium, known as Crown Ground (opened 1968)
- **Address** Livingstone Road, Accrington, Lancashire BB5 5BX
- **Capacity** 5,057
- **Best attendance** 4,368 vs Colchester United, FA Cup 3rd round, 3 January, 2004
- **Contact** 01254-356950
- **Ticket Number** 0871-434 1968
- **Email** info@accringtonstanley.co.uk
- **Website** accringtonstanley.co.uk

ACCRINGTON STANLEY

"Tottenham Hotspur, who are they?" "Exactly!" It doesn't have quite the same ring, does it? If it had stayed that way, then the 11 lines of that famous milk advert would probably have been forgotten forever – lost in the dust of time along with the dozens of other commercials we were bombarded with back in 1989. "That's the way the original script should have read, but Spurs objected, so the National Dairy Council picked another team," says Carl Rice, who played the lead all those years ago. There may be some Accie fans who wish it had never been changed, but like it or not, it certainly helped put the team back on the football map and it's gone down in marketing folklore as one of the most repeated adverts in history. At the time, Stanley were languishing in the seventh tier of English football – but everyone knew who they were. During the Saturday results ritual on Grandstand, as scores sprinted across the bottom of the screen, and Steve Rider brought a nation up to date on what Cloughie thought of Forest's last minute winner, there were certain games that leapt out. Liverpool vs Aston Villa, Chelsea vs Arsenal, Accrington Stanley vs Bamber Bridge. Bamber Bridge? Who are they?

But then Accrington Stanley wasn't just a name off the telly. By 2003 Stanley had climbed the football ladder to achieve Conference status – and by the end of the 2005/06 season they were champions – accomplishing the dream of gaining Football League status. As the milk board always attested, milk is essential for growth and development, and Stanley obviously took this to heart. They may have had a few ups and downs over the past couple of years, but one thing's for sure, Accrington Stanley is now established as a footballing name that's here to stay.

RIVALS

Morecambe, plus local rivals Rochdale, Blackburn and Burnley.

Greatest moments on this ground

"First was after securing the Conference title and we played Scarborough at home. The ground was rammed and we sang 'Bring out the Champions' for 20 minutes before kick-off. We had achieved 'The Impossible Dream'. The season after we defeated former European champions Nottingham Forest in our first League Cup tie." Rob Russell, chairman, Accrington Stanley Supporters Club.

Lowest moments on this ground

"Getting relegated for the first and only time in the nineties was a particular low moment." Rob Russell.

Heroes of the sideline

"John Coleman and Jimmy Bell. Appointed as manager and assistant in 1999 and have since won three promotions, taking us from the old Northern Premier Division One back into the Football League, where against all odds we have stayed for three seasons to date. Never once have supporters called for their heads in 10 years. That speaks for itself." Martyn Robinson, Editorial and Communications Manager, Vital Accrington Stanley.

VILLAINS

"Not many really but it will take a while for people to get over Kenny Arthur leaving us. He could have gone a lot higher than bloody Rochdale." Rob Russell.

Heroes of the turf

"Paul Mullin, record holder with over 400 appearances at the Crown Ground, still scoring goals to date. Brett Ormerod played for us in our non-league days, scored 34 times in just over 50 appearances. On selling him to Blackpool a clause was that Stanley got a quarter of any future transfer fee. Ormerod was sold on to Southampton for £1 million. One of the main reasons for our return to the Football League." Martyn Robinson.

Zeroes of the turf

"Alan Rogers came with a big fat reputation but was just fat and lazy – and a thug. Justin Jasckon, one of the first 'big name' signings we made, was just fat and lazy then disappeared, presumably to the nearest pie shop." Rob Russell.

"We've had more than our fair share of these. Mauro Almeida, Portuguese defender signed after a trial and came with a CV boasting FC Porto and Bulgarian Division One side Vihren Sandanski (no I haven't heard of them either) as previous clubs. A handful of appearances followed before he was released and disappeared off the football map. The number of Scouse flops we have had has been unbelievable, because of the Liverpool connection!" Martyn Robinson.

PUB QUIZ

HOME AWAY

Pubs for home fans
The Crown Inn, Whalley Road, just behind the ground (and actually owned by the club) has sports screens, a beer garden and a good mix of Stanley and away supporters. Visiting fans also very welcome. The Grey Horse, Whalley Road is a Thwaits pub and also gets packed with Stanley fans but welcomes the away contingent also.

Good food near ground
Tracys Fish Bar and Oaklea Fish & Chip shop opposite. Grey Horse, on Whalley Road are handy for those walking to the ground. Heading into town, The Chicken Shop, Little Blackburn Road does a great range of sandwiches and all types of chicken.

Pubs for away fans
As well as the above, The Nags Head, Blackburn Road is just by Accrington station, and serves real ale. Peel Park Hotel, Turkey Street is a slight detour but worth it for the real ale fan. It also overlooks one-time Stanley ground Peel Park.

Top tips
The away stand is totally open to the elements so dress accordingly – still it's no worse than it is for your 11 on the pitch!

The ground

The Fraser Eagle Stadium, formerly the Crown Ground, is a small ground with two terraces behind the goals – the open **Coppice Terrace** for away fans at one end, and the **Sophia Khan Stand**, which has just received a roof, for home fans at the other. On the near side is the modern stand that looks like a single structure but is actually split into the **Main Stand** and **Thwaites Stand** which together offer 1,200 covered seats, while the **Whinney Hill** covered terrace runs the length of the pitch.

Getting there

By Road/Parking The ground is on the northern edge of Accrington. From the north: Exit M65 junction 7 taking the A6185 exit for Clitheroe. Turn right onto Blackburn Road/A678 and right onto Whalley Road. Left onto Livingstone Road, ground on left. From the south follow M66, continue onto A56. At roundabout, left onto A680/Blackburn Road, follow onto Whalley Road. Right onto Livingstone Road. Road parking plus club car park.

By Train Accrington station is about a 20-minute walk from the ground. Leaving the station head towards the large roundabout. Straight over the roundabout onto

DON'T MENTION THE...

"Ball boys in the fields. With the Sophia Khan Stand being low, the ball often ends up being hoofed over, into some of the longest grass I've seen. When five youngsters are cluelessly deployed it does make quite good viewing, as they really have no idea where the ball is. At least they get a bit of a run around I suppose." Martyn Robinson.

GETTY IMAGES

▼ Paul Mullin scores against Nottingham Forest at the Fraser Eagle Stadium.

- **Nicknames** The Shots
- **Founded** 1992
- **Ground** EBB Stadium at The Recreation Ground (opened 1926)
- **Address** The Recreation Ground, High Street, Aldershot, Hampshire GU11 1TW
- **Capacity** 7,100 (standing)
- **Best attendance** 7,500 vs Brighton, FA Cup 1st round, 18 November, 2000
- **Contact** 01252-320211
- **Ticket Number** 01252-320211
- **Email** enquiries@theshots.co.uk
- **Website** theshots.co.uk

ALDERSHOT TOWN

Aldershot fans have been through the school of hard knocks, and finally graduated with honours. They're one of the 'phoenix from the flames' clubs, a team reborn out of the ashes of a former club forced out of existence by a combination of financial disaster and lack of success. Many league clubs have been lost through the years – Bradford Park Avenue, Gateshead, Leeds City, Halifax Town, Accrington Stanley and, most famously, Wimbledon, to name but a few. It takes the passion, hard work and commitment of true fans to build a new club from the ruins of an old one, but this is what's happened at many of these defunct sides. It can be a long road back, but Aldershot Town are proof that it's possible.

Born in 1992, the club badge signifies the club ethos – a phoenix rising again. Luckily for the embryonic club, the Recreation Ground was saved from debtors and formed a nucleus around which the new team could be built. Starting five leagues below their old level, ground zero was the Isthmian League Division Three. The new club needed momentum, and luckily this arrived on the pitch in the form of a squad built from scratch by former player Steve Wignall. They quickly set about climbing the ladder once more.

In 2002 they reached the Conference, a division full of teams hungry for a place in the Football League, and in 2004 Aldershot Town made the decision to become a full-time professional team. The season from 2007/08 was a historic time, as The Shots finally regained League status. It had taken 16 years of hard work, hard knocks and a gruelling education that saw them grow from the grass roots up. For those on the financial precipice, Aldershot are an example of just what can be accomplished.

RIVALS

Reading. Non-league rivals include Farnborough Town and Woking.

Greatest moments on this ground
"The greatest moment for the reformed Aldershot Town has been our return to the Football League. It took 16 seasons and five promotions, climbing the ladder. Although the non-league was fun, there's nothing like being back in the 92." Pat Llanwarne, editor, *Redan Blue* fanzine.

Lowest moments on this ground
"The lowest moment was when we were wound up and went out of business in 1992." Pat Llanwarne.

Heroes of the sideline
"Our groundsmen. Dave Tomlinson was with the old club and continued to look after the pitch until he retired in 2006. Currently riding the mower is ex-player Andy Nunn, who

IAN MORSMAN

HOME AWAY

Pubs for home fans
"There are two pubs close to the ground," recommends Pat Llanwarne. "Almost opposite the main entrance, on Crimea Road, is The Crimea, which has a nice garden (plus football and military memorabilia). At the Top of Redan Hill (after which the fanzine is named) by the away turnstiles is La Fontaine, on Windmill Road." It has Sky Sports, decent food and beer and also welcomes away fans.

Good food near ground
Aldershot town centre covers all your basic food groups. There's a Burger King on Wellington Road, a Subway on Union Street, and plenty of Chinese and Indian takeaways, pizzerias and fried chicken shops.

Pubs for away fans
The Red Lion, Ash Road, is large with sports TV and good range of beers. Royal Staff, Mount Pleasant Road, is a basic boozer on the hill behind the ground. It welcomes home and away fans. The Beehive, High Street, is fairly standard with a token ale or two.

Top tips
Do not park on Ordnance Road or on grass verges with double yellows – ticket wardens are very active. Away fans enter from Redan Road – about a 10-minute walk from the main turnstiles.

keeps the turf in excellent condition – as you'll see when you visit us. Promotion-winning managers – they would be Steve Wignall (our first manager, who played for the old club), Terry Brown and Gary Waddock." Pat Llanwarne.

Don't mention the…
"War – unless you don't mind us going on about all the top players who played for Aldershot while they were stationed here in the army." Pat Llanwarne.

Villains
Spencer Trethewy. This property developer and momentary saviour of Aldershot is often blamed, somewhat unfairly, for the demise of the club. In 1990 the then eager 19-year-old came to the ailing Aldershot's rescue, promising them a £200,000 lifeline based on projected profit from a future property deal. Unfortunately, his business acumen didn't match his football enthusiasm and he was unable to make good on the cash. In an interview with *The Non-League Paper*, Trethewy explained how an ill-considered attempt to save the club by settling one of its old debts with a £65,000 charge against his own home had sent him into bankruptcy, off the club's board of directors, and into the tabloids branded a fraud. Less than a year later Aldershot went bang to the tune of £1.1million. Like his former club, Spencer has risen from the ashes to become the owner/manager of a new club, Chertsey Town, under his new name, Spencer Day.

The ground
The EEB Stadium at the Recreation Ground may be a bit of a mouthful, but who cares if it brings in money to a club that has seen more than its fair share of financial troubles. **The North Stand** runs the length of the pitch and offers seating for home fans. **The East Bank**, with its barrelled roof, is the noisiest part of the ground and is behind the goal. It's a covered terrace occupied half by home fans, with away fans sharing the stand and the southeast corner of the ground, wrapping around into the eastern side of the South Stand. **The South Stand** has a section of covered seating that straddles the halfway line. At the far end, behind the other goal, is the **High Street Terrace**, an open stand for home fans with a new electronic message board.

Getting there
By road/Parking Right in the centre of the town, the stadium can be accessed from both the M25 and the

M3. From the M3, exit junction 4 following the A331 for A323/Farnham/Farnborough/Aldershot for just over five miles. Take the A323 exit and follow the A323/Ash Road, becoming the High Street. The ground is on the right. From the M25, exit at junction 10 and follow the A3 towards Guildford. After Guildford exit onto the A31/Farnham Road and follow. At the roundabout take third exit onto the A331 for Aldershot/Camberley. Exit onto the A323 for Aldershot and follow. The ground is on the right. There's limited parking at Parsons Barracks car park, but it fills up early. It's better to park at one of the pay and displays or the multi-storey car park in town.

By train Aldershot station is less than half a mile from the ground. From Station Road turn right onto Arthur Street and right onto Windsor Way. Next turn right into Victoria Road and cross over the High Street. The ground is right in front of you.

⌄ Scott Donnelly slots the ball home against Coventry City.

GETTY IMAGES

That's quite interesting
"Arthur English, who played caretaker Mr Harman in *Are You Being Served?*, was club president and designed the club badge when we reformed. Other famous fans are Peter Alliss, the golf commentator, and Shaun Udal, the cricketer." Pat Llanwarne.

Not a lot of people know that
"The Aldershot to Waterloo railway line runs right beside the ground, but we've never scored a goal while a train is passing." Pat Llanwarne.

PUB QUIZ

HOME COLOURS

- **Nicknames** The Gunners
- **Founded** 1886
- **Ground** Emirates Stadium (opened 2006)
- **Address** Highbury House, Drayton Park, London N5 1BU
- **Capacity** 60,355
- **Best attendance** 60,161 vs Manchester United, Premier League, 3 November, 2007
- **Contact** 0207-619 5003
- **Ticket Number** 0207-619 5000
- **Email** info@arsenal.com
- **Website** arsenal.com

The mighty Emirates Stadium.

GETTY IMAGES

RIVALS

Tottenham Hotspur, Chelsea, Manchester United.

The Gunners had been written off before they even boarded the coach in North London. After all, Arsenal hadn't won a game at Anfield in 13 visits and Liverpool were unbeaten since early January. Not only did they need to win, they needed two clear goals to snatch the League title from Liverpool's grasp. As the clock ticked past 90 minutes, Steve McMahon prowled around the centre of the pitch barking at the Liverpool players, trying to keep them focused. Arsenal were a goal up, but John Barnes had the ball and pushed the Reds forward. A moment later, however, the ball was down the other end thanks to a lofted pass. "Thomas, charging through the midfield…" (Bursts into the box.) "Thomas, it's up for grabs now…" (Subtle lob over the advancing keeper.) "Thomas! Right at the end!" (Collapses on the floor and kicks his legs in the air.) That short burst of Brian Moore commentary has become as imprinted on the psyche of Gooners, as Kenneth Wolstenholme's immortal "Some people are on the pitch…" is on the brains of every England fan. In injury time, in the last two minutes, the last game of the 1988/89 season, you couldn't have got away with this ending even in a cheesy American 'soccer' movie with a moral. Many on the Kop still wonder to this day how Arsenal scored from a Liverpool attack, but it's gone down as the most dramatic climax to a League Championship ever. So much for 'Boring, Boring Arsenal'. Manager George Graham could be a dour Scot, and at times his side seemed to revel in the art of the 1-0 victory, but he brought silverware to Highbury and re-introduced a title- and cup-winning mentality.

Today, in Arsène Wenger The Gunners have found the archetypal anti-Graham. He has assembled a set of players who have blended into a cohesive unit that no one could accuse of merely grinding out a result. And when the seemingly irreplaceable – such as David Seaman, Sol Campbell, Patrick Vieira, Dennis Bergkamp and Marc Overmars – are lost, he somehow finds a more than suitable alternative from deep within his little black book. While many would baulk at the prospect of having to replace goal-scoring legend Ian Wright, Wenger simply looked under S for striker and called on a young player he had helped bring through the ranks at Monaco called Thierry Henry. Henry shattered Wright's record despite the early misgivings of many about his ability to adapt to the English game. Under the French manager's vision of total football, Arsenal have produced some sublime displays, their interplay is world class and truly internationalist. They have become one of the most successful clubs in English and European football with four FA Cups and three League titles, while the five runner-up spots and one Champions League final appearance hint at what could have been. And this is the rub. Watching Arsenal can sometimes be akin to having an itch you just can't quite scratch. A mixture of joy, occasional pain and a hint of 'nearly there'. If Wenger's side can click once more, and iron out those midweek losses away to Bolton in February, then they could again prove to be unstoppable – just as they were in the unbeaten season of 2003/04.

Greatest moments on this ground

"I've got to pick two. The first, more recent memory, was when Arsenal defeated Everton 4-0 at Highbury in May 1998 to clinch the Premiership title, Wenger's first at the club. Tony Adams capped the day when he tore down the pitch to latch on to a Steve Bould through ball and lash it into the net. The upper tier of the North Bank stand that day was visibly bouncing as Tony lifted the trophy after the final whistle. A great day. Then there's the second leg of the 1970 Cup Winners' Cup final against Anderlecht. We had won nothing for years and had

GETTY IMAGES

≫ HEROES OF THE SIDELINE

"Herbert Chapman, because without him it's unlikely Arsenal would be the club they are today. He was a true visionary and without question one of the greatest managers in the game. George Graham, who left under a cloud but was still responsible for the greatest night of my life (so far) – Anfield 1989. Arsène Wenger, who I feel privileged to have watched as he has revolutionized the club in a similar way to Herbert Chapman 70 years previously and had us playing some of the most sumptuous football any fan can ever hope to see."
Mike Francis, founding editor, *The Gooner*.

DON'T MENTION THE…

"The Pires/Henry farcical penalty against Manchester City. Even Sunday League players at their worst would have been ashamed."
Editor, A Cultured Left Foot.

❮ Thierry Henry, rainy night in Blackburn.

even managed to lose to Swindon in the previous year's League Cup final (*Swindon* for goodness sake!), so trailing 3-1 after being outplayed in the first leg, no-one was particularly confident. But Arsenal rose to the occasion and ran out 3-0 winners on the night to win their first European trophy. Since then it's often been remarked at how magical Highbury was under the floodlights on a European night; there has never been a more magical night than that." Mike Francis, founding editor, *The Gooner*.

Lowest moments on this ground

"Definitely the Champions League semi-final in May 2009. The place was rocking and the atmosphere electric, but within 13 minutes the game was over. Kieran Gibbs slipped to let Park score, and Ronaldo's free kick meant the game was over as a contest. Crushing." Andrew, editor, Arseblog.

Heroes of the turf

"Thierry Henry – the leading goal-scorer of all time. Dennis Bergkamp – his signing heralded a new era for Arsenal. Robert Pires – he was pure class and always scored against Spurs. Patrick Vieira – when he came on for his debut it was obvious he was something special. Liam Brady – he would have fitted into Wenger's Arsenal beautifully, shame we didn't have the team to match his talent back then." Andrew, arseblog.oleole.com.

"Tony Adams – quite simply, Mr Arsenal. Anders Limpar – he was way ahead of his time, with skill, vision and thought. He wouldn't have been out of place under Wenger's tutelage; in fact, he'd be talked of as one of the game's greats had he been playing now." Editor, aculturedleftfoot.wordpress.com.

"Charlie George – for being the epitome of the fan turned player. He used to stand on the North Bank before the North Bank made him their idol and is still great entertainment today as a tour guide working for the club. David Rocastle – he loved the club so much he cried when he was told he was being sold to Leeds. Taken from this life far too soon." Mike Francis.

Zeroes of the turf

"Igor Stepanovs – not so much failed to live up to the hype, as so awful that no hype could be generated.

∧ Arsenal legend Charlie George with team mate and future Gunners manager George Graham, 1971 FA Cup final. George scored the winning goal in extra-time to beat Liverpool 2-1.

That's quite interesting
"Before he signed for Arsenal, Emmanuel Petit held talks with Spurs. Spurs then paid for a taxi, which they thought would take him to the airport. Instead he arrived at Highbury, held talks with Arsène Wenger, and became an Arsenal player." Andrew, arseblog.oleole.com.

Not a lot of people know that
"In 1928 Arsenal were the first club to pay a five-figure transfer fee, £10,890 for David Jack." Andrew, arseblog.oleole.com.

> IT'S OFTEN BEEN REMARKED AT HOW MAGICAL HIGHBURY WAS UNDER THE FLOODLIGHTS ON A EUROPEAN NIGHT…

Francis Jeffers – supposed 'fox in the box' who turned out to have the predatory instincts of a toothless hamster. Gus Caesar – great name, crap defender." Editor, aculturedleftfoot.wordpress.com.

"Jermaine Pennant – £2million for a 15-year-old. Great things were expected; they never happened. Jose Antonio Reyes – he obviously had talent, he just never settled in England." Andrew, arseblog.oleole.com.

"Lee Chapman – he was bought to replace Frank Stapleton in the early eighties but failed miserably, and yet he always managed to score against us after he left. Glenn Helder – he had an amazing debut by all accounts against Nottingham Forest, but his Arsenal career went downhill from that point onwards." Mike Francis.

Villains
"Ashley Cole for throwing away the chance to become an Arsenal legend for a few extra quid. Being the person he is I doubt that he regrets it, but he should." Mike Francis.

"Emmanuel Adebayor – he left not so much under a cloud as a full-on tsunami. I can't ever recall a player bringing so much negative opinion upon themselves – we're no angels, but prostituting yourself around the biggest clubs in Europe before leaving for financial gain, disguised as a great football project, pretty much sealed his fate as a permanent villain." Editor, A Cultured Left Foot.

The ground
While Highbury was bemoaned as undersized, The Emirates (or The Grove) is the resultant arena fit for the new global Arsenal brand. The four-tier bowl has comfy seats and leg room, though some criticize the lack of noise. The upper and lower tiers are the standard seating areas and hold 26,646 and 24,425 respectively. Away fans are seated in the lower tier of the south-east corner but the allocation can be expanded to 9,000 for big games and cup matches with upper and lower tiers utilized, expanding into the south stand as well.

Getting there
By road/Parking The stadium is located in North London just off the A1. On match days there is restricted access/road closures surrounding the stadium including parts of Hornsey, Benwell and Gillespie roads. For details on drop-off/pick-up points: T020 7704 4030. Parking is also an issue so it is a better idea to drive to the outskirts, park and hop on to a connecting tube/train.

By train Arsenal Tube (Piccadilly Line) is closest and less than five minutes' walk away. Finsbury Park (Victoria and Piccadilly Line plus GNR) and Highbury & Islington (Victoria Line plus GNR) are good alternatives and are around a 10-minute walk to the ground. Note: Holloway Road tube is not usable on match days.

HOME AWAY

Pubs for home fans
As recommended by Arseblog editor Andrew, Bank of Friendship is an excellent little local boozer/old-man's pub with decent real ales, sports TV and a beer garden. The Gunners is full of Arsenal memorabilia. Both are on Blackstock Road. Other good choices include The Wig and Gown, with large sports screens and memorabilia, as well as the The Herbert Chapman, both on Holloway Road (accessed via Highbury & Islington on match days). Finally, Highbury Barn on Highbury Road is a popular, large, gastro-pub type of affair.

Good food near ground
"My personal fave is The Tollington on Hornsey Road," says Andrew. It's modern, with cask ales, lagers and Thai food. The usual Wetherspoons is here in the form of The White Swan, Upper Street, Islington.

Pubs for away fans
The Drayton Arms has long been the away fan's pub of choice and now, since the move, overlooks the stadium. It's, unsurprisingly, very busy. At Finsbury Park both The Twelve Pins and the insalubrious Blackstock welcome away fans.

Top tips
A residents' parking zone is fully enforced and requires permits. It is easier to drive to an underground/rail station on the outskirts of London to catch a connection in. See tfl.gov.uk for tube maps.

THE LAST WORD

onlinegooner.com
aculturedleftfoot.wordpress.com
arseblog.oleole.com
goonerholic.com
arsenal-world.co.uk

- **Nicknames** Villa, The Villa, The Villains, The Lions
- **Founded** 1874
- **Ground** Villa Park (opened 1897)
- **Address** Aston, Birmingham B6 6HE
- **Capacity** 42,640
- **Best attendance** 76,588 vs Derby County, FA Cup quarter-final, 2 March, 1946
- **Contact** 0121-327 2299
- **Ticket Number** 0800-612 0970
- **Email** ticketsales@avfc.co.uk
- **Website** avfc.co.uk

GETTY IMAGES

Take the Darwinian approach to English league football, and you'd have to say that the early building blocks, the primordial soup, were heavily laced with Aston Villa. As teams with incredible names, such as Thursday Wanderers and Corinthians, milled around playing local rivals, the game was in danger of stagnating. It needed a lightening strike to kick-start the transformation, a spark provided by a Scotsman called William McGregor. McGregor moved to Birmingham in 1870 and soon found himself involved with the fledgling Villa. He realized that regular competitive matches were needed to help the team improve, and the game evolve. At the time there were some regionalized competitions, mostly based in the West Midlands and the northwest of England. McGregor wrote to all the major clubs, set out his views and canvassed opinions. It was a kind of football lonely hearts letter – 'club director seeks like-minded for regular dates, excitement and long-term commitment.' Nobody read the fine print – 'may one day lead to mullets, WAGS and Ronaldo'. A meeting was held in London at Anderton's Hotel, and in March 1888, the relationship was consummated and the Football League was born – the world's first.

It seems only fitting that a league laced heavily with Villa's DNA should see the Midlands team rise to become one of the most successful sides in the English game. If you look at their achievements, based purely on honours, they possess a trophy cabinet only slightly smaller than those of the big three of Manchester United, Liverpool and Arsenal. A 1982 European Cup win must certainly rank as their crowning glory, their Everest. At a time when British teams were enjoying regular success in Europe,

RIVALS

Birmingham City; the second city derby is ferocious in its intensity. West Brom come a close second, as well as Wolves and Coventry.

> James Milner scores for Villa in the local derby against Birmingham at Villa Park.

HOME AWAY

Pubs for home fans

All of the pubs around the ground are home fans only, they all have bouncers on the door and in some cases only allow recognized locals in or those with season tickets.

Good food near ground

Close to the ground there is very little to choose from other than fast-food vans and outlets. Birmingham city centre is a different story though, especially for Asian cuisine.

Pubs for away fans

Close to the ground there is little to chose from, The Cap and Gown, Bartons Arms and Yew Tree do allow away fans in at their discretion. For big games they may stop away fans from entering. If arriving by train, having a pint in the city centre would be a better idea before heading out to the match.

Top tips

If you've got time or are arriving by train, it's well worth heading into Birmingham city centre for both food and drink – you'll find a better quality of both here and a friendlier atmosphere.

HEROES OR ZEROES?

⪢ HEROES OF THE TURF

"There have been a few heroes at Villa Park. My personal favourites were Gordon Cowans, Peter Withe, Dennis Mortimer and Paul McGrath," Derek Wilson, fan. Also Johnny Dixon, Brian Little, Eric Houghton, Charlie Aitken, Trevor Ford, Billy Walker, John Devey, Archie Hunter and Andy Gray.

⪡ ZEROES OF THE TURF

"I'd say the worst signings we've ever made are Bosko Balaban and Djemba Djemba. Others, like David Ginola, Stan Collymore and David Unsworth, didn't really do a lot for us either, even though they were undoubtedly good players in their prime." Richard Whitfield, fan.

Villa secured a memorable victory on a thrilling May night in Rotterdam against a strong Bayern Munich side. Peter Withe's goal saw the English champions home in front of 40,000 fans. However, the season was not all plain sailing for them. The Championship-winning side of the year before had been moulded and developed by manager Ron Saunders and he had got the Birmingham-based club back into the top flight, winning two League Cups along the way. But when chairman Doug Ellis took over, Saunders sensationally quit claiming that he would no longer have full control of team affairs. This left assistant manager Tony Burton to guide Villa to the zenith of European football, not Saunders.

While the team are again back among the top half dozen sides in the country, their ground has always had a special place in the English football psyche. Villa Park is one of FA Cup football's all-time great venues; no other ground has hosted more cup semi-finals. This figure of 55 games now seems unlikely to be beaten as the FA have made Wembley the default semi-final venue. The grounds' central location and size

VILLAINS

"Premiership referees, especially when you're playing at a 'Big Four's' ground. We've dropped more points due to bad refereeing than we have bad performances in the last couple of seasons!" Richard Whitfield.

meant it was the ideal staging place for neutral games. Its grassy heart has hosted incredible battles and some of the most memorable FA Cup moments of all time: Ryan Giggs scoring in 1999 to beat Arsenal 2-1; Crystal Palace beating Liverpool 4-3 in 1990. These, and numerous others, have made Villa Park not only a special place for the home team, but also for fans from across the country. William McGregor would have been proud.

Greatest moments on this ground

"I've been fortunate to see a lot of great moments in my football-supporting life. The European Cup campaign and winning the League in 1981 has many great memories, although we won it by losing at Arsenal and that's where all the celebrations were. Seeing Villa lift the European Cup is the greatest-ever moment, there were no second chances back then. In December 1976, we thrashed then European champions Liverpool 5-1 at Villa Park, that was incredible. Every time we beat Birmingham is great too. There are too many great moments to list them all, which I suppose is the sign of a great club!" Derek Wilson, fan.

Lowest moments on this ground

"I wasn't there, but I always look at losing the League Cup final to Birmingham at home as being the darkest moment. There have been plenty of other one-off games as well, but I imagine that as the low point." Derek Wilson.

Don't mention the…

1963 League Cup final, played over two legs, Birmingham lifted the trophy at Villa Park, winning 3-1 on aggregate.

Heroes of the sideline

"Ron Saunders and Tony Barton for League and European success. George Ramsay, in the very early days, racked up six FA Cups and six League titles." Richard Whitfield, fan.

The ground

Villa Park is one of the country's great football stadiums and has been home to Aston Villa since the late 1800s. It has undergone a steady series of modernizations, making it one of the best grounds in Europe. It has hosted a number of full internationals as well as games during the European Championships in 1996. There are plans afoot for further expansion of the ground, although the club has stressed it has no plans to move to a purpose-built stadium. These expansions will mostly involve the filling-in of the corners of the stadium and will raise the capacity to just over 50,000.

Rebuilt in the 1970s, the **North Stand** looks very modern with two tiers, the lower being the smaller; it is an impressive structure. The two levels are split by a double-decked row of executive boxes. There is a large video screen between the North Stand and the Doug Ellis Stand.

Opposite is the extremely impressive **Holte End**. Once a huge open terrace, it was reopened in the mid-nineties with two large tiers seating 13,500 of the more vocal Villa fans. It is without doubt one of the more impressive end stands in the country. There is a large video screen between the Holte and the Trinity Road Stand.

The **Trinity Road Stand** was opened in 2001 and is a modern three-tiered stand with a row of executive boxes. It's fitting of one of the biggest clubs in the country and it replaced a characterful, if a little old, predecessor.

The **Doug Ellis Stand** completes the four sides and is a modern two-tiered structure with executive boxes between the two. It now also houses the away support, with up to 3,000 tickets released per game. Previously the away fans were situated on the lower tier of the North Stand. They now sit on the bottom tier at the north end of this stand.

Getting there

By road/Parking From the M6, Villa Park is both visible and clearly signposted. Take junction 6, which is signposted for North East Birmingham, and follow the signs. Street parking used to be available around the ground and was the best place to leave your car. Nowadays, close to the ground, more resident permit schemes have come into place, but if you don't mind a short walk, it's still not a problem. There are also a few car parks that are well signposted.

By train Arrive at Birmingham Central Station and then get a connecting train to either Aston Station or Witton, the second being slightly closer.

THE LAST **WORD**

astonvilla.vitalfootball.co.uk
avillafan.com
astonvilla-mad.co.uk

PUB QUIZ

That's quite interesting
Aston Villa decided not to go for a traditional sponsor in the 2008/09 season, instead opting to advertise a charitable foundation, Acorns Children's Hospice, which is ongoing.

Not a lot of people know that
Villa Park became the name of the ground due to fans referring to the stadium by that name in the late 1800s, from then on it just stuck.

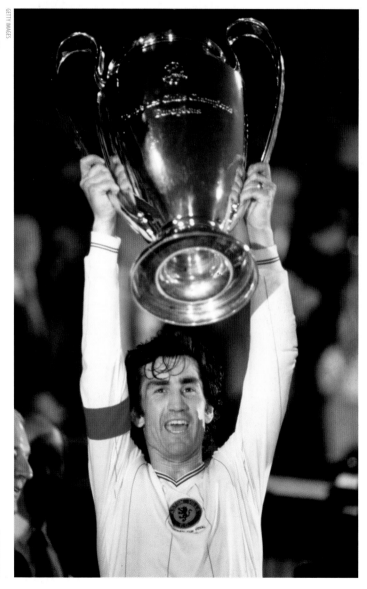

GETTY IMAGES

∨ Dennis Mortimer lifts the European Cup in 1982 after Villa defeated Bayern Munich 1-0 in Rotterdam.

- **Nicknames** The Bees
- **Founded** 1888
- **Ground** Underhill Stadium (opened 1907)
- **Address** Barnet Lane, Barnet EN5 2DN
- **Capacity** 5,568
- **Best attendance** 11,026 vs Wycombe Wanderers, FA Amateur Cup 4th round, 23 February, 1952
- **Contact** 0208-441 6932
- **Ticket Number** 0208-449 6325
- **Email** info@barnetfc.com
- **Website** barnetfc.com

BARNET

You jump aboard the train at Kings Cross with the tickets practically burning holes through your pockets – it's Saturday, match day. Excited chat reverberates around the carriage. It's not long before a stadium comes into view, bright lights already piercing through the winter gloom, dank drizzle transformed to glistening diamonds. The sight of the mighty Emirates draws the eye and sends the mind soaring with thoughts of cup draws and heroic exploits to come. One day. But it's not Emirates that really gets the heart sailing. No, onward the train pushes, on past the North Circular, to the rarefied air of Zone 5, heading northwest, out onto the fringe. New Barnet Station is the gateway to Underhill Stadium, home of the mighty Bees. It's not easy for many football clubs in London, competing with the bigger teams for fans and coverage. It'd be easy for Barnet to be lost on the periphery of the league and on the periphery of the capital. But they're not. They've built a profile that belies their size. Yes, Barnet are a small team. Their ground is diminutive, hemmed in by housing and gardens and squeezed by lawns and vegetable patches. The pitch slopes like a listing ship. Their investment's been modest. Yet they've seemingly flourished in with bigger fish. Yes, Bradford's drawn in crowds of 12,000, and Rotherham over 10,000, making Barnet's season high of under 3,000 seem modest in comparison, but they've still expanded their ground, and even managed a memorable promotion to League One. A move away from Uphill has been long mooted, but nothing concrete rests in the pipeline. It's still a great ground to visit, with a vocal and fervent support crammed into the East Terrace.

Think of Barnet and there's one image that immediately springs to mind. Barry Fry, prowling the touchline, barking orders out onto the field, arms waving in animated frustration. Like Brian Clough, Fry has always been a

RIVALS

Long-standing rivalry with Enfield.

managerial maverick, never afraid to speak his mind. His second spell at the helm here saw him partnered with the equally larger than life Stan Flashman. The then club chairman was the legendary king of the ticket touts and entertaining times followed with promotion to the Fourth Division, halcyon days, money troubles and sackings – it was a veritable footballing soap opera. Although those days of high drama are long gone, Barnet is still one of the best known lower league teams; the name still resonates. They have a solid foundation, if they can keep the local kids asking for the amber and black shirts of Barnet for Christmas, the club should have a secure future.

Greatest moments on this ground

"I've been watching Barnet since late 1999. The greatest moment at Underhill for me was seeing them win promotion back to the League by winning the Conference in 2005. We clinched promotion by beating Halifax Town 3-1." Jeffrey Benge, Barnet Mad.

Lowest moments on this ground

"Getting relegated in 2001 when we had to beat Torquay United at Underhill in the last match of the season to stay up and send them down. We lost 3-2." Jeffrey Benge.

Zeroes of the turf

"Paolo Vernazza arrived at Barnet from Rotherham in 2005. He was a former Arsenal player who had played in Europe with the Gunners, but was fairly awful at Underhill. He was much too lightweight for League Two, he kept being knocked off the ball and couldn't tackle. He's found his level in the Conference. Stephane Seanla was signed at the beginning of the 2007/08 season and was so bad he only played one game for us. His claim to fame was that he injured Ian Hendon in training, an injury which finished his career. Paul Smith arrived from Lincoln with the idea that he was going to provide the experience to help the young

That's quite interesting

"Bees players Albert Jarrett and Ahmed Deen are cousins and play for Sierra Leone, while two other Barnet players, Ryan O'Neill and Mark Hughes, are distantly related." Jeffrey Benge.

Not a lot of people know that

According to Barnet club historians, "In October 1946 the television cameras came to Underhill and televised 'live' the game between Barnet and Wealdstone – the first ever live football match to be televised."

PUB QUIZ

players in the squad. Before he made his debut, manager Paul Fairclough changed his mind and released him. Des Hamilton joined the club in 2004. Newcastle United had at one point paid a reported £1.5million for him and it was seen as a great signing for a club who were at the time in the Conference. Unfortunately, he never played for us, in fact I don't know anyone who ever saw him or ever heard of him again!" Jeffrey Benge.

Don't mention the…

"One Christmas Day, when Barnet were in the Football Conference, the pitch was frozen and manager Barry Fry was on the pitch driving a tractor trying to get it ready for a game at Underhill the next day. The police received a number of calls about someone behaving strangely at the ground and when they arrived they thought Fry was a drunk damaging the pitch. When Fry was asked to come to the station by a policeman he replied that he was Barry Fry, the manager of Barnet. The policeman replied, "And I am Father Christmas!" Jeffrey Benge.

Villains

"Mark Arber was very popular at the club but he engineered a move on a free transfer to Peterborough on a technicality concerning his contract. He lost the club probably about £150,000, which they would have received as a transfer fee for him. Arber gets a terrible reception at Underhill when he plays against The Bees. Tony Cottee became player-manager in 2000 with Barnet looking a side likely to make the Division Three (now League Two) play-offs. By the time he left we were in an unstoppable rush towards the Conference." Jeffrey Benge.

The ground

The Main Stand runs the length of the field and is a raised tier of seating that can accommodate 784 home fans. There are a couple of pillars, but it offers good views across the pitch. This stand is also home to the dressing rooms, players' tunnel and benches. At the northern edge of this side of the ground is the uncovered **Northwest Terrace**, with standing room for up to 510. The Family Stand is an area of seating on the southern side of the Main Stand with a capacity of 214.

The **South Stand** is a modern single tier of 1,016 seats behind the goals with a cantilever roof (so no restrictive pillars). The club shop, ticket office and main reception are housed here. **The East Terrace Central and South** is an area of old-school covered terracing for 1,102 home

fans. This is where the noisiest section of home fans congregate. **The East Terrace North** is where the away fans can stand, with room for over 1,022 under cover here. **The North East Family Stand** is a somewhat basic, temporary covered stand with seating for 240 away fans. Behind the goal is the tiny, uncovered area of the **North Terrace**, a thin strip of standing room that is allocated to away clubs should there be sufficient demand.

Getting there

By road/Parking The ground is in north London, handily situated between the M25, the M1 and the A1 and easily accessed via junction 23 of the M25. Follow the A1081 St Albans Road past the golf club as it feeds onto the High Street and on to Barnet Hill, passing the underground on your left. Pay parking at High Barnet tube station.

By train High Barnet tube station is in Zone 5 at the end of the Northern Line and around a five-minute walk down hill to the ground (passing the Old Red Lion on the way).

Alternatively head to the mainline New Barnet train station from where it's about a 10-15 minute walk to the ground heading along Station Road.

Pubs for home fans
The Queens Arms Sports Bar, by the Odeon, and Weavers, Greenhill Parade, are both on the Great North Road. They're decent enough spots to grab a pint. By the New Barnet train station (a mile east of the stadium) is the Railway Tavern, with sports TV and ales on tap, ideal for wetting your whistle en route to the ground.

Good food near ground
You can find a variety of food types fairly close to the ground. There's the Golden Arches and Pizza Hut on the High Street. Fresh Fry fish and chips on Great North Road is a cracking choice.

Pubs for away fans
The Old Red Lion is one of the closest pubs to Underhill and popular with away fans. The Queens Arms Sports Bar and Weavers, see above, are both on the Great North Road.

Top tips
If you really want to drive, park at High Barnet tube station to avoid the wrath of traffic officials and Barnet locals.

THE LAST **WORD**

barnet-mad.co.uk
bfcsa.co.uk

HEROES OR ZEROES?

⌃ **HEROES OF THE SIDELINE**
"Barry Fry, who took Barnet into the Football League in 1991 by winning the Conference and then took the club to promotion to Division Two (now League One), two years later. Paul Fairclough, who took over from Martin Allen in 2004 and won the Conference in 2005 and thus took The Bees back into the league. Ian Hendon, who took over last season when Fairclough had run out of ideas and the club was slumping alarmingly towards the bottom of League Two." Jeffrey Benge.

⌃ **HEROES OF THE TURF**
"Giuliano Grazioli, whose goals took us back to the League. Ian Hendon, who was such an inspirational captain taking us up and a promising manager at Barnet. Liam Hatch, who didn't score as many goals as he should but always gave 110% and was loved by most of the fans. Albert Adomah – possibly the most exciting player at Barnet in my time and loved by the fans who are a bit astonished that he is still with us. Simon Clist, who became something of a cult figure, left-back in our promotion season. Bees fans were greatly upset when he was released on a free transfer." Jeffrey Benge.

GETTY IMAGES

- **Nicknames** The Tykes, The Reds
- **Founded** 1887
- **Ground** Oakwell Stadium (opened 1888)
- **Address** Grove Street, Barnsley S71 1ET
- **Capacity** 23,009
- **Best attendance** 40,255 vs Stoke City, FA Cup 5th round, 15 February, 1936
- **Contact** 01226-211211
- **Ticket Number** 0871-226 6777
- **Email** thereds@barnsleyfc.co.uk
- **Website** barnsleyfc.co.uk

The 1997/98 season brought a new anthem to the Premier League and a new name to the fixture list. "Brazil – it's just like watching Brazil, it's just like watching Brazil." The tune may have been 'Blue Moon', but the fans were true reds. No other team has spent longer in the second tier of English football than Barnsley, so when their time came in the top league, they were going to enjoy it. Chelsea scored six goals in a televised game at Stamford Bridge, but still the Tykes sang "We're gonna win 7-6!" Soon they clinched an away win at Anfield and there was an upsurge in confidence. The return saw Barnsley on a good run and hopes were high. What followed, however, left a feeling around the Yorkshire faithful that maybe referee Mr GS Willard was an agent of the establishment and that the dice were loaded against them. At 1-1 Barnsley had Barnard sent off somewhat harshly when he clipped Owen's heels, then Liverpool went 1-2 up. Soon Morgan was controversially given his marching orders also, but still the nine Tykes managed to equalize late in the game. Mr Willard, however, wasn't finished. Darren Sheridan was sent for an early bath and Liverpool scored the winner from the resulting free kick in the last minute of the game. Barnsley finished the match with just eight men on the field, supplemented by the occasional irate fan who ran on to remonstrate with the referee.

The club never recovered, and relegation followed nine games later. Back in the second tier, Barnsley have enjoyed fluctuating form supplemented by the odd cup run. Ten years after their Premier League adventure, they famously reached a Wembley FA Cup semi-final after beating both Liverpool and Chelsea live on TV during a campaign that gripped the nation. And when skipper Brian Howard fired home that historic winner at Anfield… well, it really was just like watching Brazil.

HOME AWAY

Pubs for home fans
The Mount, Pontefract Road, has photos and cuttings of the team from the fifties onwards and big screen live sport. The Full House, Rotherham Road, Monk Bretton, is recommended by Wilky: "Official branch of Barnsley FC's Supporters Trust. Tonnes of memorabilia, much gained via regular Brian Howard, the FA Cup hero. It welcomes visiting fans, providing coaches are registered with respective clubs/supporters trusts. Great lunchtime menu and sports TV."

Good food near ground
Rigby Bar and Restaurant at the leisure centre serves up decent food.

Pubs for away fans
Rigby Bar at Metrodome leisure centre nearby. There's a decent atmosphere, views and a mix of fans. Food is available.

Top tips
The town centre is best left to the home fraternity. If passing through, keep your colours covered.

With performances like that, could we see a return of the South Yorkshire samba to the upper tier?

Greatest moments on this ground
"Most fans would probably say the home game against Bradford City (26 April 1997), when Barnsley won promotion to the Premiership. To have achieved that at home, in front of our own fans, was something special for everyone who was there. Folklore was created that day; Danny Wilson et al can still dine out 'in tarn' because of that result." Wilky, OnThePontyEnd.

Lowest moments on this ground
"The injury sustained by Iain Hume in our derby with Sheffield United. To think that a player had a fractured skull as a result of a football challenge was pretty sickening to witness." Wilky.

Heroes of the sideline

"Alan Clarke – he breathed new life into the club when he arrived at Oakwell. He brought excitement back and as a player-manager began Barnsley's recovery, which culminated in promotions and our eventual arrival to the Premiership. Danny Wilson – the man that got the Reds to the Premiership, what more can you say? As a coach or manager, his career has never hit those heights since." Wilky.

‹ Oakwell.
⌄ Neil Redfearn during the 97/98 Premier League season.

Heroes of the turf

"Eric Winstanley – Mr Barnsley himself. A stalwart of the Reds, joining as a schoolboy, representing them for almost 13 years, then joining the coaching setup. Neil Redfern – our Captain Fantastic, justly rewarded by winning promotion to the Premiership with Barnsley. A fierce midfield general, he could batter a ball into the net from 40 yards. Ronnie Glavin – or 'God' as he was known to the Oakwell faithful. I was just a bairn and couldn't believe that Barnsley had a superstar. Craig Hignett – 20 goals from midfield in a season that saw Barnsley appear in their first Wembley final at the play-offs. Brian Howard – the winning goal at Anfield during our 'Giant Killing' run in the FA Cup during the 2007/08 season." Wilky.

Zeroes of the turf

"Kayode Odejayi – despite his winner against Chelsea at Oakwell (FA Cup semi-final) he never realized the same heights. With just the keeper to beat and four yards of empty net to aim at, he put it wide and ended our dreams at Wembley. Hero to zero in 90 minutes. Craig Rocastle – he came on loan from Chelsea in 2004, with huge expectation. He had five very brief appearances,

'Cocoon' by Time Rider is the tune that rings around Oakwell as the players appear. It was also the theme tune to the late eighties after-pub show *The Hitman and Her*, hosted by Pete Waterman and Michaela Strachan. Now, that's hardly Gladiatorial is it?

THE LAST WORD

onthepontyend.com
barnsley-mad.co.uk

PUB QUIZ

That's quite interesting
Barnsley failed to gain promotion to the newly expanded First Division in 1919, despite finishing third in the Second Division in 1915. Following the First World War, Arsenal, two places below the Reds, were elected into that position. Exactly how Arsenal owner Sir Henry Norris nobbled the Football Management Committee is still not known. You can't fail to wonder, what if?

Not a lot of people know that
Offended by the local rugby football team's decision to play a match on Good Friday, Reverend Tiverton Preedy set about forming a club that played association football instead. Barnsley St Peters, later Barnsley FC, was formed.

then his loan was terminated. Being a Chelsea player and the cousin of a famous international (David Rocastle) didn't do him any favours here. Ian Woan – another disastrous loan signing. After a decade with Nottingham Forest, Woan joined Barnsley for just three unspectacular appearances. On evidence, Premiership players do not always have the pedigree to succeed at Oakwell." Wilky.

Villains

"Neil Warnock – a Barnsley player during his career, he always gets his fair share of stick when bringing his teams to Oakwell. While not an out-and-out villain, he's the one you love to hate. Daniel Nardiello altered his journey to Oakwell, apparently to re-sign and extend his contract with the club, instead heading down the M1 to sign for QPR. Michael McIndoe's brief stay left a sour taste in the mouth, after only 18 appearances he activated a clause in his contract to sign for Wolverhampton Wanderers in 2007." Wilky.

The ground

Oakwell is an excellent mixture of the modern and the old. Three boxy new stands hem in **The West Stand**, the only part of the original ground still standing. It is all seated, but a large part of the 4,752 capacity terrace is open to the elements. Behind the goal **The North Stand** was built in 1999 to replace the Kop with a capacity of 6,000. This is where away supporters are housed with The Academy adjacent. Running the length of the field, the two-tier **East Stand** was opened in 1992 and has executive boxes and the family area, with a combined capacity of 7,492. The **CK Beckett Stand** was built in the mid 1990s to replace the Pontefract Road (Ponty) End.

Getting there

By road/Parking Exit the M1 at junction 37 following the A628/Dodworth Road to Barnsley and passing Alhambra Shopping Centre on the left. Take a right at Pontefract Road/A628, then a left to Grove Street. The ground is on the right. The club car park is on Pontefract Road; there's also a large car park on Queen's Road.

By train Barnsley station is half a mile from the ground. Turn left onto Kendry Street towards the dual carriageway. Go under the bridge. Take a left onto Bala Street, becoming Belgrave Road. Grove Street is at the end.

BIRMINGHAM CITY

- **Nicknames** The Blues
- **Founded** 1875
- **Ground** St Andrew's (opened 1906)
- **Address** St Andrew's Stadium, Birmingham B9 4NH
- **Capacity** 30,009
- **Best attendance** 66,844 vs Everton, FA Cup 4th Round, 11 March, 1939
- **Contact** 0844-557 1875
- **Ticket Number** 0844-557 1875
- **Email** ticket.office@bcfc.com
- **Website** bcfc.com

⌄ Trevor Francis, Birmingham legend.

When Birmingham City moved to St Andrew's in 1906 it was still a piece of wasteland with Romany travellers living on it. The then directors turfed the travellers off the land and in return, received a 100-year-curse on the club. Little was thought of it at the time, but in those 100 years Birmingham, one of the biggest clubs in the land, has tasted virtually no success. They have yo-yoed around the top two divisions, never really looking like they were going anywhere in particular. They have long tried to dispel this blight. During the first full season under the curse, they were relegated from the top flight. Manager Barry Fry allegedly urinated in every corner of the pitch, as he had been told this would break the hex, and Ron Saunders put a crucifix on every floodlight pylon and painted the soles of the players' boots red. Neither seemed to work.

In the 100 years since the malediction, the only piece of major silverware Birmingham have won is the League Cup in 1963. One bright point was that this did come at the expense of arch-rivals Aston Villa, who they beat in the final. Birmingham also hold two European records that are often overlooked. They were the first English club to ever compete in Europe, where they reached the Inter Cities Fairs Cup semi-final in 1956, losing to Barcelona over two legs. They also went one better than this and became the first English side to reach a European final in the same competition, again losing to Barcelona over two legs.

The curse apparently ended on 26 December 2006. Birmingham beat QPR 2-1 and went on to win the Championship playoffs. From now on, managers will not have to urinate on the pitch, use crucifixes or any other kind of superstition – unless they'd like to that is.

Greatest moments on this ground
"Three spring to mind: the 3-1 win over Aston Villa in the first leg of the League Cup final in 1962/63 season,

PUB QUIZ

That's quite interesting
Birmingham City were the first English club to play in European competition in 1956.

Not a lot of people know that
Birmingham City only became Birmingham City after the Second World War. Previously they were known as Small Heath and then simply Birmingham.

Birmingham went on to draw four days later at Villa Park to win their only piece of silverware; the 4-1 win over Ipswich Town in the semi-final of the League Cup in 2001; the first derby against Villa in the Premiership, where we won 3-0 including a hilarious own goal by their keeper, the ground was banging." Graham Hughes, fan.

Lowest moments on this ground
"The mid- to late eighties were bad all around. We slipped as far as the third tier under ex-Villa man Ron Saunders, there was the terrible day of rioting with Leeds which saw a young lad die, and we lost to Altrincham in the cup around then too." Graham Hughes.

Heroes of the sideline
"Although Steve Bruce ditched us mid-season, he did get us back to the Premiership after years in the wilderness. Current manager Alex McLeish has all the hallmarks of becoming a future legend if we continue to improve and stay in the top flight. Back in the sixties, Gil Merrick took us to League Cup glory and a European final." Graham Hughes.

RIVALS
Aston Villa are the main rivals, their history goes back to their formation, but also West Brom, Coventry and Wolves all have their place.

GETTY IMAGES

VILLAINS
"There is only one set of villains in Birmingham – Aston Villa and anyone who has played for them."
Ben Tucker, fan.

Don't mention the…

Fact that Birmingham's city neighbours, Aston Villa, have had so much success and the city's name-bearers have had so little.

The ground

St Andrew's is on three sides a modern and attractive stadium, and on one side a throwback to the sixties and seventies. Redevelopment took place in the early nineties and could not come too soon for what was then an ageing ground. The Tilton Road end and The Spion Kop opened in 1994 and then, after some legal issues over land, The Railway End Stand was completed and opened in 1999.

This left just one side undeveloped and the **Main Stand** does stick out like a sore thumb in what is an otherwise modern stadium. With two tiers and a row of executive boxes it runs the length of the pitch. Supporters at the front are open to the elements in bad weather.

The **Railway End Stand** is separate, with a large bottom tier and a smaller gallery-style tier above. It is quite distinctive, with its smaller upper tier that is allocated to home fans only. The lower tier houses away fans and, depending on the match and support, tickets allocated number between 2,500 and 4,500.

The **Spion Kop** runs the length of the field and is a very impressive single-tiered structure befitting a club of Birmingham's size. At the very back of the stand is a row of executive boxes. The whole stand is one continuous sweep around the corner into the Tilton Road end.

The **Tilton Road** end is identical to the Kop side of the ground, with a large single tier with executive boxes at the back. The whole structure is very impressive and St Andrew's is, on three sides at least, an incredible stadium.

Getting there

By Road/Parking As St Andrew's is situated just off the A45, it is pretty straightforward to find. From the M6 turn off at junction 6 onto the A5127 Aston Expressway, continue for about a mile until the junction with the A4540; it is signposted St Andrew's. Continue along this road for a about a mile and you will see the ground on your left.

From the M42, turn off at junction 9 for the A45, signposted Airport. Stay on this road towards the city centre until you see the ground on your right after a couple of miles.

Parking-wise there are plenty of opportunities to street park. There are a couple of match-day car parks in the area that are clearly signposted, and to the city centre there are several pay-and-display car parks.

By Train The main station in Birmingham is New Street; it's walkable at just over mile from the ground and handily placed in the centre of the city. Alternatively you can get a local train to Bordesley Station, which is within five minutes of the ground.

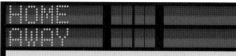

Pubs for home fans
Near the ground, all pubs are Blue; most will have a bouncer on the door for big matches and away fans will be turned away.

Good food near ground
There are many fast-food vans around the ground that serve palatable grub; there is also a Subway on the Kop side. There is a retail park next to the ground with cafés and a Morrison's supermarket. Birmingham, being the multi-cultural hub that it is, has pretty much every cuisine you could dream of available, mostly closer to the city centre.

Pubs for away fans
You can get a pint in the ground, but if you want to drink on the way you'd be advised to do it in pubs a little further out. The city centre pubs, which are about 20 minutes away, offer everything from sports bars to real ale joints, but as you come out of the centre towards St Andrew's they become more and more partisan and aren't worth the bother.

Top tips
If you want a pint or something to eat stick to the city centre, there are more options and a friendlier atmosphere.

THE LAST WORD

bcfcfanzine.com
smallheathalliance.com
keeprighton.co.uk

⌄ Birmingham versus Villa; Gallagher beats Little to the ball.

BOB THOMAS/GETTY IMAGES

HOME COLOURS

- ⊖ **Nicknames** Rovers
- ⊙ **Founded** 1875
- ⊕ **Ground** Ewood Park (opened 1990)
- ⓘ **Address** Ewood Park, Blackburn, Lancashire BB2 4JF
- ⊕ **Capacity** 31,367
- ✪ **Best attendance** 62,522 vs Bolton Wanderers, FA Cup 6th Round, 2 March, 1929
- ⓒ **Contact** 0871-702 1975
- ⊕ **Ticket Number** 0871-702 1975
- @ **Email** tickets@rover-mail.co.uk
- Ⓦ **Website** rovers.co.uk

BLACKBURN ROVERS

RIVALS

Burnley ARE public enemy number one at Ewood Park, and this worsened with the rival's recent success. Also, Bolton, Manchester Untied, Manchester City and Preston.

Which football fan hasn't dreamed the dream of taking over their beloved club, installing the best manager in the land and then backing him with the money to go and get the job done – to transform the club and wrestle the league title away from the trophy room of Old Trafford or Stamford Bridge? Well, Jack Walker was one fan who did exactly that. A lifelong Rovers supporter and local steelworks owner, the 1990/91 season saw Walker take the proceeds from the sale of his factory and buy the less-than-fashionable Rovers, a team languishing in the frustration and ignominy of the old Second Division. For the new season Sir Jack brought in Liverpool legend Kenny Dalglish as manager, the wily Scot making some radical changes that helped take Rovers to the top of League Two. Despite a bout of nerves that meant having to go through the trauma of the play-offs, Rovers managed to triumph and take their place in the newly formed Premier League. The English transfer record proved no barrier for Sir Jack and soon Alan Shearer, along with a number of other high profile signings, propelled Rovers to fourth in the Premiership at the first attempt. The following season they spent big on David Batty and Tim Flowers and then broke the English transfer record again with Chris Sutton, a snip at £5 million from Norwich City. The legendary SAS (Shearer and Sutton) partnership helped fire Rovers to the Premiership title in 1994/95, Sir Jack realizing his dream of making Rovers the best team in English football. He had achieved his goal in under five years, and had succeeded in putting Blackburn back on the football map. Suddenly their claim to fame was no longer that they had been one of the three clubs who could boast being founder members of the both the Premier League in 1992 and the Football League way back in 1888. He was the first of the modern-day football millionaire owners changing the fortunes of a team, and,

unlike some of the overseas business consortiums, Sir Jack was a true fan who left a lasting impression on his home town club.

Greatest moments on this ground

"Monday 8 May, 1995 vs Newcastle United. Shearer scored in a 1-0 win and Tim Flowers was outstanding (he had bottle!). That game won us the Premier League." Peter Anslow, 4000holes.co.uk.

Lowest moments on this ground

17 August 2000, the day Jack Walker died.

Heroes of the sideline

"There can be only one – Kenny Dalglish!" Peter Anslow.

PUB QUIZ

That's quite interesting
Mike Newell scored the fastest hat trick in Champions League history during the 4-0 win over Rosenberg – three goals in nine minutes.

Not a lot of people know that
Blackburn are the only professional team to win the FA Cup in three consecutive seasons: 1884, 1885 and 1886.

HOME AWAY

Pubs for home fans
The Ewood Arms and The Aqueduct Inn are strictly home fans only pubs, they often have bouncers on the door and will bar anyone they deem not local. Other pubs around the ground include The Havelock Inn and The White Bull and all serve decent food as well as ale.

Good food near ground
The Fernhurst is a good bet for decent pub food, it has a large restaurant and the food is spot on. In the town centre there are the usual fast-food outlets and other pubs and vans around the ground. There is a McDonald's over the road from the ground on Bolton Road.

Pubs for away fans
The Fernhurst is best known to be an away pub. Towards the town centre, just a 20-minute walk away there are more options, from traditional to modern Weatherspoon-style pubs. The Golden Cup is about 20 minutes from the ground in the Bolton Road, and usually has a good atmosphere and mix of supporters. The Fox and Hounds also allows away fans in, although in crunch games with rival teams it may be home fans only.

Top tips
For a quick getaway post match it's advisable to park closer to the M65, it is closer to the away end and the area directly around the ground gets very congested.

> Shearer celebrates his second goal in a 2-0 victory against Manchester United in April 1994.

Villains
Mark Hughes for leaving the club and joining rivals Manchester City.

Don't mention the…
Attendances; despite consistent position in the Premiership, the ground is rarely full and they have one of the lowest average attendances in the division.

The ground
Extensively redeveloped in the mid-nineties, Ewood Park was one of the first top-flight grounds to really take on a modern stadium feel. Two ends and one side were totally rebuilt and are impressive two-tier structures, that really enclose and impose upon the pitch. Only the single-tier Riverside was not rebuilt, although it had been in the mid-eighties. There are plans afoot to develop this stand, which would push the capacity to around the 40,000 mark, though there are question marks over the financial sense of this as they struggle to fill their current stadium.

When built, the **Darwen End** was one of the most impressive modern end stands in the country, with two tiers and a row of executive boxes. It is home to away support, taking up a number of blocks in the lower tier, depending on the size of support and the competition. FA Cup games, for example, will see the visiting support taking up the whole lower tier of up to 4,000 seats and for really big games, the whole end. Although all corners are open in the ground, there is a screen filling the one corner by the away fans and a large scoreboard on the Darwen End stand itself.

Home to the core of Rovers' support, the **Walkersteel Blackburn End Stand** is another very impressive two-tiered structure, particularly due to the large lower tier and excellent acoustics. There is also a row of executive boxes mirroring the Darwen Road end.

Named after the famous local benefactor, the **Jack Walker Stand** is a two-tiered affair with executive boxes splitting the tiers. It is also home to the dressing rooms.

The only single tier, undeveloped side, the **Fraser Eagle Stand (Riverside)** does look a little dated compared to the rest of the stadium. The front of the stand is also open to the weather but offers uninterrupted views of the pitch, which is more than can be said for the back rows. There are supporting pillars, which do cause minor obstruction to views in some areas.

Getting there
By Road/Parking Ewood Park, like most Premiership grounds, is well signposted. The easiest way to get to the ground is to approach along the M65 and at junction 4 leave and take the A666 signposted Blackburn and Ewood Park. After about half a mile you will see the ground and you are in the best area to start looking for a car park that will ensure a quick getaway from the ground.

Street parking close to Ewood Park used to be straightforward, but like a lot of Premiership grounds, the introduction of residents' permits has made this much more limited, especially for weekend games. It's easier to park in one of the many car parks near the ground, all are well signposted and reasonably priced, although these do fill up early for big games and are a nightmare from which to make a quick getaway from the ground. A short walk from the ground there are some industrial areas that offer parking for £3 to £5 and are clearly signposted, these are the best places to park for a dash onto the M65.

By Train Blackburn station is approximately 1½ miles from Ewood Park. Mill Hill Station is approximately one mile away from the ground. There are direct trains from Manchester Victoria, Salford Crescent and Preston. The walk from the main station will take 20 to 25 minutes, however there is a bus station opposite the rail terminal. From here, there are buses which pass Ewood Park every 10 minutes, the numbers 1, 5a/5c, 19, 225 and 237 are all suitable.

THE LAST WORD

4000holes.co.uk
boards.rovers.co.uk
roversretu… ₁e Grounds
…lackburn Rovers /

^ The lethal SAS celebrate eliminating the competition.

BLACKPOOL

- **Nicknames** The Pool, The Seasiders, The Tangerines
- **Founded** 1887
- **Ground** Bloomfield Road (opened 1899)
- **Address** Seasiders Way, Blackpool FY1 6JJ
- **Capacity** 13,500
- **Best attendance** 38,098 vs Wolverhampton Wanderers, Division One, 19 September, 1955
- **Contact** 0871-622 1953
- **Ticket Number** 0871-622 1953
- **Email** info@blackpoolfc.co.uk
- **Website** blackpoolfc.co.uk

The ball's crossed in, a high lofted trajectory looping into the box. The crowd in the North Stand rise as one as the ball hangs in the air, begging for a right foot volley. The striker in orange steadies, slows and prepares to pull the trigger, but at the last minute a lunging boot from the sliding central defender sends the ball ricocheting away to the near touchline. The bright, modern stadium fills the screen, but as the camera pans away the stands end abruptly. Blue sky crashes into the scene and, pulling back, the stadium suddenly takes on the appearance of a film set, like a two dimensional illusion quickly constructed by an art department, hopeful that no one will slam the door too hard causing the set to wobble and the bubble of reality to burst. Indeed, it's a strange sight to see a two-sided football ground. Many clubs have modernized their once humble abodes by adding new stands, some through a closed season rush, but Blackpool's extended spell as a team with only half a ground made Bloomfield Road a somewhat surreal stage for Championship football.

Blackpool set themselves some pretty high standards when they chose their team colours. While teams from abroad often imitated the strips of mighty English football clubs (think of Juventus, who famously copied Notts County), the team from the Lancashire coastline adopted the striking colours of the Dutch national squad, meaning the Tangerines have some pretty lofty role models to emulate. Cruyff, Gullit, Van Basten and Bergkamp spring to mind. Yet during the fifties the team was filled with the high-flyers every young player hoped to become. This was a decade when Blackpool shone brightly, with its Golden Mile, golden sands and spectacular illuminations drawing people to the town from far and wide. The Tangerines were giants of the First Division, vying for League titles and fighting out three FA Cup finals. In 1953 they won

the famous 'Matthews Final', which saw the Seasiders fight back from 3-1 down to take the trophy home to Bloomfield Road. Football legends Stanley Matthews and Stan Mortensen combined to make this one of the FA Cup's most memorable games. As with many of this era's greats, Blackpool suffered through the seventies and eighties, but they returned to the Championship under young manager Simon Grayson and have established themselves as a solid team, maintaining consistent form, even after Grayson's departure in December 2008. With wealthy backers, the Seasiders may prove to be dark horses, pushing for a Premiership place and following a tradition set by other giants of the fifties, such as local rivals Burnley. Hopefully the club's newly opened Jimmy Armfield South Stand will soon be joined by a new sibling, creating a stage finally fit for the bright lights of the big league.

Greatest moments on this ground

"In the 'new' ground, Keigan Parker's curler in the last minute of the play-off semi-final against Oldham was special. In the twentieth century, Eamonn O'Keefe's 30-yard strike against Chesterfield to seal promotion in the eighties." Jack Gaughan, Vital Blackpool.

Lowest moments on this ground

"Applying for re-election in 1983 was a low, along with nearly going out of business around the same time. In the late nineties, a 5-0 home defeat at the hands of Bury was dismal." Jack Gaughan.

Heroes of the sideline

"Joe Smith – who can argue with an FA Cup winner? Billy Ayre – for his charismatic style and bringing the club together after a difficult 1980s. Simon Grayson – for winning promotion to the Championship for the first time in three decades." Jack Gaughan.

Heroes of the turf

"Jimmy Hampson – 247 goals in 360 games. Jimmy Armfield – he was a one-club man, the original 'overlapping' full-back and England captain. Stanley Matthews – architect in the 1953 Cup Final and won the European Footballer of the Year while at Bloomfield Road. Stan Mortensen – the hat trick hero of that 1953 Cup Final. 'Morty' has a statue outside the Kop end. He was the scorer of nearly 200 seaside goals and 23 for England in just 25 appearances. Alan Suddick – dubbed 'king' of Bloomfield Road, the midfielder was the first player to curl a ball in the

That's quite interesting
"In the nineties, managers of Blackpool always seemed to leave for better things despite not pulling up any trees at Bloomfield Road. Sam Allardyce and Nigel Worthington were both sacked but ended up in the Premiership, while Gary Megson left after a poor stint and is also in the top flight. Something in the water, obviously!" Jack Gaughan.

Not a lot of people know that
"Blackpool captain Jimmy Armfield received his 1966 World Cup winner's medal 43 years late after missing out on the finals through injury." Jack Gaughan.

"South Stand. Finally, the wasteland (or novelty car park if you wish) at the south end of the ground has been built on. For years that's been the brunt of many jokes from away supporters. It looks smart now though – pity about the rust on the 'new' stands, which are under 10 years old! But ssh, let's rejoice at a four-sided ground." Jack Gaughan.

▼ The 2010/11 season saw fans of The Pool celebrating in the top flight.

GETTY IMAGES

POPPERFOTO/GETTY IMAGES

◀ Stanley Matthews is hoisted by team-mates Jackie Mudie and Stan Mortensen after the famous 'Matthews Final', 1953.

late sixties. New signing Charlie Adam is becoming the darling of the club just like Suddick was." Jack Gaughan.

Zeroes of the turf
"Chris Malkin – he signed for a club record fee of £275,000 in 1996 but the striker was hugely injury-prone and only scored six times in tangerine. Tony Diamond – despite only playing three games for the club (and actually scoring), Tony was voted the worst player ever to grace the tangerine shirt. John O'Kane – the former Man United and Everton man came with great pedigree, but his performances in midfield were abysmal, ending with home fans actually baying for him to be sent off as a referee cautioned him." Jack Gaughan.

Villains
"Sadly for Richie Wellens he'll always be booed at Blackpool – despite being a terrific midfielder for the club – because of the way he left for Oldham Athletic and his constant transfer requests. David Eyres – the popular winger was sold to rivals Burnley and then went on to sign for bitter rivals Preston seven years later, bad-mouthing The Seasiders in the process. In more recent times, 'Pool fans take great delight in pointing out that most players who choose to leave end up in a worse situation just months down the line. Wes Hoolahan is a prime example of this, manipulating his way out and then finding himself relegated not long after with Norwich." Jack Gaughan.

The ground
Bloomfield Road's been subject to a long renovation, with **The North** and **West** stands first to be completed back in 2002. The long, vacant area of the **South Stand** was opened in 2010 by, and named after, club legend Jimmy Armfield. The three completed stands are single tier, all-seater covered structures, which flow through the corners to create a large enclosed arena. The **Sir Stanley Matthews**

West Stand runs the length of the field and the dug-outs are on the halfway line here. Opposite sits an open, temporary **East Stand** where away fans have traditionally been housed. There's no cover against the often inclement weather. A statue of Stan Mortensen has been erected outside the north stand, or Kop, which bears his name.

Getting there
By road/Parking On the west coast, Blackpool is easily accessed via the M55 (reached from junction 32 of the M6). Follow the M55 west to its conclusion. Then turn right at the roundabout onto Preston New Road (A583), left onto Waterloo Road (A5073), right onto Central Drive and Bloomfield Road is on the left. Pay and display parking is over the road from the stadium.

By train There are two train stations here. Blackpool South Station is the closest (around a 10-minute walk), but is served by fewer connections. North Station is well served, but a 25-minute walk from the ground. Manchester Square is the nearest tram station.

HOME AWAY

Pubs for home fans
Just north of the club, the Swift Hound pub, Festival Park, Rigby Road, is a popular spot (but probably because it's one of the closest pubs to the ground as opposed to selling top-quality ales). There's usually a good mix of home and away supporters.

Good food near ground
Festival Park, half a mile north of the ground, has a few eateries, including a Frankie & Benny's restaurant and a McDonald's.

Pubs for away fans
Blackpool is set up for the pleasure seeker so there's no shortage of suitable watering holes for the thirsty to search out, especially in the city centre. The Waterloo, Waterloo Road, is a decent family-friendly spot with sports TV. Old Bridge House, Lytham Road, is a small, local pub with some decent enough real ales. The Auctioneer, Lytham Road, is a handy stop-off for those coming via Blackpool South – a Wetherspoons with decent food.

Top tips
While the East Stand remains open, a cold wind can whip in off the sea and the ground there can become incredibly wet underfoot. Cheer yourself up afterwards with a trip to the famous Pleasure Beach!

THE LAST WORD

blackpool.vitalfootball.co.uk
blackpool-mad.co.uk
bfcblog.co.uk

HOME COLOURS

BOLTON WANDERERS

- ✪ **Nicknames** The Trotters
- ✪ **Founded** 1874
- ✪ **Ground** Reebok Stadium (opened 1997)
- ✪ **Address** Burnden Way, Bolton BL6 6JW
- ✪ **Capacity** 28,723
- ✪ **Best attendance** 28,353 vs Leicester City, Premier League, 28 December, 2003
- ✪ **Contact** 0844-871 2932
- ✪ **Ticket Number** 0844-871 2932
- ✪ **Email** asktony@bwfc.co.uk
- ✪ **Website** bwfc.co.uk

GETTY IMAGES

RIVALS

Manchester United,
Manchester City,
Blackburn, Bury,
Wigan and Preston.

Bolton could be viewed as a footballing limpet. They battled and fought to gain a berth in the top flight and they won't be giving up this privileged place easily – it'll have to be prised from their cold, dead hands. However, that metaphor would be unfair; yes, they are purveyors of the never say die, tough, physical game, but their success cannot be attributed to that alone. They've played in Europe against class teams producing some flowing, stylish football. Ex-manager Sam Allardyce assembled a team for a task, blending a backbone of home-grown steel with a selection of foreign journeymen and flair players. Some surprising names have lined up in the white of Bolton. 'Big Sam' seemed to have something of a magic touch, blending temperamental characters such as El Hadji Diouf and Nicolas Anelka with the likes of Jay Jay Okocha, Ivan Campo and Youri Djorkaeff – players who had graced the greatest teams and greatest stages around the world. However, had you told Bolton fans back at the end of the 1986/87 season that their squad would soon be laced with players from Real Madrid and Inter Milan as well as a host of internationals, they would have thought you'd lost your marbles, for that was the year the team dropped into the bottom tier for the first time in its history. It was a hard road back.

This is a club with a long and proud heritage. It features FA Cup wins and extended periods as First Division giants. They're one of those teams whose successes seem to always be played out in grainy black and white against a backdrop of cloth caps and rattles; when players seemed to knock around balls that weighed eight stone while wearing workman's boots. They were four-time winners of the FA Cup, including the famous White Horse Final

➤ The Reebok.

That's quite interesting

"Despite spending the majority of our history in the top flight (over 70 years), Bolton have never won the league title. No other club's spent as many years in the top flight without winning it." Chris Deary.

Not a lot of people know that

"When Bolton sacked manager George Mulhall in 1982 we made an audacious attempt to make Pelé our next manager. Unfortunately, the Brazilian legend turned us down and the slightly less glamorous John McGovern got the job instead." Chris Deary.

∧ Big Sam and Little Sam.

of 1923. Officially a crowd of 126,000 swarmed into Wembley Stadium that day, but many put the figure nearer to 300,000. The mass was so great that thousands spilled onto the pitch and the police had to push the crowd back to the touchline so the game could go ahead. The defining image was policeman George Scorey mounted on a white horse trying to clear the masses. The crowd filled every centimetre of the arena down to the very edge of the touchline.

During its illustrious history the club's boasted legendary players such as Nat Lofthouse, the Lion of Vienna, a one-club player who averaged more than a goal every two games in a career that ran from 1946 to 1960. As an England player his strike rate was even better – virtually a goal per game.

Under Big Sam, Bolton became a permanent fixture in the upper half of the league table, a regular thorn in the sides of more fancied teams and League Cup finalists in 2004. However, this is a club that appreciates what can happen to a team used to life in the top flight when tides turn. Their relegation in 1962 established the club as perennial fallen giants. They know just how hard it can be to fight the currents back to the top – and just how hard you need to fight to hold on when you get there.

DON'T MENTION THE…

"Miss by Dean Holdsworth in the FA Cup semi-final against Aston Villa in 2000. It was an open goal to book us a place in the last final at Wembley, instead he blasted it over. We lost on penalties." Chris Deary.

Greatest moments on this ground

"The entire final season at Burnden Park was something of a fairytale: we won the First Division by 18 points, scored 100 goals (60 at home) and signed off from the old ground with a 4-1 hammering of Charlton. I think the Reebok Stadium's always lived in the shadow of that momentous season a little bit, but the game that stands out for me is when we beat West Ham near the end of the 2002/03 season. We were head to head for the final relegation spot and the joy of seeing Joe Cole's tantrum at the final whistle was bettered only by the screamer from Jay-Jay Okocha that won it for us." Chris Deary, Manny Road.

Lowest moments on this ground

"Relegation in our first year at the Reebok was a massive anti-climax after what had gone before. Moving to the Reebok was meant to give us a better chance of surviving in the Premier League and, although that did prove to be the case eventually, in the short term we were left wondering if we'd got a little big for our boots with our shiny new stadium." Chris Deary.

Heroes of the sideline

"Bruce Rioch completely transformed the club in the nineties, taking us from the third tier to the Premier League. When I was at school everyone supported Liverpool and Manchester United. You wouldn't have been seen dead in a Bolton Wanderers shirt. Kids in Bolton grow up supporting Bolton these days and that's because of what Bruce Rioch did. Sam Allardyce took it to another level. If you'd told me back in the early nineties that we'd play in Europe one day, I'd have taken you to the nearest lunatic asylum." Chris Deary.

Heroes of the turf

"Jussi Jaaskelainen – he joined Bolton in 1997 and has stayed loyal to the club ever since. There's no doubt he is highly regarded around the world and he's had his chances to walk away, but he's always stayed where he's wanted. Gudni Bergsson – a bargain buy from Tottenham in 1995, Gudni went on to captain the Wanderers and stayed with the club he loved through thick and thin. He originally planned on retirement in 2001, but after promotion back to the Premiership, he stayed on until 2003. Kevin Davies – Bolton took a chance on Davies in 2003, a risk that paid off as he's gone on to become one of the most feared players in the English game, the work ethic he brings is hard to beat. Youri Djorkaeff – hoping to earn a place in

France's 2002 World Cup squad, Djorkaeff moved to Bolton in the hope that English football would get him noticed. He took to the Premier League with ease and was part of the side that reached the League Cup final in 2004. Jay-Jay Okocha – after showing some of his magic in the 2002 World Cup, Okocha was a shock signing for Bolton. He lit up the Premier League in his first season before taking the captain's armband." Chris Mann, Burnden Aces.

Zeroes of the turf

"Mario Jardel came with a huge reputation, but the only thing that turned out to be huge about him was his waistline, which left him barely able to move, let alone score the numbers of goals he'd scored in Europe. Most of the players signed by Sammy Lee were a disaster, especially the ones whose CVs consisted of little more than a few well-watched videos on YouTube (I'm looking at you Daniel Braaten)." Chris Deary.

Villains

"Michael Ricketts is the most obvious candidate, mainly because he thought he was leaving for bigger and better things (Middlesbrough). After failing for several lower league clubs he was last seen trading off his one England cap for the mighty Tranmere." Chris Deary.

"The biggest villain isn't a player, but a manager. No doubt Sam Allardyce will be remembered for the job he did at the club, but in his final two years things became stale as he set his sights on becoming England manager. In April 2007 he resigned, stating his wish for a break from the game. Just two weeks later he was unveiled as boss of Newcastle United, much to the displeasure of fans. He was sacked just months into his tenure at St James' Park, much to the delight of many Bolton fans, before he turned up down the road at local rivals Blackburn Rovers!" Chris Mann.

The ground

The all-seater Reebok Stadium was built in 1997 and when viewed from a distance has an appearance of a circus big top. Inside the ground, the seating is divided into four main stands, each with an arching roof that joins in the corners. The design is such that there are no corner terraces of seats. The **Bolton Evening News North Stand** is away behind the goal, a two-tier structure for home fans, the upper tier being the family stand. The two-tier **West Stand** runs the length of the field and is home to the dug-outs. At the far end, behind the goal, is the **Woodford Group South Stand** where away fans sit. The **Nat Lofthouse East Stand** is

also a two-tier structure, opposite the **West Stand**. All have executive boxes between the two levels, giving the ground a very symmetrical feel.

Getting there

By road/Parking On the western peripheries of the city, the Reebok Stadium is easily reached from the north and south via junction 6 of the M61. Following the A6027, the stadium is clearly visible from the road on the left-hand side. Car parking is available at the ground for £6. Alternative (and cheaper) match-day parking can usually be found around the industrial estates near the ground.

By train Horwich Parkway station is literally yards from the stadium with regular connections from Bolton's mainline railway station taking around 10 minutes. Bolton supporters can use the BWFC bus service, which is subsidized by the club. It costs £1 single and £1.50 return to the stadium, see bwfc.co.uk for route details.

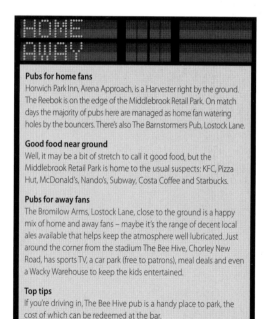

Pubs for home fans
Horwich Park Inn, Arena Approach, is a Harvester right by the ground. The Reebok is on the edge of the Middlebrook Retail Park. On match days the majority of pubs here are managed as home fan watering holes by the bouncers. There's also The Barnstormers Pub, Lostock Lane.

Good food near ground
Well, it may be a bit of stretch to call it good food, but the Middlebrook Retail Park is home to the usual suspects: KFC, Pizza Hut, McDonald's, Nando's, Subway, Costa Coffee and Starbucks.

Pubs for away fans
The Bromilow Arms, Lostock Lane, close to the ground is a happy mix of home and away fans – maybe it's the range of decent local ales available that helps keep the atmosphere well lubricated. Just around the corner from the stadium The Bee Hive, Chorley New Road, has sports TV, a car park (free to patrons), meal deals and even a Wacky Warehouse to keep the kids entertained.

Top tips
If you're driving in, The Bee Hive pub is a handy place to park, the cost of which can be redeemed at the bar.

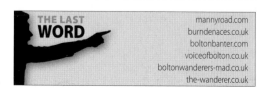

THE LAST **WORD**

mannyroad.com
burndenaces.co.uk
boltonbanter.com
voiceofbolton.co.uk
boltonwanderers-mad.co.uk
the-wanderer.co.uk

HOME COLOURS

- **Nicknames** The Cherries
- **Founded** 1899 (as Boscombe FC)
- **Ground** Dean Court (opened 1910)
- **Address** Dean Court, Kings Park, Bournemouth, Dorset BH7 7AF
- **Capacity** 10,700
- **Best attendance** 9,632 vs Leeds United, League One, 6 November, 2007
- **Contact** 01202-726300
- **Ticket Number** 01202-726338
- **Email** enquiries@afcb.co.uk
- **Website** afcb.co.uk

AFC BOURNEMOUTH

RIVALS

Southampton, Brighton and Portsmouth

Portsmouth fans were apoplectic when Harry Redknapp left them for local rivals Southampton. Saints fans were apoplectic when he then went the other way after Southampton's relegation. However, for all the south coast giants' bickering and gloating, they all seemed to miss the point that Redknapp's natural home is actually AFC Bournemouth. While not the team that he is immediately associated with, Harry gave four years as a player and seven years as a manager to The Cherries, bringing unprecedented success to Dean Court. After taking over as manager in 1983 and helping the team avoid relegation to the bottom tier, Redknapp consolidated his side, and the following year The Cherries beat the mighty Manchester United 2-0 in the third round of the FA Cup. May 1987 saw Bournemouth crowned champions and take their place in the second tier for the first time in their history. Redknapp used his wheeler-dealer skills to assemble a side that included the likes of Luther Blissett, enjoying three seasons in Division Two. He also brought through his son Jamie, who began his professional career with The Cherries before attracting the attention of Liverpool.

Recent financial troubles hit the south-coast side hard. After nearly two decades in the third tier of English football, the club suddenly found itself struggling in the basement. Life has not been rosy for the Cherries – administration and the fact that the newly rebuilt Dean Court remains a three-sided affair stand testament to that. However, a new consortium of owners and promotion in 2010 point to a brighter future at Dean Court, one where The Cherries blossom.

Greatest moments on this ground

"Since the new stadium: either the play-off semi-final win that sent us to the Millennium Stadium and on towards promotion or the final home game of the 2008/09 season, where the club secured Football League safety despite a huge points deduction… I'll go with the Grimsby game and narrow the moment down to Fletch's goal to fire us into a 2-1 lead. The script couldn't have been written any better; a returning hero scores the goal to secure safety and cements his place in club history." Dave Jennings, editor, Up The Cherries, Vital Bournemouth.

Lowest moments on this ground

"The home defeat to Barnet in the 2008/09 season. The culmination of a poor few months on and off the pitch: the club had been deducted 17 points, sacked Kevin Bond and installed Jimmy Quinn, who changed our style of play and results for the worse. Following this game many fans couldn't have imagined how the club was going to survive past the end of the season." Dave Jennings.

Heroes of the sideline

"Harry Redknapp started his managerial career at Dean Court and took the club to its highest position on the Football League ladder, winning the old Third Division title and breaking various records along the way. Mel Machin achieved the Great Escape in his first season, steering the club to safety despite having just nine points at Christmas. He led the club through administration and on to Wembley (Auto Windscreens Shield Final 1998) the following season. Sean O'Driscoll, for winning the play-off final in 2003. John Bond would be in contention. Eddie Howe and the success in 2008/09 – the Greatest Escape following the side's 17-point deduction." Dave Jennings.

Don't mention the…

"9-0 at Lincoln when the kit man packed the wrong studs so that our lads couldn't stop slipping over on a half-frozen pitch!" Steve Brown, Vital Bournemouth photographer.

PUB QUIZ

That's quite interesting
"At the old ground, opposite the South Stand used to be called the Brighton Beach End, as a little dig at our south-coast neighbours, due to the fact that it was covered in gravel." Steve Brown.

Not a lot of people know that
"We have the second-largest car park in the Football League (Plymouth's is bigger)." Steve Brown.

Villains

"Warren Feeney – a protracted contract negotiation ended with Feeney opting to leave and join Stockport. Feeney scored for Stockport on his Dean Court return and duly celebrated in front of The Cherries supporters like he had won the FA Cup, despite his goal being a simple consolation in a 2-1 defeat for his new side." Dave Jennings.

"Howard Goddard – he left for Newport and did an interview on their PA at a game against us. He said he left as Bournemouth was too small for his ambitions. He re-signed a few years later and went and scored the goal at Bradford that got us promoted." Mick Cunningham, Bournemouth FC programme editor.

The ground

Dean Court underwent a complete renovation at the start of the new millennium, and to overcome the problem of being hemmed in by local housing, the pitch was moved through 90 degrees and new stands built around it. The **North Stand** behind the goal is where the core supporters gather; it's a single-tier all-seater stand with great views. The **East Stand** runs the length of the pitch and is again single tier; the southern end of it has 1,200 seats available for visiting fans. The **Main West Stand** has a row of executive boxes at the back and a single tier of seating for home fans. There are still plans for a south stand to be built, but there's no concrete date yet.

Getting there

By road/Parking East of the town centre, the ground is just of the main A338. From the M3, exit junction 13 for Bournemouth joining the M27. Follow to its conclusion and go onto the A31 through New Forest National Park. Exit onto the A338 for Bournemouth/Christchurch. Turn left at Bournemouth Hospital onto the A3060/Castle Lane East. At the roundabout take the A35/Christchurch Road. Go right onto Clarence Park Road becoming King's Park Drive. Parking is available at the ground.

By train Pokesdown Station is a 15-minute walk from the ground. Head up Clarence Park Road before cutting across Kings Park.

⌃ Cherries midfielder Danny Hollands crosses the ball at the Fitness First Stadium.
⌄ Dean Court.

Pubs for home fans
The Cherry Tree, which can be found at the ground, is a popular haunt for the home contingent.

Good food near ground
The Wetherspoons is a good bet for a pre-match bite; there's also a Maccy D's on Christchurch Road, Boscombe.

Pubs for away fans
"The Queens Park pub, Holdenhurst Road, is a few minutes walk from the ground – the traditional pub for away supporters," says Dave Jennings. It has ale, basic bar food and sports TV. "There is a Wetherspoons (Sir Percy Florence Shelley, Christchurch Road, Boscombe), which is further away, but offers the usual cheap meals."

Top tips
For the most part there is little or no trouble. If you're a Leeds fan however, they won't be best pleased to see you. Bournemouth fans have very long memories!

THE LAST WORD

afcb.vitalfootball.co.uk
fansonline.net/afcbournemouth

HOME COLOURS

- **Nicknames** The Bantams, The Citizens
- **Founded** 1903
- **Ground** Valley Parade (opened 1903)
- **Address** Coral Windows Stadium, Valley Parade, Bradford BD8 7DY
- **Capacity** 25,136
- **Best attendance** 39,146 vs Burnley, FA Cup 4th Round, 11 March, 1911
- **Contact** 01274-773355
- **Ticket Number** 01274-770012
- **Email** bradfordcityfc@compuserve.com
- **Website** bradfordcityfc.co.uk

BRADFORD CITY

RIVALS

Bradford fans consider Leeds United their biggest rivals. Also Huddersfield Town, Barnsley, Sheffield United and Wednesday.

The difficult second season, as it's become known, is a bit like a band's difficult second album. Clubs promoted from the Championship seem to survive the first year in the Premiership on adrenalin, but it's the next campaign that seems to be the toughest. For many clubs it's become a game of financial poker as they decide whether to stick or twist in a bid to compete, or at least survive at the top table. For Bradford City, life in the fast lane went from the difficult second season to a slightly crazy 'Premier League Part Deux'. Having avoided relegation back to the Championship through a heroic final day victory against Liverpool, The Bantams looked forward to the 2000/01 fixtures with renewed relish. They may have survived with an all-time low of 36 points, but the club approached the oncoming fixtures with a plan. After the departure of manager Paul Jewell, Bradford invested heavily in big wages for the likes of Dan Petrescu, Benito Carbone and Stan Collymore. Results, however, did not follow spending and the club found itself in freefall and financial meltdown. Soon the club was crippled by debt. Having survived two spells in administration, City found itself kicking off the 2007/08 season in the bottom division for the first time in its history.

Bradford City is a club whose large fan base and community support are tightly linked to the tragic events that unfolded on 11 May, 1985. The Bradford fire disaster galvanized the city behind the club. The flames that ripped through the wooden stand and claimed 56 lives shocked the football world and changed the way we watch football and treat our supporters.

Bradford City have pioneered an innovative pricing policy at the rejuvenated Valley Parade that aims to put the cost of football around the same price as a trip to the cinema. As a result, during the 2009/10 season, City regularly hosted the biggest crowds in League Two and that support transferred into a fine away following. The club hopes they can surf this groundswell of support back up through the leagues. Bradford is a city large enough to support a Premier League team, all the club needs to do now is deliver success to its 'Premier League' supporters.

Greatest moments on this ground

"The afternoon against a Europe-bound Liverpool in 2000 in which David Wetherall's headed goal gave City a 1-0 win. It kept the club in the Premiership against all odds and predictions. The afternoon saw both clubs share a sombre minute's silence at the anniversary of the fire of 1985 – a grief empathized with at Anfield – which gave way to a cracking football match that The Bantams won on a knife edge. The future – a future that would take the club nearly out of business twice in 10 years as a result of that win – looked technicolour-bright and brilliant." Michael Wood, editor, Boy From Brazil.

Lowest moments on this ground

"The fire of 1985 in which 56 people died, obviously, is the lowest moment and it is a tragedy that's still keenly felt by the supporters and the whole city. While it represents the depths of despair for any club, there were good things to come out of the disaster, such as the linking of the fans with the largely Asian community around the ground, many of whom took in injured victims on day. The day rightly overshadowed the football, which saw City's young captain Peter Jackson lift the Third Division Championship trophy and start the day celebrating promotion. Many of the players on that day spent the following months going to funerals and supporting the injured with hospital visits. A stark contrast to the image of the modern footballer." Michael Wood.

Heroes of the turf

"Ces Podd –he holds Bradford City's league appearances record with 502 games played from 1970 to 1984. Podd was one of the first black players to establish himself in league football and was probably the first to receive a testimonial game. Stuart McCall – he had two spells as a player and then three seasons as manager. He was the driving force in midfield, which saw City win the Third Division championship in 1985 and almost gain promotion to the old First Division in 1988. He returned to the club 10 years later after successful spells with Everton and Rangers, and then helped lead City to the Premiership in 1999. Frank O'Rourke – he scored 88 league goals between 1907 and 1914 and was City's record goal-scorer for 69 years. He helped City gain promotion to the First Division in 1908 and also won an FA Cup winners' medal in 1911. Bobby Campbell – he broke O'Rourke's record, and his total of 121 league goals scored between 1980 and 1986 still stands today. Campbell was City's key goal-scorer in the successful promotion campaigns of 1981/82 and 1984/85. Sam Barkas – he was part of the successful side that won the Third Division North Championship in 1928/29, which scored a record 128 goals. He spent six

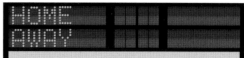

Pubs for home fans

Michael Wood recommends The Fighting Cock, Preston Street, for the best pint. Although not technically on the way to the ground, as a traditional ale house it's definitely a worthwhile diversion, with a good selection of real ales, guest beers and a good atmosphere; it's even away-fan friendly. The Corn Dolly at the bottom of Bolton Road is a two-minute walk east of Forster Square Station and another cracking spot to sup a real ale or two.

Good food near ground

"The best pint and scran is at The Fighting Cock, which boasts real ale, great pie and peas and a friendly atmosphere," recommends Michael Wood, editor, Boy From Brazil.

Pubs for away fans

The Cartwright Hotel, north of the ground at the top end of Manningham Lane has a decent bar for a pre-match pint. Mellow real-ale aficionados would do better searching out The Fighting Cock or Corn Dolly, see above.

Top tips

When in Rome… Bradford is well known for its quality curry houses so don't leave the city without sampling some of its spice.

DON'T MENTION THE…

"In March 2000, with all City's goalkeeper's injured, 41-year-old Neville Southall made his one and only appearance in goal for City in a televised home game against Leeds United. City lost 2-1." Mike Harrison.

GETTY IMAGES

> Stuart McCall – player, manager, legend, fashion icon.

further seasons playing for City in Division Two before he was sold to cover mounting debts at Valley Parade. He went on to win the League Championship with Manchester City as well as play for England." Mike Harrison, editor, The City Gent.

Zeroes of the turf
"Benito Carbone, Dan Petrescu, Ashley Ward, David Hopkin, Andy Myers, Peter Atherton and Ian Nolan were all signed during the six weeks of madness in the summer of 2000. All of them underachieved as, instead of consolidating City's position in the Premier League, The Bantams headed straight for the trap door of relegation." Mike Harrison.

Villains
"Having retired now, it seems unfair to recall former Huddersfield Town defender Kevin Gray, who in a local

derby game launched a two-footed tackle on new signing Gordon Watson. It was described in court as 'the worst tackle I have ever seen in my life' by Chris Waddle and saw Watson – who almost lost his limb – awarded £1million in damages." Michael Wood.

That's quite interesting
"David 'Bronco' Layne holds City's record for number of goals in one season at 36 in 1961/62. After this feat he was transferred to First Division Sheffield Wednesday. He was one of the players later embroiled in the betting scandal that saw him banned for life." Mike Harrison.

Not a lot of people know that
"Most people must know by now that the present FA Cup was designed in Bradford and City were the first winners of the new trophy. What is less well known during that cup run is that, after beating Norwich City 2-1 in the second

▼ The great escape 2000.

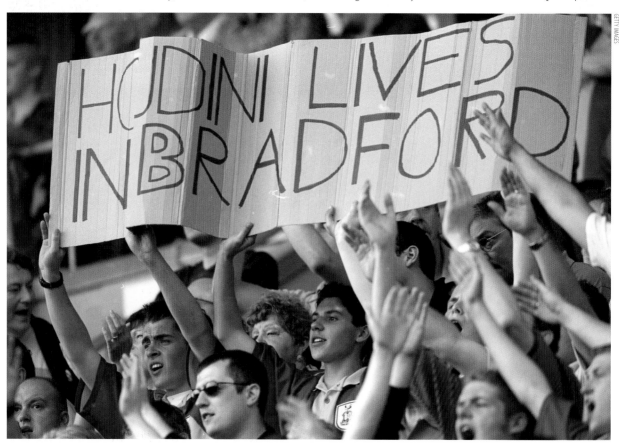

round of the FA Cup in 1911, City went 11 games without conceding another goal until being defeated 3-2 against Barnsley in the quarter final the following season. This record of clean sheets in the FA Cup is unlikely ever to be beaten." Mike Harrison.

The ground

Valley Parade is a ground that's undergone a transformation since the dark days of the eighties. The new ground has developed in a slightly lopsided way, half Premier League stadium and half Football League. The Main Stand, or **Sunwin Stand**, is an impressive two-tier structure that runs the length of the field. It's the largest stand holding 9,004 fans. Like the rest of the all-seater ground, it's resplendent in claret and amber. Behind the goal is the towering two-tier **Carlsberg Stand** or Kop, which can seat 7,492. The **East Stand**, or Midland Road Stand, looks a little dwarfed, but is still a decent-sized single-tier structure that has no pillars to obscure the views for the 4,500 fans it accommodates. **TL Dallas** or Bradford End is the smallest stand, a two-tier area for 1,800 home fans behind the goal. The northwest corner is the infill area between the two large stands and is the **Pulse Family Stand**; it can hold 2,300.

Visiting fans used to be allocated the Bradford End, but up to 1,800 are now accommodated in a section of the East Stand.

Getting there

By road/Parking Approach from south of the city via the M62, exiting at junction 26 onto the M606 signed for Bradford. Turn right onto the Ring Road. Valley Parade on the northern perimeters of the city is well signposted. There's no parking at the stadium on match days and limited street parking.

By train Valley Parade is a 15-minute walk north of the Bradford Forster Square Rail Station via either Midland Road or Manningham Lane. Trains also run to Bradford Interchange Rail – a 25-minute walk southeast of the ground (bus connections are also available).

THE LAST **WORD**

boyfrombrazil.co.uk
thecitygent.co.uk
claretandbanter.com
bradford.vitalfootball.co.uk
bradfordcity-mad.co.uk

BRENTFORD

- **Nicknames** The Bees
- **Founded** 1889
- **Ground** Griffin Park (opened 1904)
- **Address** Braemar Road, Brentford TW8 0NT
- **Capacity** 12,763
- **Best attendance** 38,678 vs Leicester City, FA Cup quarter-final, 26 February, 1949
- **Contact** 08453-456442
- **Ticket Number** 08453-456442
- **Email** enquiries@brentfordfc.co.uk
- **Website** brentfordfc.co.uk

Think back to the golden era of Association Football – when men in tweed jackets were squashed onto terraces like sardines, when the sound of wooden rattles resonated around huge open grounds and when a cloth cap and a scarf were all the protection one needed from a biting wind on a chilly Saturday afternoon. In the period between the wars Brentford were giants. OK, maybe not giants, but they certainly held their own with the big boys during the mid-1930s, when they battled in the upper reaches of Division One. Times have changed slightly. Today, this is a proud club that regularly battles it out in the top six, jostling for a place at Wembley and a chance to see that famous approach seething under a sea of red and black. Granted, it may no longer be the top flight title they're challenging for, but Brentford fans still enjoy the thrill and excitement of an annual battle for either a league title or the possibility of a trip across town for a play-off final.

Brentford's had its fair share of financial difficulties, but the club's been carried across turbulent waters on the shoulders of loyal supporters from the terraces, meaning it's managed to stay afloat where others have foundered and sunk. In 2006 the Brentford Supporters Trust took control of the ailing club with former BBC helmsman Greg Dyke assuming the chairman's responsibilities. Optimism is high for the future and there are plans for a new all-seater stadium. On the pitch, cup exploits have been good for the club's profile; they famously disposed of Premiership Sunderland shortly after the Supporters Trust took the reigns, with goals from DJ Campbell. In 2009 they sealed a memorable campaign by taking the League Two title against Darlington, securing a berth in a division inhabited by the likes of Leeds United, Norwich City, Charlton and Southampton. With a secure top ten finish in 2010, the foundations are there for the future – it could be honey time for The Bees.

Greatest moments on this ground

"In recent years it was the 2-1 win over Sunderland in the FA cup, with DJ Campbell dumping Gary Breen on his backside in the last minute for a win against the Premiership side. Our championship celebration in May 2009 was pretty good too – we even got one of those podium things on the pitch (even if the people assembling it hadn't read the instructions very well). A 2-1 win against Bournemouth to complete 'The Great Escape' from relegation under Martin Allen also sticks in the mind." Jon Restall, editor, Beesotted.

Lowest moments on this ground

"Losing 3-2 to ex-non-leaguers Dagenham and Redbridge just seemed like an all-time low at the time it happened – although they subsequently turned out not to be a bad side. There was a relegation six pointer a few years back against Chesterfield where we took the lead in the 92nd minute only to concede an equalizer. That was pretty awful too." Jon Restall.

Heroes of the turf

"The Terrible Twins – George Francis and Jim Towers. Got to count 'em as one because they were so lethal playing alongside each other. They were both tremendous goal-scorers and team players. Mel Scott – the classiest centre-half of all time. As a stop-the-others defender he makes John Terry look like a carthorse; as a football-playing defender he makes Rio Ferdinand look like a carthorse. Johnny Brooks – sheer class. Ken Coote – skill, loyalty and a lovely man; holder of The Bees record appearances. Steve Phillips – a pugnacious little so-and-so who not only scored plenty but made plenty. Ron Greenwood – a terrace supporter who went on to play for The Bees and eventually to manage England. He was cool under pressure, just a short head behind Mel Scott, but ahead of Ian Dargie, Peter Gelson and Jamie Bates as Brentford's best-ever centre-half. Billy Dare – a bit of a short-arse (he was only 5-ft 6-in), but he could score goals. He signed for West Ham for £5,000 in front of the telly cameras! Billy Gorman – a bald-headed full-back, but my, could he tackle. And, although he looked old, he was as nippy as a two-year-old on something uplifting. Terry Hurlock – he made Ron 'Chopper' Harris look like a pussy cat. I think the expression is 'tough tackling' – in reality, he terrified opponents into giving the ball away. I would have added Jimmy Hill, but he became a Foolham player!" Larry Signy, journalist, Beesotted.

RIVALS
Fulham and QPR.

That's quite interesting

"We're well known for having a pub on every corner. TV's Bradley Walsh was once on our books and we were the first team to lose in Cardiff's 'lucky changing room', which surprised no one who supports the club." Jon Restall.

"After getting off the bus on his way to games, George Francis would often drop into one of the four corner pubs for a bevvie with the fans; ditto Stan Bowles." Larry Signy.

Not a lot of people know that

"Brentford has a trophy cabinet – and that there's something in it apart from the 2008/2009 League Two Championship. I believe it's the West Middlesex County Cup or something like that, though." Larry Signy.

HEROES OR ZEROES?

⤢ **HEROES OF THE SIDELINE**

"Steve Coppell – an intelligent manager that had us playing wonderful football and scoring goals for fun. Martin Allen – his tactics were fairly mundane (getting big players to stand in the right places), but his enthusiasm was completely infectious. Andy Scott – the current gaffer got us out of the bottom division and appears to be an astute and hard-working young manager." Jon Restall.

"Malcolm MacDonald – he built great, winning teams and was a fun man to interview (my oft-quoted favourite was: 'The status is remaining quo'). Bill Dodgin Jnr – he also built good footballing teams. He was a neighbour of mine, and we often met. I listened in awe as he told me about football and footballers." Larry Signy.

Zeroes of the turf

"Lorenzo Pinamonte – the big Italian striker was very, very poor indeed and apparently earned a fortune. Murray Jones regularly features in any conversation of worst-ever players. He was just dreadful on every front. Neil Shipperley – supporters hoped he was the man to save us from relegation. By the time he reached us he was enormous and a complete drain on resources – he looked a bit like the Honey Monster." Jon Restall.

Don't mention the…

"Game in which we lost 4-1 to Swindon in the LDV Trophy. Swindon were later fined for fielding an understrength team." Jon Restall.

Villains

"Ron Noades and Dave Webb both left the club in a far worse state than they inherited it in and are largely blamed for our current financial debts – Ron was effectively playing *Championship Manager* in real life." Jon Restall.

The ground

The best-known fact about Griffin Park is that it boasts a pub at each corner. The name supposedly originates from the griffin in the Fullers brewery logo – they used to own the land on which the ground was built.

One of the most striking features is the **Brook Road Stand**, behind the goal. Nicknamed The Wendy House, it's more a two-storey stand than a two-tier structure. It holds 1,600 away fans, 600 seated above a terrace for 1,000. On the far side is the **Bill Axbey Stand**, an all-seater single-tier covered structure that runs the length of the field. There are pillars at the front supporting a roof that acts as a giant advertising hoarding for planes on approach to Heathrow. The stand was named after a longtime supporter who came to watch The Bees for 89 years before passing away

in 2007. Opposite is the main **Braemar Road Stand**, a single tier of covered seating for home fans, while behind the goal is the small covered **Ealing Road Terrace**.

Getting there

By road/Parking Griffin Park is on the western outskirts of the big city. North of the river and just off the M4 it's easy to reach. Exit the M4 at junction 2 and follow the A4 (circling around the Chiswick Roundabout to head back the way you came). At the roundabout turn left onto Ealing Road, the ground will be on your right. There's road parking – try the side roads near Brentford train station.

By train Brentford station is a 10-minute walk to the ground – go right onto Station Road, right onto Orchard Road, right onto Windmill Road and then left onto Clifden Road. The stadium is dead ahead. Alternatively, Kew Station is just over half a mile east, following an easy route along Green Dragon Lane. In terms of tube stations, South Ealing and Northfields are around a mile north of the ground.

Pubs for home fans

It may sound like an election campaign promise, 'a pub on every corner', but that's exactly what there is at Griffin Park. The Royal Oak, New Road, has sports TV and Courage beers, while Princess Royal, Ealing Road, is a Fullers pub. The Griffin, Brook Road South, is a Fullers pub with sports TV, a beer garden and decent grub, as well as a good mix of home and away fans.

Good food near ground

Brentford High Street has a number of decent independent cafés or, for a quick fix, there's always McDonald's.

Pubs for away fans

The New Inn, New Road, has a beer garden, sports TV and the odd ale as well as a good mix of home and away supporters, making it a good choice. Princess Royal, Ealing Road, is a Fullers pub making up the fourth corner. The Wagon and Horses, Kew Bridge Road, is a handy stop-off for those coming via Kew Bridge Railway Station. For those in the market for a decent real ale, try the Magpie and Crown, High Street, or the Brewers Tap, just off Catherine Wheel Road.

Top tips

Although there's a pub on every corner, The Royal Oak and Princess Royal are not the best places to head to in opposition colours.

THE LAST **WORD**

brentford.vitalfootball.co.uk
beesunited.org.uk
griffinpark.org
brentford-mad.co.uk

- 🔵 **Nicknames** The Seagulls
- 🔵 **Founded** 1901
- 🔵 **Ground** Withdean Stadium (opened 1999/00)
- 🔵 **Address** Tongdean Lane, Brighton BN1 5JD
- 🔵 **Capacity** 8,850
- 🔵 **Best attendance** 8,729 vs Manchester City, League Cup 2nd round, 24 September, 2008
- 🔵 **Contact** 01273-695400
- 🔵 **Ticket Number** 01273-776992
- 🔵 **Email** seagulls@bhafc.couk; tickets@bhafc.co.uk
- 🔵 **Website** seagulls.co.uk

BRIGHTON & HOVE ALBION

RIVALS

A strong rivalry has developed with Crystal Palace, with all the intensity of a local derby.

"**A**nd Smith must score." Four words that haunt any Brighton fan – more than perhaps any stadium move, ground sale or relegation battle. They so nearly beat Manchester United in the 1983 FA Cup final. Stellar performances from the headband-wearing Steve Foster at centre-back and midfield dynamo Jimmy Case, combined with a late equaliser from Brighton legend Gary Stevens had brought Brighton, already relegated from the top flight, close to lifting the cup in a thrilling final. Then, with seconds left on the clock, Gordon Smith was gifted the opportunity to win the game. It seemed easier to score than miss, and one of the most famous quotations to have fallen from a commentator's lips was uttered. To be fair, it was not all Smith's fault – United goalkeeper Gary Bailey pulled off a good save too. You don't usually get two bites at the cherry and Brighton went on to lose the subsequent replay. That result, and their relegation from the old First Division, was to be the beginning of turbulent times for the south coast outfit.

A decade of decline then began, and despite a brief revival in the early nineties, the club spiralled into financial problems that ultimately led to the end of the Goldstone Ground. Its sale by chairman Bill Archer and his board in 1997, when the team were at the foot of the Football League, was meant to halt the club's slide into bankruptcy. However, the sale angered fans and it was claimed the club gained little financial reward in return, especially as they were now homeless. When a ground was found, it was 70 miles away

in Gillingham. Eventually the new owners negotiated the return to Brighton and the Withdean Stadium. This is a temporary move and after a bit of a financial scrape, a marathon planning battle and some novel fund-raising schemes, Brighton and Hove Albion should be settled into the purpose-built Falmer Stadium by the start of the 2011/12 season.

Greatest moment on this ground

"The last game at Goldstone was emotional as not only were we leaving the ground, but we also had to win, and did, which was exciting. Recently, winning the League One title at a canter in 2001/02 season had many great moments, just a shame Micky Adams left us too soon." Nick Jackson, fan.

Lowest moments on this ground

"There have been plenty of low moments, it was never much fun driving all the way to Gillingham for a 'home' match to see us lose, but the saddest moment was probably the last game at the Goldstone Ground, even though we won 1-0." Carl Richards, fan.

Heroes of the sideline

"Got to be Alan Mullery – two promotions and a spell in the top flight." Nick Jackson.

Heroes of the turf

"Steve Foster (not only for the headband), along with the likes of Jimmy Case, Gary Stevens, Bobby Zamora, Stuart Storer, Peter Ward and Mark Lawrenson." Carl Richards.

VILLAINS

Most Brighton fans consider the chairman and board behind the sale of the Goldstone Ground the biggest villains in the club's history.

Zeroes of the turf

"Anyone who ever pulls on a jersey and doesn't give 100 % is a zero in my book, and we've had a few of those. Although he did score another goal in the FA Cup final, Gordon Smith for 'hitting' Gary Bailey's legs and not the back of the net almost qualifies him too!" Nick Jackson.

Don't mention the…

…sale of the Goldstone Ground.

The ground

The Withdean Stadium is a council-owned multi-purpose stadium, with an athletics track around the perimeter, making for a ground that is

> Withdean Stadium, complete with running track.

LAURA COLLINS

low on atmosphere and soul. It's no surprise that Brighton are so keen to get their new ground underway. It's taken them ten years to gain planning permission for the Falmer Stadium, which will hold an impressive 23,000 supporters.

The **North Stand** is the only permanent structure and the only stand with a roof. Unfortunately it is also unavailable for away supporters. It will be the only stand left when the club leaves for a permanent home.

The **East Stand**, or stands, are a collection of temporary, small seated areas for home support only. The view is OK considering the running track, and extra atmosphere is generated by the home fans utilizing the temporary structure by banging their feet on the wooden planks.

The **South Stand** is the biggest seating area. Raised up a bank, it is open and backed by woods, and offers great views to home support only. Its open nature makes it a miserable place to be in bad weather.

The **West Stand** houses the 900 away fans; this can be split if the support is small though. It is the furthest away from the pitch with a running track and then a large oval area making the action quite distant. The atmosphere is better than one would expect though.

Getting there

By Road/Parking The ground is about two miles outside the city centre. There is no parking within a mile of the stadium, as this was one of the conditions for the club being able to use the stadium. So if driving, it is best to head to either one of the park and rides, which are specifically opened for match days, or park a little distance away. Fans from either direction will be travelling along the A27 or coming down the A23 from London.

Either way, at the junction of the A23 and A27 is the Mill Road park-and-ride; it is clearly signposted and is perfect for a quick getaway post match. The buses are fast and efficient both before and after the game. The park and ride service is free with a valid match ticket.

By Train Preston Park is the closest station and is served from London Victoria, King's Cross, London Bridge and Brighton's Central Station, should you wish to park in the middle of the city. From there it is a 10-minute walk to the ground.

ALL OF THE PUBS AROUND THE GROUND ARE HOME FANS ONLY, THEY ALL HAVE BOUNCERS ON THE DOOR AND IN SOME CASES ONLY ALLOW RECOGNIZED LOCALS IN OR THOSE WITH SEASON TICKETS.

THE LAST WORD
theseagulllovereview.blogspot.com
brighton-mad.co.uk

HOME AWAY

Pubs for home fans
Brighton fans who fancy a pint before the game usually do so in the city centre hence there are no specific pubs as there are so many, and then get the train out to the ground. The only pub close to the ground is The Sportsman which is packed and has a friendly atmosphere.

Good food near ground
As mentioned above the local pubs serve bar meals and The Sportsman does a carvery. There are a few-fast food vans around the ground too, but if you want something a little more interesting to eat then it is best to head into the city centre where you will have far greater choice.

Pubs for away fans
Near the ground The Sportsman, behind the North stand, is the best bet, although it gets rammed. It also does bar food and a carvery. Near the station on the main A23 is The Preston Brewery Tap, it's about a mile walk away and gets busy, but also serves food, all the pubs will admit away fans and the atmosphere is generally excellent.

Top tips
No alcohol is served in the ground, so if you're gasping for a pint quench that thirst prior to entry or you will be disappointed.

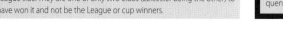

PUB QUIZ

That's quite interesting
The song 'Tom Hark (We Want Falmer)' reached number 17 in the charts in January 2005 and was vital to help raise funds to keep the club going in its quest for planning permission for its new ground.

Not a lot of people know that
In 1910, Brighton won the Charity Shield, their only national honour, beating Aston Villa (League champions) 1-0 when only a Southern League side. They are one of only two clubs (Leicester being the other) to have won it and not be the League or cup winners.

BRISTOL CITY

- ⊕ **Nicknames** The Robins
- ⊕ **Founded** 1897
- ⊕ **Ground** Ashton Gate (opened 1904)
- ⓘ **Address** Ashton Road, Bristol BS3 2EJ
- ⊕ **Capacity** 21,497
- ⊕ **Best attendance** 43,335 vs Preston North End, FA Cup 5th round, 16 February, 1935
- ⊕ **Contact** 0871-222 6666
- ⊕ **Ticket Number** 0871-222 6666
- @ **Email** enquiries@bcfc.co.uk
- ⊕ **Website** bcfc.co.uk

The 'Ashton Gate Eight' are without a shadow of a doubt the most important eight players who ever wore a Bristol City jersey. The eight players (Gerry Sweeney, Dave Rodgers, Peter Aitken, Geoff Merrick, Chris Garland, Trevor Tainton, Jimmy Mann and Julian Marshall), became national football celebrities in 1982, not for anything they ever did on the football pitch, but simply for tearing up their contracts. Had they not done so, Bristol City would no longer exist as a football team. Three years before, the club had been in the First Division, but successive relegations followed and when they hit the fourth tier, bankruptcy beckoned. The club were losing thousands a week, and with the early eighties seeing falling crowds and revenues, there seemed to be no way back. A new company was formed in 1982, Bristol City Football Club Limited emerged, but they still had a huge problem – how to refinance.

These top eight players, The Robins' highest earners, were all on long-term contracts and unless they could be persuaded to forego these, the team could not survive. Intense negotiations went on for days, players were essentially being asked to put the club first while potentially putting themselves into financial difficulty. It was a nail biting eleventh-hour decision – minutes before the deadline the 'Ashton Gate Eight' emerged blinking, into the bright lights having agreed a life saving deal which saw them walk away and the club begin its fight back. And while Bristol City survived to play another day it took several years of consolidation, team rebuilding and restructuring, before they started to climb the league again. It took them until 1990 to leave the basement division, although even this achievement had a slightly bittersweet edge as they finished runners-up to deadly rivals Bristol Rovers. But it was significant nonetheless, as

RIVALS

Bristol Rovers by far, although the proximity of Swindon doesn't go unnoticed nor does the England/ Wales rivalry when Cardiff come visiting from just over the river Severn.

they had survived a tumultuous 10-year period and were once again heading in the right direction. Recent years have seen them established as a top Championship side with realistic Premiership ambitions, something that was only a dream before the 'Ashton Gate Eight' helped bring the club back from the brink.

Greatest moments on this ground
"In recent times the 3-1 home win over Rotherham, which sealed promotion to the Championship, was incredible. Any time we've beaten the Gas at home is a great moment too." Simon Rosher, fan.

Lowest moments on this ground
"The early eighties, around the 'Ashton Gate Eight' saga was truly awful, there seemed to be no future for the club and we'd all have to start watching Rovers!" Simon Rosher.

Pubs for home fans
There are a number of pubs around the ground that are home favourites, The Hen and Chicken and the BS3 bar are amongst the most popular.

Good food near ground
The city centre, which is about a 20- to 30-minute walk away is the best bet for grub, with everything from restaurants to fast food. Around the ground there are vans selling the usual pre-match food.

Pubs for away fans
All pubs near the ground are strictly home fans only. If you want a pint it is best to drink near the city centre or on the Waterfront, both are about a 25-minute walk from the ground. No alcohol is available in the ground.

Top tips
The pubs close to the ground really are locals only, if you fancy a pleasant pint it's better to drink nearer the city centre.

PUB QUIZ

That's quite interesting
Despite having had little success, they have star-studded support that includes Jenson Button, John Cleese, Banksy and The Wurzels, who wrote their theme song 'One For The Bristol City'.

Not a lot of people know that
Despite being an English club, Bristol City won the Welsh Cup in 1934, beating another English club – Tranmere Rovers – in the final.

Heroes of the sideline

Gary Johnson got them promotion to the Championship and was highly regarded by fans until his 2010 departure. Alan Dicks had tenure of 13 years from 1967 to 1980, which included leading Bristol City into four years of top-flight football.

Don't mention the...

2002/03 season when, despite scoring a whopping 106 goals, they ended up in the play-offs in Division Two where they lost in the semi-finals to arch rivals Cardiff City.

Villains

"Tony Pulis, he was ex-Bristol Rovers, which meant things started badly and then he jumped ship to Portsmouth. Russell Osman also had a torrid time as manager and player." Mark Knighton, fan.

The ground

Ashton Gate has been slowly modernized over the last ten years to bring it in line with rules regarding all-seater grounds. However, it still looks like a bit of a throwback to the seventies with the whole ground in desperate need of modernization. Plans have been on the table to rebuild the oldest of the stands, most notably the Wedlock Stand, but this has continuously been put on hold, and now seems to have been shelved completely in favour of moving the club to a new purpose-built stadium on the edge of the city in the near future.

The **Wedlock Stand**, better known as the **East End** was traditionally a home supporters' terrace, but after seating the ageing single-tier structure was used to house away fans in the southeast section. It's a tight stand, with some restricted viewing due to pillars, but has excellent acoustics.

The **Williams Stand** doesn't quite run the length of the pitch; it is pretty unremarkable and is starting to show its age. It contains directors and press areas and offers almost uninterrupted views of the playing area.

The **Dolman Stand**, named after the late, great chairman, is by far the most impressive. It has two levels of seating, although you hesitate to call them tiers. It offers uninterrupted views and is home to the family areas.

The **Atyeo Stand** is the most modern, built in the mid-nineties to replace a large open terrace. It also houses the training facilities and dressing room. Named after the late, great player John Atyeo, it was opened in 1994, sadly one year after the legend's death.

Getting there

By Road/Parking The best way to approach Ashton Gate is to go around Bristol and down the M5. At junction 18, take the A4 Portway and follow signs for the airport. Continue along here over the Brunel Way swing bridge and then take a left into Winterstoke Road where you will soon see the ground.

Parking is possible on streets a little way from the ground, although some roads are permit-only. There are some car parks but it may be easier to park closer to the town centre and walk back.

By Train Bristol Temple Meads is the mainline station in the city, it is a fair walk from the ground, a solid 45 minutes, so it's best to either hop on a bus or get a taxi.

bristolcitynet.com
bcfc3lions.co.uk
ziderheads.co.uk

▼ Nicky Maynard celebrates 'One for The Bristol City'.

⊖ **Nicknames** Pirates, Gasheads, The Gas
⊙ **Founded** 1883
⊕ **Ground** Memorial Stadium (opened 1921)
ⓘ **Address** Filton Avenue, Horfield, Bristol BS7 0BF
⊕ **Capacity** 12,393 (limited to 11,916)
✪ **Best attendance** 12,011 vs West Bromich Albion, FA Cup 6th Round, 9 February, 2008
ⓒ **Contact** 0117-909 6648
ⓒ **Ticket Number** 0117-909 8848
@ **Email** info@bristolrovers.co.uk
Ⓦ **Website** bristolrovers.co.uk

BRISTOL ROVERS

There's no doubt it's rare to be able to say a club has become as famous for its smell as it has for its football, but back in the days when Bristol Rovers played at Eastville Stadium they had this dubious honour. Fumes from a nearby storage facility would fill the air around the ground with the pungent odour of gas, an association that still lingers in the air, despite the club having left the ground long ago. Bitter rivals Bristol City used to taunt Rovers with the name 'Gasheads,' but as the years passed, this derogatory term was taken by Rovers' fans as a badge of honour, one they have worn with pride ever since. Back then, Eastville Stadium could turn its hand to anything. It hosted football, speedway, greyhound racing, American football and cricket, but even this creative system of multi-usage could not save the club from financial woes. In 1986 the team were evicted and forced into exile at Twerton Park, home of non-league Bath City. This ignominious move was like manna from heaven for fans of the equally fiscally-challenged Robins.

Rovers were originally formed by a young schoolteacher back in 1883, when they were called the Black Arabs FC, due to their all black kit and because they played on the pitch next to the Arabs rugby team. Over the following years they became Eastville Rovers and then Bristol Rovers. Their history is not one overflowing with trophies, in fact they spent years hovering in the mid-two tables dabbling in relegation and promotion between Second and Third Divisions until, in 2001, they found themselves relegated to the Fourth Division. The following year they very nearly dropped into non-league football, but 'the Gasheads' fought back, crucially finding a permanent home at the Memorial Stadium. Although initially a 'time-share', the football team now own the ground, and have big plans for hosting football in the upper leagues, an

RIVALS

Bristol City, their neighbours from across the town, are the most hated of teams. Cardiff City and Swansea also rank highly as do Cheltenham Town.

area that Bristol Rovers have had little taste of in recent years, but are aiming to make a steady push towards. Here's hoping they come up smelling of roses.

Greatest moments on this ground

"Has to be 2 May, 1990 at home to Bristol City at Twerton. Our 3-0 win not only secured our promotion from the old Third Division, but also knocked City off the top of the table and allowed us to claim the title on the following Saturday." Geoff Sayer, gas-trust.org.

Lowest moments on this ground

"Probably Wycombe's second goal in the game that sent us down to the bottom tier for the first time in our history. Ironically, also 2 May, in 2001. It ushered in six miserable years." Geoff Sayer.

▲ Jason Roberts scores against City in a 2-0 win over The Robins

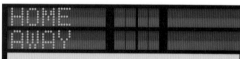

Pubs for home fans
The Wellington on Gloucester road is popular, it can be a home pub only for certain games such as derbies and when Welsh clubs are in town.

Good food near ground
There is a wide range of eateries in the area, from Asian to fish and chips and greasy spoons. The Bristol Fryer and the Big Bite Café on Ashley Down Road come recommended.

Pubs for away fans
The Gloucester Road area and the surroundings are packed with good pubs. The Victoria on Gloucester Road has a mix of both fans. In general all of the pubs in the area, which is also popular with students, have a good match-day atmosphere.

Top tips
As most parking is residential arrive early or expect a good walk.

Heroes of the turf

"I never saw him, but it's generally accepted that Geoff Bradford was Rovers' greatest ever player. He played in the 1950s and is the only player ever to represent England whilst still playing for The Gas. The early seventies saw Bruce Bannister and Alan Warboys, known as 'Smash and Grab', scoring for fun, particularly in the 1973/74 promotion year. I'd say they were the most potent strike partnership we've ever had," says Geoff Sayer. Also Marcus Stewart (he tarnished his reputation though by later joining Bristol City), Nathan Ellington, Andy Tilson, Ian Holloway and David Williams.

Zeroes of the turf

"There have been some really terrible players over the years, plus at times, in the darker days, we were just grateful someone wanted to wear the shirt! Andy Spring and Bob Lee are two I can remember though." Ben Smithe, fan.

Villains

"Obviously, anyone with an association with Bristol City always gets a warm reception! Also, Jim Gannon, until recently Stockport County manager, is much disliked amongst Gasheads, after accusing the club of cheating by watering the pitch to get a game postponed. It was quite sweet when we pipped them to the play-offs on the last day of that same season." Geoff Sayer.

Don't mention the…

…fact that they have never yet been in the top flight of English football.

The ground

After 89 years in the same spot, Bristol Rovers went through a period when they were, perhaps, better known for their ground-moving exploits than their football. However, their nomadic existence is now over. The Memorial Stadium is Bristol Rovers' home, and the club has grand plans for redevelopment. The new 18,500 all-seater stadium will be built on the same spot and should provide facilities for both football and rugby. There were talks of the team having to go into exile whilst the development took place, but it seems more likely they will develop around the playing surface.

The **Das Stand**, which has a row of executive boxes at the back with a terrace in front looks a little like a pavilion and straddles the halfway line on one side of the pitch. Either side of it are two smaller structures – one is the family stand and is covered, the other is the Guinness stand

HEROES OF THE SIDELINE

"For me, Gerry Francis, who took a team of average players and turned them in to champions in the 1989/90 season, is one of the legends. Sadly he returned some years later to manage us again, which was a bit of a disaster in all honesty." Geoff Sayer.

BRISTOL CITY, THEIR NEIGHBOURS FROM ACROSS TOWN, ARE THE MOST HATED OF TEAMS.

which is just a small area of terrace. The stand houses the changing rooms, television gantry and scoreboard.

The **Uplands Stand** is the tallest structure and like the Das Stand straddles the halfway line but does not run the full length of the pitch. It has an upper level of seating with terrace below. There are two additional areas of terrace either side; both are open to the elements with one housing the away fans.

The **Becks South Stand** is a semi-permanent stand that fills half of the end; it has been nicknamed the tent due to its temporary nature.

At the other end is the **Bass Terrace**, more permanent in nature and home to the core Rovers fans, it is tight and low but has good acoustics, although old-fashioned supporting pillars do impede viewing a bit.

Getting there

By Road/Parking From the north (east and west) turn off the M4 towards Bristol on the M32. At junction 2, turn off and take the exit signposted Horfield, the stadium is then clearly signposted.

From the south on the M5 take junction 16 signposted Thornbury on the A38. Continue on the A38, Gloucester Road, passing Filton Airport until you get to Filton Avenue where you will see the ground.

Parking close to the ground is tricky, residential streets are the best options as you move a bit further away form the ground. Try Muller Road or Gloucester Road, or the surrounding streets.

By Train The only mainline station is in the centre of Bristol at Temple Meads. From here trains go to Montpellier and Parkway stations, both of which are about two miles from the ground. Alternatively there are regular First Great Western buses to the ground from the centre of town.

THE LAST **WORD**

gas-trust.org
bristolrovers.rivals.net

PUB QUIZ

That's quite interesting
The ground's multi-use system even included firework displays and a visit from the Harlem Globetrotters.

Not a lot of people know that
'Goodnight Irene' by Lead Belly, is a distinct yet slightly unusual club anthem sung on the terraces. No one can pin down its exact origins but it would appear to come from a 1950s tie with Plymouth. With Rovers beating the Pilgrims convincingly, fans sang the song to the Plymouth fans departing early.

- ⊖ **Nicknames** The Clarets
- ⊙ **Founded** 1882
- ⊕ **Ground** Turf Moor (opened 1983)
- ⓘ **Address** Harry Potts Way, Burnley BB10 4BX
- ⊕ **Capacity** 22,546
- ✪ **Best attendance** 54,775 vs Huddersfield Town, FA Cup 3rd round, 23 February, 1924
- ⓒ **Contact** 0871-221 1882
- ⓒ **Ticket Number** 0871-221 1914
- @ **Email** info@burnleyfc.com
- ⓦ **Website** burnleyfootballclub.com

BURNLEY

May 25, 2009 will go down in Burnley history. After 33 years in the comparative wilderness of the lower leagues, The Clarets roared back to the Premiership, the top table, a league that in the post-war period up until the early seventies, saw the team as one of the most consistently dominant forces in English football. During this period they won the First Division championship twice, were twice runners up and made two cup finals and quarter finals of the Fairs Cup. They were, without doubt, one of the great football teams of the era with legends such as Jimmy McIlroy and Jimmy Anderson ever-present in the team. With ex-player Harry Potts at the helm, there were a couple of seasons when they came close to being invincible.

This period of top-flight football had become all but old newsreel footage for many Burnley fans, as between 1976 (when they were relegated) and 2009, fans of the Clarets had been to hell and back. A match simply referred to as 'the Orient game' was the very bottom, and it saw Burnley needing to win and Lincoln City to lose to secure survival. They survived and the recovery began. During the wilderness years, closest rivals Blackburn Rovers became one of the richest clubs in the land, winning the Premiership trophy and playing in Europe. However, a steady climb through the league followed and some good cup runs saw the team from Turf Moor finally established in The Championship under Steve Cotterill through the noughties. But it wasn't until manager Owen Coyle stepped in and Wade Elliot delivered that vital killer punch to beat Sheffield United, that they returned to the promised land. While their trip to the Premier League was a brief affair, the Clarets faithful relished every moment and reminded some of the opposing teams what real, passionate support was about.

RIVALS

Blackburn Rovers are their main rivals, although Preston and the seaside club Blackpool also come in for some stick.

Pubs for home fans
Most town centre pubs are home fans only, especially places like the Turf Hotel.

Good food near ground
The Bridge and The Talbot pubs do excellent bar meals. In the town centre there are a number of fast-food restaurants as well as the usual vans around the ground.

Pubs for away fans
Near the ground The Bridge and The Talbot are away-fan friendly; both serve good food as well as good beer.

Top tips
The town centre of Burnley can get a bit rowdy on match days, some pubs frown upon away colours being worn for fear of trouble.

PUB QUIZ

That's quite interesting
The Bee Hole end couldn't have a roof added in the seventies due to the foundations being situated on the old Bee Hole Mine, thus they couldn't support any extra weight. It was said that the stand moved when Burnley scored.

Not a lot of people know that
Burnley is one of only three teams to have won all four English league titles.

Greatest moments on this ground
"It wasn't an achievement, just a rescue from potential oblivion. A 2-1 win against Orient on 9 May, 1987 that ensured we would continue in the Football League the following season when anything other than a win would have seen the club either playing non-league football or, even worse, go out of business." Tony Scholes, editor, *Clarets Mad*, claretsmad.co.uk.

Lowest moments on this ground
"Again, there's no doubt that the era in the second half of the eighties was the worst. We had our worst-ever team and our worst-ever players and with that came our worst-ever results. We'd lost our previous home game to Rochdale 3-0, and that was a horrible performance, but then we suffered a 6-0 defeat to Hereford. With no disrespect to Hereford , that sort of result should never have been possible." Tony Scholes.

Heroes of the sideline
"The winners are the heroes, so John Haworth and Harry Potts are the managers who have brought the top honours to Turf Moor. Then there are those such as Cliff Britton, Jimmy Adamson and Owen Coyle who have all won promotion to the top flight." Tony Scholes.

Don't mention the…
"George Oghani, striker from 1987 to 1989, who in his first season scored 20 goals. In his second season in 1989 he was arrested buying an ironing board from Asda as he hadn't paid for the screws he had on his person. When confronted by a security guard as he left the store, he hit him over the head with the board." Richie Crossley, fan .

Villains
"There are probably too many to mention. The worst referee I ever saw at Burnley was a Mr George Hartley from Wakefield who won the game for Wolves almost single-handedly in January 1970. Some might say an impartial referee could never have conjured up the sort of decisions he did that day. Anyone who played at Turf Moor in blue and white halved shirts. I think Burnley fans from the sixties might just say Mike England." Tony Scholes.

The ground
Turf Moor has been home to Burnley since 1883, making it one of the oldest grounds in the Football League. Over those years it has been through a number of redevelopments, the first being the Longside, a stand that was covered for the cost of £20,000, which back in 1954 was a small fortune and reflected the status of the club. Since then the most notable was the rebuilding of the James Hargreaves Stand (formally the Longside) and the Jimmy McIlroy (formally the famous Bee Hole Stand) in 1996. The other two stands remain undeveloped, although plans are afoot to modernize.

Opened in 1996 the **James Hargreaves Stand** is a an impressive two-tier stand running the length of the pitch. Executive boxes separate the two decks and the modern nature offers excellent views with a capacity of 8,100.

During the same period of construction in 1996 the **Jimmy McIlroy Stand** was also opened as part of the modernization of Turf Moor. Two tiers with executive boxes, it replaced the whole Bee Hole end with a modern cantilevered stand capable of holding 6,200 fans.

The **Bob Lord South Stand** is a throwback to the seventies and is a classic single-tiered main stand, which is now looking somewhat dated. It is due for a revamp though, a planned second tier would add 4,500 seats to the current capacity at just under 4,000. The development would also add hospitality suites and a cinema.

The **David Fishwick Stand**, also known as the Cricket Field Stand is also planned for redevelopment. Currently, it is an old single-tiered affair with some pillars, which used to harbour the core of home fans but has lately been used for away support and holds up to 4,100.

Getting there
By Road/Parking If coming from the south, north or west, exit the M6 at junction 29 and join the M65. Continue on the M65 until junction 10 and follow signs for Towneley Hall. This road eventually passes the ground. From the east, the above applies, but you can also leave at junction 12 and take the A682 towards Burnley, after about two miles turn left onto the A6114 and continue on this road until you see the ground.

Most of the surrounding streets have parking restrictions on a match day (Saturday and Tuesday), so it is advisable for away supporters to use the cricket club next to the ground or the road spaces further up Ormerod Road near the fire station.

By Train The nearest station is Burnley Manchester Road. On leaving the station, proceed down Centenary Way, Turf Moor should now be visible. At the roundabout, turn right into Yorkshire Street, which then becomes Harry Potts Way.

If arriving at Burnley Central, head for the town centre then bear left towards Gala Bingo. Join Yorkshire Street, which will take you to the ground.

Burnley's Brian Jensen celebrates victory in the 2009 Wembley play-off final.

THE LAST WORD

clarets-mad.co.uk
thelongside.co.uk

HOME COLOURS

- **Nicknames** The Brewers
- **Founded** 1950
- **Ground** Pirelli Stadium (opened 2005)
- **Address** Princess Way, Burton on Trent DE13 0AR
- **Capacity** 6,912
- **Best attendance** 6,192 vs Oxford United, Football Conference, 17 April, 2009
- **Contact** 01283-565938
- **Ticket number** 01283-565938
- **Email** bafc@burtonalbionfc.co.uk
- **Website** burtonalbionfc.co.uk

BURTON ALBION

RIVALS

Derby County, Tamworth and Stafford Rangers.

Burton Albion are like a modern Aesop's Fable. While some teams seem to revel in the bipolar boom to bust of euphoric league title wins and big name signings followed by the crashing lows of relegation and administration, the Brewers have adopted a more Zen-like approach towards the beautiful game. For most of their recent history the club has been famous for its affiliation with the name Clough – their manager from 1998 to 2009 was former England and Nottingham Forest player Nigel Clough. In management terms the name brings a lot of expectation, but at Burton he built steadily and patiently and the club progressed into the Conference where results improved year on year – from ninth to sixth to fifth. By 2009 the team were looking odds-on favourites for promotion, and Clough was lured away by Derby County, a club where his father enjoyed huge success as manager.

Burton Albion's greatest moment came over two legs against Manchester United in the FA Cup in January 2006. Clough's side valiantly held the mighty reds at home without conceding, with on-loan keeper Saul Deeney earning the plaudits for keeping out the United star strikers. The team fought for a hard-earned draw, gaining the reward of an away day at the Theatre of Dreams for the Conference team. The Brewers took

PUB QUIZ

That's quite interesting
"Pirelli gave us the space to build our stadium, giving them the naming rights." Chris McNeill.

Not a lot of people know that
"The Pirelli Stadium, when the club was in the Football Conference, was mostly maintained by the players themselves. Darren Stride could regularly be seen with a pot of paint and a brush." Chris McNeill.

11,000 followers to Old Trafford, still a record for away fans at the ground. The result? Well, let's just say they put up a good showing. The club had now tasted the big time in front of 53,000, and left with a renewed determination to achieve league status. Today, the goal is to build on that steady progress, climb the table, and push on for promotion. In terms of league football, the Brewers are the new kids on the block. This is a team that was plying its trade in the Birmingham and District League during the 1950s, and didn't gain promotion to the Conference until the new millennium had well and truly dawned. But with the shiny, new Pirelli Stadium and the ability to play the passing game on the pitch and the long game off it, they're certainly equipped for life in the professional ranks. Hares watch your backs, don't doubt the opposition. Remember: slow and steady wins the race.

Greatest moments on this ground
"There are two moments that come to mind. First, when we had Manchester United come visit the Pirelli Stadium in the third round of the FA Cup and the Brewers held them to a 0-0 draw. We later lost at Old Trafford, but the experience was fantastic. The second is obviously 2008 at Torquay, when we were crowned Conference champions and promoted to the Football League. Both are fantastic moments in the Burton Albion history." Aaron James, Vital Burton Albion.

Lowest moments on this ground
"We've had it quite good so far, fingers crossed. The stench of the yeast around Burton isn't pleasant." Chris McNeill, Burton Albion Mad.

Heroes of the sideline
"Nigel Clough is by far the biggest hero. He was at Burton for 11 years and created the Albion we see today. Without him, we wouldn't be where we are." Aaron James.

Don't mention the…
"Amount of time it took us to become champions of the Football Conference… one point was needed in our last three games and we

VILLAINS
"Anyone playing for Nuneaton, Tamworth, Gresley or Stafford Rangers." Chris McNeill.

▲ Young Burton midfielder Jacques Maghoma breaks away into space.

got nothing – talk about nail-biting. We had to rely on other teams losing their games." Chris McNeill.

The ground

The Pirelli Stadium grew opposite the old Eton Park. It's named after the tyre brand as they were the previous owners of the land. This shiny new ground looks a little like a superstore from the outside, but that might be being a little unkind. The **Main Stand** is a single tier of seating for 2,000 that's covered by a high roof, though there are no pillars. The **Coors East Stand** behind the goal is for away fans and is one of three virtually identical covered terraces. Along with the **Popular Stand** opposite the Main, and the **West Stand** behind the far goal, all are modern, covered terraces with no obstructing pillars and good views.

Getting there

By road/Parking In the centre of the country, Burton-on-Trent is fairly easy to reach with the M6 running to the west and southwest, the M42 terminating just to the south and the M1 taking up the eastern flank, not to mention the A38 that runs right through the centre. From the M1 north, exit at junction 28 onto the A38, signed Derby/Matlock. Continue for 20 miles before exiting onto the A5121, Derby Road (signed Burton North). The stadium will be on your right. From the M1 south exit at junction 23 and follow the A50 to junction 4, exiting onto the A38 and following the route as above. From the south take the M42 to junction 11 and follow the A444 to Burton. Turn left onto the A511 Bridge Street and at the roundabout take the third exit onto the A5121 Derby Road. The ground is ahead. There's pay parking at the ground as well as the nearby Rykneld Trading estate. Street parking also.

By train Burton train station is about a 25-minute walk to the ground heading northwest along Derby Street.

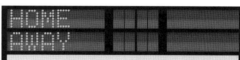

Pubs for home fans
The Great Northern, on Wetmore Park Road, is a favourite meeting spot for many Brewers fans. Owned by the local Burton Bridge Brewery, there are obviously plenty of quality ales to sup as well as sports TV to watch. The Beech Inn, Derby Road, is another good choice and the closest watering hole to the new stadium.

Good food near ground
Close to the ground, there's a McDonald's on Derby Road, just past the Beech Inn.

Pubs for away fans
Close to Burton train station, on Station Street, are a couple of good pubs. The Roebuck, otherwise known as Burton Ale House, has a decent selection of local ales and sports TV. The Devonshire Arms, tied to Burton Bridge Beers, has a good range of ales as well as decent food. On Derby Street, The Alfred is also tied to Burton Bridge Brewery.

Top tips
With a team nicknamed the Brewers, it would seem churlish to overlook the town's heritage and leave without sampling at least some of the local culture. Whether you feel that purpose is best served by visiting a museum or an actual living, breathing pub is entirely up to you!

THE LAST **WORD**

burtonalbion-mad.co.uk
burton.vitalfootball.co.uk
burtonalbion.com

⩔ **HEROES OF THE TURF**
"Kevin Poole – going into the 2010/11 season as the oldest player in the Football League at 47. Our keeper has come out of retirement twice to continue his long career. Nigel Clough – the club's longest-serving manager. Gary Crosby – Clough's assistant and deserves a lot of credit. Darren Stride (Mr Burton Albion) – he's seen it all with well over 600 appearances for the Brewers. He was captain for nine years and always a reliable and consistent performer. When people talk of Burton Albion, the name Darren Stride always gets a mention; he's a legend. Matt Duke – he only played three seasons for us but was a fantastic keeper and possibly the most famous. He went on to ply his trade at Premier League Hull City and deservedly so. Daryl Clare – a former league striker who in two seasons scored 37 goals in just over 80 games and a real hero amongst the younger Brewers fans, who will always give him a cheer every time he returns to the Pirelli." Chris McNeill.

⩔ **ZEROES OF THE TURF**
"Too many to mention." Chris McNeill.

GETTY IMAGES

HOME COLOURS

BURY

- **Nicknames** The Shakers
- **Founded** 1885
- **Ground** Gigg Lane Stadium (opened 1885)
- **Address** Gigg Lane, Bury, Lancashire BL9 9HR
- **Capacity** 11,840
- **Best attendance** 35,000 vs Bolton, FA Cup 3rd round, 9 January, 1960
- **Contact** 0161-764 5521
- **Ticket number** 0161-763 3103
- **Email** info@buryfc.co.uk
- **Website** buryfc.co.uk

The Bury crest reflects the industrial heartland from which the town draws its support. There's the anvil for metalwork and manufacturing, the crossed shuttles of textiles, the fleece of the wool industry and the culms of papyrus (no, me neither) that represent papermaking. Crowning the crest there are two branches of the cotton plant and, in case we missed anyone, there's a bee representing industry. It's an appropriate symbol, not just of the hard-working northwest but also of the industry and resolve demonstrated by the fans, who succeeded in hauling the club back from the precipice of extinction.

In March 2002 the League One club was sinking in a financial mire with administration looming and debt spiralling. The fans immediately mobilized, forming the 'Save our Shakers' campaign. A mass charity drive was organized, spearheaded by Gary and Phil Neville's father Neville, who helped coordinate fund-raising dinners, seat sales and auctions. Fans rattled buckets and, with a massive groundswell of support, the club was able to pull itself out of the quagmire and out of administration. Matt Dunham, of the club's joint administrators RSM Robson Rhodes, said: "Without the hard work of the supporters the sale could not have been achieved and it is probable that the club would by now be closed."

Forever Bury, the supporters' association formed to coordinate the SOS campaign, now have representation on the board in recognition of the amount of money they raised and their titanic efforts to save the club. It's a testament to Shakers fans that the team lived on to see its 125th birthday in April 2010. Formed the year the motorcar was invented, the club has gone on to claim two FA Cup wins and has spent much of its history in the top two tiers of English football. Relegations have meant that Bury are currently fighting to return to these levels, but with the club moto 'vincit omnia industria' (hard work conquers all),

a set of fans that have put their money where their hearts are and a badge that literally covers all forms of industrious labour, this team certainly can't be beaten on effort.

Greatest moments on this ground
"It's 6 January, 1976 – the FA Cup 3rd Round replay. Having beaten Doncaster Rovers (4-2) and Spennymoor (3-0) at home in rounds one and two, the Third Division Shakers reward was a tough away trip to high-flying, First-Division Middlesbrough. A hard-fought 0-0 draw brought the tie back to Gigg Lane on a cold, damp Tuesday evening. I was one of thousands still queuing outside when the game kicked off and Middlesbrough took an early lead. After missing the first 15 minutes I got into the ground to find we were 2-0 down. From then on it was one-way traffic as Bury battered away at their loftier opponents, pulling level as both Jimmy McIlwraith and Kevin 'Reggie' Hulme scored. The roof was finally lifted off Gigg Lane when Andy Rowland netted the winner. What a night!" Dave Giffard, chairman, Forever Bury.

Lowest moments on this ground
"Again, a cup game. FA Cup 1st round on 11 November, 1995. Bury had what seemed an easy first round draw against non-league Blythe Spartans. However, the Spartans certainly had other ideas. An awfully embarrassing 90 minutes later saw virtually every Bury fan line the pitch to applaud the underdogs on their lap of honour after winning 2-0. They outfought us, were more skilful, fitter, faster... it was truly embarrassing." Dave Giffard.

Heroes of the sideline
"Stan Ternent – quite simply the most successful Bury manager of all time, leading us from third from bottom of the lowest tier to the First Division (now Championship) with a double promotion in the nineties. Bob Stokoe – he joined the club in 1960 as part of the deal that took John McGrath to Newcastle. He immediately became player-manager and led the club to the Third Division Championship that season with a team that scored 108 goals. If goal difference was involved then Bury's would have been +63." Dave Giffard.

That's quite interesting
"Bury FC can lay claim to a number of records. Their 6-0 victory over Derby County in the 1903 FA Cup final is a record score that still stands today. They're also the only club in the entire league to have scored over 1,000 goals

RIVALS

Rochdale, Bolton, Preston, Stockport County and Oldham.

HEROES OR ZEROES?

⌃ **HEROES OF THE TURF**

"Les Hart – player, coach, physio and manager; 44 years at one club, an absolute legend. Greg Farrell – "the greatest player to ever grace the game". Not my words, but those of legend John Charles. Chris Lucketti – captained Bury through the mid-nineties when they won double promotion. Nicky Daws – the 'three lunged' engine of Bury's midfield serving almost 10 years at the club. Dean Kiely – his penalty save in the dying minutes of the final away game at Watford in 1997 earned Bury the one point needed for promotion." Dave Giffard.

⌄ **ZEROES OF THE TURF**

"Dave Hickson signed from Liverpool in 1961 and managed to create an appalling disciplinary record in just eight games – he was sold on after being sent off for picking a goalkeeper up and throwing him in the net. Ade Littlejohn – signed by Neil Warnock. The fans never took to him yet he still managed 112 games in nearly three seasons that saw us nosedive down the leagues to almost oblivion. Fortunately, he followed Warnock to Sheffield United." Dave Giffard.

---

in each of the top four professional leagues in England. They're now also the only league club to have been thrown out of the FA Cup." Dave Giffard.

Don't mention the…

"Time our mascot, Robbie the Bobby, lost his head. There was a mass of media attention and Sky Sports filmed an appeal with a headless Robby. I don't think I've laughed so much in all my life." Dave Giffard.

Villains

"Stan Bowles – he played for us in 1970 on loan from Manchester City. He was a real character and the fans took to him straight away, but he couldn't conform to rules and regulations, which often got him into trouble. He'd only played five games for us when Bury terminated his loan. The story goes that he had turned up very late for the team coach for an away game at Chesterfield. He got into a row with then manager Les Hart, who stopped the coach before it had got 50 yards from the ground and threw him off.

Terry Fenna. He wasn't a villain or unpopular. He was a big, strapping striker that played for the reserves but had one serious problem – he couldn't see without heavy glasses. He couldn't wear them in games so the lads had to learn vocal cues to help him through. However, he still kept getting booked or sent off for kicking out at players when he caught a glimpse of some movement and thought he was kicking the ball." Dave Giffard.

Not a lot of people know that

"The 2009/2010 season saw Bury FC celebrate its 125th anniversary and I organized the sixth annual Forever Bury Beer Festival to coincide with the date the club was formed. The festivals so far have raised £47,000." Dave Giffard.

The ground

Gigg Lane is an impressive mix of old and new. Half the all-seater stadium is single tier, running from the **East Stand** or Cemetery End, behind the goal and around through the **South Stand** along the pitch. These covered seats are mostly pillar-free with only a few supporting the roof of the South Stand. Behind the far goal the Manchester Road End is again a single tier of seating with a high roof, but the stand doesn't run all the way to the corner, stopping instead at the edge of the penalty box. This where the away support is housed, an allocation of up to 2,000. There are three supporting

pillars but mostly excellent views. The **Main Stand** is also all-seater and slightly elevated, as the old terraces in front are no longer in use.

Getting there

By road/Parking Easily reached via the M66, M62 or M60, the ground is on the southern reaches of the town. From the M60, exit at junction 17, signed A56 Whitefield, and follow the A56. Gigg Lane is a right turn. From the M66, exit at junction 2 onto the A58 Rochdale Road and follow through three roundabouts. Turn left onto Market Street and right onto Gigg Lane. Street parking available.

By train Bury Metrolink is about a mile from the ground. Turn left out of the station and left again by Chicago Rock Café and head over the crossroads onto Knowsley Street. At the end turn left along Manchester Road, then left onto Gigg Lane. A number of buses run from the station down Manchester Road by Gigg Lane if you can't face the walk to the ground.

Pubs for home fans
The Bury Social Club is a decent choice for enjoying a bit of pre-match chat and a pint. The Staff of Life, Manchester Road, is the closest pub to the ground with generally good beers, a good vibe and a decent mix of home and away fans.

Good food near ground
On the A56 there's a McDonald's as well as a number of takeaways (from Italian to Chinese). Man Sons Chinese Takeaway, Manchester Old Road, is another decent bet, closer to the ground.

Pubs for away fans
You can grab a swift half pre or post match at Bury Social Club for a £1 entry fee provided it's not too packed. Manchester Road is home to a number of decent pubs including the Swan and Cemetery – a family-friendly spot close to the ground with decent ales. The Pack Horse, closer to the ground, is another popular spot for the away contingent.

Top tips
For the short-term, FC United of Manchester, who have a pretty strong and loyal following, also use the ground to stage their home matches. This is some of the best attended non-league action around, and worth a look if you're in the area.

foreverbury.org
themightyshakers.co.uk

HOME COLOURS

- **Nicknames** The Bluebirds
- **Founded** 1908
- **Ground** Cardiff City Stadium (opened 2009)
- **Address** Leckwith Road, Leckwith, Cardiff, South Glamorgan CF11 8AZ
- **Capacity** 26,828
- **Best attendance** 26,033, vs Leicester City, Championship play-off, 12 May, 2010
- **Contact** 02920-221001
- **Ticket Number** 0845-345 1400
- **Email** club@cardiffcityfc.co.uk, tickets@cardiffcityfc.co.uk
- **Website** cardiffcityfc.co.uk

CARDIFF CITY

W hen you think of great British European teams you rarely pluck Cardiff City's name out of the air, unless of course you are a Cardiff fan. Then you'd know that the sixties and seventies saw a feast of European football come to Ninian Park. Of course, at the time Cardiff were mainly plying their trade in the old Second Division, but with a virtual monopoly of the Welsh Cup from 1964 to the end of the seventies, European competition was an annual expectation. It wasn't a token round or two either, as you might expect from a Second Division outfit. In the 1964/65 season they made it to the quarter-finals of the competition before losing to top Spanish side Real Zaragoza. Two seasons later they went a step further and made it to the semi-finals and played German giants Hamburg, with two young strikers, Brian Clark and John Toshack forming a spearhead in attack. They drew the away leg 1-1 only to be beaten at home 2-3 in front of a massive 43,000 fans. But this wasn't the highlight of their European forays, that was saved for the 1970/71 season. The team again went way beyond what was expected of them into the quarter-finals of the Cup Winners' Cup where they faced Spanish giants Real Madrid. Over 47,000 crammed into Ninian Park. Incredibly, Cardiff, who were flying high in the Second Division at the time, won 1-0 with Brian Clark heading the winner. The return leg, however, shattered the fairytale with Real winning 2-0, but nevertheless Cardiff had beaten the best in Europe.

Of course, The Bluebirds have another slightly more famous claim to fame; they are the only club from outside of England to win the FA Cup. They achieved this feat in 1927, a period when the team was a powerhouse in British football, finishing runners-up in the First Division in 1924 and runners-up in the cup in 1925. This was a success they came close to repeating in 2008, losing out to Portsmouth, by a single goal to nil.

RIVALS

Swansea without a doubt, but all English clubs come in for some stick, especially Bristol City and Rovers.

▼ Below: Joe Ledley wins a header against Arsenal's Aaron Ramsey in the FA Cup.
▼ Bottom: 1927 FA Cup final, Wembley. Cardiff 1 Arsenal 0.

GETTY IMAGES

POPPERFOTO/GETTY IMAGE

Greatest moments on this ground

"I would say that my greatest moment was Cardiff beating Real Madrid 1-0. I was there, but was so young all I can remember is burly blokes swearing and the overwhelming stench of fags and burgers." Mike Slocombe, urban75.

HEROES OR ZEROES?

Lowest moments on this ground
"I can't pin down a single low, the eighties and early nineties saw numerous relegations into the bottom tier, finishing third from bottom of the old Fourth Division in 1996 was just full of painful moments." Clive Stanton, fan.

Heroes of the sideline
"Dave Jones got us to the 2008 Cup final, and could become a hero if he can do more for us this season. In the sixties, Jimmy Scoular." Clive Stanton.

"Has to be Eddie May for having such a wonderfully chant-friendly name. After drinking six pints of Theakston's XB before our game at Doncaster, I managed to put myself into a trance-like state, singing 'Eddie May's Barmy Army' for the entire duration of the game." Mike Slocombe.

Villains
"Lee Trundle and fellow Jack, Alan Tate paraded around the Millennium Stadium having won the Football League trophy, with anti-Cardiff messages on a Welsh flag. Trundle wore a shirt which was highly offensive. They were arrested though and Trundle made things worse by moving to Bristol City!" Clive Stanton.

That's quite interesting
Cardiff City are the only team to have won the FA Cup, in 1927, that do not come from England.

Not a lot of people know that
The new stadium is just across the road from Ninian Park.

The ground
Cardiff finally left Ninian Park in 2009, the ageing ground having come to the end of its days. Cardiff City Stadium was built for their push to achieve Premiership status. The ground is an all enclosed arena with a high roof. The main **Grandstand** is a two tier structure, a row of executive boxes along the back topped by a high second tier of seats. Behind the goal is the **Canton End**, a single tier of seating that wraps through the **Ninian Stand** and along to behind the far goal and the **Grange**.

Away fans have an allocation of 2018 in the south east corner, accessed through gate 7. The corners have huge exits that make it feel less bowl-like. Great atmosphere.

Getting there
By Road/Parking Most fans will be coming from the west, so take the M4 and turn off at junction 29 onto the A48 (M), follow this road as it turns into the A48 around the edge of the city centre. As you are starting to come out of the city, just before the river, turn left onto the A4161, continue for about a mile and then right into Leckwith Road. The athletics stadium next the ground is well signposted. There is a big car park at the ground. If you want to avoid the city, or are a Swansea supporter, then turn off at junction 33 of the M4 and follow the A4232 all the way into the city, which again has clear signposting for the athletics ground.

There are ample-sized car parks around the ground, alternatively there are city centre car parks should you want to check out Wales' capital prior to a game.

By Train Ninian Park Station is only a short walk from the ground and is served by trains from Cardiff Central Station.

HOME AWAY

Pubs for home fans
All pubs within a 5- to 10-minute walk of the ground are home fans only.

Good food near ground
The Lansdowne Hotel serves excellent bar meals. Close to the ground there are fast-food vans, but if you want more variety Cardiff city centre has everything you want.

Pubs for away fans
Cardiff is an intimidating place to visit as an away fan; all the pubs close to the ground are strictly home only. Pubs in the city centre are a little better, although there is obviously a big rivalry between Wales and English teams. But keep a low profile and most banter is good humoured. The exception close to the ground is The Lansdowne Hotel on Beda Road, it serves good food as well as beer and advertises on its website that it welcomes away support, all reports of the establishment have been positive as home and away fans mingle.

Top tips
It's worth getting to Cardiff early and having a look around, the city centre is like you would expect of a capital city and is full of life. It's worth having a quick look at the Millennium Stadium, too, which is spectacular.

THE LAST WORD

urban75.org./cardiff
cardiffcity-mad.co.uk

HOME COLOURS

CARLISLE UNITED

- **Nicknames** The Cumbrians, The Blues
- **Founded** 1904
- **Ground** Brunton Park (opened 1909)
- **Address** Warwick Road, Carlisle, Cumbria CA1 1LL
- **Capacity** 16,981
- **Best attendance** 27,500 vs Birmingham, FA Cup 3rd round,
  5 January, 1957 and vs Middlesbrough, FA Cup 5th round,
  7 February, 1970
- **Contact** 01228-526237
- **Ticket Number** 0844-371 1921
- **Email** enquiries@carlisleunited.co.uk
- **Website** carlisleunited.co.uk

PUB QUIZ

That's quite interesting
"Sam Hunt played one season for the club in 1938-1939 and scored 33 goals in 32 games. Who knows what a player he would have been had World War Two not come along." Tim Graham.

Not a lot of people know that
"Player/manager Ivor Broadis was the first manager to sell himself when he arranged his own transfer and fee to Sunderland for £18,000 in February 1949." Tim Graham.

Jimmy Glass is probably Carlisle's most famous player. Ask people to name one and he'll probably spring to mind before even Bill Shankly or Peter Beardsley. For a goalkeeper to score is unusual enough to make headlines, but for one to score with the very last touch of the season, to keep a team in the Football League, was the stuff of fairytales. Were it not for the fact that regular keeper Tony Craig was sold to Blackpool, Glass would not even have been at the club for the end of the 1998/99 campaign, let alone on the pitch. Drafted in on an emergency loan from Swindon Town, Glass went up for the last-minute corner and on to national stardom. That volley from five yards assured the team from Cumbria their survival, and Glass became an instant hero to the Carlisle faithful. As the commentator screamed "Jimmy Glass! Jimmy Glass!" thousands of fans piled onto the pitch and on top of the prostrate keeper. Even the ref was mobbed by celebrating supporters as the ground was swamped by the mass of a shell-shocked Blue Army. Glass returned to Swindon Town at the end of the season and retired from professional football soon after.

Carlisle endured some lean years around this period, and in 2004 slipped into the Conference. Many fans look back at this as a watershed moment for the club, who have returned stronger and secured successive promotions to climb into League One. They missed out on a Wembley League One play-off final by a last gasp goal in a thrilling climax to the 2008 season. Maybe now they're ready to break through that glass ceiling into the Championship?

Greatest moments on this ground
"Without doubt the events of 8 May, 1999. On loan goalkeeper Jimmy Glass goes up for a corner for what will be the last action of the season. Scarborough have drawn and are celebrating survival until the unbelievable happened – the corner falls to Glass, who hammers it in the net to win the game 2-1. Cue pitch invasion at Brunton Park and the greatest escape ever." Simon Clarkson, Carlisle United Supporters Club, London Branch.

Lowest moments on this ground
"How long have you got? There are numerous opportunities to pick in the latter days of the Michael Knighton regime, but perhaps the most disappointing game I remember is being 2-0 up at home to Charlton in the penultimate game of the 1985/86 season only for the Addicks to come back and win 3-2. A defeat at Oldham two days later was our last-ever game at what is now Championship level." Tim Graham, editor, Carlisle United Mad.

Heroes of the sideline
"Bill Shankly – he played and managed United and look what he went on to do at Liverpool. Bob Stokoe – he managed on three occasions bringing plenty of success. Mick Wadsworth – he was manager of the rampant 1994/95 champions." Simon Clarkson.

Villains
"I think it's rather obvious to all that Michael Knighton is the main one. His threat to lock the gates of Brunton Park and withdraw our registration from the Football League while saying, "The people of Carlisle do not deserve a football club", didn't exactly endear him to the Cumbrian public. Player-wise Karl Hawley's actions in his last few months with the club before he went to Preston certainly left something to be desired." Tim Graham.

The ground
Looking at the ground from the comfort of the smart single-tier **Story Homes East Stand** you could be mistaken for thinking you were looking back on another era of football. With so many small clubs now nestled in purpose built all-seater arenas, Brunton Park is a real blast from the past with its banks of uncovered terraces. The East Stand has an area for away fans at the northern end. The **Warwick Road End** is a covered terrace behind the goal, and generates great noise from the home support there. The roof is distinctive for its three apexes. The long **West Stand** has a large, open standing terrace at the front, known as **the Paddock**. These are backed by a series of boxed seating areas. Away fans also occupy the **Petteril End**, a shallow uncovered terrace behind the far goal.

Getting there
By road/Parking East of the centre, the ground is easily accessed from the motorway. Exit the M6 at junction 43 following the A69/Warwick Road for just over a mile, and the ground is on the right. The main car park is behind the CBS stand – turn right through the gates at the third set of traffic lights.

By train Carlisle Citadel Station is in the centre. Head straight out of the station, cross Botchergate and walk along The Crescent. Turn right into Warwick Road and follow for about 15 minutes.

> Bob Stokoe, manager of Carlisle on three occasions.
< Richard Prokas models the Eddie Stobart coloured strip of the 99/00 season.

Pubs for home fans
Tim Graham, editor of Carlisle United Mad says, "The nearest pub to the ground is The Beehive, Warwick Road; it's the busiest match-day pub for Carlisle fans." Away supporters are also allowed. Further along try the White House. In town try The William Rufus, Botchergate. "The landlord is a Carlisle fan who does pre- and post-match deals on beer and food."

Good food near ground
The Tesco superstore on the way in from the motorway has a handy café. There are several good cafés on Botchergate near the station, as well as a Subway sandwich bar.

Pubs for away fans
The Beehive and, for those not sporting away colours, The White House accept visiting fans, both are on Warwick Road. "The Rugby Club, 100 yards past Brunton Park on the way in from the motorway, is highly recommended," says Tim. "A good pint and they actively encourage away fans to visit." The Cumberland Inn, Botchergate, serves some decent ales and is handy for the train station.

Top tips
Be aware that there's a residents' parking scheme in operation by the ground.

THE LAST WORD

carlisleunited-mad.co.uk
carlislelondonbranch.org
kynson.org.uk

BOB THOMAS/GETTY IMAGES

HEROES OR ZEROES?

⌃ HEROES OF THE TURF
"Jimmy Glass – if that goal hadn't gone in, I don't think the club would have survived. Chris Balderstone – he played for the club for nine years and in our only top tier season. Allan Ross – a goalkeeper with a club record 542 League and cup appearances. Jimmy McConnell – a striker in the late twenties/early thirties who scored 132 goals in 160 games. Hughie McIlmoyle – he had three spells at the club and has a statue outside the club shop." Tim Graham.

⌄ ZEROES OF THE TURF
"Eric Gates – the worst signing ever. Jermaine Beckford – absolute garbage for us. Jean-Claude Pagal – only one appearance sums it up." Simon Clarkson.

DON'T MENTION THE...

"The Floods in 2005 saw Carlisle unable to play at their ground for over a month. The tale is that a goldfish was found swimming in the goals!" Simon Clarkson.

HOME COLOURS

CHARLTON ATHLETIC

- 🎯 **Nicknames** The Addicks
- 🏆 **Founded** 1905
- 🏟 **Ground** The Valley (opened 1919)
- ℹ️ **Address** Floyd Road, Charlton SE78BL
- 🎯 **Capacity** 27,111
- ⚽ **Best attendance** 75,031 vs Aston Villa, FA Cup 5th round, 12 February, 1938
- ☎ **Contact** 020-8333 4000
- 🎫 **Ticket Number** 0871-226 1905
- @ **Email** customerservices@cafc.co.uk
- 🌐 **Website** cafc.co.uk

A two-nil win over Stoke City hardly seems like a scoreline that would put a club into mourning, but that day in 1985 Charlton Athletic fans walked away from their beloved Valley for possibly the last time. An early victim of football's increasing boom and bust, Charlton's bubble burst in 1984. The Addicks had seemed to be enjoying such a positive period – promotion from the old Third Division and new owners who appeared to have ambition and deep pockets, but it was too good to be true. Overspending, coupled with low crowds, soon led to a club staring into the abyss. Charlton fans rallied around and a trust was formed to purchase the Addicks, but the ageing Valley, once the largest league ground in London, was now in a sorry state of repair. Here was a stadium that could no longer meet league standards for safety and a newly formed supporters' consortium that could not afford the necessary upgrades. Not only that, but the Valley was still the property of the previous owners. Fans left a make-or-break meeting knowing that to save the club they would have to become the first team in the football league to ground share. And so in 1985, the Addicks moved in with local rivals Crystal Palace.

The turmoil off the pitch didn't halt Charlton's success on it though, as they were promoted to the then First Division for the first time in 30 years under the managerial guidance of Lennie Lawrence. They remained up despite low crowds and poor league performances and in 1989 they announced their intentions to return to the Valley, having reunited club and ground. The struggle wasn't over yet though, as Greenwich City Council refused planning permission to rebuild the ground. Undeterred Charlton fans formed The Valley Party, with a single agenda – to pass the necessary permission for the stadium's redevelopment. They won a massive 14,838 votes, enough to show the council the depth of local feeling and help secure a positive planning notice for the ground, bringing football back to the heart of the community where it belonged. Even then, it wasn't quite plain sailing, as to help finance the redevelopment, the club had to make the painful decision to sell local lad and star player Robert Lee. After a brief spell lodging at Upton Park, an emotional 1-0 win over Portsmouth brought The Addicks back to the green, green grass of home on 5 December 1992.

Greatest moments on this ground

"Beating a very expensive Chelsea side 4-2 at The Valley in 2003 ranks highly for a lot of fans, I think we were 4-1 up at one stage. We also went top of the League for the first time in 60 years when we panned Southampton 5-0 in 1998, that was a special moment and confirmed our return to top-class football. They were great, but the day I'll always remember was 5 December 1992, a 1-0 win over Portsmouth, our first game back at the Valley." Clive Pearson, fan.

Lowest moments on this ground

"The last game at the Valley in 1985 – we beat Stoke but at the time it felt like we would never come back." Simon Lawrence, fan.

Heroes of the sideline

Alan Curbishley is the number one hero of the modern game; he created a Premiership side that for a few years became a competitive force for other smaller clubs to aspire to. Back in the glory days Jimmy Seed led Athletic to runner-up position in the First Division after two successive promotions and an FA Cup win. Also Lennie Lawrence.

VILLAINS

Some fans blamed Michael Gliksten, owner of The Valley, when they had to leave. Also Greenwich Council, who refused planning permission when the club wanted to return, thus sparking The Valley Party.

RIVALS

Crystal Palace, fuelled by the stadium share, Millwall and West Ham.

PUB QUIZ

That's quite interesting
The last goal at the old Valley was scored by Robert Lee, he had started work for Charlton as a turnstile operator.

Not a lot of people know that
The Valley Party won double the amount of votes of the Liberal Democrats at the local elections.

Don't mention the…
1984/85/86 season; Charlton very nearly went out of existence.

The ground
The rebuilt Valley is impressive, although it was always one of the smaller grounds in the Premiership. It lay derelict for almost a decade and there were times during that sad period where it seemed unlikely that the weed-covered terraces would ever see action again. However, the Valley has never looked back, and despite Charlton's collapse through the divisions it has remained a ground that is big enough yet tight enough to create an excellent atmosphere.

The **Jimmy Seed Stand** is home to the away support. It is the oldest stand in the ground and is single-tiered. It offers excellent views as it is slightly raised above pitch level, although there is one supporting pillar right behind the goal, which can be annoying. It will seat up to 3,000 and on occasion, when away support does not require the whole end, home fans may be seated in the end.

Opposite is the impressive two-tiered **North Stand**, which is home to the core of Charlton support. It is part of the revamped Valley and the corners sweep round to meet the two side stands. The stand was completed in 2002 and will hold almost 9,000 fans.

The **West Stand** sweeps round to join the North and is the largest of the four sides over two tiers. Built in the 1990s as part of the first wave of redevelopment, it is unusual amongst many Premier-standard grounds of its age, as it has no executive boxes. Those boxes are confined to the single-tier **East Stand** that also houses a television gantry and was built on the site of a former massive open terrace, which was reputedly the largest terrace in the country at one point.

The ground has no floodlight pylons, but rows of lights across the stands and a large video screen between the Jimmy Seed Stand and the East Stand.

Getting there
By Road/Parking The simplest way into the Valley is to exit the M25 at Junction 2 and then head towards London on the A2, the A2 will then become the A102 (M); you then need to take the A206 turning which is signposted Woolwich. Continue towards Woolwich and you will soon see the ground, but don't get too close.

It's mostly street parking, but you can't get too close to the ground as there are residents' permits and roads regularly get blocked off on match days. The closer to the A2 the better. There are also some industrial areas just past the ground, although parking this side of the ground makes leaving a slower process.

By Train Charlton Station is a mere two blocks from the ground and the stadium is clearly visible when you leave the station. It is served by trains from Charing Cross, London Bridge and Waterloo East stations.

◀ Clive Mendonca notches up a hat trick in a 5-0 win over Southampton, August 1998.

Pubs for home fans
The Royal Oak and The Bugle Horn are the two real Charlton-only pubs, although they don't openly refuse entry to away fans, but do get packed prior to matches.

Good food near ground
The Spanish Galleon, Anchor and Hope and The Antigallican all serve good pub grub at lunchtime and in the evenings. There are also a number of fast-food eateries and cafés especially around the station.

Pubs for away fans
The Antigallican Pub close to Charlton Station on Woolwich Road is a firm favourite with visiting supporters, although it has to be said most of the area's pubs are friendly. It's generally a good atmosphere and most pubs will allow entrance as long as colours are not overtly worn. The Rose Of Denmark is also popular.

Top tips
Don't try and park too close to the ground, parking permits are enforced and the area gets congested post-match.

charltonathletic-mad.co.uk
addickted.net
forever.charlton.net

HEROES OR ZEROES?

⪢ **HEROES OF THE TURF**
"From back in the day, legendary goalkeeper Sam Bartram, flat cap and all. He gave Charlton 22 years as their number one shot stopper." Simon Lawrence. Also Mark Kinsella, Derek 'Killer' Hales, John Hewie, Clive Mendonca and Richard Rufus.

⪢ **ZEROES OF THE TURF**
Taher El Khalej and Dennis Rommedahl.

CHELSEA

- **Nicknames** The Blues
- **Founded** 1905
- **Ground** Stamford Bridge (opened 1919)
- **Address** Fulham Road, London SW61HS
- **Capacity** 42,055
- **Best attendance** 82,905 vs Arsenal, Division One, 12 October, 1935
- **Contact** 0871-984 1955
- **Ticket Number** 0871-984 1905
- **Email** see website
- **Website** chelseafc.com

ADRIAN DENNIS/AFP/GETTY IMAGES

∧ Zola holds off Arsenal's Gilles Grimandi.
❯ The Cat vs Manchester United, Christmas Eve 1960.

Long before Russian oil magnates rolled into the capital, Chelsea were renowned for attracting, as well as producing, larger-than-life characters. Its location helped inspire this with a fan base composed of both working-class West Londoners as well as the moneyed from the nearby wealthy boroughs. This mixture of the rough with the smooth has been reflected on the pitch and transferred into the stands, helping to shape Chelsea into one of the best supported and most feared teams in the land. It hasn't always been roses though. Chelsea history has been rocky at times, with a sprinkling of success, but it's certainly always been colourful.

Ten years after they were formed in The Rising Sun pub (now The Butchers Hook), opposite the ground, Chelsea reached their first FA Cup final in 1915. Although they lost, they were establishing a name for playing thrilling and attractive football, a reputation that would help them sign some of the biggest names of the time, establishing a policy that would become the hallmark of Chelsea FC right up to the modern day. It wasn't until the 1954/55 season that they tasted their first proper success as, under the managerial guidance of ex-England centre forward Ted Drake, they claimed the League title. This larger-than-life figure rid the club of its old image, rejuvenating both the crest and the nickname, getting rid of 'The Pensioner' moniker along the way. He also built a team of exciting players, and brought on notable youths such as Jimmy Greaves. The sixties saw Chelsea emerge as a major power, narrowly missing out on Championships and losing in semi-finals but eventually winning the League Cup all under the guidance of Tommy Docherty. Dave Sexton brought the team's first FA Cup of the modern era, beating Leeds United in an enthralling 2-1 replay, a game that long lives in the memories of the two clubs and has fuelled an intense rivalry that exists to this day. The next season they

went on to beat Real Madrid in the final of the Cup Winners' Cup to achieve their first European success.

The rest of the seventies and the eighties were a decidedly rocky period, for everything from industrial relations to the British car industry, as well as fans of the West Londoners. Stadium redevelopment almost brought the club to its knees, star players were sold and the club plummeted to the verge of relegation to the third tier before Ken Bates purchased the club for £1. 'Uncle Ken' helped to turn fortunes around, eventually getting the club back on a level financial footing. The team also returned to the top flight, though many fans believed they were always destined to fall into a 'big-club-underachieving' bracket.

Then former European Player of the Year Ruud Gullit joined as player manager, building a classy team that took the 1997 FA Cup. Gianluca Vialli and Claudio Ranieri followed winning League, FA and Cup Winners' Cups over the next six years. Things were pretty good for Chelsea fans. Then it all became the stuff of dreams – the most highly publicized sale in football history. Russian billionaire Roman Abramovich purchased the club, pumped in millions of pounds on and off the pitch and established Chelsea as not only one of the big four in England, but also Europe. Back to back Championships

RIVALS

Fulham is the closest but not the fiercest. Tottenham, Arsenal, Manchester United, Liverpool and a particularly bitter rivalry with Leeds United.

That's quite interesting
Chelsea has the honour of winning the last FA Cup at the old Wembley Stadium and the first at the new one.

Not a lot of people know that
In 1928 along with Arsenal, Chelsea became the first side to wear numbers on their shirts.

PUB QUIZ

followed, along with FA and League cups under new manager José Mourinho, 'the Special One'. But the elusive Champions League trophy has just remained out of their grasp. Failure to win here cost Mourinho his job and then a bad start to the competition saw 'Big Phil' Scolari axed too in the quest to become kings of Europe. When suspect refereeing denied Gus Hiddink's side a birth in the final, some people began to wonder if Chelsea would ever be the ones to put a London club's name on the trophy for the first time.

Greatest moments on this ground
"The highlights of watching Chelsea at Stamford Bridge are too numerous to mention, but definitely include Chelsea 4 Liverpool 2 (1997 FA Cup 4th round). Ruud Gullit's side were two-down at half-time but came back thanks to Gianluca Vialli, Mark Hughes, Gianfranco Zola and company. The Cup Winners' Cup semi-final the following season. Losing 1-0 from the first leg, Chelsea went a goal down but came back to win 3-1 on the night and qualify for the final where they beat Stuttgart 1-0 courtesy of Gianfranco Zola. Winning the Premiership in 2005 at Stamford Bridge. Watching Chelsea winning the English League Title is something I never thought I'd see." David Johnstone, CFCUK.

Lowest moments on this ground
"The worst match at Stamford Bridge for me was in 1988 when Chelsea were relegated in the First Division relegation play-off against Middlesbrough." David Johnstone.

"I have only been a season ticket holder for 15 years so the dark days were before my time, but the lowest moment I have experienced was the daylight robbery that was the 2009 Champions League semi-final against Barcelona – I am angry just thinking about it!" Michael Baker, fan.

Heroes of the sideline
Tommy Docherty, Eddie McCreadie, Ruud Gullit and Gianluca Vialli, José Mourinho is by far and away the most successful, although the pressures of a lack of Champions League win or the egos around the club signalled his demise. Gus Hiddink – short but brilliant with an FA Cup win.

Villains
"The biggest villains in my eyes include referees David Ellery (awarded Manchester United two penalties in their 4-0 FA Cup final rout of The Blues in 1994), and Graham

∧ Mark Hughes celebrates Chelsea's second goal in their 1997 FA Cup final victory.
◀ Terry stretches to block Blackburn's Ryan Nelsen.

Poll. Then there is Tom Henning Overbo, the Norwegian referee who denied Chelsea four penalties in their Champions League semi-final against Barcelona in 2009. As far as opposition players are concerned, everyone who has ever played for Spurs, Leeds and Liverpool. In qualifying that, Chelsea supporters were pleased with the job former Blues' chairman Ken Bates was doing at Leeds United, helping them to languish in League One." David Johnstone.

Don't mention the…
Semi-final defeats against Liverpool and Barcelona in the Champions League, or the final defeat to Man United, it's the one major trophy that has eluded them.

The ground

Chelsea have played their football at Stamford Bridge since their inception in the pub just across the road. The club has grown from its roots way back in 1877 until it finally got one hell of a makeover in the nineties, making it one of the greatest arenas in the country. Prior to this metamorphosis it was famous among fans for three things: the huge three-tier East Stand, the legendary Shed End and the fact there seemed to be a car park behind one of the goals. The building of the East Stand almost brought the club to its knees in the 1970s as the cost forced the sale of the ground's freehold to developers. It was later bought back by the Chelsea Pitch Owners, a non-profit group composed of shareholding fans, which guarantees nothing can happen to the ground unless in the best interest of the supporters.

The **East Stand**, despite its cost to the club, was for several decades the most impressive stand in English football. Its huge three-tiered cantilever design made it stand out like no other stand in the seventies and eighties. It now sits as part of an all-seated stadium but is no less impressive.

The **West Stand** has been redeveloped into a modern and very impressive three-tier structure with the added modern accessory of executive boxes. It also has a totally transparent roof to allow light onto the now enclosed pitch.

The North Stand, renamed the **Mathew Harding Stand** after the late benefactor of the club, fills both corners of the ground sweeping its two tiers to join the West and East keeping true to the bowl shape that the Bridge used to be famous for.

The opposite end is the **Shed End**, another two tier affair with the upper being significantly larger that the lower. A police control room hangs like some Orwellian watchtower. This is also where away fans will find themselves and depending on their number, they can be in either tier or side of the Shed.

There are large video screens in the corners between the Shed and East Stand and the Mathew Harding Stand and the West stand.

Getting there

By Road/Parking From all directions use the M25 to Junction 15, then the M4 towards London. The M4 becomes the A4 to Hammersmith. Use the Hammersmith Flyover before turning off for Earl's Court after about a mile and a half. Go past Earls Court station, cross Old

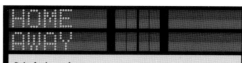

Pubs for home fans
The Sofa So Bar and The White Horse are a couple of lively favourites, but any pub within a short walk of the ground will be strictly Chelsea. The Butchers Hook (Chelsea were formed in this pub) is now a gastro pub.

Good food near ground
The Kings Road has a number of eateries and most of the local pubs sell food, all can get very busy pre games in the evening and prices are excessive in some cases. There are the usual vans near the ground for pies and so on.

Pubs for away fans
Most pubs near the ground are to be avoided; the home fans are less than tolerant of groups of away fans in their boozers. There are a number of pubs on The Kings Road, which is about a mile away, which are fine for a low-key drink. Nearer the ground The Slug and Lettuce is probably the safest bet, opposite Fulham Broadway Station. Inside the ground, beer is served at what can only be described as interesting prices, even for London.

Top tips
If you fancy a drink before a match its best to do it away from the ground, the local pubs are very partisan.

transparentsport.com/cfcuk
theshedend.com

Brompton Road, then turn right at Fulham Road; the ground is then about half a mile away.

Like anywhere in the capital, parking is tricky. A lot of the surrounding roads are permit-only but some have meter systems, these often only apply up to 1800 so night games are a little easier to park for. There are some car parks near the ground, most notably at the station at Fulham Broadway but it is advisable to get to these nice and early and don't expect easy getaways. Depending on your direction of approach it is also worth looking at parking at a station on the outskirts of the city and travelling in for the last bit.

By Train The nearest tube station is Fulham Broadway on the District line. Take a train to Earls Court and change for Wimbledon-bound trains.

HEROES OR ZEROES?

⌃ **HEROES OF THE TURF**
Tommy Lawton and Roy Bentley. Peter Bonetti 'The Cat' was so named for his lightning reflexes; he was a charismatic keeper in the sixties, renowned for his incredible displays of goalkeeping during the Fairs Cup run, especially in the wins over Roma, Barcelona and AC Milan. Peter Osgood, Charlie Cooke, Alan Hudson, Kerry Dixon, Pat Nevin, Ruud Gullit, Gianluca Vialli, Gianfranco Zola, Joe Cole, John Terry and Frank Lampard.

⌄ **ZEROES OF THE TURF**
Chris Sutton, he did nothing at Chelsea, Robert Fleck, Jody Morris, Christian Panucci and Slavisa Jokanovic.

CHELSEA HAVE PLAYED THEIR FOOTBALL AT STAMFORD BRIDGE SINCE THEIR INCEPTION IN THE PUB JUST ACROSS THE ROAD.

HOME COLOURS

CHELTENHAM TOWN

RIVALS

Gloucester City, Rushden and Diamonds, Bristol City and Rovers, and Yeovil.

- **Nicknames** The Robins
- **Founded** 1887
- **Ground** Abbey Business Stadium (opened 1932)
- **Address** Whaddon Road, Cheltenham, Gloucestershire GL52 5NA
- **Capacity** 7,200
- **Best attendance** 8,326 vs Reading, FA Cup 1st round, 17 November, 1956
- **Contact** 01242-573558
- **Ticket number** 01242-573558
- **Email** info@ctfc.com
- **Website** ctfc.com

That's quite interesting
"The Cheltenham Town youth system has started to be taken seriously by the bigger clubs. We've recently sold a 16-year-old to Arsenal for what could earn the club a large amount of money. We also have a host of Premier League clubs interested in our other talent." Pidge.

Not a lot of people know that
"Before 1999 we had never played League Football." Pidge.

Cheltenham: visions of flared nostrils, sweat evaporating in a steamy mist, the smell of warm leather, the thunder of hooves, sudden raised voices blasting out coded chants over the sea of heads while arms wave in curious patterns. The crowd gripped with anticipation, ready for the off. And then, of course, there's the horse-racing festival too. But this is no one-horse town, no one-trick pony. As well as being the home of Gloucestershire's premier football club, this is a town that has spawned mighty talents, from musical titan Gustav Holst to Olympic hero Eddie 'the Eagle' Edwards.

The club was promoted into the ranks of the Football League in 1999, following hot on the tail of an FA Trophy win at Wembley in 1998. The Robins were guided by local-born manager Steve Cotterill, who established the Whaddon Road outfit as a real force in the fourth tier. The team had a strong self belief and progressed as far as the fifth round of the FA Cup, beating Burnley along the way. By the end of the 2001/02 season Cheltenham had earned an away day in Cardiff for the play-off final. Rushden and Diamonds were their adversaries that day and the Cheltonians headed across the border to the Millennium Stadium in large numbers. The fans were rewarded with a thrilling 3-1 victory and the club rose into the third tier of the Football League for the first time in its history.

The past decade hasn't been an easy sprint along the flat. Instead, the club's been over many fences and laboured through several ditches with the highs of promotions and the crashing lows of relegations and near administration. However, today visitors to the Abbey Business Stadium will find a smart, modern ground that still retains great character, and a team that's established itself as a firm fixture on the Football League calendar. Unlike The

GETTY IMAGES

^ Mark Yates, former Cheltenham player and club captain who returned as manager in December 2009.

Festival, Whaddon Road isn't a natural haunt of the Royals, but then again, there's always the chance they'll draw Reading in the cup.

Greatest moments on this ground
"I'll always remember back in 1999, the goal that ensured promotion from the non-league to the Football League for the first time. I'm sure that it was Jamie Victory's goal, but to this day, it's been credited to Mike Duff." Pidge, Robins Nest Forum.

Lowest moments on this ground

"The Hereford game back in 2008/09. We lost 3-2, and I've never been so ashamed to be a Cheltenham fan. Some fans were calling for the managers head, and there was effectively a 'sing off' between haters and supporters of Martin Allen." Pidge.

Heroes of the sideline

"Steve Cotterill – FA trophy, four promotions, zero relegations. His record speaks for itself. John Ward – he never played the most entertaining football, but he took a club on its knees in the bottom half of League Two, stabilized it, and got them into League One." Pidge.

Don't mention the…

"Cheltenham player Julian Alsop, who was sacked by Oxford in October 2004 after an incident involving a youth team player, and, allegedly, a banana." Pidge.

The ground

Whaddon Road's two modern stands balance well with the traditional half of the ground. Behind the goal is the **Carlsberg Stand**, an all-seater structure opened in 2005 that can hold 1,100 fans. Running along the pitch the **In2Print Stand** is an impressive, modern structure with a capacity of 2,034; the high roof has no pillars to obstruct views. Half the all-seater allocation goes to away fans. Behind the far goal at the Prestbury Road End is the home **Cheltenham and Gloucester Stand**, a covered terrace with a low roof behind the goal and a capacity of 1,980. The **Stagecoach West Stand** holds 1,074 fans in an area of terracing known as the Paddock and Tunnel Enclosures, while an elevated section of covered seating rises behind with a capacity of 1,068. It doesn't run the full length of the pitch, straddling the halfway line and running to about level with the start of the D. The 2010/11 season sees arch rivals Gloucester City as tenants at the Whaddon Road stadium.

Getting there

By road/Parking Cheltenham is easily accessed via the M5. From the south exit at junction 11 onto the A40. At the second roundabout exit left onto Princess Elizabeth Way and follow through one roundabout. At the next roundabout exit right onto Tewkesbury Road, the A4019, and follow, turning right onto Swindon Road/A4019. Turn left onto Fairview, becoming Portland Street, right onto Clarence Road and left onto Prestbury Road. Follow Prestbury through one roundabout, then go right onto Whaddon Road and left to stay on Whaddon Road. The ground is on the left. From the north exit the M5 at junction 10, the A4019, becoming Tewkesbury Road, and follow the directions above. There's limited street parking, but you can park at The Parklands Social Club, Wymans Road (accessed via Whaddon Road) for £4. There's also a free park and ride from Cheltenham Racecourse.

By train Cheltenham Spa is the nearest station, two miles from the ground. Regular buses are available running to the town centre, from where it is a 15-minute walk; alternatively take a connecting bus on to the stadium.

Pubs for home fans
The Robins Nest club bar has a good vibe, decent beer and food available. The large Fox and Hounds, on Prestbury Road, is another popular spot close to the ground. For those in need of some real ale, it's worth searching out The Kemble Brewery Inn, Fairview Street.

Good food near ground
The Whaddon Fish Bar, Whaddon Road, is a good bet if you're feeling peckish.

Pubs for away fans
Coming from the town, the Sudeley Arms, Prestbury Road, is about five minutes' walk from the ground and a popular spot for the away contingent with some decent ales. The Parklands Social Club, Wymans Road, behind the ground, has a great atmosphere, sports TV, well-kept beers as well as 'with-chips' style grub that fills a hole. Parking also available for £4.

Top tips
If the horses are racing and you're coming via car, leave plenty of extra-time to reach the ground.

THE LAST WORD

robinsnestforum.co.uk
cheltenham.vitalfootball.co.uk
ctfctalk.co.uk
cheltenhamtownyears.com
cheltenhamtown-mad.co.uk

VILLAINS

"...ean Windass, for squeezing ...hn Finnigan's testicles and ...etting him sent off during a match against Bradford in 2006." Pidge, Robins Nest Forum.

HEROES OR ZEROES?

⌃ HEROES OF THE TURF
"Jamie Victory – an absolute gentleman. Tony Naylor – he was an incredible player and could do things I wouldn't have thought possible. John Finnigan – he was our Captain Marvel. He gave 100% for the team, week in, week out, and you could see that he cared. Bob Bloomer – a fantastic player for us. Why he wasn't picked up by a bigger club, I have no idea. Damien Spencer – he changed my whole idea of players 'giving 100%'. He'd run around the pitch all day and force mistakes and nine times out of 10 he'd win his headers. It's a shame he had a thing for the corner flag." Pidge.

⌄ ZEROES OF THE TURF
"Mickey Bell – an awful player, he only had one good game for us. Andy Smith – his attitude was poor, and when he was dropped to the bench he wanted out. Aaron Ledgister – he came to Cheltenham on a three-year contract with the manager claiming he was the next big thing. Three years and no starts later, he's playing for Weymouth in the non-league." Pidge.

- 🌐 **Nicknames** The Spireites
- ⚽ **Founded** 1866
- 🏟 **Ground** B2net Stadium (opened 2010)
- ℹ **Address** Sheffield Road, Whittington Moor, Chesterfield S41 9BN
- 🏢 **Capacity** 10,600
- ➕ **Best attendance** 30,561 vs Tottenham Hotspur, FA Cup 5th round, 12 February, 1938 (at the Recreation Ground)
- 📞 **Contact** 01246-209765
- 📞 **Ticket number** 01246-209765
- @ **Email** sallyswain@chesterfield-fc.co.uk
- 🌐 **Website** chesterfield-fc.co.uk

CHESTERFIELD

Pubs for home fans

There are two pubs next to the ground. The Donkey Derby is just to the south on Sheffield Road and has two rotating guest ales and Sky Sports. It also does pub food. Opposite the ground on Sheffield Road is the Rose and Crown, while nearby there's also the Darby Tup as well as the Travellers Rest to choose from.

Good food near ground

Opposite the ground there are a host of take-outs ranging from Pastry Plus and Kate's Pantry to a Tesco next to the ground.

Pubs for away fans

The Darby Tup on Sheffield Road is part of the Tynemill chain and offers a wide range of local ales, plus four or five guest beers. The Industry Inn on Queen Street used to be popular with visiting fans as it was the nearest pub to the away end at Saltergate.

Top tips

Chesterfield is famous for the crooked church spire.

RIVALS

Mansfield Town, Sheffield United and Sheffield Wednesday.

To dream the impossible dream, part one. Own your own football club. Darren Brown (no, not *Derran* Brown, *Darren* Brown) took over as chairman of Chesterfield FC in 2000. The club had enjoyed some success but many fans were frustrated at what they perceived as a lack of investment in the club by then chairman Norton Lea. When 29-year-old Brown appeared on the scene, with his media-savvy spin and grand plans for the future, fans were delighted. But for all the hype and expectation, behind the scenes Brown was 'magicing' money out of the financially stable team, and using it to prop up his other business interests – which included Sheffield Steelers ice hockey team. Soon, players' cheques were bouncing and fees for the influx of new signings weren't paid. It was clear there was something of the smoke and mirrors going on, and eventually the suspicions of the glacial FA were aroused. The Spireites had been used and abused by their chairman, who was eventually forced out of the club leaving behind debts of £1.6million. Far from the promises of pushing on into a new era, Chesterfield found themselves in administration, fined for financial irregularities and docked points. It took a consortium of fans to save the Saltergate club from going bust. The disastrous end to the season had one silver lining – as the team were 15 points clear at the top of the third tier, they still managed to gain promotion to League One as third-placed finishers despite the docking of points. As for Brown, after his curtain call in court, he went down for four years. He couldn't Houdini his way out that one.

To dream the impossible dream, part two. Play in an FA Cup final at Wembley. And that's the old Wembley, twin towers and all, when you only got to play there in finals. For a club from the third tier of the English Football League to walk out onto the neutral turf of Old Trafford to face up to Premier League opposition in an FA Cup semi-final was the stuff of Hollywood films. To be leading 2-1 by the 60th minute was the stuff of dreams, but that's exactly what happened in the 1996/97 season as Middlesbrough wilted under the Spireites onslaught. Then the pivotal moment as the ball was blasted from five yards, hit the Middlesbrough crossbar, bounced down behind the line and out. Referee David Ellery waved to play on and the moment was gone. It was still a magical day as the Spireites came from 3-2 down with a last minute of injury time equalizer from local boy Jamie Hewitt, but fans were left with a haunting feeling. What if that goal hadn't been ghosted away?

Greatest moments on this ground

"Clinching an FA Cup semi-final place after beating Wrexham 1-0 in an all League Two affair on 9 March 1997. Running a close second would be Glynn Hurst's last-gasp 88th-minute winner against Luton Town, which leapfrogged the Spireites out of the relegation places in May 2004." Richard Stacey, webmaster, Chesterfield FC.

Lowest moments on this ground

"The old ground survived two world wars, witnessed The Spireites relegated and saw players injured, but in reality the lowest moment is probably the last league game on the green, green grass of Saltergate." Richard Stacey.

Heroes of the sideline

"Jimmy McGuigan – led the Spireites to the Fourth Division title in 1969/70 playing some fantastic football that has lived long in the memories of those fortunate to witness it. A definitive players' manager. Jamie Hewitt – current physio and long-time servant of his hometown club. No one will forget his equalizer at Old Trafford against Middlesbrough in the 3-3 epic semi-final of 1997. John Duncan – arguably The Spireites most successful manager. Two promotions and an FA Cup semi-final are pretty hard to beat during his two tenures in the Saltergate hot seat." Richard Stacey.

Heroes of the turf

"Herbert Munday – showed loyalty beyond the scope of modern understanding. He joined Chesterfield Town in the summer of 1893 and quickly began to establish a name for himself. He scored their first (Football League) goal. He continued to score regularly and turned down offers from almost every other league club in that time. Ernie Moss – the club's record scorer and rare 'three-time' Spireite. A Chesterfield career that saw 469 league appearances produce 162 goals. Sam Hardy – England's greatest goalkeeper – before Gordon Banks! He made 21 England appearances between 1907 and 1920, at a time when England usually played only three games a season and the nation went to war for four years. Any keeper enjoying a 14-year spell as his country's first choice at the end of the 20th century would have earned around 140 caps, knocking Peter Shilton's record into a cocked hat. Alan Birch – he played as if touched by the Gods. He graced a Chesterfield side enjoying its best spell for 30 years. His tightly curled perm made him instantly recognizable as he executed the 'roving brief' that Arthur Cox gave him. Gordon Dale – arguably our best post-war player and, for years, the Spireites record 'sale'. In the eyes of many older supporters, Gordon was the most naturally gifted player to wear the blue since the second world war." Richard Stacey and Stuart Basson, Chesterfield FC.

Villains

"Terry Curren was always a villain when playing for the Owls and made a substitute appearance for the Spirietes at Grimsby where he was booed by both sets of fans. Ben Strevens got Lloyd Kerry sent off at Dagenham after a tweak to Lloyd's neither regions. The diminutive midfielder's reflex punch/slap to Strevens stomach left the 6-ft striker rolling on the floor." Richard Stacey.

The ground

For the 2010/11 season, Chesterfield have moved to the state-of-the-art B2net Stadium, an all-seater arena for over 10,000 fans. The **HTM Main (West) Stand** has a capacity of more than 3,000 seated in a single tier stand with arched roof and no pillars to obstruct views. This stand will also be used to house the media and is the location of the player's tunnel, dug outs and dress rooms. The **Midland Co-Op (East) Stand** again has a capacity of more than 3,000 featuring an identical arched roof. The family area is housed at the south end of this stand with 1,000 seats, while the north end can be used for additional away fan allocations should the need arise. The **Karen Child (South) Stand** is behind the goal. This flat-roofed, single-tier stand has a capacity of more than 2,000 home fans, while behind the opposite goal is the architecturally identical **Printability North Stand**, where away fans reside.

Getting there

By road/Parking B2net is located just off the main A61 Chesterfield to Sheffield Road, about a mile outside the city centre. Exit the at junction 29 on the M1, following the A617 to Chesterfield (four miles). At the roundabout take the fourth exit, signposted Sheffield/A61. At the next roundabout turn left on to Lockoford Lane. At the mini roundabout take the third exit, and the B2net stadium is on the right.

By train It's a short ride or 25-minute walk from the centre along Sheffield Road to the stadium. The number 25 Stagecoach runs up Sheffield Road and stops outside the ground.

⊻ ZEROES OF THE TURF

"The biggest zero really has to be the Spireites record £250,000 signing Jason Lee, signed allegedly by the then chairman Norton Lea and not the then manager John Duncan. Jason only managed two goals for the Spireites and actually managed to get sent off twice." Richard Stacey.

GETTY IMAGES

⋀ Spireites goal-scorer Andy Morris holds off Gianluca Festa of Middlesbrough in the FA Cup semi-final at Old Trafford.

Former chairman – jailed for defrauding the club.

THE LAST WORD

chesterfield-fc.co.uk
thecfss.co.uk/forums
chesterfield-mad.co.uk

PUB QUIZ

That's quite interesting
The Karen Child South Stand is sponsored by a local lottery winner.

Not a lot of people know that
"There can't be many grounds that have doubled up as three other famous venues on the big screen. In *The Damned United*, about the brief tenure of Brian Clough at Leeds United, Saltergate featured heavily as it resembled Derby's old Baseball Ground. Also, sections of it were used to represent the old Wembley and Carrow Road." Richard Stacey.

HOME COLOURS

COLCHESTER UNITED

- ❷ **Nicknames** The U's
- ❷ **Founded** 1873
- ❷ **Ground** Weston Homes Community Stadium (opened 2008)
- ❶ **Address** United Way, Colchester, Essex CO4 5UP
- ❸ **Capacity** 10,000
- ❸ **Best attendance** 9,559 vs Leeds United, League One, 4 April, 2009
- ❶ **Contact** 01206-755100
- ❶ **Ticket Number** 0871-226 2161
- @ **Email** ticketing@colchesterunited.net
- ❷ **Website** cu-fc.com

RIVALS

Ipswich Town by far, at just 17 miles up the A12 it is the closest East Anglian derby. Southend United, Wycombe Wanderers (due to battles in the conference and lower leagues vying for titles and relegation).

Back in 2007 Colchester were the top dogs and their fans had bragging rights over all their local rivals. The proof? The U's were awarded the title 'Pride of Anglia', an event that coincided with local television station Anglia TV awarding a trophy to the winners for the first time. They had finished above the likes of Ipswich Town and Norwich City, a dream for their fans, a nightmare for their rivals. Ipswich fans especially would have found it hard to swallow, as traditionally the title has only ever been fought between the Suffolk and Norfolk sides, never in recent times with the club from down the road in Essex. That season a tenth place in the Championship saw The U's record their highest ever finish, and there was even talk of a play-off place and dreams of the Premiership. Had that been achieved, the decrepit Layer Road ground, still in use at the time, would have been useless, its wooden away terraces a throwback to pre-war stadia. Access to the top tier would have meant sharing a ground with their arch rivals from Suffolk, a delicious prospect for Colchester fans at the time, with Ipswich struggling. The next season however brought heartbreak for The U's, finishing bottom of the Championship and dropping into League One. They also bid farewell to Layer Road, as the ground that had been home since their formation was replaced by the 10,000 all-seated purpose-built Cuckoo Park.

Colchester United has always been synonymous with one great cup upset. In 1971, the Essex side drew Don Revie's all-conquering Leeds United, who arrived in Essex hot favourites, and left with egg on their face as the relative minnows unseated the First Division outfit 3-2 in a pulsating cup-tie. More recently, the two have been regular sparring partners, something that wasn't lost on the Colchester faithful whenever Leeds visited.

Greatest moments on this ground

"Personally for me it has to be season 2006/07, our first in the Championship, and our home game against Hull City. Pre-season our then manager Phil Parkinson (the man responsible for our promotion the previous year) sensationally quit to take over as manager of big-spending Hull City. Despite spending a lot of money on his new squad, Hull were struggling ahead of this fixture. Layer Road on a cold Tuesday evening turned into a nightmare for Hull and Parkinson. Colchester United ran out 5-1 winners, his expensive squad of players were humiliated and he was sacked a week later after only four months in charge!" Dan Humphries, CUSA Member.

Lowest moments on this ground

"Home to Stoke in May 2008, we were relegated back to League One and it was also our last-ever game at Layer Road. To many an outsider, Layer Road was a dump, but it had character and was our home. It gave the Colchester fans memories that will last a lifetime, with many a giant falling on the hallowed turf over the years." Dan Humphries.

Heroes of the sideline

"In a word 'Parky' (aka Phil Parkinson) the man who took over a League One club going nowhere and in a season transformed them into a Championship team." Dan Humphries.

That's quite interesting
Football in Colchester started with Colchester Town before United was formed, originally both teams lived alongside each other until the Essex FA insisted they merge.

PUB QUIZ

Not a lot of people know that
The Eagle on Colchester United's badge is a symbol of the town's Roman heritage. Once one of the biggest towns in England, legions from Colchester would carry a golden eagle at the head of their columns.

Getty Images

▲ Weston Homes
Community Stadium.

HEROES OR ZEROES?

⌃ **HEROES OF THE TURF**
"Peter Wright. Micky Cook, a legend with the record of appearances. Vic Keeble, an incredible striker who ended up being lured away to Newcastle United. Also Martyn King and Bobby Hunt. Mark Kinsella was a key player on our rise out of the Conference and in the FA Trophy win. Tony Adcock came through the youth team to become an awesome goal-scorer. Most recently Jamie Cureton, Chris Iwelumo and Lomana Lua Lua." Clive Daly, fan.

⌄ **ZEROES OF THE TURF**
Fabrice Richard, Sagi Burton, Brian Launders, Danny Granville and Adam Tanner.

Don't mention the…
George Burley. The ex-Ipswich Player joined as player manager in 1994 and made a promising start with an unfashionable team. Just when things were looking up after 20 matches in charge, he left for arch-rivals Ipswich Town where he took them to fifth in the Premiership.

Villains
"Jamie Cureton, a player picked up off the football scrap heap by Colchester, he scored over 20 goals in our Championship season, finishing the league's top scorer, only for him then to demand a transfer saying we 'lacked ambition', he eventually signed for Championship rivals Norwich. To make matters worse he was seen kissing the badge on his return to Layer Road, much to the disgust of the home fans who had adored him the previous season." Dan Humphries.

The ground
Colchester left Layer Road at the end of the 2007/08 season; the ground was a somewhat ageing throwback. The new ground, The Western Homes Community Stadium is an ultra-modern stadium, and situated on the outskirts of town by a business park. Although lacking the character and personality of the former ground, it offers modern facilities and excellent views. Good disabled seating is available in each stand and much improved access.

The **South Stand** is single-tiered and holds around 2000 supporters; it was home to the away support but the club moved its core support into the South Stand after a season and it is home to the most vocal part of the crowd.

The **West Stand** differs from the other three in that it is slightly taller and has a row of executive boxes running along the back. It is the most impressive of the four sides and also houses the changing rooms, directors' and press seating as well as all hospitality and administration.

The **East Stand** is unremarkable but smart, opposite the main stand. With no supporting pillars it offers unrestricted views of the ground. It is a much more family-orientated stand housing a specific family enclosure.

The **North Stand** is the new home for the away support, simular to the South Stand it differs only in its lack of a police control room. Good views and excellent disabled access make it a well-appointed stand for the travelling supporter.

Getting there
By Road/Parking From all directions come off the A12 at junction 29 and take a left onto the A1232. When at the top of this road, bear right back over the A12 towards the traffic lights. Go straight over the lights, you should be on Ipswich Road. At the next set of traffic lights, turn right onto Severalls Lane. Follow this road to its conclusion, where you will pick up signs for the stadium. You then head through the business park, where several of the factories and units offer match-day parking, there is also a car park at the ground but this fills early and is expensive. Parking around the ground is very difficult.

By train Colchester North is the nearest station and is on the main Liverpool Street line. It is around two miles from the ground so either get a taxi or the shuttle bus to the ground.

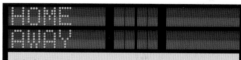

Pubs for home fans
The Dog and Pheasant is the closest pub to the ground on the Nayland Road, but is still almost a mile away and is strictly home fans only.

Good food near ground
Again, being on the edge of town there is little other than burger vans and food inside the ground, so it is best to head into the town centre or eat on the way.

Pubs for away fans
Being on the outskirts of town there are no pubs nearby, the closest being the Dog and Pheasant. Best bet is to have a pint in the town centre or near the station before heading to the ground.

Top tips
There is only one way in and out of the area of the ground so congestion is bad for big games, so unless you're in a hurry it's worth taking your time leaving, at least until they build a new exit onto the A12, which is just yards from the stadium.

THE LAST **WORD**

clubfanzine.com/colchester_united
colchester.vitalfootball.co.uk

HOME COLOURS

- ⊗ **Nicknames** The Sky Blues
- ⊙ **Founded** 1883
- ⊙ **Ground** Ricoh Arena (opened 2005)
- ⊙ **Address** Phoenix Way, Foleshill, Coventry CV6 6GE
- ⊙ **Capacity** 32,500
- ⊙ **Best attendance** 31,407 vs Chelsea, FA Cup quarter-final, 7 March, 2009
- ⊙ **Contact** 0870-421 1987
- ⊙ **Ticket Number** 0844-873 1883
- @ **Email** ticket.office@ccfc.co.uk
- Ⓦ **Website** ccfc.co.uk

COVENTRY CITY

Coventry City have found chances to get their hands on a bit of silverware hard to come by in their long history. When the opportunity finally did arrive in the 1987 FA Cup final, they made sure it was one to remember. Despite trailing twice to Tottenham they kept coming back, eventually winning in extra-time through an own goal. Although this has been Coventry's only piece of bling, they were, at the time, a permanent fixture in the nation's top division and made several semi-final appearances in the League Cup as well as numerous FA Cup runs. When finally relegated to the Championship in 2001, they had spent an impressive 34 years at the top level, something that, at the time, teams like Manchester United or Chelsea could not come close to boasting.

Since then it's been a rocky road for the Sky Blues, they've gone through 14 managers or caretaker managers, have narrowly avoided administration and relegation to League One but, on the plus side, have relocated to a swanky new stadium. Their old home, Highfield Road, was of interest as it was the first all-seater ground in the country, replacing terracing with seats in 1981. The then chairman Jimmy Hill claimed, "You can't be a hooligan sitting down." Creative thinking Leeds fans proved him wrong, ripping up seats and using them as missiles when they lost a League Cup quarter-final game. The stadium was re-terraced in 1983. Perhaps in an act of solidarity with the Sky Blues trophy cabinet, home fans visiting the Ricoh exist in a environment where their silverware is no good, neither is their copper or paper for that matter. The internal market is ruled by the power of plastic – rechargeable pre-payment cards are the currency of choice – bet they wished topping up the trophy cabinet was that easy.

Greatest moments on this ground

"One of the best games was beating Liverpool 4-0 in 1983. They were champions and League leaders. Coventry had just avoided relegation the year before, but Bobby Gould had built a new team. Nicky Platnauer scored the fastest-ever goal in under a minute and we led 3-0 at half time. Terry Gibson had scored the other two and with six minutes to go he got his hat trick to complete the score," Kevin Adams, fan.

Lowest moments on this ground

"The 2001 relegation season from the Premiership had a lot of low moments, the lowest being away from home, the defeat to Sutton United. My father was at the 1-2 home defeat to King's Lynn in 1961 which is probably the lowest of all time," Malcolm Wright, fan.

Heroes of the sideline

Jimmy Hill manager and later chairman. John Sillet, a legend on the pitch and then as a manager winning the FA Cup.

Heroes of the turf

Tommy Hutchinson's silky skills graced Highfield Road during the seventies and he was our Player of the Year three times and was adored by the fans for his attacking runs down the wing. Also Cyrille Regis, Darren Huckerby, David Speedie, Dion Dublin, Gary McAllister, Ernie Hunt, Clarrie Bourton, Brian Borrows, George Curtis and Steve Ogrizovic.

Zeroes of the turf

Peter Reid (manager) and Terry Butcher (manager).

The ground

The Ricoh Arena was officially opened at the beginning of the 2005/06 season. Due to some building delays, Coventry had to play their first three games of the season away from home. The first home game was eventually played against

QPR and saw the Sky Blues win convincingly 3-0, with Claus Bech Jorgensen netting the first-ever goal. The out of town ground was also built as a centre for other events and attractions for the local community and thus houses a casino, exhibition hall, shopping and conference facilities and is regularly used for concerts.

Like a lot of newly built stadiums in the English game the Ricoh Arena is an impressive but fairly characterless affair. Three sides are essentially the same with the corners filled, so it is one continuous area of seating. These three sides, the **Jewson South Stand**, The **Tesco East** and **Evening Telegraph North Stand**, are steep and offer good unobstructed views of the playing area. Away supporters are tucked away in blocks six and seven of the **South Stand** and the view is OK, but distance from the pitch is a bit of an issue. For league games there are up to 3,000 tickets available for travelling supporters and all turnstiles are operated remotely using bar code scanners to let supporters into the ground. Between the South and East stands in the corner sweep there is a large video scoreboard.

The **Telent West Stand** is the only side of the stadium with two tiers, the upper one being a narrow area backed by executive boxes. It is also home to the dressing rooms and television gantry. It is most striking as it has a large back to the seating with Ricoh logos, it gives it an almost Italian-style feel to the stand, this due to the exhibition centre that backs onto it.

COVENTRY CITY FOOTBALL CLUB

∧ Ricoh Arena.

Getting there

By Road/Parking From the M6 leave at junction 3, then take the second exit onto Phoenix Way – A444 (signposted Coventry). At the next roundabout, take the first exit onto Rowley's Green Lane. At the roundabout take the second exit onto Judds Lane and arrive at Ricoh Arena.

All match-day car parking for the Ricoh Arena's A and B car parks work on a pre-book-only basis. Bookings will need to be received at least a week in advance of the particular match. There is some road parking back into the city in the Longford Road area, but it is limited and a good 10- to 20-minute walk from the ground. Car park C at the Ricoh Arena, however, is available for cash parking on a match day.

Match-day car parking costs £10 per game or fans can take up the option of a season ticket pass at £216, which covers all of the Sky Blues' league and cup matches. There are a number of park-and-ride options nearby.

By Rail Coventry's train station is about three and half miles away from the stadium and really is too far to walk. There is a shuttle bus that operates from the bus station to the Tesco/Arena stadium complex.

HOME AWAY

Pubs for home fans
Being out of town there are no pubs, although 15 minutes away there are several on the Longford Road which are the supporters main watering holes. Either that or get to the ground early for a pint.

Good food near ground
There are 20 bars and eating establishments in and around the Ricoh Arena, its edge-of-town situation means this is really your only option for food unless you stop on the way to the ground. There is a Tesco nearby.

Pubs for away fans
It's either get to the ground early for a pint or stop in the town centre or on the Longford Road. The Black Horse is the main away pub but is a solid 20 minutes from the ground.

Top tips
If you want to get a parking space near the ground, arrive early as the spaces fill up quickly, or book ahead via the stadium website.

THE LAST **WORD**

Gary Mabbutt's Knee fanzine
coventrycitybanter.co.uk

DON'T MENTION THE...

Leading 0-2 at half time against arch rivals Aston Villa in 2001 on the last day of the season. Coventry had to win to stay up, but they went on to lose 3-2 and were relegated. Oh, and the Sutton Utd game.

HOME COLOURS

- ☻ **Nicknames** The Railwaymen, The Alex
- ☻ **Founded** 1877
- ☻ **Ground** Alexandra Stadium (opened 1906)
- ☻ **Address** Alexandra Stadium, Gresty Road, Crewe, CW2 6EB
- ☻ **Capacity** 10,153
- ☻ **Best attendance** 20,000 vs Tottenham Hotspur, FA Cup 4th round, 6 January, 1960
- ☻ **Contact** 01270-213014
- ☻ **Ticket Number** 01270-252610
- @ **Email** info@crewealex.net
- Ⓦ **Website** crewealex.net

PUB QUIZ

That's quite interesting
Goalkeeping legend Bruce Grobbelaar scored for Crewe against York City.

Not a lot of people know that
David Platt started his career at Gresty Road, amassed a total of £22,150,000 in transfer fees. He left Crewe for just £200,000.

What came first, the station or the town? Usually a station is built to feed a community. Here in Crewe it was the other way round, with the town growing up around the station and its railway works and it has become famous the world over for its association with all things locomotive. However, mention Crewe to some people and something entirely different will spring to mind; images of precision and class, smooth running and perfect finishing. Yes, Crewe is home to Bentley too. Bentley was a small-time car company after the Great War, a collective of a passionate few, besotted by speed and the excitement of the race. The Bentley Boys took on the might of the French Bugattis, the lightweight favourites who mocked the British vehicles as the 'world's fastest lorries'. Still, the Bentley's came and they conquered, winning away from home, taking four consecutive Le Mans from 1927 to 1930.

Local football club Crewe Alexandra are a hybrid of these two industries. They possess the engine room of a locomotive, combined with the desire, the work ethic, the craft of Britain's finest automobile. They possess a precision and intelligent design that has seen them rise way beyond where they should. This small team has reached higher than many with bigger budgets and bigger reputations.

In manager Dario Gradi they found a man with a vision and a plan. Gradi assembled an organisation of which the team was the final product. He developed an excellent scouting network, he put an emphasis on youth development and brought through many scholars into the team. Without the big budgets of his rivals, he knew that this was the only way to compete. Gradi took over the managerial reigns in June 1983 when Crewe was a pretty dark place; it had just had to apply for re-election to the Football League. Its very existence as a professional club was at stake.

Under Gradi the club rose to the dizzying heights of the second tier of English football. He brought through some of British football's biggest names. Danny Murphy joined The Railwaymen as a trainee and made his debut as a 16-year-old, coming on to score the winner against Preston North End. He stayed with the club from 1993 to 1997 and was a key part of the Crewe midfield. David Platt started his career here with a three-year stint and both Dean Ashton and Neil Lennon were products of the Gradi school of football. Many of the players who shone in The Alex team eventually moved on, but they attracted big money, a welcome income for the club. Ashton made a £3 million pound move to Norwich and Seth Johnson went to Derby County for the same amount. Rob Jones, Ashley Ward, Rob Hulse, Craig Hignett, Geoff Thomas and Dele Adebola – all ex-Railwaymen.

The last few years have been tough for The Alex. Gradi moved upstairs in 2007 as the club's technical director but found himself back on the sidelines just a couple of years later in the role he made his own, facing a climb back up the League ladder. But with the ruthlessness of teams in the upper reaches discarding young players in favour of foreign imports, as well as a good youth system, Crewe should be able to fall back on what they do well. You can bet on two things; one, that there will be many scouts from across the country heading to Gresty Road this season; and two, that there won't be many Bentleys in the Gresty car park.

Greatest moments on this ground
The last game of the 2002/03 season saw Cardiff come to Gresty. 9,500 fans were there to see Richard Walker score and Crewe take a point, earning runners-up spot in League One and promotion back to the second tier.

Lowest moments on this ground
On 2 May, 2009 Crewe lost 3-0 at home to Leicester City to be relegated back to the bottom tier.

RIVALS

Stoke,
Port Vale.

Heroes of the sideline

Dario Gradi. He joined the club in 1983, guided them to the second tier and established an amazing youth policy that has seen the club consistently out perform bigger spending teams.

Heroes of the turf

Danny Murphy started as a trainee, went on to become a legend before leaving for Liverpool. Combative midfielder Neil Lennon had six years at Gresty Road and went represent Northern Ireland. David Platt, a stand out in midfield where he played from 1985 to 1988 before attracting the advances of Aston Villa. Tommy Lowry played a record-breaking 475 times for Alex. Terry Harkin, a goal-scoring legend who scored 34 goals in the 1964/65 season. Dean Ashton, another scholar, five years of scoring bag-fulls in the Championship.

Don't mention the…

In 1955 Crewe did not win away from home in 56 matches.

The ground

The Alexandra Stadium, more commonly known as Gresty Road, is a fairly modern, tidy ground with an impressive main stand. The **Air Products Main Stand** or Railtrack Stand was built in 2000 and accommodates 6,809. It is a large cantilever structure and a huge single tier of seats. It is by far the biggest stand in the stadium and would easily grace any ground. The **AB Nutrition Stand** or the Gresty Road End sits behind the goal, an all seater stand which holds 982 home fans in a compact covered single tier. The **BMW Bluebell Stand** or Pop Side runs the length of the field and is an all seated single tier for away fans. It has a low roof that covers most rows but the front few are a bit exposed but it does help generate some good volume. Its capacity is 1,680 with a few restricted views due to pillars. The **Wulvern Housing Stand** or Railway End is behind the other goal has a capacity of 682, mostly accommodated in seating but with room for fourteen wheelchair users and their carers. This is quite a small stand but with a similar girder and corrugated roof design as the other three. This is sometimes given to away fans with a large following.

Getting there

By Road/Parking Exit the M6 at junction 16, following signs for Crewe/A500. At the next roundabout take third exit for Crewe A5020/Weston Road and follow through two roundabouts. At next roundabout exit left signed to the station onto the A534 and follow taking the first left onto Gresty Road, stadium will be on the left. Parking available on site, often restricted to the home contingent. Away fans directed to Weston Road industrial estate for parking – a 10-minute walk from the ground.

By Train Crewe train station could not be more convenient and is literally a five-minute walk to the stadium. Head left out of the station along Nantwich Road, taking the first left onto Gresty Road.

Pubs for home fans
The Royal Hotel, Nantwich Road, isn't one to cut off its nose to spite its face. Instead they have two bars available – one for the home and one for the way contingent.

Good food near ground
There are a number of cafés and a couple of Indian restaurants on Nantwich Road, while the ground is circled by a ring of fryers: one on Nantwich Road en route from the station, one on Gresty Road opposite the stadium which does a roaring trade pre-match and another further along the road. At the Grand Junction Retail Park, just off Earle Street, north of the station, is a KFC.

Pubs for away fans
Clancy's Bar, in the Royal Hotel, has sports TV and bar snacks and is close to the train station. Just up the road the British Lion has a couple of ales on tap while the Brocklebank Pub, Weston Road, is a Brewers Fayre so carries all the usual fizzy lager offerings associated with the chain. It is heading away from the ground, but Borough Arms, Earle Street, has a cracking range of ales from local micro breweries to continental exotics. There's a also a handy KFC close by.

Top tips
If you win the pools, Bentley Motors is just a couple of miles north west of the ground.

crewealexandra-mad.co.uk
crewe.vitalfootball.co.uk

- 🔹 **Nicknames** The Eagles
- 🔹 **Founded** 1905
- 🔹 **Ground** Selhurst Park (opened 1924)
- 🔹 **Address** London SE25 6PU
- 🔹 **Capacity** 26,309
- 🔹 **Best attendance** 51,482 vs Burnley, Division Two, 11 May, 1979
- 🔹 **Contact** 0208-768 6000
- 🔹 **Ticket Number** 0871-200 0071
- 🔹 **Email** boxoffice@cpfc.co.uk
- 🔹 **Website** cpfc.co.uk

CRYSTAL PALACE

I t's no accident that Crystal Palace play in the same colours as Aston Villa. The claret and blue strip is a result of Palace employing one Edmund Goodman, who ran the business side of the club as it was formed. He was a former Villa player and employee and was recommended to the club by the then Villa chairman. It is therefore ironic that perhaps Palace's greatest moment actually took place at Villa Park, in the 1990 FA Cup semi-final, when in extra-time, they beat Liverpool 4-3 to set up their only final appearance in a major competition. This was a game considered by many to be one of the best FA Cup ties of all time. The final itself was against Manchester United and was also a classic, with Ian Wright first equalizing for Palace to take the game into extra-time and then putting the London club into the lead, only for Mark Hughes to equalize and force a replay. The second game was far less dramatic; Palace lost to a single goal and United took their first trophy in five years.

The 1990/91 season also saw the same FA Cup final team record Palace's highest-ever league finish, with an impressive third behind Arsenal and Liverpool. However, the season ended up on a slightly disappointing note for Palace fans. Liverpool, at the time banned from European competition, had their ban suspended earlier than expected and this meant that Crystal Palace missed out on the chance of European football. In recent years, consistency has been hard to come by and a string of promising managers have been through the Selhurst Park hotseat. Just when a period of consolidation as a strong Championship team looked likely, the end of the 2009/10 campaign saw The Eagles' wings clipped as they were plunged into administration and avoided a last day relegation by the skin of their beaks.

RIVALS

Milwall and Brighton rank the highest, with Charlton close behind.

Greatest moments on this ground

"Palace 2, Burnley 0 – last day of the season 1979. A record crowd saw Palace clinch the Division Two Championship with two second-half goals, a draw would have got Palace promoted but a win meant we pipped arch rivals Brighton to the title." Gareth Gurney, fan.

Lowest moments on this ground

"There have been a few! But I'll choose losing 1-6 to Liverpool on the first day of the 1994/95 season – all hope was gone on the first day." Gareth Gurney.

Heroes of the sideline

Steve Coppell's nine years in charge during the eighties and early nineties makes him the greatest modern-day manager.

Heroes of the turf

Ian Wright. Palace pulled the England player out of non-league obscurity and started him on his way to legend status. As well as being their main striker in the run to the FA Cup final, he went on to become an England legend too, but tarnished his rep at Selhurst by kissing his Arsenal badge after scoring for the Gooners. Also Dougie Freedman, Johnny Byrne, Peter Burridge, Ian Evans, Kenny Sansom and Attilio Lombardo, quoted by many as the best player to wear a Palace shirt.

Zeroes of the turf

Rudi Hedman and Thomas Brolin. "Leif Anderson – he didn't really look or appear to be a football player!" Martin Shaw, fan.

Don't mention the…

Probably the lowest moment at Selhurst Park was when Manchester United player Eric Cantona launched a kung-fu style attack into a part of the Palace crowd.

The ground

Selhurst Park has been Crystal Palace's home since 1924 and a couple of the stands are most definitely ageing, but it has got an excellent atmosphere at big games, something that larger, more modern grounds often lack.

The **Holmsdale End** is the most impressive

VILLAINS
Ron Noades – he almost brought the club to its knees as chairman and then as ground leaseholder. Alan Mullery for two disastrous years of management having previously managed arch rivals Charlton and Brighton.

BOB THOMAS/GETTY IMAGES

∧ Desperate lunges from the Manchester United defence fail to stop the ball hitting the top corner in the 1990 FA Cup final.

allow parking for permit holders or vehicles displaying a valid pay-and-display ticket, however a lot of the pay-and-display areas allow only for a maximum of two hours, so check before you park. The area a little further away around Thornton Heath station has a little better parking. There are very limited amounts of space in match-day car parks so get there early if you want to utilize one of these.

By Train Selhurst Park has three overground stations nearby. Selhurst and Thornton Heath are the closest with regular trains to London Victoria, London Bridge, Clapham Junction and East Croydon. A little further away is Norwood Junction, which can also be reached via the affor mentioned stations.

and modern stand. A two-tier structure behind the goal, it is home to the majority of the hardcore Palace fans. The lower tier is over hung by the upper, allowing a good level of noise to be generated by the faithful.

At the other end of the ground is the **Whitehorse Stand** (Corydon Advertiser Family Stand), it is single-tiered with two rows of executive boxes at the back. A large video screen/scoreboard sits precariously on the roof. The **Main Stand** is really starting to show its age, single-tiered with many supporting pillars and still some old wooden seats, it's a bit of a throwback to the sixties or even earlier. There are plans to redevelop should the club regain their Premier League status.

The **Arthur Wait Stand** is another single-tiered stand although slightly more modern looking than its opposite number. It is here that there is accommodation for 2,000 away supporters who sit at the Helmsdale End of the stand.

Getting there

By Road/Parking From outside London approaching from the West, exit the M25 at junction 7 and follow signs for Croydon on the A23. Keep on the A23, following signs for Croydon passing the town centre, stay on the A23 until you reach the Thornton Heath roundabout where you take the A235, then turn immediately left into Brigstock Road. Go past Thornton Heath Station and go right into High Street then at the next roundabout turn left into Whitehorse Lane and you will see the ground. However, it is wise to look for parking a little further away around the station or Brigstock road.

Street parking around Selhurst Park on match days is extremely limited. Most streets around the ground only

HOME COLOURS

- **Nicknames** The Daggers
- **Founded** 1992
- **Ground** Selhurst Park (opened 1924)
- **Address** Victoria Road, Dagenham, Essex RM10 7XL
- **Capacity** 26,309
- **Best attendance** 5,949 vs Ipswich, FA Cup 3rd Round, 5 January, 2002
- **Contact** 020-8592 1549
- **Ticket Number** 020-8592 7194
- **Email** info@daggers.co.uk
- **Website** daggers.co.uk

DAVID SIMPSON

DAGENHAM & REDBRIDGE

RIVALS

Greys Athletic and most other Essex non-League sides. In league terms the closest team is Leyton Orient.

PUB QUIZ

On paper, Dagenham and Redbridge FC seems like a mere baby in the football world. However, on the terraces it's a different matter, the 1992 birthday merely the latest incarnation of a club that can trace its roots all the way back to 1881. Like Dr Who, The Daggers have undergone a series of regenerations, each time appearing in a new form. The story starts when Ilford FC (1881) merged with Leytonstone FC (1886) in 1979, to became Leytonstone/Ilford FC. They merged with Walthamstow Avenue (1900) in 1988 and in 1989 the club was renamed Redbridge Forest. Meanwhile from the other side of the family tree Dagenham FC (1949) arrived to marry Redbridge Forest in 1992 to form Dagenham and Redbridge FC, who took Forest's position in the Conference. Are you still with me? They had a respectable first year and finished sixth before being relegated the next season to the Isthmian League – it took them some time to get out of the lower tier but in 1999/00 they climbed back into the Conference and immediately finished third as well as making a third-round FA Cup appearance, a feat they would become familiar with.

The 2002/03 season went down in club history due to the notorious 'Bostongate' fiasco. The FA decided to dock points from Boston United, Conference Champions, for financial irregularities. However the Football Association allowed those points to be deducted the following

That's quite interesting
They are the only side in the League to be sponsored by an undertaker.

Not a lot of people know that
Dagenham and Redbridge are actually an Essex side, despite being continuously referred to as a London side.

season after their promotion, thus robbing Dagenham, Conference runners-up, of a chance to go up. A cup run the following year saw them defeat Plymouth 2-0 live on television and they made the fouth round only to be robbed at Norwich City. Despite these performances, it took the non-leaguers until 2007 to reach the hallowed turf of League Football.

Greatest moments on this ground
Winning the Conference title by beating Aldershot Town on 7 April, 2007. After several near misses the young side exceeded all expectations and ran away with the title after Christmas. Promotion was sealed by beating Aldershot Town 2-1, sparking a pitch invasion and wild celebrations, which went on long into the night.

Lowest moments on this ground
"28 April 2002. Dagenham beat Chester City 3-0, but lost out on the title and promotion by goal difference to Boston United. The two teams had been neck-and-neck throughout the season, and started the day level on points. Rumours came through as the afternoon went on that Boston were losing in their game at Hayes, but all were false, and Boston's 2-0 win meant they were champions. Despite the win it was the biggest anti-climax, and many wondered if the chance of becoming a league club was gone forever. The disappointment increased as it became apparent Boston were in trouble with the FA for financial

VILLAINS

Boston United and the League for deducting points the season after they got promoted rather than in the season they infringed the rules.

irregularities, but had points deducted from the following season." Paul Middlemiss, upminsterdaggers.co.uk.

Heroes of the sideline

"Three were outstanding. Ted Hardy took the club to Wembley in the FA Trophy in 1997, Gary Hill twice nearly took the club into the Football League and took the club to the FA Cup third round in three successive seasons. John Still built a young side and got the club promoted to the League." Paul Middlemiss.

Don't mention the...

Bostongate.

The ground

Unsurprisingly, the London Borough of Barking and Dagenham Stadium (better known as Victoria Road) has a tight lower division/non-league feel. The stands and terraces are close to the pitch and it's the sort of place big teams hate to come to, and may go some way to explain The Daggers' excellent cup runs.

The main **Carling Stand** (built in 2001) is the newest stand. It is slightly elevated and has six rows of seats, holding 800. It is free from obstructions like pillars. This stand only runs for three-quarters of the pitch, though, as the last quarter is taken up by a more old-fashioned stand which houses 200 fans. This is reserved for travelling fans and, whilst covered, there are some obstructing pillars.

Opposite the main stand is the **North Terrace**, affectionately named by home fans as 'the sieve' as the roof used to leak like one! It's a really old-fashioned-looking low stand which offers some covering towards the rear with a low boxy sort of roof. It also has a TV camera gantry perched precariously on top.

The **Bury Road End** is where most hardcore home fans gather, is open to the elements and just a few steps high. There is also a scoreboard and a small police control room.

The opposite end is an open terrace just six steps high that houses the away fans. Open to the elements, the **Pondfield Road End** has capacity for up to 1,200 fans and sits tight to the pitch.

Getting there

By Road/Parking Use the M25 and leave at junction 27 and follow the M11 until it finishes. Continue on the A406 towards docklands and then join the A13 and follow signs for Dagenham, follow this road until the A1306, then continue on until the third set of traffic lights. Here, take

⌄ Legend Paul Terry puts The Daggers one nil up against Plymouth Argyle in the FA Cup 3rd Round.

a left and follow the road to the Bull Roundabout where you take a left into Rainham Road, Victoria Road is about a quarter of a mile further on.

There is plenty of on-road parking in the area as well as a free car park next to the ground; this does tend to fill up early though.

By Train The District line takes you to Dagenham station in about 40 minutes from central London. The ground is then about a five-minute walk away and is clearly signposted.

Pubs for home fans
The Social Club at the ground is very popular but only for home fans; there is no beer for sale in any other part of the ground.

Good food near ground
The area doesn't have a lot in the way of eateries, near the station are a couple of chippies and a café, whilst catering vans serving the usual grub can be found around the ground.

Pubs for away fans
The Railway is popular and is close to both rail and tube stations and about a five- to 10-minute walk from the ground.

Top tips
If you want a parking space in the area for a big game arrive early.

THE LAST WORD

diggerdaggers.com
upminsterdaggers.co.uk

HOME COLOURS

DARLINGTON

RIVALS

Hartlepool and
Carlisle.

⊖ **Nicknames** The Quakers, Darlo
⊙ **Founded** 1883
⊌ **Ground** Northern Echo Darlington Arena (opened 2003)
ⓘ **Address** Neasham Road, Darlington, Co Durham DL2 1DL
⊕ **Capacity** 25,000
✪ **Best attendance** 11,600 vs Kidderminster Harriers,
Division Three, 16 August, 2003
ⓒ **Contact** 01325-387000
ⓞ **Ticket Number** 0871-855 1883
@ **Email** reception@darlington-fc.net
ⓦ **Website** darlington-fc.net

The cold, damp summer that preceded the start of the 2009/10 season saw the financial vultures swirling around the cool thermals of the northeast, casting long shadows over the long summer grass. Newcastle United might have monopolized the national headlines as the rudderless team from St James' Park careered towards the rocks of the second tier, but they had managed to retain most of their playing staff and the majority of their coaching setup, and they had a huge core of support behind them. The real storm was brewing just to the south, where Darlington faced the very real possibility of footballing extinction. The club floundered in administration as they approached the start of the season with a manager charged with assembling a squad while just two players were on the books. There weren't even ground staff to tend the rampant field growing in the middle of their huge arena.

The 27,000-seater stadium, built by former multi-millionaire chairman George Reynolds and christened the White Elephant Stadium by rivals, was the ultimate example of an 'If you build it they will come' mentality. However, this was a team that drew around 4,000 people through its turnstiles at their old ground on a good day, and now averages about the same in their swanky new surroundings. Reynold's folly appeared to sum up his reign at the club – this gleaming new bathtub of a stadium that only filled with a quarter of an inch of fans provided just the right depth to drown in – he went bankrupt and ended up in prison. In January 2004 an all-star charity match organized to raise money for the club saw 14,000 seats filled, while in May 2009 a similar match attracted just 3,000 diehard followers. It seems that being in the financial trenches for so long had left the local fans cold and tired. Plans were made by a core of supporters for a new club should the old one go bust.

In new manager Colin Todd, The Quakers hoped to have a man who could calm the waters. He assembled a team, brought in Dean Windass as his assistant and even got the ground staff back to work. However Todd's attempt at bailing and Staunton's subsequent work with a sticking plaster were not enough to stop Darlo's hopes of staying in the League going down the plug hole.

Greatest moments on this ground
"The 2-1 play-off semi-final win against Rochdale. A last-minute Ian Miller winner gave Darlington fans a rare but very real chance of a trip to Wembley going into the second leg." Daniel List, Sky Sports FanZone, Darlington correspondent.

Lowest moments on this ground
2010 and relegation to the realms of the Football Conference.

Heroes of the turf
"Marco Gabbiadini – one of the greatest players we've ever seen. Craig Liddle – he stuck with us even when our chairman tried to force him out. Mario Dorner – a bit-part player, but a cult hero. Robbie Blake – our most successful youth product. Kevan 'Smudger' Smith – he captained us to two promotions." Simon Hawkins, loidland.net.

HOME
AWAY

Pubs for home fans
"The best place for a pint before the game is The Carling Bare, located at the southwest corner of the stadium," recommends Daniel List. "It has a good mix of home and away fans and a friendly atmosphere."

Good food near ground
The local area is not laden with pubs – one of the closest is The Copper Beech on Neasham Road. In the town centre there are a number of good choices including The Tanners Hall Wetherpoons on Skinnersgate and, for real-ale drinkers, Number Twenty 2, Coniscliffe Road, which has quality hand-pumped refreshments. Food is available but football colours are not welcomed.

Pubs for away fans
"The stadium offers a carvery pre-match that is always well received and is excellent value," says Daniel.

Top tips
A Saturday match-day bus service runs between Tubwell Row (town centre) and the ground. Buses run every 15 minutes between 1.15pm and 2.30pm. Return service runs 4.45pm until 5.30pm.

That's quite interesting
"Bar Rochdale, Darlington had spent the most consecutive seasons in the bottom tier of English football without promotion or relegation." Daniel List.

Not a lot of people know that
"Darlington are the only team to be knocked out of the FA Cup twice in one season (after being drawn as the 'lucky losers' in 1999/00, when Manchester United withdrew from the competition)." Simon Hawkins.

HEROES OR ZEROES?

⌃ HEROES OF THE SIDELINE
"'David Hodgson – the real man for a crisis. He saved the club from relegation in his third stint at the helm and then saved the club from folding soon after by organizing an all-star charity game. Dave Penney – he took the club as close to promotion as we have been since our move to the Darlington Arena and led the team with real dignity despite not getting paid during administration." Daniel List.

"Steve Foster – the Darlington captain who stayed with the club throughout the administration period (without getting paid) and after, even when the rest of the squad left for pastures new. Ian Miller – he was the only other senior player to stay loyal to the club after the administration season." Daniel List.

Zeroes of the turf
"Nathan Porritt, came on loan from Middlesbrough. He was involved in Panorama-gate with Chelsea a couple of years ago. Craig Russell – he scored goals galore at Sunderland, but scored no goals for us." Simon Hawkins.

The Faustino Asprilla signing that wasn't – George Reynolds announced that former Newcastle striker Faustino Asprilla was set to sign for Darlington. It made the national news only for Asprilla to do a no-show on the day of the contract signing. Simon Johnson – he played like a world-beater in pre-season, but what followed was nothing but disappointment. Dean Windass – we thought we'd got a real coup, how wrong we were. " Daniel List.

Don't mention the…
"Probably anything to do with former owner George Reynolds, the ex safe-cracker who was declared bankrupt after building us a 25,000 all-seater stadium. He was famous for turning up on the doorstep of any fan who dared to criticize him, but shortly after putting us into administration he was arrested for tax evasion with £300k in the boot of his car." Simon Hawkins.

GETTY IMAGES

> The team huddles together before the kick off of a game at the Northern Echo Stadium.

Villains
"Asprilla – not quite our player. Clyde Wijnhard was sacked by the club for continually breaking club rules, however he was one of the best forwards we've had for a while. Kevin McBride/Ian Harty – two Scottish players signed in the summer of 2007. Both left under a cloud." Simon Hawkins.

The ground
The Northern Echo Darlington Arena is an amazing facility once you get over the vast space for such a small club. The stands sweep around in a large single-tier bowl with a suspended roof. The **South Stand** houses the changing rooms and has a row of executive boxes. Away fans sit in the **East Stand** behind the goal, while the home fans occupy the **North Stand** as well as the **West Stand** behind the far goal. There are excellent facilities, but away fans may find they are all together in one block.

Getting there
By road/Parking From the south exit the A1(M) at junction 5 and follow the A66(M) signed Darlington. This becomes the A66/Bridge Road. Turn left at Neesham roundabout; the ground is on the right. From the north, and to avoid getting snarled up in the city centre, exit the A1(M) at junction 59, following the A167. At the roundabout turn left onto the A1150/Salters Lane and follow through one roundabout. At the next roundabout, take the second exit onto the A66 signed Darlington, and follow for just over three miles through two roundabouts. At Neesham roundabout, take the third exit onto Neasham Road and the ground is on the right.

Parking at the ground costs £5 (available in advance and on the match day). There's limited street parking towards the town.

By train Darlington Station is just over a mile from the ground. Take the north exit and turn right at the end of the car park onto Parkgate, crossing under the railway bridge. Turn right onto Neasham Road and follow for around a mile (passing the Copper Beech for light refreshment). The ground is on the left.

THE LAST WORD

loidland.net
skysports.com/fanzone/blogs
dafts.co.uk
the-tinshed.co.uk
darlington.vitalfootball.co.uk

HOME COLOURS

- **Nicknames** The Rams
- **Founded** 1884
- **Ground** Pride Park (opened 1997)
- **Address** Pride Park Stadium, Derby DE24 8XL
- **Capacity** 33,597
- **Best attendance** 33,378 vs Liverpool, Premier League, 18 March, 2000
- **Contact** 0871-472 1884
- **Ticket Number** 0871-472 1884
- **Email** derby.county@dcfc.co.uk
- **Website** dcfc.co.uk

RIVALS

Nottingham Forest, Leicester City, Leeds United.

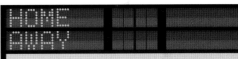

HOME
AWAY

Pubs for home fans

Close to the train station you'll find The Waterfall, which is a decent pub that gets very busy on match days. The beer is good but you will pay a bit of a premium for your pints here. Other pubs near the station well worth visit include the Brunswick, which has a great selection of real ales, and the Merry Widows, a cosy little place which also does a decent pint. Be prepared for some queuing on a match day though as these places get really busy.

Good food near ground

There is a good selection of food takeaways in the centre and most pubs do food.

Pubs for away fans

Away fans arriving by car should head towards The Navigation Inn on London Road which is away friendly and usually has a snack bar outside selling burgers, hot dogs, etc. Away fans travelling by train can either head to The Crown and Cushion or The Harvester. If you leave the station through the main entrance you will come out onto Midland Road. Walk straight up the road, past the Post Office sorting depot on your left, up to the traffic lights at the top. On the corner you will find The Crown and Cushion, which is an away fans pub. If you leave the train station through the rear exit, which leads onto Pride Park, you will see a Harvester. This pub does not always allow away fans in though.

Top tips

Pride Park is considered one of the best grounds to visit. Passionate fans and great facilities.

When Nigel Clough walked in through the reception at Derby County Football Club in January 2009, the personification of calm confidence, there must have been an unshakable feeling of déjà vu about the situation. Pride Park is just another modern stadium, but for Clough it must have carried a huge gamut of memories and feelings and emotions. The weight of expectation and the sense of anticipation must have been palpable, like the cloying heat that muscles in on equatorial afternoons, crying out for the relief of a tropical downpour to ease the tension. Derby's previous home, the Baseball Ground, would have been a second home to the young Clough. He might have been found playing in the corridors, our out near the practice pitches; after all, his dad was the boss.

For it was here his father, Brian Clough, forged a managerial reputation in the fires of one of English football's most glorious eras. It was a time of huge clubs, rousing choruses echoing from huge terraces, a time of hard players and new tactics, flying wingers and bruising defenders, of Busby, Shankly, Ramsey and Revie. When 'Old Big Ed' joined Derby in the summer of 1967, the club was languishing in Division Two. As a player Clough Snr had been a spectacularly prolific striker, but his career had been cut short by injury and he had cut his managerial teeth in the northeast at Hartlepool. But it was at Derby County that he would carve his name as a great.

He took charge of the Midlands club with his right hand man Peter Taylor and they proceeded to piece together a team, bringing in a succession of new faces. The likes of John McGovern, John O'Hare, Roy McFarland and Dave Mackay all joined the Rams, who went on to claim the 1968/69 Division Two title at a canter. Their first season in the top flight ended in a respectable 4th place in the league, however by the 1971/72 season the East Midlanders were battling it out with the great Liverpool and Leeds teams for the title. It went down to the last Saturday, but Derby were champions.

However Clough's relationship with his board was becoming fractious. He signed players without their permission and became increasingly controversial. They were beaten in the semi-final of the European Cup by Juventus, who he labelled "cheating bastards" (knowing what we know now, maybe he was right). By October 1973 he and Taylor had resigned. The fans were up in arms, but the board moved swiftly to appoint Dave Mackay as manager and Clough was forced to move on. The incidents around this period became a central theme in the David Peace book *The Damned United* and the film that followed. Mackay won the title in 1974-75 but then the Rams began a steady decline until they slipped into Division Two in 1980.

Followers of Derby County have enjoyed a couple of spells back in the top flight, both in the late eighties and late nineties. While more recently the 2007/08 season

⌃ Kevin Hector beats Manchester United's Steve James to score for Brian Clough's Derby and help beat Manchester United 1-0 at Old Trafford, in September 1973.

allowed another taste of the big time as fans found themselves again following the Rams to Liverpool's Anfield, Manchester's Old Trafford and Arsenal's Emirates. It was not a season of great success on the field, but fans won plaudits wherever they went for their passionate support of the team in white and black.

Now Clough Jnr has his chance at the helm. There is the weight of great expectation. He has to fight this gravity and gain the momentum. He handled it as a player, where he was admired for his calm head and skill under pressure. Fans here are hoping he can deliver just some of the success brought by his father. Then the legend will be complete.

Greatest moments on this ground

"If we're talking about Pride Park rather than the Baseball Ground, then my personal favourite moment was the play-off semi-final when we beat Southampton. The away game had been a great game now promotion was dependent on beating Southampton on a very wet Tuesday night.

Southampton were managed by former Rams boss George Burley and had two ex-Rams in the team. The game was a draw after extra-time so it came down to penalties. After several tense penalties, Southampton's chances of reaching Wembley fell to Inigo Idiakez, the former Rams midfielder and dead ball specialist. He stepped up to take his kick and duly whacked it over the bar thus sending us on our way to Wembley where we went on to win promotion to the Premier League." Martin Broadhurst, RamBalls.

Lowest moments on this ground

"Take your pick from nearly any of the 2007/08 season home games. In a season which saw us finish with the lowest ever Premier League points total, we took a few beatings at home including a 6-0 loss to Aston Villa and a 5-0 hammering against West Ham." Martin Broadhurst.

HEROES OR ZEROES?

⌄ HEROES OF THE SIDELINE

"Brian Clough. He was the greatest manager England never had and there is nothing else I can say about "Sir Brian" that hasn't already been said. He was a true legend. Dave Mackay was in charge for Derby's League Championship win in 1975 and is often overlooked for his achievement because people say it was still Clough's team. The fact remains that he was in charge and is therefore a legend at the club. Jim Smith, The Bald Eagle, guided the Rams into the Premier League and kept us there, finishing 12th in our first season and 8th in 1998/99. Under Jim Smith we played some excellent football and signed some world class players who entertained the Pride Park crowd week in, week out." Martin Broadhurst.

Heroes of the turf

"Steve Bloomer. You're probably thinking Steve who? He is Derby County's all time highest goal-scorer and football's first superstar. He had a stunning goal-scoring record – in 14 consecutive seasons he finished as the Ram's top scorer. In 1895 he won his first England cap, a game in which he scored a brace, and he went on to score 28 goals in 23 games for England.

"King" Kevin Hector. The King joined Derby in 1966 and went on to make over 450 appearances in a Derby shirt over two stints with the club. Hector was a key player during both of the Championship winning seasons, but only managed to earn two England caps during his career.

Dave Mackay was signed by Brian Clough from Tottenham in 1968. He steadied the ship and helped win the Second Division Championship in his first season. He later went on to the manage the club and lead The Rams to their second League Championship.

Stefano Eranio. The Italian maestro came to Derby from AC Milan in 1997 during the Jim Smith era. His quality consistently shone through as he showed a level of skill and flair that has rarely been seen at Pride Park since.

Igor Štimac. It's fair to say that when the Croatian centre-back joined Derby in 1995, we weren't pulling up any trees. His debut saw us lose 5-1, although he did score the consolation goal. But his arrival heralded a new belief and we won promotion to the Premier League when we secured second place in the league following a 20 game unbeaten run. He stayed with the club for four years before joining West Ham for £600,000." Martin Broadhurst.

Zeroes of the turf

"Francois Grenet was signed by Colin Todd for £3m and Derby fans were told he was the second best right-back in France, behind Lilian Thuram. It didn't take Rams fans long to realise he wasn't even the second best right-back in the city of Derby.

That's quite interesting

"Pride Park is the only football ground to be opened by the Queen, despite Arsenal trying to share the honour. She was due to open the Emirates Stadium, but had to cancel due to a back injury. The Queen's opening of Pride Park isn't her only visit to the stadium. She returned in 2002, proving she is a Derby County fan." Martin Broadhurst.

Not a lot of people know that

"Derby County were one of the founder members of the Football League and have played in the top two divisions of English football in all but four seasons since the league was created." Martin Broadhurst.

Derek Hales joined the Rams in 1976 from Charlton where he had a goals-to-games ratio of one-in-two. His record at Derby was very different as he managed a feeble four goals in 23 League appearances for the Rams. Needless to stay, his spell at the Baseball Ground was short lived.

Derby have wasted millions on terrible defenders and Bjorn Otto Bragstad is just one of several I could mention. The £3m we paid for him makes Joleon Lescott's £22m move to Man City look like a car boot sale bargain." Martin Broadhurst.

Don't mention the…

"Disastrous 2007/08 Premier League season, which saw us rewrite the "How Not to Play Football" handbook. We were the first team in Premier League history to be relegated in March, which wasn't surprising given the fact we finished the season with a pathetic 11 points and only one win on the board. It was a nightmare season, which went from bad to worse, as managerial sex scandals and stories of players fleeing the club through the training ground windows made the headlines.

The one consolation was winning a Fans of the Year award from *Nuts* magazine. Still, we'd have rather had a few more points on the board." Martin Broadhurst.

Villains

"In recent years, Derby fans have been relatively nice to former players who have returned to Pride Park. There have been some pretty fierce reactions to certain players returning to the club though, notably Mark Pembridge who left the club in 1995 to join Sheffield Wednesday where he decided he would make comments about Derby. This secured him the fate of being the most booed player to play at Derby. On one occasion, because of the reaction he got every time he touched the ball, he was substituted.

More recent examples would include Lee Camp, a former Rams keeper and supposed life-long Derby supporter, who joined local rivals Notts Forest and celebrated like a chimp who had just received a crate of bananas when they beat us for the first time in six years. Needless to say, this hasn't gone down well with the Derby faithful." Martin Broadhurst.

The ground

Pride Park was opened in 1997, replacing the aging Baseball Ground. It is an arena-style ground with seating wrapping around the corners. The largest stand is the main **West Stand**, an impressive two-tier structure that runs the length of the pitch, but finishes as it reaches the corner to accommodate a block of corporate boxes and media suites. The roof angles down to the **North Stand** behind the far goal, which is a slightly smaller and lower one tier structure for home fans. This wraps around and joins with the **East Stand**. Behind the near goal the **South Stand** is again a one-tier structure, the western side of which is allocated to away fans. The allocation varies with demand but is usually around the 3,000 mark.

Getting there

By Road/Parking Take junction 25 of the M1 and follow the A52. There is on-street parking on London Road,

although you have to get there early. There is also the Ascot Drive industrial estate close by, which usually has free spaces for weekend games. The stadium is approximately a five- to 10-minute walk from here.

By Train Pride Park is just a 15 minute walk from the mainline station. When leaving your train, use the footbridge from the station directly into Pride Park.

THE LAST
WORD

martinblogs.co.uk/ramballs
therams.co.uk
derbycounty-mad.co.uk
popside.com

GETTY IMAGES

> Nigel Clough, back at Derby County.

HOME COLOURS

- **Nicknames** Rovers, The Vikings
- **Founded** 1879
- **Ground** Keepmoat Stadium (opened 2007)
- **Address** Stadium Way, Lakeside, Doncaster DN4 5JW
- **Capacity** 15,231
- **Best attendance** 15,001 vs Leeds United, 1 April 2008, League One, 1 April, 2008
- **Contact** 01302-764664
- **Ticket Number** 01302-762576
- **Email** info@doncasterroversfc.co.uk
- **Website** doncasterroversfc.co.uk

DONCASTER ROVERS

RIVALS

Barnsley,
Rotherham United,
Scunthorpe United
and Hull City

Huge, black, winged creatures circled the ground, casting shadows of despair across the gathered Vikings as the visiting Seagulls took to the pitch at Belle Vue on that grey October Saturday in 1997 – somewhat distracting when you're looking for your first away win in 19 matches. Glancing around the 2,351 gloomy South Yorkshire faces, Brighton knew this was their chance. Banners of the home fans draped over the railings demanded 'Richardson Out!' But Doncaster chairman Ken Richardson was going nowhere. Having dismissed manager Kerry Dixon, the wayward owner was now running and picking the team with his sidekick, manager Mark Weaver. Few would recognize the squad he put out that day. Making their first appearances were Andy Thorpe, a 37-year-old who'd last played full time six years previously, and a bloke called Rod Thornley. The away support crowed as their team peppered the Donny goal from all parts of the field – until the rumour reached them that rotund keeper David Smith only made the cut because he was Doncaster manager Weaver's neighbour. Still, the long drive home to Brighton was a happy one for the south coasters, leaving the swirling black cloud of Belle Vue behind, and Doncaster to face a charge from the FA of fielding an under-strength team. Rovers final record that season: P46, W4, D8, L34, GD-83 and a total of 20 points. The committed few who could bear to watch held a mock burial as the team was consigned to the cemetery of non-league football.

By 1999 the club had a new owner and saviour in Jon Ryan; Richardson meanwhile was in prison for conspiracy to burn down the ground. At the time, you could have got pretty good odds from any Vikings fan against their beating neighbours Leeds United at Wembley inside 10 years, but by 2008 they had earned a deserved place in

the Championship via just such a play-off victory. With a brand-new stadium to boot, it appears that Doncaster have emerged from the depths of their desperate Dali-esque nightmare as a shining example of how a modern club should be run. But, more importantly, local kids, who once favoured the strips of the Premiership, can now be seen having a kick about proudly sporting their Donny replica shirts – the red, white and black are back!

Greatest moments on this ground
"Beating Southend 5-0 in the League One play-off semi-final. An all-round classy performance that really put us in a good frame of mind to head to Wembley." Nathan Batchelor, editor *Popular Stand*, and founder of footballhelp.co.uk.

Lowest moments on this ground
"The lowest point during our time at Belle Vue was under ex-chairman Ken Richardson, who hired somebody to burn down the main stand. He ended up going to jail for the crime. We were then relegated out of the Football League in 1998, I honestly thought I had seen my last game following Rovers when we played Colchester on the final day of the season. All I can say is thank god for new chairman John Ryan." Daz King, Vital Doncaster.

HOME
AWAY

Pubs for home fans
Salutation, on South Parade, is quite a trek from the ground, but is a friendly spot with sports TV and a good range of ales, including one in support of the club. Good scran also. The Park Hotel, Carr House Road, is another spot that has traditionally attracted fans.

Good food near ground
"There's a Pizza Hut, KFC and McDonald's next to the ground," says Nathan Batchelor. "There's also a family pub, The Cheswold, on the other side of the lake that serves food."

Pubs for away fans
"With a lot of local derbies in our league it might vary from match to match," explains Nathan Batchelor. "For example, when we played Leeds the whole town was dry before (and I think for a short period after) the match." The Lakeside Beefeater, White Rose Way, can be fine, if not particularly inspiring.

Top tips
Has a reputation for not being the most away-fan-friendly of spots so it's best not to dwell around the town.

GETTY IMAGES

▲ Doncaster have gone from the grey skies of non-league football to golden days as Championship contenders. Spurs come to the Keepmoat.

Heroes of the sideline

"Billy Bremner – he took over in 1978 when we were perennial re-election candidates, within three years he'd got us promoted. We were established as a Third Division side by the time he left in 1985. Dave Penney – he led us back into the League in 2003 and the following season we were Division Four champions. We had our best-ever cup run under him, reaching the quarter-finals of the League Cup in 2005, beating Man City and Aston Villa on the way and eventually losing to Arsenal on penalties after leading going into injury time. Sean O'Driscoll – he took over from Penney and led us to our first-ever final to win the Johnstone's Paint Trophy. The following season won us promotion to the Championship when we beat Leeds 1-0 at Wembley. He established Rovers as a mid-table Championship side on limited resources playing passing football." Daz King.

Heroes of the turf

"Paul Green – he joined our youth team at 16 and rose up the through the divisions with us. A real 100%er. Alick Jeffery – many claim there's been no better player to wear the Rovers shirt. He would have no doubt gone to play for England if injury hadn't curtailed things. Syd Bycroft – an old-fashioned, no nonsense defender who would tackle a brick wall, but was a gentleman off the pitch. Dave Penney – he joined us when everyone else in football must have been advising him not to. He brought some grit and determination to the side." Nathan Batchelor.
Also Ian Snodin, Peter Kitchin, Francis Tierney and Michael McIndoe.

Zeroes of the turf

"Carl Alford – he joined with a huge reputation in 2000 having scored more than a goal a game during his time at Stevenage. He managed only one goal for Rovers! Justin Jackson – we paid a

lot of money for him after he'd been quite prolific at his previous two clubs. Again, he didn't manage to do the same, netting only a handful of goals. Steve Brooker – still at the club. He joined originally on loan and scored within 10 minutes of being on the pitch. He got injured, signed while still injured and since then has spent all the time on the treatment table. The club has announced that he needs a further operation." Daz King.

Don't mention the...

"In the eighties burly Gerry Daly got into a fight with a St John's Ambulance man during a game and chased him around the pitch." Daz King.

The ground

Doncaster played their last-ever game at the old Belle Vue ground in December 2006, before moving to this new purpose-built all-seater arena. The Keepmoat Stadium isn't the prettiest in the Football League, resembling a large Ikea store from the outside, but it is smart and modern. The seating is single tier wrapping around the pitch continuously. The **Success Doncaster Stand** runs along the length of the field. Behind the goals is the **Polypipe South Stand**, while the rest of the home support sits in the **West Stand**. Away fans are seated behind the other goal in the **Case Construction North Stand**, with an allocation that can run to just over 3,000.

Getting there

By road/Parking Southeast of the centre. Exit the M18 at junction 3 following the A6182/White Rose Way for Doncaster. At the second roundabout, go straight over onto Wilmington Drive, passing the shopping centre on the left. At the next roundabout turn left into Stadium Way. The ground is on the right. Parking at the ground costs £5. Park in and walk from the former Belle Vue car park (there are signs).

By train Doncaster station is about a 35-minute walk to the ground. The better bet is to take the regular bus from Frenchgate Bus Interchange – five minutes' walk away (First Bus 72 and 75).

VILLAINS
"They don't come any greater than Ken 'He burns down stands, he's hated by the fans' Richardson." Nathan Batchelor.

EVERTON

- **Nicknames** The Toffees, The Blues
- **Founded** 1878
- **Ground** Goodison Park (opened 1892)
- **Address** Goodison Road, Liverpool L4 4EL
- **Capacity** 40,157
- **Best attendance** 78,299 vs Liverpool, Liverpool, Division One, 1948
- **Contact** 0871-663 1878
- **Ticket Number** 0871-663 1878
- **@ Email** everton@evertonfc.com
- **Website** evertonfc.com

From the very birth of popular culture, there has been a Mersey beat at its epicentre. It has provided a cauldron of musical talent, and the eighties were no exception. A Flock of Seagulls, OMD, Echo & The Bunnymen and Frankie Goes to Hollywood were storming the charts, along with many other Liverpool bands. Some, such as the Reynolds Girls, are best forgotten. But during this decade, Merseyside was also the swirling eye of the football world. While Derek Hatton was doing his best to paint the city red, Liverpool was feeling distinctly blue.

After years of domestic dominance, the team from Anfield suddenly had a very real rival – one that was very close to home. Everton, under the stewardship of Howard Kendall, had assembled a Championship-winning side, and set about adding some silverware to the Goodison trophy cabinet. Having won the FA Cup at Wembley in May 1984, Kendall knew the following year would be make or break. The team was set – Neville Southall was in goal, and Gary Stevens, Trevor Steven, Peter Reid, Andy Gray and Graeme Sharpe were the backbone. Fighting on three fronts, The Toffees were on course for a treble coming into the home straight. The League title was clinched with the final standings, leaving Everton 13 points clear of runners-up Liverpool. A thrilling European campaign culminated in a trip to Rotterdam, where the blues took on Rapid Vienna for the European Cup Winners' Cup. Goals from Gray, Steven and Sheedy saw the trophy come back to Merseyside and set up a treble showdown at Wembley just three days later against Manchester United. In the FA Cup final a crowd a whisker shy of 100,000 had gathered in the shadows of the twin towers. In a thrilling game, the battling blues were only denied by an extra-time goal from Norman Whiteside.

The Kendall era had seen titles come to Goodison in 1985 and 1987 and runners-up medals in 1986. They were runners-up in the FA Cup in 1985 and 1986, as well as League Cup finalists in 1984. In 1987 Kendall moved on, and an era was over.

Everton have tried relegation, they didn't really like it much, so they decided not to do it again. They have spent over a century in the top flight, longer than any other club. Longer than their Merseyside rivals, they'll keenly point out – but then, they have been around longer, for it was Everton that first occupied the hallowed turf at Anfield. In fact, Liverpool FC was born out of a split between the Anfield owner John Houlding and the Everton board. Everton moved to Goodison as a result, and Houlding formed a new club, Liverpool FC. That sort of makes them family, and there is a unique rivalry between the red and blue halves of Liverpool.

In 1925, a young player called Dixie Dean joined the Merseyside team from rivals Tranmere. A boyhood fan, he went on to become the most prolific striker English football has ever seen. In his first full season he scored 32 League goals in 38 games, then, the next year, 21 in 27, but it is the 1927/28 season he is most remembered for. In 39 games he bagged a grand total of 60 goals. Dixie stayed virtually a one-club man, with a stunning record of 383 goals in 433 appearances in royal blue. Dean was never booked throughout his career and his statue stands at the Park End of Goodison with the fitting inscription "Footballer, Gentleman, Evertonian."

Greatest moments on this ground
"Dixie Dean scoring his 60th goal of the season against Arsenal in 1928 probably ranks up there with the greatest moment to happen at Goodison Park. Reports said that the cheer that went up when he scored sent pigeons scattering on the docks – some three miles away! In recent history, the 3-1 European Cup Winners' Cup semi-final win over Bayern Munich in 1985 probably steals it." Simon Paul, NSNO (Nil Satis Nisi Optimum).

Lowest moments on this ground
"3-0 defeat at home against Tranmere in the FA Cup in 2001." Steve 'Kipper' Jones, Blue Kipper.

Heroes of the sideline
"Howard Kendall – Everton's most successful manager,

VILLAINS
"Wayne Rooney is the typical cartoon villain. He was 'one of us' and left in search of glory elsewhere after famously declaring: 'Once a Blue, Always a Blue." Simon Paul. "Nick Barmby left for Liverpool, and Joleon Lescott – a money-grabbin' and mediocre player." Steve 'Kipper' Jones.

RIVALS
Liverpool.

winning two League titles, an FA Cup, the European Cup Winners' Cup and three Charity Shields. Harry Catterick – he had the team playing great football, hence 'the school of science' with players like Young, Vernon, Ball, Kendall and Harvey. Joe Royle and his 'dogs of war' winning the FA cup in 1995 and David Moyes bringing European football back to 'The People's Club.'" Steve 'Kipper' Jones.

Heroes of the turf

"Dixie Dean with 60 goals in a league season – a record that will never be broken – and he was a real man of the people. He would get the tram to the ground for a match along with the fans! Dave Hickson – 'The Cannonball Kid'. He would put his head where most players wouldn't have put their feet in the pursuit of victory for Everton. Quoted as saying he would break every bone in his body for any other club, but he would die for Everton. Alan Ball – with his white boots and silky skills, Ball was the linchpin of the trio he formed with Colin Harvey and Howard Kendall in the sixties. Known as the Holy Trinity, they were an unbeatable combination. Bob Latchford – he scored 30 goals in the 1977/78 season, and the famous terrace

HOME
AWAY

Pubs for home fans
"For a pint I'd recommend The Brick on County Road, Walton," says Simon Paul. "It's always busy but easy to get served at, and you're just down the road from Goodison Park – a minute's walk". Royal Oak in Kirkdale, on Walton Road, is another spot with a decent atmosphere.

Good food near ground
"You'd probably be best going to one of the burger vans on Goodison Road if you want something to eat" says Simon Paul. Also on Goodison Road, The Goodison Supper Bar is that winning combination of Chinese takeaway meets chippie! McDonald's is on Walton Road.

Pubs for away fans
Thomas Frost (Wetherspoons), on Walton Road, is around 15 minutes from the ground with a decent mix of home and away supporters and a good atmosphere. The Vines, right by Liverpool Lime Street station, is a handy stop-off, as is The Melrose Abbey by Kirkdale Station.

Top tips
If travelling via train, ask for a return to Goodison Park and an extra £1 covers your Soccerbus travel between the station and the stadium; see merseytravel.gov.uk.

⌄ Andy Gray scores in 1984 FA Cup final at Wembley, against Watford. Everton win 2-0.

^ Tim Cahill (out of picture)
scores at Goodison.

chant claimed he 'walks on water'. He met Dixie Dean after scoring his 30th and was told: "Remember son, you're only half as good as I was!" Neville Southall – the most successful Everton player ever. Played 750 games for the Blues and won two League Championships, two FA Cups and a European Cup Winners' Cup." Simon Paul.

"Duncan Ferguson – he was sent off seven times, but was a footballing braveheart with the Everton crest tattooed on his arm. He regularly turned it on and scored against the reds**te." Steve 'Kipper' Jones.

Zeroes of the turf

"Brett Angel – he signed from the lower leagues as a goalscoring beanpole and returned to the lower-league simply as a beanpole a season later. Glenn Keeley – he made one appearance for Everton, and was sent off, in the 5-0 defeat by Liverpool in 1982. Per Kroldrup – he signed as a footballing defender to take Everton into the Champions League. Rumours went around that he couldn't head the ball, and he was sold six months after signing having made just one start." Simon Paul.

88 | Around the Grounds
| Everton

Don't mention the…

"Haka – Everton launched the 2009/10 away kit with a special version of the haka. The Maori people haven't taken too kindly to it, and nobody understands the relevance of it. The kit is black with pink stripes (!), which is bad enough on it's own, but the haka was said to represent the 'all black' away kit…" Simon Paul.

The ground

Goodison Park is one of the older grounds in the top flight and, as such, falls into one of two categories depending on your viewpoint – either it needs modernizing, or has great character. There have been long-term plans involving a move to Kirkby, but this relocation out of Liverpool is unpopular with many fans.

The **Main Stand** was opened in 1971 and runs the length of the pitch, seating a total of 12,664. There is a pitch-side family enclosure that runs along the front of the stand and the Main Stand area that sits below the lofty top balcony. The area of seating in the main section towards the Park End seems to peter out at the back of the stand, with the upper rows angling away. This is due to the fact that Goodison Road runs at an angle to the Main Stand so effectively slices a corner off the back of it. The benches and the players' tunnel are on the halfway line here, but aren't very visible. The floodlights are mounted on the roof of the Main Stand and on the Bullens opposite.

At the south end of the stadium behind the goal is the single-tier **Stanley Park End**, which backs onto the fringes of Stanley Park. This is a free-standing structure with no pillars to obscure views; it has a capacity of 5,922. A statue of Everton legend Dixie Dean stands outside and there is an electronic scoreboard mounted on the roof.

Bullens Road sits opposite the main stand and is separated into three areas: the Paddock sits at the front, the Lower Bullens behind and the Upper Bullens on top. Its current capacity is 10,784. Away fans can be allocated both the Upper and Lower tiers of the Bullens Stand at the Park End side of the structure. This can hold about 3,000 away fans. The Paddock offers unobscured views, but there are pillars in the upper and lower stand.

The **Gwladys Street Stand**, or the 'Street End' is a two-tier area opposite the Park End behind the goal. It has a capacity of 10,788. The roof extends around and joins the Bullens Road Stand roof and the corner between the two is filled in with seating. There are pillars about two thirds back in the Street End. Between the Gwladys Street Stand and the Main Stand there is the church of St Luke the Evangelist, which occupies a whole corner of the ground; it is one of the stadium's most famous landmarks.

Getting there

By road/Parking From the south, exit the M6 at junction 21a onto the M26 towards Liverpool. Follow to its conclusion, turning right onto Queen's Drive Stoneycroft A5058. Follow for around three miles and go left into Walton Lane. At the corner of the ground, turn right into Spellow Lane, becoming Goodison Road. From the north, exit the M6 at junction 26 onto the M58 for Liverpool. Follow to conclusion, turning left at the gyratory onto the A59/Ormskirk Road (passing Aintree racecourse). Continue straight over the roundabout onto County Road. Go left into Spellow Lane and left onto Goodison Road. Parking is available half a mile from the ground at Stanley Park for £8. Early arrivals may find some parking along Walton Lane.

By train Kirkdale Station (Merseyrail Northern Line) is closest, around one mile from the stadium. From the station cross over the railway bridge and walk up Westminster Road. Turn left onto Goodall Street (becoming Harlech Street). Cross County Road into Andrew Street, at the end of which is Goodison Road, St Luke's Church and the ground. Alternatively take the train to Sandhills. The Soccerbus runs between the station and the stadium for two hours before and 50 minutes after the game, every 15 minutes.

PUB QUIZ

That's quite interesting

"Goodison Park boasts a number of firsts – it was the first stadium to have four two-tier stands and the first to host an FA Cup final outside of London. It's also the only stadium in England outside of Wembley to host a World Cup semi-final." Simon Paul.

Not a lot of people know that

"Everton were originally called 'St Domingo FC' after the church that founded the club. They also won the league at Anfield before Liverpool FC were even created – the medals given to commemorate that feat had a Blue Liver bird on them too!" Simon Paul.

THE LAST **WORD**

nsno.co.uk
bluekipper.com
toffeeweb.com
wsag.org

EXETER CITY

⊘ **Nicknames** The Grecians
⊙ **Founded** 1904
⊙ **Ground** St James Park (opened 1905)
ⓘ **Address** Wells Street, Exeter EX4 6PX
⊙ **Capacity** 8,830
✪ **Best attendance** 21,014 vs Sunderland, FA Cup 6th round replay, 4 March, 1931
ⓒ **Contact** 01392-411243
ⓒ **Ticket Number** 01392-411243
@ **Email** reception@exetercityfc.co.uk
ⓦ **Website** exetercityfc.co.uk

Back in 1914 Exeter City players boarded an ocean liner for South America. This football tour of Brazil and Argentina would forever ensure The Grecians a place in world football history. The simple feat of going on a tour in South America in 1914 (only two years after the Titanic sank) was impressive, but one game on that tour gave birth to the world's greatest-ever football side. On 27 July at the Laranjeiras Stadium, Rio de Janeiro, Exeter played Brazil in the international team's first-ever football match. Exeter lost 2-0, (although in some quarters there is a belief that the game was a 3-3 draw), one of only two defeats. Brazil returned the favour in 2004 sending an all-star team to play Exeter in a special centenary game at St James Park.

Exeter City is also well known for their nickname, The Grecians, a moniker which appears not to have a definitive origin. The club took the name from the parish of St Sidwells, whose old boys were some of the co-founders of the club. They have been known as The Greeks, or Grecians for over 300 years. Some believe that the area, being situated beyond the city walls, was an area where ruffians and criminals resided, resembling the Greeks beneath the walls of Troy, hence the name. In the 16th and 17th centuries the word Grecian was also used to describe itinerant labourers and immigrants, something that the area was also known for. Others believe it came from the Bible as a term simply for outsiders. Whichever it was, Exeter City will forever be known as The Grecians, but still no one will quite know why.

In the domestic game, Exeter City's best years were in the late seventies and early eighties when they had a spell in the then Third Division. Unfortunately, since then financial trouble and a general decline saw them slip into the Conference. However after four years they won the play-off back into the league in 2007/08 and

then finished runners up in the now Second Division, and have returned to the third tier of English football, a return which many fans didn't believe would happen after the spectre of financial ruin that hung over the club for such a long time.

Greatest moments on this ground
"The greatest moment was actually at Rotherham. Gaining promotion back to the third tier of English football after years of financial and football heartbreak was overwhelming." Raymond Carter.

Lowest moments on this ground
"Impossible to single out as there have been so many. Although the last couple of years have erased most from my memory, one does stick out – a chilly evening against

Pubs for home fans
The Brook Green Tavern is a home fan favourite as is The Black Horse, although away fans are admitted. In general you will find all the pubs are a mix of support, and the atmosphere is friendly.

Good food near ground
There is every sort of eatery you can imagine in the city centre, which is just a 15-minute walk away. The aforementioned pubs also serve food and there are the usual array of fast-food joints close to the ground.

Pubs for away fans
There are plenty of pubs within 15 minutes of the ground, especially in the town centre. Most will welcome a number of low-profile away supporters. Close to the ground The Victoria is popular with both sets of support as is the Bowling Green Pub, both serve food too. There are sometimes restrictions for local derbies.

Top tips
There is a military presence in the town, hence the clubs and pubs can get rowdy, so if you're planning a night out keep a watchful eye out for trouble.

PUB QUIZ

That's quite interesting
Exeter turned professional in 1908 and successfully got elected to the Southern League, replacing Tottenham Hotspur.

Not a lot of people know that
Exeter City's draw away at Old Trafford in the third round of the 2005 FA Cup was a shock, but also the gate receipts from the game and the subsequent replay virtually wrote off the clubs debts, thus securing their future.

Kidderminster, where we lost 2-5. We lost a local derby to Plymouth 2-3 in the dying seconds as well, that was a heartbreaker, although an exciting game." Raymond Carter.

Heroes of the sideline
"Paul Tisdale is the obvious choice, winning back-to-back promotions in the last two seasons. From the late eighties, Terry Cooper for delivering the Fourth Division title, Alan Ball also deserves a mention." Raymond Carter.

Don't mention the…
Police raiding the club and taking the chairman away for questioning.

The ground
St James Park is a compact ground and although its size and shape are reminiscent of an old stadium, two of its stands have actually quite recently been built or refurbished.

The **Stagecoach Grandstand** is a real throwback to yesteryear. A short, single-tiered stand, it doesn't run the full length of the pitch but instead straddles the halfway line. It is covered and both ends provide shelter from inclement weather. There are 300 seats in this stand for away supporters, although this is not where the main contingent of away fans will be.

The **Flybe Stand** was opened in 2001 and is a modern single-tiered stand for home supporters only. There is a row of executive boxes at the back straddling the halfway line and the all the seating is undercover.

St James' Terrace is the smallest stand in the ground and is open to the elements and home to the bulk of away fans. Anyone travelling to the ground with a ticket for this end would be wise to bring some weatherproof clothing, as there is no cover.

Re-opened in 2000 the **Big Bank Stand** is home to the core of home support. Capable of holding 4,000 fans, the terrace is now covered, and although referred to as the Big Bank still, the club officially renamed the stand after twenties and thirties Exeter and Arsenal legend Cliff Bastin.

Getting there
By Road/Parking Most fans will arrive by the M5 and should leave at Junction 30 following signs for Middlemoor. At the following roundabout take the exit marked for Heavitree and continue along this road for just over two miles towards the city centre. At the bottom of the long hill turn right at the roundabout into Western Way and then at the next roundabout take the second exit. The second left is Stadium Way leading to the ground.

By Train Though the nearest train station to the ground is St James Park, there are no direct out-of-county services to the station, and so visitors need to change at either Exeter Central or Exeter St David's. The ground is walkable from both mainline stations, although they are on opposite sides of the city centre to the ground.

THE LAST WORD   exeweb.com

▾ Exeter's Scott Hilley goes past Wayne Rooney in an FA Cup 3rd round replay.

GETTY IMAGES

VILLAINS
"Anyone who has ever played for Plymouth or Torquay. There were many villains behind the financial problems of the club, but the mismanagement was so deep it's impossible to single out anyone." Stuart Biggs.

HOME COLOURS

- 🌐 **Nicknames** The Cottagers
- ⚽ **Founded** 1879
- 🏟 **Ground** Craven Cottage (opened 1894)
- ℹ️ **Address** Stevenage Road, London SW6 6HH
- 👥 **Capacity** 26,400
- ✖️ **Best attendance** 49,335 vs Milwall, Division Two, 8 October, 1938
- 📞 **Contact** 0870-442 1222
- 🎟 **Ticket Number** 0870-442 1234
- @ **Email** enquiries@fulhamfc.com
- 🌐 **Website** fulhamfc.com

PUB QUIZ

That's quite interesting
"Fulham are the oldest professional football club in London." David Harris.

Not a lot of people know that
"The original 'Cottage' was built in 1780, by William Craven, the sixth Baron Craven, and was located on the present centre circle. The surrounding land used to be woodland in which Anne Boleyn would go hunting." Stuart Mackie.

When Fulham hit rock bottom in the mid-nineties, wallowing in the depths of the bottom league of English football, there seemed a real chance that the oldest professional club in London might just fall out of the Football League, either due to poor form or lack of financial backing. The Cottagers had undergone a steady decline, a string of chairmen and owners had come and gone – most seemed more interested in the potential of the club's ground than the performance on the pitch. The sale of Craven Cottage, a prime piece of London real estate, was brought up on many occasions. The possibility of Fulham having to ground share, most likely with deadliest rivals Queens Park Rangers, was also floated. It wasn't until ex-player Jimmy Hill stepped up that the fans saw some hope; he took over as chairman and pledged that Fulham would be staying at Craven Cottage in the heart of the community where they belonged. This was the first stage of stability for the west London club, but finances and form were still in a bad shape, and when Mickey Adams took over, the club was in the bottom four of the Football League and seemingly going nowhere. Adams first stabilized the team and, on a very tight budget, got them promoted the next season, just missing out on winning the league on goals scored. Ironically they had a better goal difference but chairman Hill had been one of the backers of the new goals scored scheme at the Football League, thus depriving his own team of the title.

There then followed the re-birth of Fulham FC with the dramatic entrance of new club owner Mohamed Al-Fayed. Never a shy type, he pledged to the fans that he would place the club back onto a firm financial footing, rejuvenate the ground and more importantly, have them playing in the Premiership in five years time. He proved good to his word – first under Ray Wilkins, then Kevin

Keegan and ultimately Jean Tigana, a formidable side was moulded, with up-and-coming French forward Louis Saha spearheading the attack. The striker helped fire them into the top flight in 2001, a year ahead of schedule, and with a massive 101 points in the bag. After just over a season in the Premiership, Tigana was released by the club and Chris Coleman, one of the club's legendary players whose career was cut short due to a car crash, became the youngest manager in the top flight. He had five games to keep them up and he achieved that and went on to manage for almost five more seasons as Fulham battled and fought for their place at the top table.

Now, experienced manager Roy Hodgson seems to be thriving at the helm and in his first season when relegation seemed certain, he steered the club out of trouble in what many fans still refer to as 'the great escape'. 2009 saw the team qualify for Europe finishing seventh, their highest-ever finish. There is now a new confidence around The Cottage and the club might just be on the verge of something big.

Greatest moments on this ground
"Instinctively, one brings into vivid focus 19 March, 2006, when Fulham beat Chelsea for the first time in 27 years. However, although momentous and euphoric, it was, ultimately, a one-off event: a necessary exorcism. Thus, this occasion is prevailed over by a date loaded with significance for the long-term future of the club, both in terms of its geography and its identity. Regulations outlawing terracing sentenced the club to two years of enforced exile at QPR's Loftus Road ground. This period was bedevilled with the not unfounded fear that it would be a one-way trip, and Fulham Football Club without Craven Cottage is an unresolvable paradox. On 21 August, 2004, we returned." Stuart Mackie, White Lines.

Lowest moments on this ground
"In May 1994, having avoided the threatened merger with QPR but still in a perilous financial state, we travelled

⌃ HEROES OF THE TURF

Fulham and England Captain Johnny Haynes is without a shadow of a doubt, the club's greatest-ever player, spending 18 years at The Cottage and thrilling supporters throughout his stay. Also Sean Davis, Chris Coleman, Rufus Brevett, Arthur Stevens, Alan Mullery, Brian McBride, Luis Boa Morte, Gordon Davies, Jimmy Bullard and Louis Saha.

⌄ ZEROES OF THE TURF

"When we were in the lower leagues and dropping most of the team! I wasn't keen on Alan Cork as he was at the end of his career at Fulham and was poor. Steve Marlet was a pretty bad signing too, although he wasn't totally useless." Mike Blewitt, fan.

◀ Andrew Johnson.

THE JOHNNY
HAYNES STAND
IS A REAL
THROWBACK
WITH ITS
OLD-FASHIONED
ROOF AND MANY
SUPPORTING
PILLARS.

‹ Roy Hodgson takes a stroll
after Fulham's home match
against Stoke in May 2010.

to face Swansea in a must win final game. We found the occasion all too much and went out with little more than a whimper. Although it was no longer called the Fourth Division it was the first time we'd dropped into the league's basement level and was a very black day for Fulham supporters." David Harris, former editor, The Hammy End Chronicle.

Heroes of the sideline

"Under Jean Tigana, Fulham's training, preparation, and match-play were revolutionized. Possession was king, facilitated by endless movement." Stuart Mackie. "The announcement of Roy Hodgson's appointment received an underwhelming response and the first few games didn't offer us much to improve this. Slowly but surely he won us over. To take us on to our highest league finish and European final is more than even our most ardent supporters could have expected." David Harris.

The ground

Craven Cottage is one of the, if not the most, old-fashioned of the current Premiership grounds. It's not that the club haven't wanted to redevelop, it's more the cost of that redevelopment. Without any other suitable sites within the area, redeveloping the current ground has been estimated at anything from £50 to £100 million, so it is unlikely to ever be done in one hit. Possibly of most interest is the small pavilion in the corner, which looks a little out of place now but gives the stadium a sense of history. Although referred to as The Cottage, it is in fact a pavilion; the original 'cottage' was a hunting lodge dating back to the 1700s.

Of all the stands, the **Riverside** is the newest. As its name would suggest, it backs directly on to the Thames. It is a single-tiered stand with a row of executive boxes at the rear and dug outs in front.

The **Johnny Haynes Stand** is a real throwback with its old-fashioned roof and many supporting pillars. In fact, it was built just after the turn of the century (in 1905) and has worn pretty well. It gives the ground a bit of character, although tell that to someone stuck behind one of the pillars!

Away supporters are housed in one half of the **Putney Stand**, with a ticket allocation of about 3,000, this equates to just under half of the area. It is a little cramped as it is a converted terrace, and there are quite a few pillars. There is also a scoreboard on the roof.

The **Hammersmith Stand** is of similar proportions to its opposite number, but only has one pillar. It is for home fans only and offers decent views.

Getting there

By Road/Parking Craven Cottage is centrally located right by the river Thames, but apart from traffic it is actually easy to reach from all directions. If travelling from the north follow the M1 until the end, then take the A406 down to the A4 then follow signs for Hammersmith, once in Hammersmith turn right down the A219 and after about half a mile start looking for somewhere to park. If leaving from the west follow the M4 to the end and then the above directions from the A4. From the south take the A3 into the city and then A219, which crosses the river at Putney, parking can be found either side of the bridge. Parking around the ground is very limited; it's all street and is controlled by metres, which charge by the hour.

By Train By far the best way to get to the ground is by train. Putney Bridge is the closest station and is on the District Line, its about a 15- to 20-minute walk along the Thames to the ground.

Pubs for home fans
The Golden Lion is one of the closest pubs to the ground and gets packed with home fans; usually there is a check on the door to keep it home only. All of the other pubs close by, like The Cottage, are also restricted to home fans only.

Good food near ground
Most of the pubs mentioned serve bar food; on Fulham Road there are a number of cafés and restaurants. Closer to the ground there are a few fast-food vans.

Pubs for away fans
The best bet for a pint is either across the river in Putney, about a 20-minute walk from the ground, or near Putney Bridge Station, which is 10- to 15-minutes from the ground. The Eight Bells, Boathouse and Dukes Head all-come recommended.

Top tips
The local pubs do not allow away fans in, so drink a distance form the ground. If you can, travel into the area by public transport as the parking can be a nightmare.

THE LAST WORD

swsix.blogspot.com
fulhamish.blogspot.com

HOME COLOURS

GILLINGHAM

- ⚬ **Nicknames** The Gills
- ⚬ **Founded** 1893
- ⚬ **Ground** KRBS Priestfield Stadium (opened 1893)
- ⓘ **Address** Redfern Avenue, Gillingham, Kent ME7 4DD
- ⚬ **Capacity** 11,582
- ⚬ **Best attendance** 23,002 vs QPR, FA Cup 3rd round, 10 January, 1948
- ⚬ **Contact** 01634-300000
- ⚬ **Ticket Number** 01634-300000
- @ **Email** info@priestfield.com
- ⓦ **Website** gillinghamfootballclub.com

"Taylor, 2-0. Gillingham are surely there now!" With 87 minutes on the clock, the Gills end of a packed Wembley Stadium erupts. Blue flags wave, strangers hug, dancing ensues. "Party time in Kent". At the opposite end of the Stadium, Manchester City fans sit with heads in hands. City are on the ropes, teetering. Surely that's the knockout blow for the team from Manchester. Another season in the third tier beckons for them, while Gillingham can start planning for life in the second tier. But, like all the great boxing films, just when you think your man's down, beaten, he comes back from the brink. Amazingly, City score two, in the 90th and 95th minutes, then go on to win on penalties. It was a sucker punch for the gallant underdogs. For many clubs that would have been a hammer blow from which they'd never recover. "Ain't gonna be no rematch, ain't gonna be no rematch."

But The Gills are made of stronger stuff. Like a certain Mr Balboa, they went away, ate steak, worked out in a meat locker – metaphorically of course – and came back stronger the following year (2000). They had a new man in their corner, Tony Pulis having been replaced by Peter Taylor. With 43,000 fans to cheer them on, they squared up to Wigan and this time they were ready. Despite going behind, the Gills kept their heads. This time it was their turn for the fight back – they had more in the tank. The yellow shirts fought for every ball, chased every player down. Gillingham ran out 3-2 winners, earning a place in the second tier for the first time in their history. Oh how the success felt all the more sweet after the bitter disappointment of the year before.

Being the only League team in the county has its drawbacks. There isn't a great footballing tradition for one. There are also no natural local rivalries to spur on the fans, so they have adopted an adversary. Millwall fit the criteria as well as any other potential rival would. Hardly the most

popular team to start with, they seem to revel in the role of panto villain, they're a kind of dead-eyed Ivan Drago of the middle leagues. In 2009/10 The Gills looked like they could again be contenders with wins over the likes of Leeds, Southampton, Huddersfield and of course Ivan Drago. However, cruising home at the season's end, the Gills had their pockets well and truly picked, their League One status swiped from right under their noses. In a fight for survival you can't take anything for granted – time for some payback.

Greatest moments on this ground
"Hmm, there's been quite a few in recent years but I think I will go for the play-off semi-final win over Preston in 1999. We'd drawn the first leg of the game 1-1 at Deepdale, and brought them back down to Kent with us looking to get to Wembley for the first time in our history. Andy Hessenthaler scored after just two minutes and we held on gallantly for the remaining 88. It was also the last night that the Rainham End was a terrace and it was a pretty emotional place at the final whistle. Shame about what happened in the final…" Jon Phipps, Vital Gillingham.

Lowest moments on this ground
"Our relegations in recent years have both been away from home, but the place was pretty low after we drew our last home game with Swindon in 2008 after a late goal which virtually condemned us to the drop. April 1995 was pretty hard as well when we drew 0-0 with Hereford in our last home game and we all thought we'd never see the club play at Priestfield again because we were going bust. Fortunately we were saved by our current chairman Paul Scally and we've never looked back since then." Jon Phipps.

Heroes of the sideline
"Keith Peacock was in charge between 1981 and 1987 and is still viewed by most as the best manager the club has ever had. Almost got us into the second tier on a number of occasions and his sacking after a 6-0 defeat at Aldershot was the start of a decline that took almost eight years to recover from. Tony Pulis was appointed in the summer of 1995 by Paul Scally and transformed the club. We were promoted in the first season and gradually built our way up in Division Two under him, culminating in his final game being the Wembley defeat to Manchester City. Peter Taylor took Pulis' team on and changed its style and disciplinary record and, 12 months later, he led us to the promised land of the second tier for the first time." Jon Phipps.

RIVALS
Swindon, Millwall, Maidstone United.

Zeroes of the turf

"Rod Wallace and Tommy Johnson arrived together in the summer of 2002 and hopes were high. Unfortunately, both had their time at Priestfield decimated by injuries. When they were fit and firing, they were very good, but sadly for us that was far too infrequent." Jon Phipps.

Don't mention the…

"Wembley 1999. A proud day for every Gills fan spoiled by two injury-time goals and a lousy penalty shoot-out." Jon Phipps.

Villains

"Carl Asaba isn't on many people's Christmas card list after the way he left for Sheffield United. He was one of our greatest goal-scorers but didn't cover himself in glory with his departure. And, for that matter, neither did Marlon King." Jon Phipps.

The ground

The ground has undergone a programme of redevelopment since the new chairman took over in 1995. **Gordon Road Stand** runs the length of the field and is quite a shallow stand that seats 2,600 in a single tier. It was opened in 1999 but seems a little older in design with a row of central pillars. The **Rainham End** is a large single tier behind the goal, housing 2,400 fans. It is a modern design with no pillars and a high roof. The main **Medway Stand** is a two tier structure with a row of corporate boxes between the tiers. It runs the length of the pitch and houses the changing rooms and dug-outs. Underneath is the Blues Rock Café. The Town End Terrace was demolished in 2003/04 for the new **Brian Moore Stand**, but the site is currently occupied by a temporary uncovered stand that holds 3,400. This is the area currently allocated to away fans so be sure to wrap up warm and bring wet weather gear.

Getting there

By Road/Parking The ground is most easily accessed via junction 4 of the M2. Follow the A278/ Hoath Way signed for Gillingham through two roundabouts. At the next roundabout turn left onto the A2 and at following roundabout turn right onto Ito Way/ A289 passing a golf club on the left. Next roundabout, left onto Cornwallis Avenue, straight over into Canadian Avenue and right onto Toronto Rd. Then second left into Redfern Avenue and the stadium is on your left.

Street parking can be found on the roads further back from the ground (it's "permit parking only" on roads surrounding the stadium). There is a park and ride scheme from Twydall Junior School, Romany Road (£5). Parking from 1.15pm with shuttle operating until 2.45pm and post-match between 5 and 6 pm.

By Train Gillingham (Kent) Railway Station is just half a mile from the ground. On exiting the station walk straight up Balmoral Road (initially with the tracks on your left hand side), continuing straight over onto Priestfield Road. Stadium will be dead ahead.

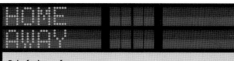

That's quite interesting
"We are the only Football League club in Kent. Maidstone United joined us briefly in the late 1980s and early 1990s, but went bust." Jon Phipps.

Not a lot of people know that
"We hold the record for the fewest goals conceded in a 46-game season, letting in just 20 in the 1995/96 promotion season, with keeper Jim Stannard keeping 29 clean sheets." Jon Phipps.

Pubs for home fans
"The home fans' pub is the excellent Cricketers on Sturdee Avenue. Cheap beer and pre-match footie is normally on the screens," recommends Vital Gillingham's Jon Phipps. In town The Will Adams, Saxton Street, is a small spot serving well kept ales. It's one of the better choices in Gillingham for those who know their beers.

Good food near ground
Handily opposite the Livingstone Arms, on Gillingham Road, is the Gillingham Fish Bar.

Pubs for away fans
Away fans should head towards the Livingstone Arms, says Jon. "Right by the stadium, it's a football pub with food available as well as a beer garden, which tends to fill up on match days."

Top tips
There is a "permit holders only" parking scheme on a number of roads around the stadium. Be aware that on match days, traffic wardens are quick, keen and in their element!

gillingham.vitalfootball.co.uk
gillingham.clubfans.co.uk

> Andy Hessenthaler during the successful 2000 Division Two play-off final against Wigan at Wembley.

HEROES OR ZEROES?

⌃ **HEROES OF THE TURF**
"Andy Hessenthaler was captain and then player-manager, a true club legend, who got us to mid-table in the second tier, as well as being a star player. Robert Taylor. A £500,000 signing from Brentford in 1998, Taylor made a slow start to his Gills career, but when he got going, he was amazing. His hat trick in front of the Rainham End against Bristol City in November 2000 was truly stunning. Brian Yeo was a legendary striker in the seventies and still the club's all-time top-scorer with 149 goals in all competitions. He also scored 31 goals in the 1974 title-winning side. Steve Bruce moved down from the northeast to start his career at Priestfield and is still fondly remembered. Tony Cascarino famously signed for a set of tracksuits. Casc was a regular scorer for the club in the mid to late eighties and his efforts almost fired us to promotion in the first-ever play-offs." Jon Phipps.

- ⊘ **Nicknames** The Mariners
- ⊙ **Founded** 1878
- ⊙ **Ground** Blundell Park (opened 1898)
- ⊙ **Address** Cleethorpes, North East Lincs DN35 7PY
- ⊘ **Capacity** 9,953
- ⊙ **Best attendance** 31,651 vs Wolverhampton Wanderers, FA Cup 5th round, 20 February, 1937
- ⊙ **Contact** 01472-605050
- ⊙ **Ticket Number** 01472-605050
- ⊚ **Email** mailbox@gtfc.co.uk
- ⊚ **Website** grimsby-townfc.co.uk

GRIMSBY TOWN

RIVALS

Hull City,
Scunthorpe
United, Sheffield
Wednesday and
Lincoln City.

Every coach and manager wrestles with the best way to motivate players, after all, each player responds in a different way. Subtle psychology needs to be employed. There's the patented 'hairdryer©' for wayward, creative midfield players, or the Glenn Hoddle spiritualist approach where defensive hard men are helped to channel their emotions with coloured crystals. But what to do if you've scooped the rest of the League and signed a former Juventus winger, who then happens to have an off night? If all else fails, why not try throwing a plate of chicken wings at him? These were the tactics employed by Brian Laws on his star player Ivano Bonetti in February 1996. And, while Fergie's boot at Beckham resulted in a mere gash, the bone china and poultry projectile that the Italian fell fowl of, left him hospitalised with a broken cheekbone. Did this motivational technique have the desired effect? Amazingly, no. The player left at the end of the season and Laws was gone not long after. Bonetti is still a firm favourite with the fans at Blundell Park. Not only was he one of the first Italians to make the jump to English football, his stylish play came part financed by the fans, with the player making up the rest of the fee himself.

Grimsby have seen some highs and lows over recent years. As Pat Bell of Cod Almighty points out, "Bill Shankly, Grimsby manager between 1951 and 1954, later described in his autobiography the side he assembled as 'pound for pound and class for class the best football team I have seen in England since the war.'" The club has since enjoyed long stints in the second flight, but over the last few years has struggled in the bottom tier, before being relegated to non-league football at the end of 2009/10. The Blundell Park faithful are looking for a manager who can come in and lift the team, by whatever

methods, back to the Championship where many feel they belong. One question though – just what was a plate of chicken wings doing in the changing rooms?

Greatest moments on this ground

"Grimsby's best moments of recent history have tended to occur elsewhere (only the desperate or impressionable could count beating Tottenham in the early rounds of the League Cup), so 3 May 1980, when Kevin Drinkell, one of several local, young players in the side, scored a hat trick in a 4-0 defeat of Sheffield United. This secured the Third Division title, a second consecutive promotion and a return to the second flight after an absence of 16 years." Pat Bell, Cod Almighty.

Lowest moments on this ground

"Losing 2-3 to Morecambe in the last minute after being 2-0 up, and 1-0 to Brentford, both in 2008/09 when relegation to the Football Conference looked odds-on." Chris Smith, Grimsby Town Supporters TRUST. The 2009/10 season when some terrible home performances saw the Mariners relegated to the Conference.

Heroes of the turf

"Matt Tees – his return to the club in 1970 put more than 3,000 on the gate. Enduringly popular with hard men of a certain age, his 27 goals the next season helped win the Fourth Division. Joe Waters – after supporters raised the money to make his loan deal permanent in 1976, for the

HOME
AWAY

Pubs for home fans
Next to Blundell Park The Imperial is the home pub. Rutland Arms, Rutland Street is half mile from the ground with some decent real ales and a happy mix of the home and away contingent.

Good food near ground
"Lots of good chippies near the ground. Barneys Café is a favourite and a two minute walk away," says Chris "Proper scran!"

Pubs for away fans
"The Blundell Park Hotel opposite the ground is good for beer and lets in away fans", recommends Chris Smith. Leaking Boot, Grimsby Road, south of the ground, is another popular spot with parking and food. Also handy is No 1 Refreshment Rooms, Cleethorpes station.

Top tips
"Don't mention fish, not because we are embarrassed by them – it's just our fish chants will be better than yours". Pat Bell.

∧ Michael Reddy tries to clear Paul Robinson with a subtle chip.

HEROES OR ZEROES?

⌃ **HEROES OF THE SIDELINE**

"Alan Buckley had three spells at Grimsby, with three promotions, no relegations and three Wembley appearances. He preached, and often achieved, a purity of football we had no right to see on the meagre transfer fees we can afford. He is naturally detested by the very vocal minority who infest the message boards and chatrooms. The charge against him is 'lack of PR skills'. This was Lawrie McMenemy's strong suit. His Fourth Division Championship win in 1972 halted a decade of seemingly irrevocable decline, but he is as much remembered for insisting the players make early morning visits to workers at the fish docks." Pat Bell.

next decade Waters was the bustling heart of the club's most successful post-war period. Paul Futcher – already a veteran when we rescued him from Halifax reserves, he never broke sweat in anchoring Town's defence to a promotion and several seasons in the second flight. John McDermott – 753 games, all for one club, over three decades, the best full-back never to play in the top flight. He ascribed his loyalty to the cheap house prices around Grimsby. Ivano Bonetti – the European Cup finalist's love affair with Grimsby briefly took us to second place in the second flight." Pat Bell.

Zeroes of the turf

"Anthony Williams, the worst goalkeeper we've had. He was over reliant on squirting water in the faces of attackers through the flower in his buttonhole. Darren Mansaram, always tried to give him the benefit of the doubt but he had the poise and balance of Bambi on alcopops. Mike Lyons fancied himself as a striker – and as a manager. I can't believe my computer didn't blow a fuse typing this. Useless." Chris Smith.

Villains

A couple of years ago, amid regular calls for Alan Buckley to sign a "20 goal a season striker", he secured Martin Butler. Unfortunately, Butler lived in the Midlands, and had no intention of moving. He had regular spells out injured (allegedly) with a bad back from driving, but he carried on taking our money even when Hereford, right on his doorstep, wanted to sign him. Ashley Sestanovich

is currently serving time for his part in an armed robbery. That happened after he'd gone, but somehow we were not at all surprised." Pat Bell.

Don't mention the…

"Fact that we ended second bottom last year (2008/2009) and would have been relegated to the Conference had not Luton been docked 30 points." Rob Sedgwick, The Fishy.

The ground

In an era of new builds, Blundell Park is proper old school, although permission has been given for a new stadium in Great Coates. The two-tier **Findus Stand** is an all-seater and sits on the half-way line, only the top tier is covered. Away fans are housed in the 2,000 seats of the **Osmond Stand**. The Osmond joins the **Main Stand** to create an L-shaped enclosure, this stand dating back to 1901 and housing changing rooms and dug-outs. At the far end behind the goal is the Pontoon Stand, where many of the more vocal fans sit.

Getting there

By Road/Parking Follow the M180 to its exit 5 conclusion and onto the A180 (signed Grimsby). Go straight on through the three roundabouts and Grimsby. Turn left onto Neville Street, and the ground is on the left. Road Parking available.

By Train Cleethorpes station is about one mile from the ground. Facing the sea turn left along the beachside promenade and use the footbridge to cross over the line to the stadium. Alternatively, go out of Station Road, left onto Poplar Road and right onto Grimsby Road. Go right into Neville Road and the ground is on the left.

PUB QUIZ

That's quite interesting
"The record crowd at Old Trafford is 76,962 and it featured… well, not Manchester United. Town versus Wolves in an FA Cup semi-final in 1939. So there!" Chris Smith

Not a lot of people know that
"On 10 August 1971, Grimsby played the Japanese national side, beating them 7-2." Pat Bell.

THE LAST WORD

codalmighty.com
gtst.net/site
thefishy.co.uk

- **Nicknames** Pools
- **Founded** 1908
- **Ground** Victoria Park (opened 1886)
- **Address** Clarence Road, Hartlepool TS24 8BZ
- **Capacity** 7,691
- **Best attendance** 17,264 vs Manchester United, FA Cup 3rd Round, 5 January, 1957
- **Contact** 01429-272584
- **Ticket Number** 01429-272584, ext 2
- **Email** enquiries@hartlepoolunited.co.uk
- **Website** hartlepoolunited.co.uk

HARTLEPOOL UNITED

RIVALS

Darlington.

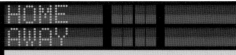

Pubs for home fans
Adam, from VitalHartlepool.co.uk, recommends Jackson's Wharf on the Marina for real ale and a good mix of home and away fans: "Just a short walk from the ground, it serves some good pub grub too." Victoria Suite Club Bar is for home support only. Millhouse Inn is the closest pub to the ground, so it's busy, with sports TV and decent enough beers.

Good food near ground
Jackson's Wharf. The Marina also has a number or fast-food joints and cafés. Asda, opposite the pub, is best for emergency supplies.

Pubs for away fans
Jackson's Wharf. Corner Flag Supporter's Club Bar is open to away fans for a tiny entry fee. The Causeway, Vicarage Gardens, has real ales and is a 15-minute walk south of the stadium, off the A689.

Top tips
Additional parking can be found at Jacksons Wharf and around the Marina. Do not park at Asda.

The Member of Parliament for Hartlepool was certainly busy through the seventies and eighties. Politics was a boiling cauldron of activity. There were strikes, campaigns and hard-fought ideological arguments along clearly defined philosophical boundaries. Mind you, the local MP had it easy, only up for re-election every four or five years; for Pools it was virtually an annual tradition. In the days before automatic relegation to the Conference, the bottom clubs in the bottom division had to reapply for election back into the Football League for the following season. Luckily for Hartlepool, they managed to keep their deposit. This electoral success also rubbed off on club mascot H'Angus the Monkey, aka Stuart Drummond. In 2002 H'Angus ran for mayor on a platform of 'free bananas for all school kids' and swept to victory. Not only that, he has just been re-elected for a record third term. If only Pools could be as successful on the field as they are at the ballot box. The Germans, however, were obviously worried about the possibility that one day the mighty Hartlepool would go on to European footballing domination, as they have taken every opportunity to bomb the ground; during the First World War the main stand was actually destroyed by a Zeppelin.

Although Hartlepool have spent most of their time battling in the bottom tier, there have been spells when Victoria Park has seen victorious seasons. In 2005 Pools were eight minutes away from the second tier. At 2-1 up against Sheffield Wednesday in the play-off final in Cardiff, the ref awarded the team from South Yorkshire one of those comedy penalties and Hartlepool were down to 10 men. Extra-time and the extra man made all the difference. Wednesday went up. Pools never recovered and were relegated the following season. Sometimes football is a cruel game. If only that Zeppelin hadn't bombed that stand, maybe a different United would have been champions of Europe by now…

Greatest moments on this ground
"In recent years the greatest moment was when Adam Boyd scored against Sheffield Wednesday in our amazing run to the play-off final. It was a Friday night, the ground was packed and in the pouring rain he scored an incredible hat trick. The third goal saw him waltz past the visiting defence like they weren't there before chipping in over the keeper." Adam, editor, VitalHartlepool.co.uk.

Lowest moments on this ground
"Relegation on the last day of the 2005/06 season was tough to take. It was the same squad that had reached the play-off final the season before, but poor signings and mismanagement saw us go from world-beaters to strangers overnight. Going back further, the years of seeking re-election to the Football League every other season from the start of the sixties to mid-eighties was not a high point in our history, to this day." Adam.

Heroes of the sideline
"Cyril Knowles – he took us from relegation certainties to promotion within a season. Sadly, ill health meant he had to retire before the end of the promotion season.

That's quite interesting
H'Angus the Monkey is inspired by the French monkey hung in Hartlepool during the Napoleonic War for spying.

Not a lot of people know that
"In the media the club are often incorrectly referred to as 'The Pool' when the nickname most often used by fans is 'Pools'. This is because the club was actually called Hartlepools United until the late sixties due to being shared between the separate towns of West Hartlepool and Old Hartlepool. They were merged into one town in 1967." Adam.

DON'T MENTION THE...

"Number of unenviable records we hold. Among other things, Pools applied for re-election more times than any other club, and also have the record for the highest number of consecutive games without scoring." John Cooper.

Neale Cooper – rather like Brian Clough (another former Pools manager), he brought out the very best in so many players." John Cooper, *Monkey Business* fanzine.

Heroes of the turf
"Kenny Johnson – a Pools player for many years and one of our highest-scoring players of all time. Bob Newton – he was one of the few shining lights in a very poor era for Pools. Brian Honour – another long-serving player who gave his all every time he got on the pitch. Joel Porter – possibly one of the most skillful players ever to wear the blue and white, and he did so at the highest level at which Pools have played. Ritchie Humphreys – an outstanding servant to the club, he made over 160 consecutive appearances and was recently named 'Player of the Century'." John Cooper.

Zeroes of the turf
"Chris Llewellyn, Michael Proctor, Darren Williams and Lee Bullock. The quartet were brought in to supposedly strengthen the side that reached the play-offs, but all were hugely disappointing and were all part of the side that were relegated." Adam.

Villains
"Chairman Garry Gibson took the club up to the Third Division but nearly took us into oblivion. He verbally attacked the fans, had the bailiffs waiting outside the ground and ended up in the High Court before being forced to sell most of the first team. The worst moment was when we played Tottenham in a memorial game for the late Cyril Knowles. The proceeds of the game were to be given to Knowles' widow, but Gibson's cheque bounced." Adam.

The ground
Victoria Park is a compact and modern ground that can generate a great atmosphere. The **Cyril Knowles Stand** is a single tier of seating with a directors' box and executive boxes, as well as the family enclosure; it has a total capacity of 1,599. Behind the goal is the **Town End**, a standing terrace for 1,775 core home supporters. The largest stand is the two-tier **Camerons Brewery Millhouse Stand**, with its seated upper tier (1,617) and lower terrace (1,832). The away support are seated in the **Rink End** behind the goal, named after a long-demolished dancehall where many Hartlepool couples first met. It holds just under 1,000 fans.

Getting there
By road/Parking The stadium is north of the city centre and just back from the North Sea (so wrap up warm). From the north, exit the A19 at the junction with the A179 and follow through five roundabouts, then go right at the next roundabout onto Marina Way. Turn right onto Middleton Road, the left onto Clarence Road and the ground will be on the right. From the south, exit the A19 at the junction with the A689 and follow through six roundabouts. Turn left onto Clarence Road and the ground is on the left. There's parking behind Mill House Stand, and street parking too.

By train Hartlepool station is just half a mile from the ground. Turn right along the main road, Church Street. Then cross over the junction with the A689 and onto Clarence Road.

THE LAST WORD

monkeybizz.net
hartlepool.vitalfootball.co.uk
pooliebunker.co.uk

HEREFORD UNITED

- **Nicknames** The Bulls
- **Founded** 1924
- **Ground** Edgar Street (opened pre-1924)
- **Address** Edgar Street, Hereford, HR4 9JU
- **Capacity** 5,300
- **Best attendance** 18,114 vs Sheffield Wednesday, FA Cup 3rd round, 4 January, 1958
- **Contact** 08442-761939
- **Ticket Number** 08442-761939
- **Email** club@herefordunited.co.uk
- **Website** herefordunited.co.uk

Twirling, lost in time, arms out, snorkel parka catching the wind, orange lining flashing with each turn. The young lad is spinning around the field in wonderment. Around him, hundreds of people are running randomly, feet slipping on the cloying, heavy earth, colliding, angling around, the perfect embodiment of chaos theory. It's a dull February afternoon in 1972. The crowd is condensing around one point, pulled in like moist air drawn to the epicentre of a swirling hurricane. Somewhere in the melee, hidden from sight, Ronnie Radford is the eye of the storm. Just 30 seconds before, Radford was running through a ploughed field, 30 yards from goal. The ball coming back from a one-two, he pulled the trigger first time, a cannon, a white blur that screamed past the diving Newcastle keeper into the top left-hand corner, and the striker was off and running, arms aloft. The Newcastle players, all in red, look on stunned as the white number 11 is buried beneath a human wave that's broken onto the field of play. It is a tsunami of flared jeans and black and white bobble hats; a surge of sideburns and huge collars, someone is even carrying a giant teddy bear. It'll take the handful of Bobbies a few minutes to clear the pitch now. But if you are going to slay a titan in the FA Cup, there has to be a degree of celebratory madness and a touch of quantum physics thrown in.

Hereford are not just a one hit wonder, famous only for a non-league giant-killing back in the mists of time. Although they have never graced the top flight, they certainly provide their fans with plenty of excitement and adventure. In 1995, former Aston Villa and Wolves boss Graham Turner took over the managerial reigns at Edgar Street, and just three years later picked up the bit and bridle also, buying not only a majority shareholding in the club but also

becoming Chairman to boot. The club was Conference bound, but under Turner's direction they built slowly and surely until eight years later they were back in the Football League via the play-offs. In 2008 The Bulls climbed into the third tier for the first time since the seventies, and although their stay was short, it has given them a taste for the higher league that they are keen to repeat.

Greatest moments on this ground

"For many it would be Ronnie Radford's pile-driver against Newcastle United. However, seeing Hereford United clinching the Third Division title in April 1976 was fantastic. Watching The Bulls go from non-league to the second tier of English football in four years was amazing!" Keith Hall, editor, Vital Hereford.

Lowest moments on this ground

"Has to be the relegation from the League in 1997, at home to Brighton. We'd not been bottom until the final week, going down on goals scored after a 1-1 draw. It was to be the start of several years of pain at Edgar Street as our financial problems were rapidly unmasked." Martin Watson, editor, Bulls News.

Heroes of the sideline

"Colin Addison achieved back-to-back promotions and was player-manager of the 'giant-killers' side in the 1972 FA Cup. Remains a fans favourite. John Sillett produced a side of flair, creativity and goals as The Bulls romped to the Division Three title in 1976. He was often outspoken but was a true motivator. Graham Turner took on the majority shareholding of the club when it was at death's door in the summer of 1998. Has slowly but surely turned the club's fortunes around, finally restoring League status in 2006. He somehow assembled a squad good enough to clinch automatic promotion to League One in 2008. The dream lasted just 12 months. and now has the task of upgrading the antiquated Edgar Street stadium into a modern facility." Keith Hall.

Heroes of the turf

"Dixie McNeil bagged 85 goals in 129 games. An astonishing marksman with a venomous left foot. Astonishingly, John Charles, the world famous 'gentle giant', became a Hereford player in June 1967. He later took on the player-manager reins, helping to build arguably the best non-league team ever seen. Ronnie Radford was the scorer of the BBC's 1971/72 Goal of the Season." Keith Hall.

RIVALS

Shrewsbury Town, Cheltenham Town, Kidderminster Harriers, Yeovil Town

"Homegrown flying full-back Chris Price will always get a nod in a Bulls top five. Stewart Phillips is the club's record league goal-scorer, and his dad built the stand!" Martin Watson.

Villains

"Aaron MacLean and referee K.A. Woolmer are linked to one incident in a play-off semi against Aldershot. One fell over and the other sent off our defender. Woolmer got a shower of red cards when he made a return to Edgar Street. MacLean had a burger thrown at him when he did a 'bull' celebration." Martin Watson.

The ground

Edgar Street is a rather old school ground, the kind that is quickly disappearing from the Football League. It has already had its capacity reduced and looks somewhat uninspiring from the outside. It has two very distinctive stands. The first is the curved **Merton Meadow End** terrace, a crescent of terracing behind one of the goals that is covered from the middle back. This is the home of the most vocal fans, the Meadowenders. Running along the pitch is the two storey **Cargill Stand**, a pitch side terrace with a tier of covered seating directly above. This tier is supported by large concrete columns which can obstruct views below. Behind the other goal is the **Blackfriars End**, another bank of covered terracing with a low roof supported by a row of pillars. The main stand is the **Merton Stand**, a raised single tier of covered seating with a high roof and no obstructing pillars. Underneath are the dug outs, as well as an expanse of windows from the bar and executive area running along the touchline. Away fans are currently housed in the Carghill Stand towards the Blackfriars End. Visiting fans also have a section of the Blackfriars Terrace too.

Getting there

By Road/Parking From the north, exit the M5 at junction 8 onto the M50 and follow to junction 2, exiting onto A417 Gloucester Road, signed Hereford. Turn left at the roundabout to stay on A417/Ledbury Road, follow through three roundabouts. Turn left at the next roundabout, onto the A438 and follow into Hereford. At the large roundabout by the Auctioneers market, turn right into Edgar Street. Then right into Blackfriars Street and left for large car park (£1) dead ahead.

From the south, exit the M4 at junction 15 onto the A419. Continue onto the A417 signed to Gloucester,

passing under M5. At the next roundabout turn right onto the A40 and follow to Ross-on-Wye. Cross the river, turn right at the roundabout onto the A49 and follow right into Hereford. Right turn into Blackfriars Street.

By Train Hereford Station is a 10-minute walk from the ground. Head left past Rockfield DIY and right onto Commercial Road, passing KFC and Wetherspoons. Right down Monkmoor Street, left onto Coningsby Street, turning left at the end, and right onto Blackfriars.

Pubs for home fans

"The club bar, Radfords, has just been refurbished and is now excellent and well priced. A lot of the singers can be found in the Exchange across from the Herdsman before the game." Martin Watson.

Good food near ground

"Pub food from the Wetherspoons or Litten Tree between ground and railway station, Commercial Road, with a KFC and McDonald's 150 yards either side of these. For anyone more adventurous there's a Chinese buffet restaurant on the same road, or a couple of chippies for the more basic." Martin Watson.

Pubs for away fans

"The away lot are usually forced into the Herdsmen around the corner from the ground. It's a pub, no frills, and not a particularly great one," says Martin Watson. The Barrels, Owen Street is a cracking spot run by the Wye Valley Brewery and consequently has a good selection of well kept (and priced) beers. Sports TV. The Victory also Owen Street is another real ale spot run by an independent local brewery.

Top tips

There is a large car park right next to the ground, which makes life easy.

PUB QUIZ

That's quite interesting

"The six goalkeepers used by the Bulls in the 2008/09 season equalled a club record set in 1982/83. Better still, the keepers were from five different countries; England, Ireland, Scotland, Cape Verde, and Hungary." Martin Watson.

Not a lot of people know that

"One of our FA Cup traditions, parading a Hereford bull around the pitch, was stopped by the foot and mouth crisis and subsequent regulations." Martin Watson.

HOME COLOURS

HUDDERSFIELD TOWN

RIVALS

Leeds United,
Bradford City,
Sheffield
United, Sheffield
Wednesday and
Barnsley.

Sibling rivalries can be intense. All brothers and sisters bicker. Usually the closer they are, the deeper and more direct the antagonism can be. But add another element to the mix where egos play an almighty part – music say – and it certainly spices things up. Ray and Dave Davies of the Kinks, forerunners of the Gallaghers brand of brotherly love, actually came to blows live on stage, during a concert. Add a sporting arena where the aim is merciless victory, and expect fireworks. How the Williams sisters maintain a working relationship, let alone share a house and train together is anyone's guess. Outside the boundaries of England's largest county, the white rose is a unifying symbol for all Yorkshire folk. But within the borders, towns are pushed apart by the matching poles generated by powerful footballing magnets.

Huddersfield Town has many local adversaries and it is a source of frustration that within the last ten years, the club's main Yorkshire rivals have all risen to enjoy spells in the top tier. Sheffield Wednesday, Bradford City and Barnsley all tasted Premier League football at the end of the nineties, both Leeds and Sheffield United have seen football in the top division within this decade, and Hull City have been revelling in life in the penthouse more recently still. It would be the equivalent of being Jamie Murray and having Andy and five other championship tennis playing brothers around the table for dinner. It still rankles the Huddersfield faithful that their team got so close, yet faltered on the brink of the play-offs in 2000. The club then slipped from a top Championship team into one now occupying the third tier of the Football League. But in Lee Clark, the fans hope that the side will finally have a manager to emulate Herbert Chapman and Bill Shankly, one with the ability to guide a promising

squad back up the footballing pyramid – and if a few old rivals are vanquished along the way, so much the better.

Greatest moments on this ground
"Beating Lincoln in the play-off semi-final second leg in 2004 to reach the final. From 2-0 down we pulled a goal back thanks to a Danny Schofield penalty and then Rob Edwards smashed in a late equalizer to put us through 4-3 on aggregate. The scene at the stadium that night was amazing, one that will last in the memory. You could see what it meant to the Town by Rob Edward's celebration, he loved our club." Sean Makin, Chief writer, Terrier-bytes.com.

Lowest moments on this ground
"Either getting relegated by a point from Division One (now the Championship) on the last day of the season in 2001 or slipping into administration in 2002/03; they were dark days." Sean Makin.

Heroes of the turf
"Andy Booth – Huddersfield born-and-bred, a true legend in the blue and white who bagged 150 goals in his career at Town. Marcus Stewart was one of the best strikers ever to play for the club, scoring 58 goals and oozing class. Darren Bullock, a tough-tackling midfielder who

back and scored a few but was let go due to our financial problems at the time. As soon as he left he slagged the club off that stood by him when he was out injured, his career soon dwindled." Sean Makin.

Don't mention the...
"Young Guns calendar. In 2006, the club (in hindsight) mistakenly chose to base a marketing campaign around a cowboy theme, which resulted in a lot of *Brokeback Mountain* references!" Jamie White.

The ground
The Galpharm, formerly McAlpine Stadium, is a modern ground of four separate stands with interlocking, arched roofs. The arena is shared between the football and rugby league teams – each have their own separate dressing rooms. The **Main Direct Golf Stand** is a two-tiered structure with a row of hospitality boxes and a capacity of 8,279 seats for home fans. Opposite sits the slightly smaller 7,333 capacity **Kilner Bank** or Antich Stand, a single tier cut into the hillside. The **Pink Link South Stand** is where up to 4,054 away supporters sit, behind the goal, while at the far end the two-tier, 4,888 seater **Fantastic Media Stand** was designed to incorporate a built-in retractable stage for arena concerts, plus leisure facilities.

Getting there
By Road/Parking The stadium is north east of the town centre, just off the A62 Leeds Road. Exit the M62 junction 24 and follow the A629 (Hudersfield/Halifax). Take the ramp onto the A62/Castlegate Slip and follow. Turn left onto St Andrew's Road, right onto Stadium Way, and the ground is on the right. From the M1 exit junction 38 onto the A637 (Huddersfield) and pass over two roundabouts. Turn left at the roundabout onto the A642/Wakefield Road and onto A629/Penistone Road. Turn right onto Firth Street and right again onto Stadium Way. Parking at the ground is £5. Unofficial car parks also spring up.

By Train The ground is 20 minutes from the station. Go left out of the station over the crossroad and onto Northumberland Street. Cross the ring road onto Leeds Road and right onto Gasworks Street (becoming Stadium Way). The ground is on the right.

always put his foot in where it hurt. He never shied out of a challenge and showed the kind of desire that Town fans love to see. Peter Jackson, a true Town hero both as a player and a manager. 155 appearances at centre-back, then two successful stints as manager. He'll always have a place in every Town fan's heart. Frank Worthington, he scored 41 goals in 171 games at Town, the first club of his career." Jamie White , Down at the Mac.

Zeroes of the turf
"George Donis, a Greek international who had played at the top level in the English game. He came on big wages but never lived up to his big earnings, with poor performances. After one season he escaped to the Greek army to serve his national service." Sean Makin.

"David Unsworth, he signed from Burnley in the 2008/09 season. He was supposed to bring a wealth of Premiership experience to our backline, instead he looked overweight, slow and no better than Conference standard. Ken Monkou, he played a handful of games and looked a class above the rest, but then lost interest and sat on the sidelines picking up his wage packet. Ben Thornley, he spent time on loan from Manchester United and looked exceptional. After we signed him, he never found that form again." Jamie White.

Villains
"Clyde Wijnhard: Dutch striker formed an excellent partnership with Marcus Stewart but after Stewart left his goals dried up and a car crash early in the 2000/01 season resulted in him being out for more than a year. He came

HEROES OR ZEROES?

≪ HEROES OF THE SIDELINE
"Peter Jackson, who saved us from relegation in the Great Escape season of 1997/98. He won promotion in his first season back, in 2004, then got us to the League One play-offs in 2006. Herbert Chapman, who guided us to two of our three successive First Division titles in 1924 and 1925 before leaving us to do the same with Arsenal. Mick Buxton, he rejuvenated a club on a downwards spiral, taking us to two promotions (1980 and 1983) before being sacked in 1985." Jamie White, Down at the Mac.

PUB QUIZ

That's quite interesting
"Huddersfield Town were the first-ever club to win the First Division three times in a row." Sean Makin.

Not a lot of people know that
"In 1999, Town signed Thai striker Kiatisuk 'Zico' Senamuang, his country's most capped player. Somewhat of a publicity stunt by the club, 'Zico' played a couple of reserve games before returning to Thailand, where he has scored 251 career goals in 339 appearances!" Jamie White.

THE LAST **WORD**

datm.info
terrier-bytes.com
htfc-world.com

HULL CITY

- 🌐 **Nicknames** The Tigers
- 📅 **Founded** 1904
- 🏟 **Ground** Kingston Communications Stadium (opened 2002)
- ℹ️ **Address** Walton Street, Hull, East Yorkshire HU3 6HU
- 👥 **Capacity** 25,400
- ➕ **Best attendance** 25,030 vs Liverpool, Premier League, 10 May, 2010
- ☎ **Contact** 01482-504600
- 🎫 **Ticket Number** 01482-505600
- @ **Email** info@hulltigers.com
- 🌐 **Website** hullcityafc.net

Since the dawn of this new millennium, the life and times of Hull City AFC seem to have been inversely linked to those of bitter rivals Leeds United. At the end of the nineties the West Yorkshire club were enjoying Champions League football, while their East Yorkshire cousins were propping up the Football League. Well, virtually. Then the great Gods of the round ball suddenly decided to mix things up a bit. The noughties were a bad time for Leeds and saw the West Yorkshire team tumble from the Premier League and crash into the second tier. Meanwhile, in Hull City a quiet revolution was underway. Under the stewardship of Peter Taylor, the team began to stealth their way up the tables. From a former fate floundering in the lower regions of the bottom tier, the team from Humberside were enjoying the plush new surroundings of the KC Stadium, and Taylor's guidance led the team to successive promotions. Hulls rise to the second tier for the 2005/06 season saw the Yorkshire rivals locked together in a duel near the foot of the Championship. Only one team would survive unscathed. Now under the tutelage of Phil Brown, Hull were scrapping to reverse a bad start. Although Leeds had edged a chilly evening clash at the KC in the January, come the end of the campaign it was The Tigers that stayed up.

The following season Hull were transformed – Dean Windass scored an iconic goal at Wembley to secure a remarkable ascent to top-flight football for the first time in the club's history. Few will forget Hull's first season in the Premier League. The team in gold blazed a trail into the top three, overthrowing Arsenal 2-1 away, drawing 2-2 at Anfield and being edged out by just one goal at Old Trafford in a seven goal thriller. It was the stuff of Hollywood. Hull survived in the top flight, Leeds meanwhile were edged out in the play-offs in their bid to escape the third. But in 2010 the Tigers discovered that

the Gods are a fickle bunch: with one hand they giveth Leeds promotion and with the other, they taketh away Hull's Premiership billing. There'll be a lot of Hull City fans praying this shift in the scales of fortune is short lived.

Greatest moments on this ground
"The move to the KC stadium transformed Tiger fortunes, we've been promoted three times since the switch from Boothferry Park. The on-pitch euphoria after the Championship play-off semi-final win against Watford, a game that secured a first-ever trip to Wembley, is paramount among many good KC moments." Les Motherby, Ambernectar.org.

Lowest moments on this ground
"Ah, the agony of choice. All relegations are awful – we were especially bad in 1978 and 1991 – but in 1996 we were demoted by some distance to the bottom division, and on the last day the corpse-like team lost to play-off chasing Bradford City, whose fans were given all the designated home ends of Boothferry Park by our witless chairman. The flames were inevitably fanned and much scrapping and public humiliation followed, and to make it worse Bradford duly scraped into the play-offs with this win, then had the nerve to win them." Editor, Boyhood Dreams.

Heroes of the sideline
"Peter Taylor – back-to-back promotions and Championship consolidation set up our eventual rise to the Premier League. His prickly demeanor made him hard to truly love, but he has our eternal gratitude and respect. Phil Brown – the media try to portray him as an attention hungry, over-tanned buffoon, but the man saved us from relegation in his first season took us up to the Premier League in his second, and kept us there in his third. Warren Joyce – he took over as boss when City were 92nd of 92 clubs and on course for the Conference and financial ruin. The mild-mannered Joyce brought in iconic players such as Justin

VILLAINS
"Most of our villains are former board members... including the malevolent asset strippers known locally as the 'Sheffield Stealers'" Les Motherby.

RIVALS
Scunthorpe United, Leeds United, Sheffield United and Grimsby Town.

Whittle and Gary Brabin and engineered a miraculous turnaround to keep us in the League." Les Motherby.

Heroes of the turf
"Chris Chilton and Ken Wagstaff, the top two goal-scorers, their statistics haven't come even close to being beaten. Tony Norman, for consistency and bravery across eight seasons in goal. Dean Windass, the local boy made (eventually) good. He was kicked out as an apprentice, but came back via local non-league. He was quite brilliant during the 1990s period when the club was going downwards. He left, reluctantly, when the club could no longer afford to turn down bids. He returned a decade later to score the goal that prevented Championship relegation and then volley in a Wembley strike to take us to the top flight. One of us, and he lived our dreams. Michael Turner – brave, disciplined, outstanding at reading the game and Ian Ashbee, as natural a leader as football has ever seen." Editor, Boyhood Dreams.

Zeroes of the turf
"Jon 'The Beast' Parkin, a cult hero for uncompromising physical play and scoring a winning goal against the reviled Leeds. It turned sour when he came back from the summer unfathomably out of shape. He seemed to no longer care and his porcine carcass was shipped off to Stoke. Stuart Green, a white-booted fop who flattered to deceive, sulked

when dropped for a game and went AWOL. Dave Bamber, an expensive (well, at the time) flop who rarely hit the target in front of goal, but was accurate when he allegedly spat at a fan who voiced disapproval of the lanky striker's efforts." Les Motherby.

The ground
The KC Stadium has a compact and modern feel to it. It is owned by the local council and houses Hull City as well as the rugby league team Hull FC. The **West Stand** has a convex roof line and runs the length of the pitch. Its two-tier structure has room for 6,000 in the lower and 5,000 in the upper sections. It also houses changing rooms with a row of corporate boxes. Behind the goal is the single-tier **North Stand** with room for up to 4,000 away fans and a large LED screen. The 6,000 seater **East Stand** is a single tier winding round to the **South Stand**, which accommodates 4,000 core home fans. The stadium complex also has a skate park.

Getting there
By Road/Parking The stadium is on the western edge of town. Follow the M62 to its conclusion and onto the A63 (Beverley/Hull). Before the centre, exit left onto Madeley Street (Royal Infirmary) and take the second exit at the roundabout onto Rawling Way. Go left onto the Anlaby Road and over the flyover. The ground is signed off to the left. Walton Street is the KC Stadium's main car park – parking £3. Park and ride – Priory Park by Clive Sullivan Way, £2 adult return.

By Train Hull station is just over a mile from the ground – a 20-minute walk. Go right onto Anlaby Road, right onto Argyle Street passing Hull Royal Infirmary and the ground is off to the left.

Pubs for home fans
Most near the ground are the preserve of home fans only, especially Silver Cod, Analby Road – one for away fans to avoid. Linnet & Lark, Princes Avenue – big screens and a good match-day atmosphere. The Lair, Anlaby Road, is a supporters' bar with pool tables and sports screens.

Good food near ground
Plenty of takeaways near the ground – Princes Avenue is lined with cafés and pizzerias.

Pubs for away fans
In the city centre, The Admiral of the Humber, Anlaby Road (Weatherspoons, one of four), is near the train station. Closer to the ground, "on Walton Street the Brickmakers Arms and Walton Street Club welcome visiting supporters" says Les Motherby. "The latter has a £3 entry fee but cheap beer and grub."

Top tips
Try parking at the nearby Royal Infirmary.

PUB QUIZ

That's quite interesting
"No serving Hull City player has ever featured for the full England national team. There was hope while Michael Turner was at the club, but alas…" Editor, Boyhood Dreams.

Not a lot of people know that
"The KC Stadium is built just yards from the site of the Anlaby Road ground, the Tigers home between 1906 and 1941." Les Motherby.

THE LAST WORD

ambernectar.org
hullcity-mad.co.uk
oncloudseven.com
thekempton.wordpress.com
boyhood-dreams.blogspot.com

GETTY IMAGES

▼ Mark Cullen scores against Wigan.

AFP/GETTY IMAGES

▲ Famous half time on pitch team talk, Boxing Day 2008.

- **Nicknames** Blues or Tractor Boys
- **Founded** 1888
- **Ground** Portman Road (opened 1888)
- **Address** Ipswich, Suffolk IP1 2DA
- **Capacity** 30,300
- **Best attendance** 38,010 vs Leeds United, FA Cup 6th round, 8 March, 1975
- **Contact** 01473-400 500
- **Ticket Number** 0870-111 0555
- **Email** enquiries@itfc.co.uk
- **Website** itfc.co.uk

IPSWICH TOWN

That's quite interesting
In the hit film *Escape to Victory* Ipswich players John Wark, Kevin O'Callaghan, Russell Osman and Laurie Sivell all starred alongside actors including Michael Caine and Sylvester Stallone as well as Pele, whilst Paul Cooper doubled for Stallone in goal and Kevin Beattie for Michael Caine on the pitch.

Not a lot of people know that
Ipswich have played in 31 European ties (62 games) and have never been beaten at home.

No English team has sacrificed quite as much to the national cause as Ipswich Town. In the early sixties, Sir Alf Ramsey led an unfashionable Ipswich team to promotion from the Second Division and then astounded the football establishment by winning the Championship the following season – a year later he was England manager and on the way to World Cup glory. Meanwhile, back in Suffolk, the Tractor Boys soon found themselves ploughing a furrow back out of the top flight. Then, during the late seventies and early eighties, a young Bobby Robson sculpted Ipswich into one of the great teams of the period, notching up the FA Cup, the Uefa Cup and finishing Championship runners up twice. But despite building a top European side, they again slipped back into the second tier after Robson moved on to a successful England career, which culminated in a tense World Cup semi-final defeat and a knighthood. These two periods of football helped define Ipswich Town, the country club from the east of England that became one of the best sides in Europe, regularly taking on and often defeating the continent's giants such as Barcelona and Roma. They boasted a wealth of home grown talent and a squad packed full of England and Scotland internationals. They also brought two of the first foreign imports into the English game, Frans Thijssen and Arnold Muhren. The two Dutch internationals added another level of class to the team as well as pioneering the way for other overseas players.

Blues fans have been raised on a diet of skilful, passing football – not for them the longball game that some teams have employed as 'route one' back

to the top flight. Since those halcyon days the club has flirted with success, most notably under George Burley, who took an excellent team to fifth in the Premiership on the first attempt, only to see them relegated a year later. He eventually followed the great Ipswich tradition, this time going on a slightly less direct route to manage the Scottish national team.

Greatest moments on this ground
"Uefa Cup final first-leg win against AZ Alkmar or the 2-0 home win against Aston Villa to clinch the title in 1962" Richard Meadows, ITFC Supporters Trust.

Lowest moments on this ground
"The 2001/02 season, 0-6 to Liverpool, after dragging ourselves out of the relegation zone the hammering destroyed all confidence in Ipswich and led to a slide out of the Premiership. Everyone in the ground knew we were doomed that day." Jake Parks, TWTD.com.

Heroes of the sideline
Sir Alf Ramsey and Sir Bobby Robson. George Burley deserves a mention for taking Ipswich to fifth in the Premiership.

Don't mention the…
League Cup semi-final defeat to Norwich in the early eighties.

The ground
Portman Road has been through several phases of modernization, resulting in a modern stadium with stands of varying ages. It is one of the few stadiums in the country, if not the only one, where away fans seem to have preference over home. Not only does the away seating

VILLAINS
Robert Fleck, the annoying Scotsman who regularly taunted the North Stand during local derbies. Clive Thomas, for disallowing a perfectly good goal in the 1975 FA Cup semi-final.

RIVALS
Norwich City and Colchester United.

offer great views, but home fans are regularly moved from their seats to accommodate visiting supporters. There are plans to redevelop the oldest of the stands, The Cobbold should the club regain Premiership status.

The **Britannia Stand**, originally built and opened in 1957 and known as the West Stand, was and still is the main grandstand at the ground. A third large tier was added in 1984, making it the largest stand at Portman Road, home to directors and television gantry, as well as a row of executive boxes.

Opened in 1971, the **Cobbold Stand** is now somewhat ageing, its two tiers are separated with a row of executive boxes. Since the redevelopment of the two ends of Portman Road it has also become home to visiting supporters and offers one of the best views in the country for away fans, although some might feel that the seating is very cramped in places, especially at the back of the stand amongst the girders.

Both ends of Portman Road are new, having been redeveloped just before and during the clubs last stint in the Premiership. The **Green King Stand** is an impressive two-tier stand formerly known as Churchman's at the tunnel end of the ground. It's never been the noisiest end of the stadium and now has the disadvantage of being next to the visiting supporters too.

The newest of the four sides, **The North Stand** is another impressive two-tier all-seater and houses the hardcore and most vocal of Ipswich fans. In the old days it was a tight terrace with home and away support, but now those vocal north standers mass in the lower tier. It's not as loud as it used to be though, as the acoustics leave something to be desired. The views from the upper tier are sensational.

Getting there

By Road/Parking Street parking around Portman road has slowly dwindled over the years as the neighbouring docks and industrial estates have been redeveloped. There is, however, plenty of match-day car parks that are clearly signposted, as well as the usual town centre car parks. Parking is a little easier in the street for evening games as some permit restrictions are relaxed; make sure you check the signs first though.

If approaching from the south turn off at the A12/A14 junction south of Ipswich and take the A1214 signposted to Ipswich. Go over five sets of traffic lights and then turn right into the West End Road, signposted Football Ground. There are various car parks surrounding the ground.

If approaching from the north take the A12 north of Ipswich, turn off onto the A1214 towards the town centre. Turn right onto the Inner Ring road. Follow the road round to the West End Road and follow the signs to the Football Ground.

Alternatively, there are three park and ride schemes which operate in Ipswich, situated at Bury Road (A14/A1156 junction), Copdock (A12/A14 junction) and Martlesham (north of Ipswich, A12/A1214 junction).

By Train Leaving the station via the main entrance, walk directly ahead over the bridge towards the town centre. After Staples, turn left into Portman Road.

THE LAST **WORD**

twtd.com
ipswichtownfirst.co.uk

HOME AWAY

Pubs for home fans
Being close to the town centre there are loads of pubs on offer, The Great White Horse is a popular pre-match watering hole and is a short five- to 10-minute walk away. In the summer it has an outdoor area. Closer to the ground is the Drum and Monkey, this used to be a boozer frequented by away support but this has now changed and is home fans only. In the town centre itself there is a wide range of excellent pubs to choose from.

Good food near ground
There are numerous burger vans around the ground serving the usual stadium grub, there is also a McDonald's and other fast-food eateries nearby as well as the standard town centre eateries. But if you want a good bit of café grub then try Jack's Café on Wilson Road, which is about 10 minutes from the ground and does excellent traditional English grub.

Pubs for away fans
With the loss of the Drum and Monkey for away fans, it means the Station Hotel, conveniently situated opposite the station, is the away supporters pub of choice. It's only 10 minutes from the turnstile and straight off the platform so in that respect it is perfect. Most pubs in town are friendly, although you should be discreet, and during derby games and high-profile visitors there is often extra security in many of the pubs.

Top tips
Away fans should try and get seats in the upper tier of the Cobbold Stand if it's raining, it offers a great view and in wet weather the lower tier is very exposed.

HEROES OR ZEROES?

>> HEROES OF THE TURF
The whole of the 1981 Uefa Cup winning side, John Wark especially. From the youth system, 'Walky' helped Town win the Uefa cup with a then record-equaling 14 goals in the competition, including one in each leg of the final. He also won the English Player of the Year award that season and boasted an impressive handlebar moustache. He left to play for Liverpool before returning and inspiring Ipswich to win the then Division Two in 1991/92 season. After two stints he retired just before his 40th birthday. From the sixties championship-winning side the two forwards Ray Crawford and Ted Philips are the obvious choices. More recently Marcus Stewart.

≈ ZEROES OF THE TURF
Finidi George, Mateo Sereni and Jim Thorburn. Thorburn was signed in the 1963/64 season, he had just been relegated with Raith Rovers in the Scottish Premiership, letting in a record number of goals. Manager Jackie Milburn declared him a fine keeper and it was his defence that let him down – two weeks later he signed the Raith centre-back. Thorburn let in over 100 goals and Ipswich were relegated.

HOME COLOURS

LEEDS UNITED

- ❸ **Nicknames** The Whites, United, The Peacocks
- ⓪ **Founded** 1919
- ⓦ **Ground** Elland Road (opened 1888)
- ❶ **Address** Elland Road, Leeds LS11 0ES
- ❸ **Capacity** 39,460
- ✪ **Best attendance** 57,892 vs Sunderland, FA Cup 5th round reply, 15 March, 1967
- ⓒ **Contact** 0113-367 600
- ⓒ **Ticket Number** 0845-121 1992
- @ **Email** tickets@leedsunited.com
- ⓦ **Website** leedsunited.com

Various theories abound as to why Don Revie changed the Leeds strip to all white. Some say it was to emulate the great Real Madrid, undisputed kings of Europe – a crown that Revie coveted for his side. Others say the real reason was that he thought players would find it easier to spot one another in the heat of battle, and the Madrid story was misdirection – a bit like the 'carrots improve your eyesight' wartime cover story for the invention of RADAR. Whatever the real reason, the Don soon established Leeds as the greatest team of the mid 1960s and early 1970s.

Revie was certainly ahead of his time in bringing in special diets and his famous team-bonding exercises. Leeds won the title in 1969 and 1974, but where they really succeeded was in that great British tradition of glorious and stylish failure – they were runners up on no less than five occasions, once by goal difference and once by a shock last-day defeat. They did notch up an FA Cup, League Cup and two Fairs (Uefa) Cups, as well as losing the 1975 European Cup final (under Jimmy Armfield).

Football at the end of the sixties was a very different, more physical ball game than the one we 'Sky Plus' today. Bundling the keeper into the back of the net with the ball in hand, two-footed challenges from behind… but Revie's side – while certainly possessing a backbone of steel, also played some sublime football. The Don's legacy was to establish Leeds as a truly global brand, one that to this day still elicits strong feelings. They're either near the top of supporters' 'love 'em' list or peaking the summit of the 'most-hated'. The fact that they still stir such emotions may seem surprising when you consider the days of 'Dirty Leeds' are more than three decades gone, and more recently the European exploits of O'Leary's kids were being lauded around the land as a pre-Abramovich challenge to Old Trafford. Maybe their ultimate crime

was flying too close to the sun with financial wings that looked sturdy enough to soar into a heady new era, but which ultimately turned out to be held together by wax.

Heroes of the sideline
Don Revie, Jimmy Armfield and Howard Wilkinson.

Heroes of the turf
John Charles, the whole Revie team – Gray, Lorimer, Clarke, Hunter, Giles, Charlton et al – Lucas Radebe, Ian Snodin, John Sheridan, Gordon Strachan and Tony Yeboah. However, rising head and shoulders above is the late, great Billy Bremner. With 17 years of service and 772 games, he was a captain who came to epitomize the spirit of Leeds United.

Zeroes of the turf
Nominees include Peter Barnes and World Cup and Champions League-winning José Vitor Roque Junior, who managed an amazing seven games and two goals (although they were against Man United). The one name that is synonymous with underachieving at Leeds has to be Tomas Brolin, the Swedish international, considered one of the best players in the world at the time he joined Howard Wilkinson's squad on 17 November 1995. Brolin made a promising start, however things quickly deteriorated to the point where he refused to rejoin the team at the start of the following season. Brolin went out on loan and things came to a shambolic end when 'Tubby' Thomas had his contract terminated in October 1997. He contributed 20 appearances, four goals and one long headache for two managers, Wilkinson and then George Graham.

Villains
Mark Aizlewood made a double two-fingered gesture to the Kop after scoring the winning goal against Walsall in a turgid end-of-season game on 1 May 1989. "He was immediately subbed, stripped of the captaincy and playing for Bradford by the end of the summer," says Kevin Markey, LeedsUtdMAD. Some would say ex-chairman Peter Ridsdale, for his financial legacy, but perhaps that's too obvious. Harry Kewell, where to start…

That's quite interesting
Former Leeds manager Jimmy Adamson (1978-1980) was actually offered the England job ahead of Sir Alf Ramsey. His reign at Leeds did not go well and many fans blamed Adamson for the team's relegation in 1981/82, the season

∧ Alan Smith tucks the ball away in a Leeds win against Deportivo at Elland Road.

after his departure. One game into the 1978/79 season, Jock Stein became Leeds manager, after an unhappy departure from Celtic. It was felt that Stein's stature and presence would be Revie-like and he could repeat his success in the English league. Forty-four day's later he was lured north of the border to manage Scotland. His time in charge at Elland Road exactly matched that of Brian Clough.

Not a lot of people know that
"Leeds used to have the tallest floodlights in Europe until they were taken down in 1992/93.

Greatest moments on this ground
"It's got to be the 7-0 win over Southampton on 4 March 1972 (we clinched our Championship mainly away from home). The team threw away the shackles of their defensive responsibilities and gave a supreme showing of how football should be played. Southampton were absolutely outclassed as seven different players scored the goals in a masterclass." Kevin Markey.

"1972 when we beat Man United 5-1 in the League. The game was against arch rivals that were really hurting as a result. Also the Champions League games against AC Milan and Deportivo for sheer pride and excitement." Dave Tomlinson, mightyleeds.co.uk.

Lowest moments on this ground
"'We've had our ups and downs' as the song goes. Losing at home to Portsmouth on 25 April 2004 was pretty much as low as it gets as it more or less confirmed our relegation from the Premiership. Nearly 40,000 fans went home shell-shocked that day." Kevin Markey.

The ground
Elland Road is an ageing ground over which the huge and impressive East Stand looms like a giant pair of open mechanical jaws. The other three sides hark back to the

age of open terraces – when Revie stalked the sidelines or when Strachan bossed the 1992 team to title-winning glory. As many clubs smaller than Leeds have moved to modern, some might say blander stadiums, Elland Road maintains an atmosphere that visiting fans relish. The ground is completely enclosed, with away fans housed at the southern end of the ground. When a big team visits, this makes for a great atmosphere, as away fans face the Revie Stand, where the core Yorkshire support congregates to generate the rousing choruses of 'Marching on Together'. Even as a club in the third tier of English football in the 2007/08 season, Leeds could generate a crowd of 36,297 for their final home play-off game.

The famous statue of Billy Bremner stands outside the ground in the southeast corner, arms raised in celebration. It was inaugurated in 1998 and has become a focal point for fans in the good times and the bad. The club superstore is open year round and on match days.

The pitch at Elland Road is towered over by the impressive **East Stand**, the first thing the players see

as they run out onto the pitch. This impressive two-tier covered area of seating can hold a massive 17,000 fans. When finished during the 2003/04 season, it was the largest cantilever stand in the world and a symbol of the club's ambition. The lower tier holds 10,000 while the upper tier can accommodate a further 7,000. A layer of executive boxes with a concourse of shops and food outlets lies between the two areas.

Completed in 1974, the **South Stand** replaced the Scratching Shed, which had stood since the 1920s. It is a two-tier stand with a row of executive boxes. The corners either side – the southwest and southeast – are filled with seating. The **Southeast Corner** is used to accommodate away fans and seats 1,710. For bigger clubs the whole of the South Stand may be used. Billy's Bar is found in the South Stand, named after the former skipper Bremner, and is open to the general public every day. The stand was revamped in 2006.

The **John Charles Stand** was named after the Leeds legend who passed away in 2004. Formerly the West

Three play-off defeats. 1-0 against Doncaster in 2008 was probably the most painful after clawing back a 15-point deduction.

◄ Don Revie celebrates a Leeds goal.

Stand, this section of the ground dates back to 1957 and contains an area of corporate seats, the radio and press area and the directors' box. This area seats 11,000 covered seats. The TV gantry is suspended over this area at the halfway line and the tunnel exits onto the turf here.

The **Revie Stand** at the northern head of the ground was formerly the all-standing Kop and is still home to the hardcore Leeds support. This 7,000 seater area is named in honour of the great Don Revie, manager of Leeds during their rise from the old first division to become a dominant force in European football.

Getting there

Roads/parking Elland Road sits next the M621 and is visible on the left as you drop down the hill towards the city. From junction 1 take the exit onto a large roundabout and take the right turn (third exit) onto the ring road (A6110), then turn left onto Elland Road (the A643). There are large car parks close to the ground. From junction 2 enter the roundabout and bear right (the third exit) onto Elland Road. The ground is on your right and car parks are on the left. There are also sneaky parking spots on the roads on the Lowfields Road-side of the M621, where there's a business park.

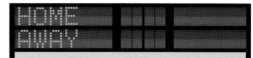

Pubs for home fans
The Old Peacock on Elland Road gets packed, but does have an outside bar in the summer. There are huge queues inside. Billy's Bar is for home ticket holders only on match days, unless you get there early.

Good food near ground
There's a Subway opposite the south stand and a McDonald's opposite the east stand.

Pubs for away fans
The Drysalters is situated at the far end of Elland Road, past the car parks and railway bridge, leading left onto Beeston Ring Road, about three quarters of a mile from the ground. It was refurbished in 2005, but is a little worn now. All away supporters are welcome and it's become an unofficial away fans watering hole on match day.

Top tips
Elland Road is actually a pretty friendly ground. The only flash points seem to be after local derbies and games involving Millwall, Cardiff or Man United, but policing is generally pretty good.

THE LAST **WORD**

leedsunited-mad.co.uk
thescratchingshed.com
leeds.vitalfootball.co.uk
waccoe.com
thesquareball.net

➤ The O'Leary team before 2001 Champions League tie away against Madrid at the Bernabeu. Leeds made the semi-final.

GETTY IMAGES

HOME COLOURS

- ❷ **Nicknames** The Foxes
- ❷ **Founded** 1884
- ❷ **Ground** Walkers Stadium (opened 2002)
- ❶ **Address** Filbert Way, Leicester LE2 7FL
- ❷ **Capacity** 32,500
- ❷ **Best attendance** 32,148 vs Newcastle United, Premier League, 26 December, 2003
- ❶ **Contact** 0844-815 6000
- ❶ **Ticket Number** 0844-815 5000
- @ **Email** ticket.sales@lcfc.co.uk
- ❷ **Website** lcfc.com

LEICESTER CITY

RIVALS
Derby County, Nottingham Forest and Coventry City.

ans learn to live with their heroes leaving. It's frustrating to see your badge-kissing captain go to a rival after pledging allegiance to your club, but unless they're able to resist the advances of bigger teams, it has unfortunately become a fact of life. Even the Big Four are no longer immune. Most leave and never look back, but some remain life-long fans, returning to watch and support the club. A select few return as managers – fewer still as saviours, but that is precisely the role played by one former goal-scoring legend. The last half of the nineties had been a joy for Leicester fans. New manager Martin O'Neill took the team into the Premier League and they became a force to be reckoned with. How many years of overachieving does it take to stop being perennial overachievers? O'Neill guided City to top-half finishes in the top flight for four years in a row, including two League Cup wins. But in the summer of 2000 O'Neill was lured away to Celtic where he won the treble in his first season, while The Foxes began a steady decline into the second tier of football. By 2002 the club and its brand-new £37 million stadium were in the hands of an administrator. Enter former Foxes legend, *Match of the Day* front man, and housewives favourite Mr Gary Lineker OBE. "I have been a Leicester fan all my life and I had eight great years playing for the club," said Lineker. "I am desperate to ensure I can still come along to watch them play in the future." The former England striker put together a consortium saving the club he supports. Today the future looks brighter. Despite a dip in the third tier, the club now boasts a new chairman in Milan Mandaric and is pushing for promotion out of the Championship, hoping that a new generation of heroes may be born to help bring redemption and top-flight football back to the club.

Greatest moments on this ground
"Two goals stand out – both against Leeds United. Lilian Nalis in our first Premiership victory at the Walkers Stadium in September 2003 with a spectacular volley past Paul Robinson. And in April 2009 with the League One title in sight, Steve Howard powered an injury-time header, virtually making us champions." David Bevan, the-blue-notes.blogspot.com.

Lowest moments on this ground
"Filbert Street – losing to Wycombe Wanderers in the FA Cup quarter final in 2001 due to an injury time header from Roy Essendoh who was signed via Ceefax in the week prior to the game. Walkers Stadium – losing regularly in 2008/09 season that saw us relegated to League One. Each game at the Walkers was torture and hard to watch." James Ireland, The Walkers Bowl.

Heroes of the sideline
Matt Gillies – he led us to our first major trophy by winning the League Cup and reached three other finals in the early sixties. Martin O'Neill – he took a second-tier side and made them a real force in the Premiership, winning trophies and playing in Europe. We won at Anfield and Old Trafford. O'Neill used a shoestring budget to build a team that was much more than the sum of its parts. Nigel Pearson – our current leader, the man who has restored hope and enthusiasm after the extended hangover since O'Neill departed. Pearson has created a side full of ability and commitment to the cause." David Bevan.

Heroes of the turf
"Frank Worthington – flamboyant, mercurial, think Eric Cantona if he'd been born in Halifax in the forties. Gordon Banks – for winning the Jules Rimet Trophy while a City player, and years of brilliance. Gary Lineker – Leicester's favourite son of a market trader, England goal hero turned media behemoth. Keith Weller – provided the trademark flair of Jimmy Bloomfield's seventies side. Arthur Chandler

PUB QUIZ

That's quite interesting
"Former City striker Emile William Ivanhoe Heskey, to give him his full name, contributed a hefty sum when Gary Lineker led a consortium to save the club from extinction." David Bevan.

Not a lot of people know that
"In the 2008/09 season, Leicester used six goalkeepers to fill the sticks; more than in any other season." James Ireland.

GETTY IMAGES

– the Football League's all-time top goal-scorer, the majority scored in the famous royal blue." David Bevan.

"Steve Walsh – most successful captain winning the League Cup in 1996 and known as Mr Leicester. Also for the Wembley play-off final in 1994. Muzzy Izzet – his career with us took him further than he could ever have imagined, including a World Cup semi-final. We got him on the cheap from Chelsea and he became a fan's favourite and a quality Premiership attacking midfielder." James Ireland.

Zeroes of the turf

"Ade Akinbiyi – £5million wasted to replace Emile Heskey. After a shocking game against Liverpool The Sun referred to him as 'Ade Akinbadbiyi'.

Junior Lewis – voted our worst player every year he was at the club – although impressing at lower levels, he was ripped to shreds by the quality of the Premiership. Zelijko Kalac – he couldn't catch a ball to save his life. Just left AC Milan and has a Champion's League winner's medal. Possibly our worst keeper ever." James Ireland

Villains

"Robert Fleck, annoying Scotsman regularly taunted the North Stand. Dennis Wise was a Chelsea legend when he arrived under the disastrous stewardship of Peter Taylor. He left Leicester under more of a thunderstorm than a cloud after attacking team-mate Callum Davidson on a pre-season tour. Despised by fans for his poor performance, the nature of his exit and subsequent claims for money." David Bevan.

∧ Emile Heskey scores against Chelsea at Filbert Street.

DON'T MENTION THE...

"Stan Collymore's infamous night with the fire extinguisher or the tour to Murcia under the reign of Mickey Adams. Hard to choose!" James Ireland.

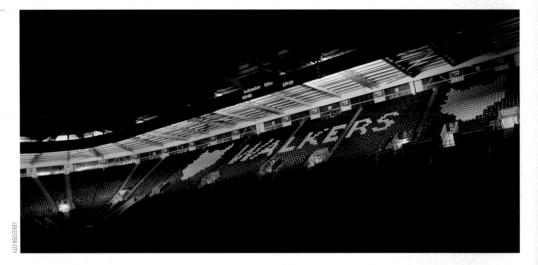

LEICESTER CITY

The ground

Completed in July 2002, the Walkers Stadium is an all-seater bowl. The **Family North Stand** behind the goal has a capacity of 5,000. The **East Stand** holds up to 7,500 home fans. The **Fosse Stand** is where the hardcore support sits and holds 7,000 – the name was chosen in a competition, though many still refer to it as the **Kop**. The main **West Stand** has 6,500 seats plus a further 2,500 corporate seats including 44 Executive boxes. Away fans occupy the northwest corner.

Getting there

By Road/Parking Exit the M1 at junction 21 (where it also meets the M69) and follow the A5460 signed for the City Centre for around three miles. Go right onto Upperton Road and right onto Easten Boulevard. The ground will be on your right. Parking at Saffron Lane Sports Centre for £3.50. Pre-book 0844-815 5000, street parking also.

By Train The station is about a 20-minute walk away. Cross over the road and head left to follow the Waterloo Way ringroad. Go right onto Lancaster Road and through Nelson Mandela Park towards the main road then left in front of Royal Infirmary onto Aylestone Road. Go right into Walnut Street, left into Burnmoor Street and the ground is ahead.

THE LAST **WORD**

lcfcwordpress.com
foxes-online.co.uk
foxestalk.co.uk
thefoxfanzine/wordpress.com
leicester.vitalfootball.co.uk
thebluearmy.co.uk
forfoxsake.com

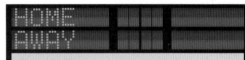

HOME
AWAY

Pubs for home fans
Most of the pubs nearest the ground are the preserve of the home contingent including The Victory and Local Hero on Aylestone Road. Meal deals on pretty average pub grub also available. Half Time Orange, Burnmoor Street is an Everards brewery pub serving up their local ales.

Good food near ground
Narborough Road has plenty of eateries from Indian and Chinese restaurants, cafés and a Subway sandwich bar. There's also a handy Morrison's nearby on Counting House Road.

Pubs for away fans
The Hind by the Station serves a selection of ales but the town centre is probably the best bet, with usual Weatherspoons including High Cross on High Street. For real ale try the large Leicester Gateway, Gateway Street with sports, simple food and a mix of fans, or CAMRA award-winning Criterion, Millstone Lane, with continental lagers and lunchtime pizzas. By the ground, The Counting House, Almond Street, with a mix of fans, is the best choice.

Top tips
The policing around Leicester home games is notably heavy-handed – best to keep your colours covered until you're in the ground.

HALF TIME

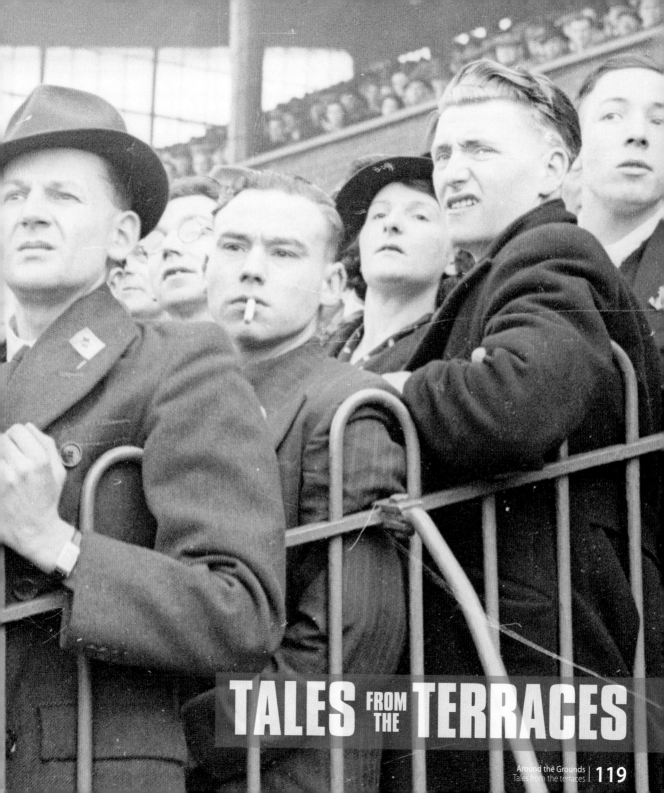

TALES FROM THE TERRACES

CATCH OF THE DAY

HOLDING BACK THE TIDE OF THE McFOOTBALL GENERATION by pete green

My football club is enduring the worst run of form in its 130-year history. In recent seasons Grimsby Town have plunged sickeningly down the Football League and out of its trapdoor into the Conference. This malaise has lasted a decade and shows no signs of ending any time soon. We've got rid of bad managers and brought in good ones, cut out the dead wood and signed decent footballers. We've tried 4-4-2, 4-5-1 and 3-4-3. We've had players from France, Australia, the Democratic Republic of Congo, even Scunthorpe. None of it has made the slightest bit of difference. We're still crap. We lost six of the first seven games in the 2009/10 season – three of those defeats by a 4-0 margin. It didn't get much better from there. After a desperate grind along the bottom of the table, we shut our eyes against the horror and hoped against hope that two other teams would somehow turn out to be even worse than us. They weren't. And we were relegated.

Would I swap places with a Chelsea fan? You must be bloody kidding.

Why? Let's kick off with kick-offs. When the fixture list comes out, and it says our games will be played at 3pm on Saturday afternoons and 7.45pm on Tuesday evenings, we know that's pretty much how it'll stay. There are no Monday nights to drag yourself out when you're reeling from work, no Sky Super Sunday lunchtime games

¡VIVA LA REVOLUCION!

to reach before the buses and trains start running. And it's not just fans who are put out by matches that begin at daft o'clock – you can set your watch by the sound of Messrs Wenger and Ferguson moaning about it. Funny how they're never quite bothered to tell Rupert Murdoch to get stuffed and give him his 50 million quid back.

Another nice thing about supporting a rubbish team is the simplicity and ease with which match tickets are procured. You want to watch the Mariners, you just roll up at five to three, breeze into the club shop, flash your debit card and you've still got time for a cardiac burger and a wee before kick off. We might be watching dross but at least we're not queuing up all day for the privilege.

In the Premier League getting tickets is like the building of the new Wembley stadium. It drags on for years, incurring unforeseen delays and extra expense, requiring the expertise of specialists and consultants to pull you through the mire. Once I tried to get tickets for Tottenham against Liverpool. I asked some Spurs fans what to do. They laughed at me. So I rang White Hart Lane and asked the club for some. They laughed at me as well. At length it emerged that to buy tickets, you have to be a 'member' of the club. What does that even mean? Eventually I ended up having to email a friend in London and persuade him to ask his work colleague, who is a 'member' of Spurs, to try and get me the tickets. It turned

out he had to send a request for them by fax. We didn't get them in the end because the fax machine in his office wasn't working that day. *Fax machine.* Can you hear that rumbling sound coming up from the ground? That's Bill Nicholson rotating rapidly in his grave, that is.

It's not just the minor practicalities. Football remains the world's most compelling game because anyone can beat anyone: what we call "the magic of the cup", the joy of the unexpected outcome, is really the magic of football as a whole. And if you support a big club, then you can never be on the right end of a cup shock. You are excluded, by definition, from experiencing the most fundamental thrill of the game. It can only be felt by supporters of smaller clubs like mine.

As Radio Humberside's John Tondeur put it after Town won at Anfield in 2001, "Liverpool fans will never have a night like we had at Liverpool."

Cup shocks are not even that rare an occurrence. After we knocked Spurs out of the League Cup in 2006, a Tottenham blog afterwards described their experience at "Blunden Park" as "the result of a lifetime for Grimsby". Which it was – as long as you're younger than 35 and you don't count Grimsby's cup wins against Everton (1979 and 1984), Newcastle (1982), Middlesbrough (1989), Aston Villa (1991), West Ham (1996) and Norwich (1998). Oh, and Liverpool (2001).

But this doesn't just apply to cup games, of course. Before our current decline we were an established second-flight club. We still had no support and a ramshackle ground, obviously, and your Wolveses and Middlesbroughs thought this meant they only had to turn up and three points were theirs'. If there's one thing better than beating a team with delusions of grandeur, it's beating a team with delusions of grandeur and watching them sack their manager afterwards. George Burley's dismissal from Ipswich in 2002 immediately followed the humiliation of defeat by Grimsby; likewise Gordon Strachan at Coventry, Steve Bruce at Huddersfield, and many more. We don't know whether it's a backhanded compliment or a forehanded insult, but it's a massive laugh.

So when a small club has a big win, it's a far greater achievement – with a far greater buzz – than when a rich club collects another silver pot. The context makes it *feel* bigger, on a scale that the complacent, success-glutted Big Four can scarcely conceive of.

When Grimsby beat a top club, furthermore, we don't just overcome the huge gulf in wealth and glamour between the clubs. We stick it to the Premier League and all that it stands for. Because the top clubs set it up explicitly to hog the cake and ruin clubs like ours. They did a Robin Hood in reverse. "When we have got 52,000 fans at each home game, the last thing we are

worried about is clubs in the Third Division," gloated the then Newcastle chairman Freddy Shepherd in 2004. He was only saying what the rest were thinking all along. They play along with all that 'spirit of football' stuff every January, for the third round of the FA Cup, but in reality they'd rub their hands in glee if Grimsby Town and all the other Davids to their Goliath disappeared tomorrow.

Then there are the plastic fans. Loads of them. Just as you could build a battleship with all the 'authentic' bits of the Crucifix, so too if every plastic fan's dad really was a season ticket holder at Man U, the Stretford End would be the size of Norway.

And if you 'support', say, Chelsea because you looked at a League table and *chose* them – rather like selecting the most appetising meal from a menu – then you have got football wrong. There is no more to it than that. You have *got football wrong*. Whatever you experience from it will always be far less than what I take from supporting Grimsby. Your team can keep winning, but you'll always be the loser.

If you support Chelsea because you're from west London, or they represent you in some other significant way concerning your identity and your culture, then no, you haven't got football wrong. But as well as daft kick-off times, faffing about for expensive tickets, and losing to Barnsley in the FA Cup, you have to put up with plastic fans sitting next to you and asking you which one's Joe Cole.

This idea that our team represents us is what everything rests on. Ultimately this is why any result matters – it's why a victory belongs to us as fans, rather than just the players who actually achieved it. It's why we call our team "we" instead of "they". But for your team to represent you, you must be linked to it – viscerally, umbilically, atavistically: in your guts and genes and blood. As a fan. Not a consumer. Your team can't represent you in any meaningful way if your only link is to have chosen it like the best brand of washing-up liquid on the shelf at Tesco.

Some of these people even know their support borders on insignificance; that a Rooney hat trick is as glorious and meaningful to them as a row of three lemons. This is why I wasn't too surprised, on the evening of 26 May 1999, when I was down the pub watching Manchester United on TV, in their Champions League final, attempting to complete a treble of trophies unique and unparalleled in the long and rich history of English football, when I glanced away from the screen and saw a man in a Man U shirt who wasn't actually watching the game. No. He was playing the fruit machine.

Most of the time, of course, supporting Grimsby is rubbish. But when we achieve anything at all, we know these little flickers of micro-success are resourced directly by the money we spend on tickets and shirts – not by the whims and loose change of a sportswear magnate or oil mogul with a God complex in the space where his charisma should be. Whoever owns the most shares or has the biggest chair in the boardroom, Grimsby Town is still, insurmountably, unconquerably and morally, *our club*; and for this reason above all else – despite the pain and the despair, the anger, and, very often, the sheer stark bloody boredom – I would never change places with a fan of Chelsea, Man U or any other rich, popular and prestigious football team you could name. You just might need to remind me gently of this next Saturday when we're losing 3-0 at home to Hayes & Yeading.

Pete Green has been watching Grimsby Town for 30 years, and since 2002 has been an editor and writer on **Cod Almighty***, a 100% independent and non-commercial online fanzine named by* **When Saturday Comes** *as one of Britain's top five web-based zines. Visit codalmighty.com.*

Grimsby were relegated to the Conference on the last day of the 2009/10 season. Mike Newell's 'Revolution' had petered out long before.

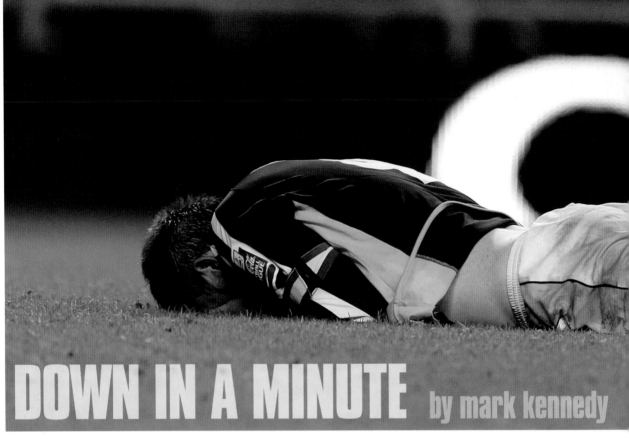

DOWN IN A MINUTE by mark kennedy

"Down in a minute, we're going down in a minute". The cry rang out from the away end at Elland Road on a sunny May afternoon. Northampton Town were 2-0 down and staring relegation in the face. The Cobblers had to get a point at Leeds, or hope other games went our way. "Que sera sera, whatever will be will be, we're going to Shrewsbury, que sera sera" soon followed from the claret and white faithful. This amusing chant, nicked from Cheltenham fans a month earlier, was the only way of humouring ourselves, with 35,000 Leeds fans taking the p*ss at our impending fate. The third goal went in and everyone headed for the exits, leaving the home fans to celebrate ahead of their play-off campaign.

Goodbye League One, hello League Two. A familiar home for the long suffering Cobblers fans. But where did it all go wrong?

Northampton Town have only once spent more than three seasons in a row outside the basement division. The glorious aberration was when the club famously went through all four divisions in the sixties, eventually playing in the top flight of English football. Then, like an especially cruel game of Snakes & Ladders, we repeated the feat, going all the way back down to where we'd started.

The rest of the time, the three season rule is king and 2008/09 campaign was to be another fateful 'third season'. Nose bleed time again for the team from the Midlands.

But fans had gone into August with the usual optimism. Stuart Gray managed an impressive ninth the previous year with a team of young Premier League and Championship loanees making up the crux of the squad. Gray was dubbed "the borrower" by fans and hopes were high. We even dreamed of maybe reaching the promised land of the Championship. New striker Leon Constantine was an instant hit with the fans. This was going to be the man to fire Town up the League. Partnered by Adebayo Akinfenwa, the floodgates were ready to open. A 4-2 opening day win over Cheltenham, including two goals from Akinfenwa and one from Constantine, was enough to raise hopes a little more.

However, it didn't take long for reality to set in. Only a week later the first stinker arrived at Milton Keynes. Because of the MK Dons' controversial background as a franchise, some fans talked about boycotting this one, but 3,500 made the short trip. They came home disappointed as the team froze on the pitch. Repeating words from the terraces would be too obscene. Perhaps we should have boycotted the game – it would have saved a lot of heartache.

It was a sign of things to come. Our highlights came outside the League routine with a mini Carling Cup adventure. After our annual cup meeting against Millwall, victory was rewarded with a trip to Bolton. Two goals from Akinfenwa gave Town a 2-1 giant killing.

Are Bolton cup giants? Who knows? The third round was a long haul to Premier League Sunderland and another cup upset looked on the cards with 10 minutes remaining. Luke Guttridge added to Colin Larkin's first half strike to put the Cobblers 2-0 and cruising. Football can be cruel and this game showed just how cruel. The Mackems scored twice in the last five minutes, saw out extra-time and won on penalties. Exiting the ground that night, it was amazing that so many home fans greeted us at the away end to congratulate us on a great performance. Many were actually gutted they beat us, a sentiment echoed by manager Roy Keane. So was that it? Was that the Cobblers' season? Well pretty much. Fans became disheartened with mediocre

performances that left everyone uninspired and expecting an uneventful mid-table finish. NTFC versus Leeds brought some early winter entertainment with the clubs being paired in the FA Cup only a week before the League fixture at Sixfields. But with Setanta showing the 1-1 draw at Elland Road and the replay, fans stayed away from Sixfields refusing to pay £22 to get in. They witnessed seven goals on the box – the visitors bagging five of them and teaching Town a footballing lesson. A week later and the big club novelty had worn off though and we won the League fixture 2-1 with a last minute goal. Hang on – our season was alive again!

The lead up to Christmas saw the comeback of all comebacks. The hardy fans who made the trip to Glanford Park, Scunthorpe, started to wish they hadn't with the home side 4-1 up. However Town rose from the dead and snatched an unlikely 4-4 draw. Christmas came and went but Northampton kept the spirit of the festive season alive and dished out some presents for the opposition with only three wins in the next 15. Two of those three may have been in style, (5-1 over Crewe and 4-0 over Stockport), but it wasn't enough. Concerns started to show, fans started to get restless. The wheels fell off another planning meeting, as the club's ongoing saga with the local council over stadium redevelopment stalled yet again. A fog of gloom and depression set in over Sixfields, as everyone started to feel the pinch. The chairman continued to pay the bills but the squad became more and more threadbare. A total of 17 loan signings were used over the season, meaning a new team photo could be shot almost every week. What's more, only three of them were really worthwhile. Leon Constantine continued to amaze fans on the pitch – amaze them in the way that he couldn't hit a cow's rear end with a banjo. Constantine replica shirts stopped selling in the club shop for good!

Town were now in it! The R word was mentioned many times. "Beware the Ides of March" and a nightmare double header of away trips; Carlisle on Saturday, Yeovil on Tuesday. With a combined total of almost 1,000 miles for travelling fans, we prayed it'd be worth it. The points return? One. The late defeat to Yeovil meant Northampton slipped below the safety line for the first time. Now for the run in. Permutations were calculated, opposition weighed up. Four wins from the final seven games would keep us up. With three wins in about 20 what hope was there?

Two games over Easter added two defeats to the balance sheet, but results elsewhere gave renewed hope – we needed three wins from five. A trip to Brisbane Road has often provided a turning point for Cobblers' seasons. In recent years, wins there have set us on the way to play-offs

or promotion… and defeats have sent us the other way. Orient were in the relegation scrap with us, although nearly safe. Town won a thrilling match 3-1 and scenes of jubilation greeted the final whistle. Players celebrated on the pitch, throwing their shirts into the crowd. Pubs near the ground were full of singing fans sporting claret and white. Hope and belief were restored. A quick check of the relegation calculator and things looked brighter. Two wins from four – this seemed easy now. Hereford were in town the following week, that would be a sure-fire three points, but next up Scunthorpe. After the eight-goal thriller in Lincolnshire, anything could happen. When the final whistle blew at Sixfields the teams had shared another six goals – our aggregate score against them was 7-7. Three games to go. Already relegated Hereford were beaten 2-1. We needed one point from two games. Easy! Ah, except those games were against promotion candidates MK Dons and big boys Leeds, the latter at Elland Road. There was hope though, with both sides resting players for the upcoming play-offs, surely Town had a chance. First MK came to town, surrounded the ref on every occasion, hit the ground whenever possible and killed the game, eventually winning by the odd goal. Fans left the ground fuming! The ref was shocking! The visitors were dirty lousy cheats! Their fans were freeloaders!

So along came May 2nd and Elland Road. A sunny spring Saturday afternoon, shorts and T-shirts. A trip up the M6 to a team who played in the Champions League a few seasons back (they mention it now and again). NTFC failed to sell out their allocation, as many couldn't bear the thought of the inevitable. All hope had evaporated for many, even before the Spring daffodils had bloomed. The relegation calculator was easy now. One point would see us safe, or Carlisle and/or Brighton must lose. Early news filtered through that Millwall really didn't want to exert themselves at Brunton Park where Carlisle raced into an early 2-0

lead. So our best hope was a miracle at the Withdean, or a bigger miracle in front of our own eyes. Things were going okay. Then just before half-time Leeds scored and 35,000 Yorkshire maniacs laughed in the face of our misfortune. But we were still above that line – news filtered through it was Brighton 0 Stockport 0. Early in the second half Leeds went 2-0 up. Even eternal optimists couldn't see Northampton pulling two back – they hadn't managed two shots on goal, let alone two goals – the whole focus centred on the Withdean. Then it happened, Brighton scored! Nobody in the away end could get a mobile signal so we were relying on the bloke in the crowd with the radio. Then a rumour spread like wildfire – Stockport had scored! Everyone went mad! "We are staying up, say we are staying up." The Cobblers were now safe! Or were they? The boy had cried wolf… talk about looking stupid. One minute of ecstasy followed by the biggest anti-climax of the day. Brighton were still winning and Town were heading to League Two again. Leeds added a third, but it didn't matter, the Cobblers faithful headed to the exits with the prospect of trips to Lincoln, Burton and Dagenham next season. Just two shots on goal in the final two games told the lacklustre story of Northampton Town's dismal season.

Oh well, back to square one. Bring on that August optimism again.

Mark Kennedy is the editor of HotelEnders and author of **We All Follow The Cobblers… Over Land and Sea**. *For every copy sold £1 will be donated to Northampton Town Football Club's youth development work. Visit followthecobblers.blogspot.com*

CANDYFLOSS AND P45s by matt lawson

"Club Faces Extinction!" screams the headline. We've seen articles like this written about enough teams to fill their own division by now, from giants like Leeds and Leicester, through to smaller teams like Accrington Stanley, Darlington and Luton Town. But they won't actually disappear, will they? Isn't it just hyperbole? Surely football clubs are sacred, somehow 'special'? Matt Lawson, editor of *Abandon Chip!*, charts the rise and demise of his team and explains just what can happen when a club runs out of financial options.

Scarborough. The first seaside resort in the UK and still as popular today as it was back in the 1700s when it was pioneered as such. It's a quiet town of just over fifty-thousand people, nestled on the Yorkshire coast between two other popular holiday locations, Whitby and Bridlington. What is Scarborough famous for? There's Scarborough Castle, Peasholm Park, the glorious North and South beaches and it is the venue of ITV drama *The Royal*. How about sport? Well, North Marine Road hosts some Yorkshire county cricket matches and is home to the Scarborough Cricket Festival. How about football? Well, that's a story worth telling…

I was on the M1 near Wakefield when the news came in over the car radio. I was just coming up to my 12th birthday and on my way back from some sort of family gathering at my Auntie and Uncles' house. It was 8 May 1999, a date which still strikes fear into the hearts of Scarborough football fans. "Jimmy Glass – a goalkeeper – has scored a goal for Carlisle United," said the excitable reporter on the local radio station. "This of course means that Scarborough are relegated to the Conference". I turned to my dad solemnly and shook my head. "Are you going to cry?" he asked me with just a hint of schadenfreude. "No. I don't think so". I wanted to, but I didn't want to show myself up in front of the family. It was only a game after all. I should have been there. We should have been there. It was my dad who got me interested in

Scarborough FC in the first place. He'd always supported the club, just like his dad before him. My dad's brother had a trial with the club in the 1970s. He used to tell us stories about running up Oliver's Mount and back – not something for the faint hearted.

I can't remember exactly how I got to my first game. It was probably on one of the painfully slow Yorkshire Coastliner buses that ran between Malton and Scarborough. As I type, memories of diesel fumes and steamed up windows come flooding back. You were lucky if you got off one of those foul machines without being either poisoned by the fumes or drenched by leaking windows. I survived the journey and on 26 October 1996 found myself outside two huge gates at the front of the McCain Stadium. "Funny name for a ground", I thought. It never occurred to me that it was a sponsor. I paid my £1.50 and entered a new world. It was to be my first serious taste of live football; one which ignited a passion which will never be extinguished until the day I die. My dad bought a programme and we took a seat in the relatively new East Stand behind the goal. "SCARBOROUGH versus MANSFIELD TOWN" the programme proclaimed in a striking font. It was a warm day for October, and I remember seeing hundreds of fans wearing red shirts as they made their way to something my dad called "The Shed". It didn't sound very glamorous to an impressionable eight-year-old, but I was intrigued by this rickety old mass of concrete and metal nonetheless. I'd never seen as many people in one place at ay one time. According to my trusty archives (the Internet), there were 2,521 fans inside the ground that day. I remember a few of the players who lined up for Boro against Mansfield. Ian Ironside in goal always struck me as a reliable sort of chap when it came to saving shots. Of course, my naivety at the time saw all the players in red as idols. There was also the fantastically named Jason Rockett, and the ever dependable Gary Bennett – one of the first black people I'd ever seen, due to my sheltered country

upbringing. Despite Boro winning the game 2-1, I missed both home goals. I was in the toilets when Rockett put us one to the good after a quarter of an hour. I did see one goal, but it was Mansfield's – in an example of true Scarborian generosity, we scored it for them through John Kay. In the second half, we moved round to the corner terrace that separated the East Stand from the Shed. Just 30 seconds or so before Gareth Williams put us back into the lead, I decided I needed another wee. Just as I was pulling my trousers back up, there was a loud cheer. Typical.

I'd arrived in the world on 22 May 1987 at Scarborough Hospital. Just over three weeks earlier, Barnet lost 1-2 to Stafford Rangers which handed Scarborough FC the Conference title. We were the first side in history to win automatic promotion to the Football League. My first seven years of life were spent two streets away from Queensgate Stadium, the home of Bridlington Town FC. But it was Scarborough, not Bridlington, that would capture my footballing imagination. I wasn't born when Boro attended four FA Trophy finals at Wembley in the 1970s, winning three of them – still a joint record to this day. I was only a twinkle in my mother's eye when Boro were made joint founder members of the Alliance Premier League, now the Conference. A decade later, I was still far too young to appreciate Scarborough's Football League heyday, if there was such a thing. Fans around the country will probably be aware of the League Cup exploits of the Seadogs in defeating Bradford City, Coventry City, Plymouth Argyle and of course Chelsea. Indeed, only a disputed Nigel Winterburn strike saw Arsenal through at our Seamer Road home by a solitary goal during that 1992/93 season.

The 1997/98 campaign saw the start of the end for Scarborough FC. Ironically, in their 12 year spell in the Football League, it was also arguably their best season. Boro faced Torquay United in the two-legged play-off semi-final. A 1-3 home reverse in the first leg meant that

Boro were always chasing this tie, and a 4-1 defeat in Devon meant we were on the end of a humiliating 7-2 aggregate thrashing. The play-offs came at a price – money the club did not have. The repercussions were the release of many of the best players, leaving Scarborough with a far weaker squad for the 1998/99 season. Just 12 months after being two games away from Wembley and promotion, Boro were relegated to the Conference. Which brings us full circle back to the sad young boy sitting in the car on the M1. But the story doesn't end there.

Things looked bright for the club during their first season in the Conference. A 5-0 opening day win over Yeovil Town had many Seadogs predicting an instant return to the Football League. The good form did continue, but only enough for a 4th placed finish. With Conference play-offs still four years away, only top spot was enough to qualify for promotion. The next few seasons were a mix of mid table finishes and financial concerns. Things started to look worrying, especially when Boro hit rock bottom of the Conference at the end of 2001. Crowds dropped as low as 616 for a midweek home defeat to Morecambe. However Russell Slade, now a Football League manager, took over the reigns in December 2001 and performed a comprehensive great escape, which saw us finish comfortably in 12th. Over 2,200 fans flocked in for the final two home games of the season. The 2002/03 Season saw Scarborough challenging for the play-offs without quite being able to sustain the push. Memories of happier times were revived by the welcome distraction of a good FA Cup run the following season. Chelsea again travelled north to the Yorkshire coastline. Boro had seen off Hinckley United, Doncaster Rovers, Port Vale and Southend United to land this plum tie. A solitary John Terry goal after nine minutes saw the Premier League side through, but many left the ground feeling the future was looking bright again. However, dark clouds were gathering. The hundreds of thousands of pounds the

club 'earned' for the tie went straight to the taxman and the warning signs were there for all to see.

Two seasons later, Boro were relegated again – this time to the Conference North – and financial irregularities meant the club would start the season on minus 10 points. Despite a brave effort, Boro again finished in the relegation zone, and the Unibond Premier League beckoned. I was at my girlfriend's house when I noticed a new post on the Surfing Seadog messageboard. The title simply said "The End of the Road…" I daren't open it, because I knew full well how the message would read. It was a strange feeling as I digested the words on the screen in front of me. It was a beautiful Summer day. The birds were singing and there was a bright blue sky smiling down on us. It made the feeling of numbness even more defined as I sank into an armchair in a barrage of thoughts and memories. I hadn't only lost a football club, I'd lost a way of life. I'd spent hours, if not days, travelling to away games all over the country with other dedicated fans, and now that'd all come to a horrible end. I was too numb to cry, but I felt like doing so. Losing a football club to some may seem a trivial matter. "It's only a game", some say. I disagree. A football club becomes part of your soul and part of your life, just as much as a job or partner does. To lose Scarborough FC was like losing a limb, a limb which still feels a sharp pain now and again when I remember what I've lost.

Although this was the end of Scarborough FC, this isn't where our story ends. As it became more and more obvious that the club was in its death throws, a Supporters Trust was formed and a 'Plan B' formulated, just in case the nightmare scenario unfolded. Plan B involved the formation of a new club, Scarborough Athletic. When the club was lost, a place in the Northern Counties East League Division One was secured for the new Scarborough club for start of the 2007/08 season. Three seasons previously, Boro had been playing the likes of Barnet, but they would now be

travelling to Barton Town Old Boys. Then there was the small matter of where to call home; Scarborough Athletic had no ground. Thankfully, our friends down the coast at Bridlington Town stepped in and allowed us to play at their Queensgate base, where we still hold our home games as of 2009/10. In the club's second season, the 2008/09 campaign, Boro marched to the NCEL Division One title, accruing an incredible 92 points from 36 games, breaking the record by netting 121 times in the process and scoring four goals or more on 20 occasions in all competitions. Boro were thus promoted to the NCEL Premier Division, where they now stand proud amongst older comrades. The 500 or so fans who make the trip to Queensgate every other week are immensely proud of the new club. Of course, the main aim is to return to Scarborough so that the people of the town once again have a senior football club to support within the borough. For the time being though, Scarborough Athletic represent the town with professionalism, prid and footballing prowess. But most importantly of all, a bank balance which sits firmly in the black. Members pay anything from £12 a year to be part of the Trust, whereby they receive one vote and the right to stand for election.

Scarborough FC gave us many memories, but Scarborough Athletic is the future of football in the town.

Follow the club's progress at scarboroughathletic.com.

Football kits come of age

by john devlin

132 | Around the Grounds
Football kits come of age

At the heart of every football team's visual identity is their playing kit. By default it is the focus of the very action on the pitch that defines the game. It distinguishes a team and today, in the age of replica jerseys, also its supporters. In addition, the club kit of today has to co-exist with shirt sponsorship and manufacturers' logos along with ever-elaborate away strips that threaten to dilute a club's identity further.

Essentially, the main functions of a football kit are:
• to make its wearers conspicuous on the football field; and,
• to distinguish one team from another during a match.

Desmond Morris in his football psychology bible *The Soccer Tribe* also suggests that a kit has the additional job of making their wearers appear distinct from other teams in their locality (i.e. Manchester United in red, Manchester City in blue). He further claims that a kit should also give a team a psychological advantage over its opponents – a battle of colour as well as football.

Prior to the 2007 FA Cup, sponsors E.ON conducted a study that illustrated how important colour was to success on the football field and in business. Its findings revealed that the most successful colour worn by teams in the competition's history was red – sported by a third of winning clubs. In second place was blue, favoured by over a quarter. A spokesman for the study said, "it's already been proven that the colour of a sports shirt may be an important factor in players' performance… It could be that people subconsciously adopt the characteristics of these colours and in turn become more successful". These findings back up Desmond Morris' interpretations of colour theory in *The Soccer Tribe*. Morris explains that red is the most fearless, bold, strong and energetic of colours. It is the brightest to the human eye and therefore proclaims its wearers as courageous and dominant. When Bill

ARSENAL
AWAY KIT: 2007

Shankly instructed his Liverpool captain Ron Yeats to add red shorts to his red shirt in 1964, he exclaimed, on seeing Yeats stride on to the pitch in the new ensemble, "Christ son, you're so big that when you lead the team out, you'll frighten the opposition to death". So was born Liverpool's famous all-red strip that ushered in a period of unparalleled success.

The popularity of blue on the football field is harder to explain, although the colour's qualities of calmness and self-assured confidence are clearly vital to any successful side. The third most popular kit colour is white – the colour of heroes, pure and virtuous and worn famously by Real Madrid whose all-white outfit was adopted in 1961 by Leeds United manager Don Revie (more of him later).

The colours of most football clubs are so ingrained in their constitution that tampering with them too much can engage the wrath of the diehard fan. In 2007 when Arsenal launched a white away kit (see above) – the colour of their fellow North London rivals Tottenham Hotspur – many Gooners were up in arms at the thought of their heroes turning out in the same colour as their hated neighbours. Petitions were signed and angry blogs posted. Of course what many of them probably didn't appreciate was that historically

white had been a staple change colour of the club. It is only relatively recently that yellow has arrived as the side's favoured away hue.

Taking into consideration this sort of passion connected to club's colours along with a kit's role as the primary differentiation between two opposing teams, football strips in both form and function can almost be seen as modern day army uniforms. Take a glance at the British Army attire from between the late 17th and 19th centuries and compare it to a football kit – its bright primary colours, trimmings and epaulets, even the placement of medals and badges – all replicated today in stadiums throughout the country.

With the arrival of the first marketed replica shirts in the mid-seventies the notion of an army uniform was extended to the terraces and the playgrounds in the vicinity. Forget scarves and rosettes, now a fan could show, without any doubt, who he followed. He was part of the extended team, the tribe that formed his club, decked out in by a bold colour scheme designed to intimidate the opposition. Newcastle United fans will remember Tino Asprilla's goal celebration in the mid-nineties when he hoisted his shirt aloft onto a corner flag, waving it vigorously like a call to arms in front of the Toon terraces.

ENGLAND
REPLICA KIT: 1970S

MANCHESTER UNITED
THIRD KIT: 1992-1994

ARSENAL
AWAY KIT: 1991-1993

ENGLAND
HOME KIT: 2009

The sportswear manufacturer Admiral led the way in the seventies replica kit initiative, primarily thanks to Don Revie's brokering of a deal with the firm whilst manager of England. The relationship saw the plain and simple, heroic white of the national side now adorned with red and blue trim and the prominent placement of Admiral logos (see previous page). The team badge still had pride of place over the heart though. There was no turning back, the replica kit was born. The trend took a while to catch on. A glance through the club shop page of a mid-late seventies programme includes replica shirts way down the list of club-branded items after keyrings, teddy bears and even ladies panties! Initially it was only purchases for children that drove sales, hence the relative rarity today of vintage 1970s replica shirts in adult sizes. The replica shirt market could also be judged to be responsible for the temporary abandonment of tradition in football apparel at about this time. Regular stripes were considered passé and replaced by varying combinations of pinstripes, panels in varying widths and sashes – all aimed at a fashionable youth eager for varying patterns and designs.

The popularity of replica jerseys in England grew steadily though throughout the eighties, gaining momentum post Italia 90 with the birth of the Premier League. Soon, with the innovation of squad names and numbers, supporters could also proudly show their favourite player on their back (for a few more pounds of course – quite a lot more, if their favourite player is Jan Vennegoor of Hesselink). It was a genius move that further integrated club, players and supporters allowing fans to further identify with, and feel part of the team. It also brought in more valuable revenue for cash-strapped clubs.

The replica shirt phenomenon reached a peak in this country with Euro 96. England went football mad and it seemed for a period that everyone; men, women and children, owned a replica jersey (either current or retro). The nineties saw further developments in the football shirt world with club colours, away from home, beginning to change more frequently with long established colour schemes going out the window. There was increased marketing of replica third strips, giving supporters another way of supporting their team. Postmodern designs became the trend, typified by Manchester United's 1992-94 Umbro third kit (see above) that revived the yellow and green halved shirt of

their Newton Heath origins, complete with lace-up neck. Home strips didn't escape change either. Driven by fabric technology, shirts got bigger and baggier, reflecting high street fashions and, with the increase of adult shirt sales, accommodating supporters whose physiques didn't quite match that of their footballing heroes. Thanks to advancements in printing techniques, kits were now adorned with all manner of patterns, spots, splatters, watermarks and abstract designs. Arsenal's "bruised banana" away kit (1991-93) as manufactured by Adidas (see above), is a prime example. By the end of the decade in answer to increasing noises amongst supporters for traditional and basic kits, designs became more restrained. Nike have led the way in recent years with simple, stylish outfits that are often conceptual in nature. Umbro have also adopted this approach with their tailored range of classic, fitted shirts spearheaded by their 2009 England home jersey that jettisoned all unnecessary embellishments and trimming in favour of a plain, white top (see above).

In 1979 Liverpool became the first professional English side to have a shirt sponsor, that of Japanese electrical giants Hitachi (see opposite page). Despite the initial refusal of TV companies to televise games featuring sponsor shirts, the phenomenon grew. By the end of the decade virtually every club kit was sponsored.

Initially deals tended to be brokered with local companies who had some affinity with the club or larger multinational organizations that had offices in the locality.

Sometimes the parochial sponsorship was confusing. Supporters cannot fail to have been bemused by Bolton Wanderers turning up at their ground in the 1981/82 season sporting shirts with "BEN" emblazoned across the front. Anyone from the Bolton area though would have been able to tell the home fans that it was in fact an acronym for a local newspaper, the *Bolton Evening News*. Dangerously, on occasion the power of the sponsor encroaches on the design and colours, and therefore the tradition of the club. After failing to attract sponsorship for some time in the mid eighties Southend United resorted to incorporating yellow into their home kit at the request of incoming partners Laing, whose corporate identity included the colour. Similarly in 1995 Carlisle adopted the corporate palette of their new sponsors local haulage company Eddie Stobart into their away kit, creating a curious concoction of green, white, red and amber

LIVERPOOL HOME KIT: 1979

(see right). A brave initiative that highlighted the close bond between a world famous firm and its local team – or a financial sell-out that weakened the integrity and heritage of the club? Ed Horton in his book *Moving The Goalposts* points out that once we identified a team by its colours, now we recognize them by their shirt sponsors.

Sponsors have a massive part to play in the modern game, bringing in valuable funds to clubs. At the time of writing Liverpool have just signed a four-year deal with Standard Chartered bank said to be worth £80 million. Some deals can backfire though thanks to club loyalties. Some Spurs fans still refuse to buy JVC product thanks to the company's close sponsorship bond with Arsenal a decade and a half ago.

People outside the game may struggle to comprehend why anyone would want to wear a shirt promoting Samsung, Emirates or in the case of Clydebank's early nineties sponsorship deal, eighties pop band Wet Wet Wet, for free. Again, it's all part of showing allegiance. Fans have few qualms declaring that they support a side backed by a major company although many still yearn for the pre-sponsorship days of plain shirts.

From its earliest and simplest function, the football kit's remit has grown tremendously. It is no longer just required to determine one team from its opponents, it now also acts as a billboard for at least two additional companies. Plus it has a responsibility to earn its keep via the replica sales that link supporters directly to the team, giving them a sense of community in this ever-fractured society.

But the power and iconic status of the football shirt is growing further. Sometimes the shirt appears as a symbolic icon of hope, strength, tribute and unity in times of tragedy. In the early nineties Italian domestic teams took to the field in their opponents shirts before switching prior to kick off to speak out against a weekend of football hooliganism that caused deaths among supporters. Off the field, the devastating Soham murders

CARLISLE UNITED AWAY KIT: 1995

led David Beckham and Manchester United leading a special request for information after the two girls who were killed, Holly Wells and Jessica Chapman, were often shown in photographs wearing Manchester United shirts. Football shirts are also now being used to support charities with Everton issuing limited edition pink versions of their home shirts to promote the fight against breast cancer. Although never worn on the pitch, replica sales raised thousands for charity.

It is clear that the football kit has grown up and although it still needs to do its job during a match it now has social responsibilities a far cry from its duties on a pitch.

John Devlin has been obsessed with football kits since he was a boy. He is the author of the **True Colours** *series of books and the only archive of football kit history that includes all away and third kits in fine detail. Visit truecoloursfootballkits.com.*

LEYTON ORIENT

- **Nicknames** The O's, Orient
- **Founded** 1881
- **Ground** The Matchroom Stadium (opened 1937)
- **Address** Leyton, London E10 5NF
- **Capacity** 9,271
- **Best attendance** 38,219 vs Tottenham Hotspur, Division Two, 16 March, 1929
- **Contact** 0871-310 1881
- **Ticket Number** 0871-310 1883
- **Email** info@leytonorient.net
- **Website** leytonorient.com

RIVALS
Millwall, Southend United, West Ham, Brighton.

What's in a name? Well, you could ask that very question to Eldrick Woods, Lucy Johnson, Archibald Leach or Maurice Micklewhite. Or you could ask Leyton Orient. This is a team that was originally born as Glyn Cricket Club. Then changed its name to Orient Football Club in 1888. There is some debate about why, but the consensus seems to be that it has something to do with the Orient Shipping Line… or the East, as they are an East London team. Or maybe they entered some kind of footballing witness protection program because since then they have gone through a number of chameleon-like changes to Clapton Orient, Leyton Orient and then back to Orient again. Then, in 1987 they entered their final reincarnation – a bit like 'The Doctor' – as the Leyton Orient of today.

It has to be said that The Matchroom Stadium, although a very smart and modern ground, does have a slightly strange design. A bit like a giant bed, with a big green mattress and a block of flats at each corner acting as the bed posts. The Matchroom is named after chairman Barry Hearn's sports promotion company. As O fan and comedian Bob Mills said, "Chelsea has Roman Abramovich and his millions made from Russian oilfields and we've got Barry Hearn who does own a rather lucrative snooker hall in Ilford." When Hearn took over the club many expected a spending spree, but what he has done instead is steady the ship, and Orient, with its seafaring roots, is certainly on an even keel. With the 2012 Olympics around the corner rumours are rife of an Orient move to the Olympic Stadium.

So what's in a name? Well you could ask Tiger Woods, or Ava Gardner, Cary Grant or Michael Caine. Or you could ask Leyton Orient, a club with one of the most recognizable names in English football.

Greatest moments on this ground
"The play-off win over Hull City in 2001. Fantastic 30 yard winner from Lockwood allied to a truly brilliant atmosphere on the night." Jamie Stripe, *Leyton Orientear*.

Lowest moments on this ground
"Getting relegated in 1983/84 at home to Bournemouth. It was a 0-0 draw and more boring than the scoreline suggests. Summed up the campaign – boring/drab/terrible/pitiful… where's that number for the Samaritans?" Mat Roper, *Pandamonium*.

Heroes of the sideline
"Martin Ling. It's funny that he's not long been sacked, but he took the job when we were bottom of the basement league (with virtually no rank and file support) and got us promoted within three seasons. It was the first time Orient had gone up automatically in 36 years and we did it with skill, guts and more than a bit of flair thrown in. In the end his poor signings in summer 2008 laid the foundation for his departure." Jamie Stripe.

Heroes of the turf
"Terry Howard – Orient stalwart with a powerful strike and his own cheer. He always gave 100% and was at the club during a great period in the late eighties and early nineties. Steve Castle – another eighties legend. He was team captain for a few seasons and typified everything about supporting a lower league club player. He was committed, passionate and a real winner. Peter Kitchen – he knew where the net was, simple as that!" Mat Roper.

"Steve Parsons – my first O's hero. He played in the midfield and could pass, shoot and he oozed class. Brilliant bicycle kick to sink Wrexham in a home game February 1981. Alan Comfort – not the fastest winger but he had a deadly left foot shot and sublime dribbling skill. He shattered many fourth division defences from 1986-1989". Jamie Stripe.

VILLAINS
"As for unpopular players – well let's just say, when do you want to publish this book – 2013?" Mat Roper.

Zeroes of the turf
"David Hunt (spelt with a silent 'c'). Couldn't pass, read a game or run about for that matter. To make matters worse he wore silver boots, which automatically

makes him a 'wrong 'un'. He got sent off needlessly on more than one occasion. Paul Hague – Sitton allegedly paid money for this bloke, which is why he's never worked in football since. You could have placed a 6-ft pile of horse manure in the centre of Orient's defence and it would have done a better job." Jamie Stripe.

"Kwame Ampadu – ex-Arsenal youth who had a great deal of experience behind him. He could only ever go backwards, he couldn't run, pass, trap or dribble – he threw-in well mind! Sam Parkin – this lumpy centre-forward came with a record of one goal in three. He couldn't hit a cow's arse with a banjo and left with no goals in 13 games! Emmanuel Vasseur – French player who helped Calais (French Third Division) to a historic cup final. 200 minutes of appearances and was last seen heading back through the Blackwall and Channel Tunnels." Mat Roper.

That's quite interesting
"Orient is the only team to have played league home games at Wembley Stadium. Back in the early thirties we took on Southend and Brentford when our own pitch wasn't up to it." Jamie Stripe.

Not a lot of people know that
"The FA and League were close to charging the club with misconduct as for two seasons O's fans took literally tons of confetti, toilet rolls, balloons etc to away games. At Reading a number of back gardens behind the away end got covered in a paper snowstorm and at Burnley officials had to send out the youth team to clear the lines of the pitch before the game could start". Mat Roper.

The ground
Brisbane Road has been the home of the O's since 1937 when the club moved from Lea Bridge Stadium. The ground has undergone extensive modernization in the past 10 years and now has a capacity of over 9,000. There are four blocks of apartments, one at each corner of the ground.

The **West Stand** has a single tier of seating below a huge façade with a directors' balcony, Olympic Suite and gallery. It was finished in 2007 with a capacity of 2,918. The changing rooms are here. The **North Family Stand** is a new 1,351 seater behind the goal while the **East Stand**, with seating for 3,636 is the oldest stand at the ground dating back to the fifties. 1,459 away supporters are accommodated in the south wing of the East Stand. **The South Stand** offers excellent views and seating for 1,336 home fans, behind the goal.

"The *Club for a Fiver* film on Channel 4 in 1995. It was both excruciating and hilarious watching the club implode and John Sitton going mad at the same time." Jamie Stripe.

Getting there
By Road/Parking Follow the M25 to junction 27, exit onto the M11 towards London. Take the right fork onto the North Circular Road/A406. As the roads merge, take the A104 exit towards Walthamstow/Woodford/A503. At the roundabout take the first exit onto the A104 and follow. At the next roundabout stay on the A104/Lea Bridge Road and follow for less than a mile, turn left onto Leyton Green Road and left again past East London Bus Company depot. Go left onto High Road Leyton and continue along for about a mile, go right onto Osborne Road, the stadium is dead ahead. Parking is in side streets.

By Train The nearest tube station is Leyton, Central Line (red). Exit the station, turn right onto Leyton High Road – from here it is a 10 minute walk, floodlights will be visible on the left.

Pubs for home fans
Leyton Orient Supporters' Club, West Stand, Matchroom Stadium is an excellent CAMRA award-winning club/bar serving up a great selection of hand-pumped real ales, bottled ales, and the usual lagers too. Sandwiches also available.

Good food near ground
There are a number of cafés along High Road Leyton including The Two Eagles greasy spoon near the tube. Further along the road (closer to Walthamstow Central Tube) The William IV is excellent, serving decent Thai food and ales.

Pubs for away fans
The Birkbeck Tavern, Langthorne Road is just round the corner from the tube, a 10-minute walk to the ground and the best pub in the area, with a good atmosphere and a rotating list of guest ales. Popular with home and away fans. Coach and Horses, High Road is literally round the corner from the ground. Family friendly, huge with Sky Sports and packed on match days.

Top tips
Watch out for match-day parking restrictions – local traffic wardens are vigilant and show little mercy.

THE LAST
WORD

leytonorientear.com
pandamonium fanzine

LINCOLN CITY

RIVALS

Mansfield Town, Peterborough, Grimsby, Boston United and Scunthorpe United.

- ⊘ **Nicknames** The Imps, The Red Imps
- ⊙ **Founded** 1884
- ⊙ **Ground** Sincil Bank (opened 1895)
- ⊙ **Address** Sincil Bank Stadium, Lincoln LN5 8LD
- ⊙ **Capacity** 10,120
- ⊗ **Best attendance** 23,196 vs Derby, League Cup 4th round, 15 November, 1967
- ⊙ **Contact** 01522-880011
- ⊙ **Ticket Number** 01522-880011
- @ **Email** lcfc@redimps.com
- Ⓦ **Website** redimps.com

Pubs for home fans
The 'Trust Suite' social club at the ground is open before all matches with Sky Sports TV and 'Lincoln City Hot Pork Roll', away fans also welcome. City Vaults, High Street, is five minutes from the ground so gets packed out on match days, bar food available, can get rowdy. The Blue Anchor, High Street is another home fans' favourite.

Good food near ground
All the big fast-food players feature on the High Street as well as some decent chippies. Alternatively wait until the ground and snag a pork roll at the supporters' club bar.

Pubs for away fans
The Golden Eagle, High Street is draped in footie memorabilia with a TV screen, pub grub and a cracking selection of real ales. The Portland, Portland Street, five minutes from the ground, is enroute from the station with decent beers and pub grub. The usual suspects are also present, including Weatherspoons who welcome visiting fans.

Top tips
Best to give the City Vaults a wide berth, especially if wearing colours.

Play-offs. You either love them or hate them. If your team snatches promotion at Wembley from an unpromising sixth place league finish, they are a godsend. If you finish third by a country mile and lose out, you feel cheated and cursed. Lincoln City fans know all about the play-offs. Five consecutive play-offs, five consecutive failures. This has to rank up there with the most unwanted of league records. In May 2003 they reached the final at the Millenium Stadium only to be thumped by Bournemouth 5-2. In 2004 they lost to Huddersfield in the semi-finals by a solitary goal and the following year to Southend in the final on another day of pain in Cardiff. The team fell at the semi-final stage in 2006 when they were edged out by local rivals Grimsby. Many hoped the Cardiff jinx would be broken when the final returned to Wembley in 2007, but a strong Bristol Rovers side denied them a day out in London over the two legs of the semi.

Yet Lincoln fans still have plenty to bang their drums about – and bang their drums they will. The Imps have a vocal and passionate following, embodied by the 'Passionistas' supporters group. Ensconced in the Stacey-West Stand, their vocal support, complete with percussion, helps raise the spirit in the ground and make it one of the most enjoyable in the division to visit. And if Lincoln do score, then a rousing blast of the 'Dam Busters' theme will get everyone aeroplaning along.

Greatest moments on this ground
"Well, previous historical moments include winning the 1975/76 title at a canter, as well as City promoted back to the League after only a season in the Conference. My personal favourite moment came at the end of the 2002/03 season. We were going into the final game on the verge of the play-offs, not bad for the team

guaranteed for relegation according to 99% of people. With five minutes to go we were looking down and out, losing 1-0 to Torquay, and Oxford were going to overtake us. Up steps Simon Yeo, hadn't scored for seven months, and he volleyed us into the play-offs." Nathan Jackson, editor, theImps.ka.

Lowest moments on this ground
"The final home game of the 2001/02 season was a sad one as it looked certain we wouldn't have a club anymore. We had entered administration and owed God knows how much money, so the final game was a bit of a goodbye to the club. Luckily it turned out not to be the case, but that was always my least fond memory at Sincil Bank." Nathan Jackson.

Heroes of the sideline
"Keith Alexander, and not just because of the results he produced on the field. He is one of the true gentleman of the game and I will always remember him for his attitude off the pitch. I remember going for the weekend in Bournemouth in 2002/03 and Alexander came back on a supporters' coach and spent time with all the fans to get to know them. Former manager, Peter Jackson, is also a legend… in his own mind." Nathan Jackson.

Zeroes of the tuf

"Not many players come to Sincil Bank with the reputation for being good. Lincoln City is the type of club where players who could be underachievers don't really come. However, I could include the majority of our squad during the period of 2007-2009." Nathan Jackson.

Don't mention the…

"The obvious one would be our record in the play-offs." Nathan Jackson.

Villains

"Ben Futcher, he was a good defender and could score a fair few goals. In 2005 he announced he was going to progress his career… a few days later he showed up at Boston United, a team who have never finished in a position higher than us. Many felt he only went for the money. He left Boston halfway through the season and joined Grimsby, eventually scoring the goal that put us out of the play-offs at the end of the year. Also Peter Gain and Leon Mettam." Nathan Jackson.

The ground

Lincoln were early leaders in ground redevelopments in the wake of the Bradford City fire disaster, probably spurred on by the fact that they were the opponents on 11 May, 1985. Two Lincoln supporters were among the dead and they are commemorated by the **Stacey-West Stand** behind the goal, which is named after them. The **Lincolnshire Co-Operative Stand** is located on the Sincil Bank side of the ground and holds around 5,700 supporters all seated in a single tier. Away fans are usually housed in an end section of this stand. The **Lincolnshire Echo Stand** opposite is a tall, narrow structure that doesn't run the full length of the pitch but straddles

the halfway line. To its right is the smaller Family Stand, separated from its larger sibling by the players' tunnel. Behind the far goal sits the small **IMPS Stand**, which was built in 1992 and also houses Executive Boxes.

Getting there

By Road/Parking From the south take the A1 north until the A46. Follow the A46 until Hykeham roundabout and signs for the city centre onto High Street. Turn right onto Scorer Street and right onto Cross Street. From the North take the A15 or A57 to Lincoln City centre and on to the High Street. Left onto Scorer Street and right onto Cross Street. Street parking is not a problem near the ground.

By Train Lincoln Central Station is about a 10-minute walk to the ground. Turn left out of the station and left onto the High Street going over the level crossing. Continue up the high street passing, if you can, the pubs along the way. Take the seventh left into Scorer Street and right into Sincil Bank.

theimps.tk
lincolncity-mad.co.uk
lincoln.vitalfootball.co.uk
theimp.lincolnfans.co.uk

> Scott Kerr at Sincil Bank.

That's quite interesting
"We had a player a few years ago called Jamie McCombe, a brilliant defender who admitted one day to the paper that he wore the same underwear to every game. He became our Captain and when he scored, would occasionally flash his underwear at sections of the crowd who used to chant 'Jamie, Jamie show us your pants." Nathan Jackson.

Not a lot of people know that
"We were the first team to win at Hull City's new KC Stadium." Nathan Jackson.

GETTY IMAGES

HOME COLOURS

LIVERPOOL

RIVALS
Manchester
United, Everton
and Arsenal.

- ⊖ **Nicknames** The Reds
- ⊕ **Founded** 1892
- ⊕ **Ground** Anfield (opened 1884)
- ⓘ **Address** Anfield Road, Anfield, Liverpool, Merseyside L4 0TH
- ⊕ **Capacity** 45,362
- ⊕ **Best attendance** 61,905 vs Wolves, FA Cup 5th round, 2 February, 1952
- ⊕ **Contact** 0151-263 2361
- ⊕ **Ticket Number** 0844-844 0844
- @ **Email** customerservices@liverpoolfc.tv
- Ⓦ **Website** liverpoolfc.tv

Most fans can boast of or hark back to a golden era. A time when their team played dream football, enjoyed a period of sustained success or were at least stylish and exciting in glorious defeat. For Tottenham fans there was the Bill Nicholson era, for followers of Leeds the reign of 'Sir' Don Revie is revered. Arsenal are revelling in the reign of Arsène Wenger, while Sir Alex transformed an erratic Old Trafford team into two-time European champions. However, Liverpool fans will feel they are blessed to be able to choose from more than one golden moment. For a start, there was the reign of Bill Shankly, the man who turned the club around, brought them back to the top tier, and established a style of play, a taste for success and a footballing dynasty that would serve the club well for decades. He brought three League titles, two FA Cups and one Uefa Cup to the club while also establishing the Boot Room, an inner circle of coaching staff. Upon his retirement, his successor rose from within those hallowed walls. Bob Paisley was a Liverpool man through and through. The Reds were the only team he ever played for, and the only team he ever managed. His figures – three European Cups, six League titles, three League Cups, one Uefa and one Super Cup. He is still England's most successful manager ever. But more than that he established a squad of household names and a style of play that conquered not just England, but Europe too. His successor Joe Fagan was another Boot Room stalwart who kept up the winning ways, packing the Anfield trophy cabinet with yet more European and English silver. When Fagan stepped down, there was really only one choice, Kenny Dalglish, Paisley's star striker and keeper of the Boot Room flame. King Kenny was an Anfield legend already; his managerial success only cemented his status. The European ban denied the Scot a chance at European trophies, but he did win three League titles and two FA Cups before his shock retirement in 1991.

The hallowed Anfield ground has always been the engine room of the Liverpool steamer, and stoking the passion of many unforgettable nights is the Kop. *THE* Kop. While other grounds may have a stand bearing the same title, there really is only the one. Its origins lie far away and in bitter conflict – more bitter than any mere local derby. The East Lancashire Regiment, made up mostly of men from Liverpool, fought a hard campaign in the Boer War. One of their great battles involved defending a hill – the name of that ridge in South Africa? The Spion Kop. The name was carried home by the returning men and given to the huge banked terrace at Anfield, one of the largest stands in the world at the time.

A stand that huge needed an anthem of allegiance. And while there are many good football songs, few teams boast one that is truly anthemic and even fewer can really rival the one that rings around the terraces of Anfield. 'You'll Never Walk Alone' has taken on an altogether deeper meaning after the fateful events at Heysel and Hillsborough, it's not only a rousing chorus but has become an enviable, unifying force. When the words ring out from the faithful, they are more than just fans and players – for those 90 minutes they are family. John Maguire of *Boss Mag* (fanzine) sums it up, "Anfield, The Kop, semi-final of the European Cup 2005 against Chelsea. The place was quite literally bouncing. Roman Abromivich must've just looked around and thought to himself, 'I've got all the money in the world, I can buy any player I want, but how the f*** can I get myself a crowd like this?' The answer is, Roman, "Ye can't!"

Greatest moments on this ground

"Thankfully there have been many great moments at Anfield but our game against Saint-Étienne back in 1977 has gone down in legend and is still considered to be our greatest ever in terms of atmosphere. Second leg of our

PUB QUIZ

That's quite interesting
"We used to win the League every May." John Maguire.

Not a lot of people know that
The flagpole at Flagpole Corner has been in position since about 1906 and is the oldest artefact at Anfield and the assembly point of the Red All Over The Land team." John Pearman.
The flagpole was originally a mast from Brunel's SS Great Eastern, one of the first-ever iron-clad ships and six times bigger than the next largest, broken up in the Mersey shipyards in 1889.

Storm over Anfield.
Famous sign in players tunnel.

European Cup quarter-final, we had lost the first 1-0, tens of thousands of Liverpool fans turned up to cheer our boys on and many thousands more were locked outside of the ground. With only minutes played Liverpool scored, the tie was now at 1-1, but despite dominating the rest of the half Saint-Étienne's stubborn defence kept the Reds at bay. Liverpool pressed on again in the second half but were then rocked when the French scored a stunning long-range goal to give themselves a 2-1 lead in the tie and the comfort of an away goal, which meant Liverpool had to score twice to go through. Time and again the Reds pressed forward cheered on by the Kop, but the French champions held firm until about 15 minutes from the end when Ray Kennedy brought the tie back to 2-2. The atmosphere in the ground

was building all the time as Liverpool pushed forward for a winner – then Bob Paisley sent on our super-sub David Fairclough. This proved to be a master stroke, with just minutes left he burst through and finished brilliantly to put Liverpool 3-2 ahead in the tie and the place went absolutely ballistic!

Liverpool went on to lift the European Cup for the first time that year but even now when I see that old footage of Fairclough's goal, it makes the hair on the back of my neck stand up. That for me was the greatest moment at Anfield and the night that The Kop sucked the ball into the net!" Gerry Ormonde, Kop Blog.

VILLAINS

"Michael Owen – money-grabbing little so and so did a runner before Rafa had even unpacked and we got Antonio Nunez [who?] and £8 million and now he's sold his soul and gone to Old Trafford. Car boot sales will be awash with Owen memorabilia, anybody want to buy a DVD?" John Pearman.

Lowest moments on this ground

"It's got to be our 2-0 defeat by Arsenal in the final game of the 1988/89 season. All we had to do was to avoid being beaten by a two goal margin to stay ahead and take the title. I'm convinced that had we gone into that game needing a victory, we would have beaten them, but our players seemed to be caught in two minds about whether they should just sit back and defend or go forward. We were very sloppy in our play. In fairness to Arsenal they knew exactly what they had to do and managed to get the victory they required with two heart-breakingly late goals. In my nightmares I can still hear that Brian Moore commentary of Michael Thomas breaking through our defence deep into injury time and scoring to put them 2-0 up and win them the title. That was a tough loss to take and I was depressed for a long time afterwards. To make matters worse, that game also launched the writing career of Nick Hornby and I'm not sure which is more painful!" Gerry Ormonde.

Heroes of the sideline

"Shankly – LFC were Second Division mid-table mediocrity. Then in December 1959, a Scottish man walked through our gates and went on to create the greatest story ever told. Paisley – in his nine seasons in charge of the Redmen, we won the European Cup three times, six League titles (finished second twice), three League Cups, one Uefa Cup, one European Super Cup and five Charity Shields. Total Domination. Dalglish – on and off the pitch – a giant of a man." John Maguire.

Heroes of the turf

"Ian Rush – the greatest goal-scorer of them all, scored all types of goals and worked for the team defending from the front. Graeme Souness – tough as nails and a great captain. John Barnes – some said he never delivered in an England shirt, but he certainly had no problem in a Liverpool one. Awesome on his day and the most skillful player I've ever seen. Steven Gerrard – there have been times when he has practically had to carry the side. The best of his type in the world and has pulled our asses out of the fire so many times that I think he should play with a fireman's helmet on! Kenny Dalglish – we have had many heroes and legends over the years, but there's only ever been one king. Kenny was quite simply the best player I've ever seen in a red shirt, nuff said!" Gerry Ormonde.

> Liverpool team of 1976 under Bob Paisley.

< Liverpool legend Stevie G.

GETTY IMAGES

Photo credit: BOB THOMAS/GETTY IMAGES

"White suits at Wembley in 1996, More The Palm Court Orchestra than Liverpool FC."
John Pearman.

Zeroes of the turf

"One of our worst was Harry Kewell. There is no denying the guy had the ability when he bothered to show it and he seemed an exciting signing. He had a decent enough first season but the rest of his time he was a waste of space. People usually tend to wait until they're dead before donating their bodies to medical science but this clown obviously wanted to get in early. He was almost constantly injured with all kinds of mysterious ailments that sometimes baffled the medical staff at the club. Amazingly, if we managed to get to a major final he would always somehow manage to recover just in time." Gerry Ormonde.

"El Hadji Diouf, Bruno Cheyrou and Salif Diao. They were supposed to be the new Henry, Zidane and Vieira but turned out to be an unfunny version of the Three Stooges." John Pearman, Red All Over the Land.

The ground

The noise generated at Anfield make this one of the most exciting grounds to visit. The two-tier **Centenary Stand** that runs the length of the pitch was renamed after the anniversary a total capacity of 11,762 including a row of executive boxes. The **Anfield Road Stand** is a two-tier stand behind the goal where away fans sit. It has a capacity 9,074 and is the end that the Shankley Gates and Hillsborough Memorial are situated. The **Main Stand** houses dressing rooms, the directors' box and a single tier of seating, (there are a couple of pillars) and a total of 12,277 seats are available including those in the Paddock. Behind the far goal lies **The Kop**, at one time a single terrace that could hold over 30,000 spectators. Its reduced capacity of 12,409 seats still makes it the largest single-tier stand in Europe. Anfield is illuminated by rows of lights fixed to the front edge of the two side stands.

Getting there

By Road/Parking Anfield is north of the city centre. Follow the M62 to its conclusion and go onto the A5058/Queen's Drive Stonecroft (Liverpool), follow for three miles. Take a left turn onto Utting Avenue, and a right for the Anfield Road and the ground. (Arkles Pub on corner.) From the M6, exit at junction 28. Limited street parking for early arrivals.

By Train Liverpool's main line station Lime Street is three miles to the ground, but onward busses run close to the ground (Arriva 26), see transportdirect.info for details. Reached via connecting train at Liverpool Central, Sandhills train station is closer – 1.5 miles to the ground with Soccerbus service.

HOME
AWAY

Pubs for home fans
Depending on what sort of pre-match banter you're after, John Mackin editor of raotl.co.uk has a few suggestions: "The obvious one is The Albert next to The Kop, packed with memorabilia, but small and gets incredibly busy. The Salisbury is re-opening shortly and should be good, but we won't know until it opens. (Both Walton Breck Road). Close by, The Flat Iron, can be busy but nowhere near as packed full of 'tourists'. Good conversation about the game, rather than the shouting and singing of The Albert can be found here." Also try The Park , opposite The Albert.

Good food near ground
There are a plethora of burger bars and takeaway joints close by.

Pubs for away fans
The Arkles, Anfield Road is the established away supporters' pub. Being close to the ground it does get packed out (queues are a common theme here).

Top tips
Make time to visit the memorial to the Hillsborough disaster.

THE LAST WORD

thisisanfield.com/kopblog
bossmag.co.uk
raotl.co.uk
redwhiteandkop.com
spiritofshankly.com
redallovertheland.sports.officelive.com

HOME COLOURS

- **Nicknames** The Silkmen
- **Founded** 1874
- **Ground** Moss Rose (opened 1891)
- **Address** London Road, Macclesfield, Cheshire, SK11 7SP
- **Capacity** 6,335
- **Best attendance** 9,003 vs Winsford United, Cheshire Cup 2nd round, 4 Feburary, 1948
- **Contact** 01625-264686
- **Ticket Number** 01625-264686
- **Email** office@mtfc.co.uk
- **Website** mtfc.co.uk

MACCLESFIELD TOWN

PUB QUIZ

That's quite interesting
"Macclesfield are owned by the Iraqi Kurd Al Khadi brothers." Matt Beresford.

Not a lot of people know that
"John Rooney, who currently plays for Macclefield, is the younger brother of England star Wayne." Matt Beresford.

Not many teams would look on a 6-1 drubbing with fond memories. There are few fans who would rank such a beating amongst their greatest highlights, but Macclesfield Town supporters look upon this scoreline with a wistful sigh and a feeling of pride. In January 2007 the Silkmen travelled to Stamford Bridge to take on José Mourinho's Chelsea in the FA Cup 3rd round. It was a massive day for the team. Bottom of the Football League, they were taking on the English champions and one of the best teams in Europe. A team valued at £40k against a squad with a street value of £220m. It was all going so well when John Murphy equalized after Frank Lampard had given the home side the lead. The Macclesfield faithful went ballistic. But the gods of football were not with the Silkmen that day. Andriy Shevchenko stumbled in the box under a challenge from the keeper and the ref went for his pocket – red card. A harsh red card. Keeper Tommy Lee was off and with no replacement on the bench, the team from Cheshire was forced to play the rest of the game not only with 10 men, but with defender and captain Dave Morley in goal. The team was further hampered when John Miles was injured and, having used all their subs, the team was reduced to nine men.

It is a testament to The Silkmen and their fans that they can look past the score, to the underlying heart and passion that the team showed, the resolve and determination to keep going when the odds turned against them. It was that fire that ultimately kept the club up that year and proved a foundation to build on.

Macclesfield sit in an area where they face fierce competition for fans from other, larger, northwest teams nearby. But they have benefitted by attracting some ex-Manchester United players to the club, both as players and managers. Sammy McIlroy became a Macclesfield legend guiding the club from the Conference to the second tier of the Football League in the late nineties, followed by ex-United player Peter Davenport and more recently Paul Ince. Former Manchester City players who've taken up the managerial role include Ian Brightwell and assistant Asa Hartford. There are also promising signs of a move to a new stadium sometime in the future as part of England's World Cup bid, which could help the Silkmen attract a larger fanbase and build for the future.

Greatest moments on this ground
"When we beat Chester City at home 3-2 in the 1997/98 season to secure promotion to the third tier. The ground was absolutely rammed that day and the atmosphere was electric. To gain back-to-back promotions was really some achievement and it meant we won the right to play Man City in a League match the following season." Matt Beresford, *Wraggs to Riches*, maccfans.co.uk.

Lowest moments on this ground
"Coming out of the Dartford game on 15 April, 1989. We'd just beat them 4-1 in the first leg of the FA Trophy semi-final and virtually booked a place at Wembley only to then go home and watch the horrendous scenes unfold at Hillsborough. It was a time we should have been celebrating, but instead our thoughts were elsewhere. I always remember that day with sadness." Matt Beresford.

Heroes of the sideline
"Sammy McIlroy. Without this guy Macc would still be meandering around the lower reaches of the Conference. Peter Wragg – 'Wraggy' – an absolute character and would have supporters in stitches. Signed some quality players as well during his time; the likes of Paul Lake, Stevie Burr and John Askey to name but a few." Matt Beresford.

Zeroes of the turf
"Andrėjus Tereškinas was the biggest let-down since Geraldo Rivera opened Al Capone's vault. He meandered

> Moss Rose.

RICHARD STANTON/ MACCLESFIELD TOWN

HEROES OR ZEROES?

⌃ HEROES OF THE TURF

"John Askey was the greatest player I've seen in a Macc shirt. Served for over 20 years and rightly deserves his legend status. Steve Burr was probably the best striker Macc have ever had. Had the knack of always being in the right place at the right time and was absolutely lethal in one-on-one situations. Steve Wood popped up with some really important goals and is probably best remembered for THAT free kick at Stevenage in 1997. Chris Byrne, a naturally gifted player. He would go past people on the pitch as if they weren't even there and some of his goals are still talked about to this day. Phil Power – the 'Maltese Falcon' – signed in 1993 and won every honour possible in non-league football before helping the Silkmen finish runners-up in their inaugural season in the Football League." Matt Beresford.

hopelessly around the pitch, barely touched the ball and was met by a chorus of boos from the Macc faithful. Kevin Sandwith was a ponderously slow left-wing-back. He made an underwhelming debut against Leyton Orient, getting skinned within two minutes, and regularly thereafter left for dead by speedy wingers. Matt Haddrell was one of David Moss's "ones for the future." He certainly made a promising start. But he never progressed." Matt Beresford.

Villains
If Macclesfield qualify for Europe and that Shevchenko is playing, he can expect to be roundly booed.

Don't mention the…
2009/10 season, when Macclesfield had the second lowest home average attendance in the Football League, at 1,934. Only Darlington were lower.

The ground
Moss Rose has gone through a series of improvements since the non-league days prior to 1997, but it hasn't lost its charm – it's one of the country's most intimate grounds. It retains a good balance of modern terraces and smart seating. The London Road side has a central **Main Stand** with covered seating, flanked on both sides with open terraces. The raised, covered seating area can house 563 fans with no obstructing pillars and offering a great view of the pitch. The terrace has room for up to 1371 but is open to the elements. Behind one of the goals is the **Star Lane End**, an unusual mix of four or five rows of seating for 486 fans backed by a covered terrace that can accommodate 835. This is where the noisiest of the home support gathers, and they can generate a great atmosphere. The **Alfred McAlpine Stand** is a modern, single tier of seating with a high roof and executive boxes at the back. It has a capacity

of 1,550 but is pretty spacious with no pillars. Finally, behind the far goal is the open Silkmen Terrace, with room for 1,530 visiting fans, but wrap up in the winter. There are also about 400 seats in the covered McAlpine stands allocated to away fans as well.

Getting there
By Road/Parking With the M6 to the west, the M1 to the east, Manchester to the north and Birmingham to the south, Macclesfield has good links to the rest of the country. From north or south, the easiest route is via M6, exiting junction 17 onto the A534 signed Congleton and follow. At Congleton follow signs for A54 Buxton, turning left at signs for A523 Macclesfield, ground will be on left. Street parking.

By Train Macclesfied Rail Station is a mile and-a-half walk from the ground. On leaving the station turn left onto Sunderland Street and follow the road until the traffic lights. Turn left onto Mill Lane and carry straight on, ground will be on your right.

Pubs for home fans
"The President's Bar at the ground is a good one," recommends Matt Beresford. Just west of Moss Rose, the Golden Lion on Moss Lane is the closest pub to the ground and usually has a happy mix of home and away support.

Good food near ground
Close to the Waters Green Tavern, west of the station is a McDonald's on Mill Street. On route to the ground, Mill Lane Chippy, is a cracking choice as is its next door neighbour, The Rainbow Café, which does a great line in greasy spoon fare (but only till 1pm on Saturdays).

Pubs for away fans
By the station, Waters Green Tavern, Waters Green, has a decent number of real ales and is handily placed to revive after a long journey. Between station and stadium and just off the main A523, The Railway View, Byrons Lane, also a good range of well kept ales and a beer garden. A popular spot for home and away crowds.

Top tips
Be aware that the number of pubs close to the ground are fairly limited.

THE LAST WORD

maccfans.co.uk
macclesfield.vitalfootball.co.uk

- **Nicknames** City, The Blues
- **Founded** 1880
- **Ground** The City of Manchester Stadium (opened 2003)
- **Address** Sportcity, Manchester M11 3FF
- **Capacity** 48,000
- **Best attendance** 47,348 vs Chelsea, Premier League, 14 March, 2008
- **Contact** 0870-062 1894
- **Ticket Number** 0870-062 1894
- **Email** mcfc@mcfc.co.uk
- **Website** mcfc.co.uk

MANCHESTER CITY

S ure, it's a bit of cliché to say it always rains in Manchester, but City fans could certainly describe their team's footballing history as a series of scattered showers and occasional thundery downpours with the odd bright spell. The great Joe Mercer made City one of the best teams in the land, bringing blue skies and a League title, the FA and League Cup, as well as a European Cup Winners Cup to Maine Road. Then there was Malcolm Allison standing in front of a metaphorical weather chart, cigar in one hand, pointer in the other, explaining how the record £1.4 million purchase of Steve Daley would lead to warm, southwesterly breezes helping them sail up the League and to prolonged outbreaks of silverware. Instead, crowds were treated to Siberian easterlies and rapidly cooling reputations as Daley blazed shots from five yards high over the bar. No wonder Allison needed that sheepskin coat. In 1998 City managed to mirror Britain's dull, wetter than average weather with Frank Clark overseeing a slide towards relegation to the third tier – the first time a team that had brought home European silverware had sunk so low.

But if football has a karmic wheel then City must be the living proof. Having dusted themselves down, rebuilt and climbed back up the League, the blue half of Manchester must now be counting their blessings. In football, 10 years can be a very long time if things are going badly – or it can go by very quickly when life is on the up, and for Manchester City a lot has happened in the past decade. In 2003 the club moved to the Eastlands site and the City of Manchester Stadium, a majestic all-seater with a capacity of 48,000. The stadium was originally built for the Commonwealth Games but was extensively remodelled into an architectural amphitheatre that has the feel of one of the country's great stadiums, complete with spiral ramps and a suspended roof. After many false dawns, the club has new owners with deep pockets who are

assembling a squad of dream-team players. A decade ago not many would have wagered that a star Argentinean striker would choose to leave the offer of a lucrative Old Trafford contract to pull on the blue jersey across town, but those days have arrived. When Messrs Hansen, Lineker and Lawrenson lounge around the *Match of the Day* studio forecasting the outlook for the season ahead, they seem to agree that the blue side of Manchester is most definitely entering a prolonged bright spell.

Heroes of the sideline

"Joe Mercer – unquestionably City's greatest-ever manager, he led us through the successes of the late sixties, before being forced out by his assistant, Malcolm Allison. The road leading up to Eastlands is now known as 'Joe Mercer Way'. Tony Book was the legendary captain of the Mercer era who came back to manage in the late seventies, presiding over the 1976 League Cup win. He filled in as caretaker in 1993." Jack Pitt-Brooke, editor of *The Lonesome Death of Roy Carroll*.

Heroes of the turf

"Bert Trautmann, a great goalkeeper; Alex Harley who scored 30 goals in a relegation season, 1962/63; Mike Summerbee, for changing the attitude of City; Colin Bell who was the complete footballer and Joe Corrigan for overcoming early stick to become an England

PUB QUIZ

That's quite interesting
"City legend Shaun Goater is honoured every 21 June in his native Bermuda on 'Shaun Goater Day'. 'The Goat' scored 103 goals in 212 games for City." Jack Pitt-Brooke. "Maine Road holds the record English attendance of 84,569 for any game other than Wembley." Ric Turner.

Not a lot of people know that
"City were once relegated whilst defending their League title." Ric Turner.

RIVALS

Every other rivalry pales when compared to Manchester United.

∧ City legend 'Franny' Lee.
❮ City of Manchester Stadium, built for the Commonwealth Games, transformed into the home of City.

international. I'll add in Andy Morrison for giving us the spirit to get out of the old Third division." Dave Wallace, King of the Kippax.

"Georgi Kinkladze – the only bright light in the otherwise dismal nineties, he was brought by Alan Ball from Dinamo Tblisi and gave us three glorious years of skill, including a goal against Southampton that is still worth finding on YouTube." Jack Pitt-Brooke.

"Colin Bell, the greatest player ever to pull on the sky blue shirt. Frank Swift, England's finest ever goalkeeper who sadly passed away in the Munich air disaster, and Alan Oakes, the most decorated player in City's history, he also holds the record number of appearances for the club." Ric Turner, bluemoon-mcfc.co.uk.

Zeroes of the turf

"Lee Bradbury – Frank Clark paid £3 mn for him in 1997 but he scored only 10 goals in a season and half, and was sold to Crystal Palace for half of what we paid for him. Wittily dubbed 'Lee Badbuy' by fans. George Weah – the former Italian league, French league and Ballon d'Or winner came to City in 2000, but left when kept out of the team by Paul Dickov." Jack Pitt-Brooke.

"Martin 'Buster' Phillips – Alan Ball said he'd become the first £10 mn player in Britain, only to sell him for a hundreth of the amount the following year." Ric Turner.

Greatest moments on this ground

"The 5-1 derby victory in 1989. United had spent heavily on the likes of Paul Ince that summer, whereas our team

◄ Keith Curle gives Eric a special Man City welcome.

► Carlos Tevez, symbol of the new City era.

Pubs for home fans
Just around the corner from MUFC is Mary D'Bemish Bar in Grey Mare Lane. It's a real sports pub with screens and an excellent match-day vibe. Food also available. By Piccadilly Station, The Bulls Head, London Road has a pre-match buzz, bar meals and hand-pulled ales.

Good food near ground
Get a bite to eat at one of the cafés in the Printworks (they have everything there from Nandos to Wagamama). Near the ground on Ashton New Road is a handy Asda for picking up snacks.

Pubs for away fans
Not masses of choice round the ground, a better alternative is to head for the city centre to Exchange Square and The Printworks leisure complex, which has a range of bars, cafés, pubs and restaurants. Tram links from Piccadilly and close to Victoria train stations. Closer to he ground The Bradford Inn, Bradford Road, is friendly and popular with away supporters.

Top tips
The police are not afraid to utilize Section 27 to send home whole groups of rowdy fans pre-match, so mind how you go in the city.

was largely made up of graduates from the 1986 FA Youth Cup winning side (Paul Lake, David White, Andy Hincliffe, Steve Redmond and Ian Brightwell). No one gave us a chance that day, but a memorable performance saw us completely outplay United. The fifth goal, scored by Hinchliffe, in front of an emptying away end was aesthetically beautiful." Ric Turner, bluemoon-mcfc.co.uk.

Lowest moments on this ground
"Probably winning 5-2 at Stoke but being relegated to the third tier of football, below Crewe, Bury and Stockport in 1998." Dave Wallace, King of the Kippax.

The ground
The City of Manchester Stadium is a wonderful oval sweep of stands surrounding a sunken pitch, excavated to remove the running track from the Commonwealth Games stadium and allow an extra tier of seating to be added, bringing the crowd nearer to the action and increasing

VILLAINS
"Joey Barton, guaranteed a bad reception after assaulting Ousmane Dabo in training and repeatedly dragging the club's name through the dirt in his time at City." Jack Pitt-Brooke.
"Manager Howard Kendall leaving City (his mistress) to go back to Everton (his boring wife)." Dave Wallace.

the capacity. There is a lip of Perspex on the inside edge of the roof, and a band around the top of the stand to let more light into the arena. **The East Stand** (the Kippax) is a three-tier side of the ground, part of the continual sweep of seating. There is a row of executive boxes between the second and third tier. The second steeper-tier overhangs the lower tier slightly. **The Colin Bell Stand** opposite is identical. Behind the goals are the two-tier **North Stand** and the identical **Key 103 Stand** (South Stand). A section of The Key 103 Stand houses away fans – between 3,000 to 4,500.

Getting there

By Road/Parking The ground is east of the city centre. Exit the M60 at junction 23 onto the A635 (towards Manchester). Take the A662 turning for Manchester (Droylsden Rd) and follow for around three miles. The ground will be on your right. Parking restrictions on the residential roads Around the Grounds apply in about

a mile radius. Nearby pubs including Mary D's and Manchester offer match-day parking for around £5. A number of other unofficial car park also operate around Ashton Road for around £5, as well as at Ravensbury Primary school round the corner.

By Train Manchester Piccadilly is around a 25-minute walk to the ground. Victoria is about 30-minute walk. Smaller Ashburys station is south of the stadium – around a 15-minute walk (follow the A6010 north).

GETTY IMAGES

HOME COLOURS

MANCHESTER UNITED

RIVALS

Manchester City, Liverpool, Leeds United, Arsenal and Chelsea.

- ⊖ **Nicknames** United, Red Devils
- ⊕ **Founded** 1878
- ⊕ **Ground** Old Trafford (opened 1910)
- ⓘ **Address** Sir Matt Busby Way, Old Trafford, Manchester M16 0RA
- ⊕ **Capacity** 76,100
- ✪ **Best attendance** 76,098 vs Blackburn Rovers, Premier League, 31 March, 2007
- ⓒ **Contact** 0161-868 8000
- ⓒ **Ticket Number** 0161-868 8000
- @ **Email** website.comments@manutd.co.uk
- ⓦ **Website** manutd.com

MAN UTD VIA GETTY IMAGES

PUB QUIZ

That's quite interesting
"Mark Hughes' real Christian name is Leslie. Norman Whiteside is a qualified podiatrist." Barney Chilton.

Not a lot of people know that
Manchester United also lose. Their most recent heavy defeat was a 6-0 thumping by Ipswich Town, on 1 March 1980.

The Theatre of Dreams. The name conjures images of a magical stage, bright beams casting a surreal white light that dazzles mere mortals while a pensive audience sit in shadowed awe, the craftsmen weaving wonders on the raised stage below. Whether the poetic musings of an ex-player, or the contrived product of a marketing department, this is more than a mere name, it is a promise of something very special: it's a statement of intent. Few clubs could lay claim to such a moniker with a straight face, but Manchester United are one of a very small number that can. To some it is a symbol of their collective arrogance, to others a true reflection of the talent and skills on offer here. Which ever camp you fall into, there is no denying there have been plenty of very real nights on this turf, nights that have seemed like pure fantasy. European victories over the likes of Real Madrid and Barcelona, 7-1 demolitions of Roma, last-gasp Michael Owen winners against City, the clinching of yet another League title at the expense of close rivals. There is a sense of grandeur that permeates the very essence of Old Trafford, a certain feeling, a spirit, an aura. Few grounds have it. The old Wembley stadium had it in spades, the Bernabeu in Madrid, San Siro in Milan, Camp Nou in Barcelona also. Places that cause hairs to prickle on the back of even a seasoned professional's neck. But whoever you play for, whoever you support, everyone in the game has two dreams: winning at Wembley and winning at Old Trafford. It's an occasion and everyone is watching.

A banner hung from the Stretford End proclaiming "Form is Temporary, Class is Permanent." It is a mantra that United have taken to the very heart of their club. They never lost the belief that they belonged at the top – even when they were rubbish. Looking at this resilient team today,

it is easy to forget that they haven't always been the masters of English football. They claimed three titles in the fifties, were the pioneers of English clubs in Europe and recovered from the horrors of the 1958 Munich air disaster to build a team of dazzling talent. At a time when football was just starting to trickle onto TV screens and into newspapers, the coverage was dominated by the club from Old Trafford. Matt Busby built a team around the skills of Bobby Charlton, George Best and Denis Law, leading them on to claim the 1968 European Cup and into football folklore. Best became football's first superstar, a player of unmatched talent on the field who lived the rock star lifestyle off it. But Busby retired in 1969 and United drifted through the next two decades with a distinct absence of success. Then, in November 1986 a Scottish manager by the name of Alex Ferguson arrived at Old Trafford.

"Yeah, but Alex Ferguson was only one game away from being sacked." Said with knowing shrug and a suck of the teeth laden with meaning, this is a well-worn mantra for pundits, whether prime time or pub time, when discussing the managerial merits of whoever's neck is currently on the block. And while it may be true, having survived an early period of consolidation, Fergie has followed a course of building, rebuilding, then rebuilding again, teams that will consistently win on field, supported by a mechanism off the pitch that has made the club arguably the biggest in the footballing world. He produced a conveyer belt of world class talent, either brought up through the club's youth academy or bought up with clubs financial muscle. The likes of Robson, Scholes, Bruce, Cantona, Keane, Giggs, Irwin, Schmeichel, Beckham, Van Nistelrooy, Ferdinand, Ronaldo and Rooney are a few of those to have graced the Theatre of Dreams. He has instilled a 'never say die' attitude in a team which truly believes that it will be victorious, whatever the state of play and whoever the opposition. Fergie himself plays by his own rules whether he's casting out the biggest player in the world, proving that footballers are replaceable or presenting a closed door to the BBC and proving he isn't.

United stand as a strange dichotomy. As well as being arguably the most popular team in the land, they are also the most hated. Whether these two reactions spring from their recent successes, their single-minded determination to win and win well, their financial strength or a fanbase that stretches not just across the UK but around the globe, it is clear that they are something of a Marmite club. But the facts of the matter are they strive to play attractive, fast, entertaining and winning football, and for all their supporters and detractors, one chant you will never hear directed at this team that thrives on stage under the bright lights is "boring, boring Manchester United."

Greatest moments on this ground

"Brian Kidd and Sir Alex Ferguson running on to the pitch, Kiddo getting down on his knees and clenching his fists, after Steve Bruce scored the second of his two late goals against Sheffield Wednesday in 1993. We had gone 1-0 down to a second-half penalty and looked to be losing our grip on the title. But Bruce's second goal gave us belief that the title was returning to Old Trafford for the first time since 1967." Scott the Red, RepublikOfMancunia.org.

Lowest moments on this ground

"We've had despair and sadness and Arsenal beating us a couple of times as they headed to recent titles didn't help. But thankfully Fergie has ensured our highs have been so high that our lows at Old Trafford haven't really registered for long (losing the League at Upton Park is an entirely different matter). Saying that, playing Spurs in our final game after losing the League to Leeds in 1992 hurt. But Fergie said we'd come back, and look what followed!" Barney Chilton, *Red News*.

Heroes of the turf

Dennis Law was the 'King of the Stretford End'. Eric Cantona was the catalyst for United's success and helped

DON'T MENTION THE...

2010 FA Cup home defeat to League One Leeds United.

King Eric, 1996 FA Cup final. United beat Liverpool 1-0.

AFP/GETTY IMAGES

HEROES OF THE SIDELINE

"Sir Matt Busby was a pioneer for English football in Europe. Against the wishes of the FA he took his young team to the European Cup. With that young team he won three league titles and the FA Cup. He created the United mentality which continues to this day, where young players must be brought through from the academy and we must attack, attack, attack. United were European champions, the first English club to manage it. The holy trinity, Best, Law and Charlton, were all from Busby's era." Scott.

"Fergie. Enough said really. And doing it in the Sir Matt Busby manner too. How blessed Utd fans are." Barney Chilton.

bring the title back to Manchester for the first time in 26 years. The following season he bagged 25 goals and the season after he guided a team of 'kids' who'd 'never win anything' to the second double in three seasons. He retired when he was still at his best in 1997, having won the League in four of his five seasons with us. Roy Keane was everything a good captain should be; dedicated, passionate, driven, a dreadful loser, and always hungry for more. Ryan Giggs' story is a fairytale. Sir Alex Ferguson turned up on Giggsy's doorstep on his 14th birthday and asked him to be a Manchester United player. 11 league titles, two European Cups, four FA Cups, 806 appearances (and counting), several other medals later, and 21 years later, he's still here. He officially became the player with the most Manchester United appearances when he came off the bench in the European Cup final in 2008. George Best was discovered by United scouts when he was 15, with a telegram being sent back to Sir Matt which read "I think I've found you a genius!". He was the club's top-scorer for six consecutive seasons and he once scored six goals in a game. His career came to a sad end but it's undeniable what a big impression Best left on our club. So many people in the sixties and seventies became United fans because of the dazzling football Best played, and he is remembered by many as the greatest ever. Sir Bobby Charlton has probably enjoyed the best football career ever. Part of the first and only England team to win the World Cup, part of the first Manchester United team to win the European Cup. He spent 19 years as a player with United, before taking on his role as ambassador with us." Scott the Red.

Zeroes of the turf

"Djemba-Djemba, so bad they named him twice." Scott, RepublikOfMancunia.org. "Not really a Zero, because he was undoubtedly gifted, but it's hard to explain why the Veron signing didn't come off for us. Right player, maybe just wrong timing. Ralph Milne was a figure of fun back in the late 1980s when things weren't going well. Mark Higgins is the worst player I've seen in a United shirt." Barney Chilton.

Villains

"Paul Ince was a cocky bastard, but players like that are usually popular when they play for your team. Fancied his chances abroad, so left United for Inter Milan in 1995. A few years later he joined Liverpool. With weeks remaining in the 1998-99 season, and United going toe for toe with Arsenal, Ince scored an equalising goal against us in the dying moments. He celebrated like he had just scored in a cup final, kissing the Liverpool badge. Carlos Tevez said he wanted to leave United to play more football, signing for our hated rivals City. Maybe because City could afford to pay him twice what Liverpool or United would? Then he couldn't stop bad-mouthing the manager." Scott the Red.

The ground

Old Trafford is the largest league football ground in England. With all the corners filled in the stadium is more of an arena, overlooking a pitch that is elevated.

North Stand is a three-tier structure, the largest in country as it will hold 25,500 and runs the length of the field. It also houses the Manchester United museum.

West Stand or **Stretford End** sits behind the goal and was traditionally home to the most vocal supporters, with the East Stand opposite.

The **South Stand** is the former main stand and the noticeably lowest structure after the recent expansion. The dug-outs are on the half way line of this single tier of seating. This was home to the old tunnel, but a new tunnel is now in the south west corner. The capacity is 11,500 and future development may be limited due to the railway line that runs behind the stand.

The away contingent are tucked into a corner stand housing 3,000 who, thanks to the acoustics can make their presence known.

MAN UTD VIA GETTY IMAGES

◁ You'll never win anything with a bunch of kids… and Roy Keane.

∧ Top: European Cup winners 1968.
∧ Above: Sir Alex, Champions League perennial.

for the privilege. It may also be worth trying the Lowry Outlet Mall multi-storey in Salford Quays, around a 10-minute walk to the stadium, parking from around £4, unless of course you combine the footie with a spot of shopping in which case it's free! Alternatively, park at a Metrolink station down the line and ride in to th haven't really registered for that long e station.

By Train The stadium has its own train station Manchester United FC Halt, only accessible on match days. Via Metro, the Old Trafford Metrolink (Altrincham line) at Warwick Rd is a 10-minute walk to the ground. Exchange Quay Metrolink (Eccles Line) is an alternative. Both the metro and train station are easily accessed via Manchester's City Centre stations.

Getting there

By Road/Parking On the south west edge of Manchester, the stadium is easily accessed via the M60 which circles the city, fed by the M66, M62, M67 and M56. From the south exit M60 junction 7 and follow the Chester Rd/A56 signed for Manchester United, turn left onto Sir Matt Busby Way. From the North, exit M60 junction 9 and follow A5081 for The Quays/ Manchester United through two roundabouts before turning right onto Sir Matt Busby Way. (Access to Sir Matt Busby Way from Chester Road is closed 90 minutes prior to kick-off). There are a number of small car parks that open up around the ground for match days but be aware these fill up fairly quickly. Old Trafford Cricket Ground is handily placed but costs £10

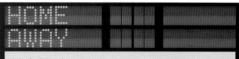

Pubs for home fans
"For a sing song close to the ground head to the Bishop Blaize," recommends Barney Chilton, editor of *Red News*. On Chester Road, the Wetherspoons pub gets packed out and the pre-match atmosphere is fantastic. Other popular pubs close to the ground include The Trafford, on Chester Road, the Village Inn, on Third Avenue in the industrial park nearby, the large Sam Platts on Old Trafford Road and the Toll Gate Inn, on Seymour Grove, opposite the Trafford Bar tram station.

Good food near ground
There are a number of takeaways close to the ground. Other options include the Harry Ramsden's fish Bar in the Castlemore Retail Park, just five minutes from the ground, but feels like you pay a premium for the privilege. There's also a KFC in the park. Pizza Hut, White City Retail Park is around five minutes to the ground.

Pubs for away fans
"For away fans, it's probably best to have a pint in town and get the tram or a cab in," says Barney Chilton.

Top tips
Visiting supporters are usually held back by police and officials for a good 15 minutes after the game to avoid any problems – be aware of this when planning your train connections and return journey.

RepublikOfMancunia.org
rednews.co.uk
redissue.co.uk
manutdtalk.com
red11.org
m-u-f-c.co.uk
stretfordend.co.uk

HOME COLOURS

- ⊖ **Nicknames** Boro
- ⊙ **Founded** 1876
- ⊕ **Ground** Riverside Stadium (opened 1995)
- ⓘ **Address** Riverside Stadium, Middlesbrough, TS3 6RS
- ⊖ **Capacity** 34,988
- ✪ **Best attendance** 34,800 vs Leeds United, 26 February, 2000
- ⓘ **Contact** 0844-499 6789
- ⓘ **Ticket Number** 0844-499 1234
- @ **Email** enquiries@ mfc.co.uk
- ⓦ **Website** mfc.co.uk

MIDDLESBROUGH

Sunderland supporters arrive at the Riverside clad in white chemical suits and dust masks. "What's it like to see the sun, what's it like to see the sun?" sing the Newcastle fans to the visiting Middlesbrough contingent. By 2003 the Boro bosses had had enough and banned gas masks, NBC suits and any such paraphernalia from the ground – they felt it was, "both insensitive and intimidating to wear such outfits, particularly in the current international situation." Actually. The source of this long running ridicule? The backdrop to the Riverside – a large petro-chemical and industrial plant that lines the banks of the river Tees. Boro fans were christened 'The Smoggies' by their close neighbours and rivals, so the home fans decided to adopt the name as their unofficial title. Banners with 'Smoggies on Tour' have since graced stadiums across the continent, accompanying the Teeside team on their European adventures and continental cup runs. Perhaps this environmental banter is a progressive, right on move by Northeast fans – a greening of terrace chants. What about, "Your team coach has higher particulate emissions than ours!" or, "We might not have qualified for Europe but at least that means our carbon footprint will be cut!" That'll tell 'em.

But it would seem that casting aspersions on the region's air has not had a detrimental effect on attracting some of the world's most exciting football talent to Cleveland. Or is it Teeside? Or is it Yorkshire? After all you'll see Cleveland Bobbies outside the ground for Tyne Tees derbies against Newcastle as well as the Yorkshire derbies against Leeds. But wherever the county lines have been drawn, some of football's brightest stars have managed to shine here, through the Teeside miasma. During the mid-90s, Bryan Robson assembled a team of talent from across the globe. There was a promising young Brazilian called Juninho, who surprised the football world by choosing Boro

over so-called bigger clubs. Another signing was Italian legend Fabrizio Ravanelli, who came wearing a glinting Champions League winners medal from Juventus. They were playing in the squeaky new Riverside Stadium, having relocated from Ayresome Park. It was a far cry from just ten years before, when the team sat in the third tier of the English game, a mere ten minutes from liquidation. A last minute rescue deal from club director Steve Gibson pulled the club back from the brink. Two promotions in two seasons saw the team back in the big time, their near death experience banished to the mists of time.

Today Middlesbrough have become firmly established as one of English football's biggest teams. Perhaps not in the realm of Chelsea or Man U, they still succeed in attracting big time players and splashing not inconsiderable sums of cash around. Under Steve McClaren, Middlesbrough brought in promising talent including Massimo Maccarone, Franck Queudrue, George Boateng and the returning Juninho. Other big names followed, some proving to be more junk bonds than prime gilt investments, while Mark Viduka was just a bit over ripe.

Boro have a little 'Spurs-esque' side to them, perhaps finding the humdrum of the League a little tiresome, but really coming to life in the gladiatorial arena of the knock-out environment. How else could you explain the fact that they reached both FA Cup and League Cup finals in 1996/97, the year they were relegated from the top flight? They graced the League Cup final in '98 while in '04 they took the trophy home. 2006 saw a storming run to the final of the Uefa Cup, while under Gareth Southgate they qualified for three successive FA Cup Quarters. This is a club that always looks to the silverware from the bright Riverside Stadium, glinting on cold February FA Cup nights, illuminated against the vast Redcar works, where red flames light up the horizon in an otherworldly panorama. From here, Boro are scanning the fixture list, like a giant Eye of Sauron, looking past the opposition to the precious ties ahead and path to the final. Looking through the shimmering mist, they are focused on the goal. Wembley.

Greatest moments on this ground
"Greatest moment at the Riverside – I never thought the cup heroics under Bryan Robson would be topped but that they were not once but twice in the most incredible and dramatic way possible. To come from the dead 0-2 down to Basel and win in the last minute of our Uefa Cup quarter-final in 2006 was amazing. To do it again in the

GETTY IMAGES

⬈ HEROES OF THE SIDELINE

"Jack Charlton – turned a perennial 2nd string club into runaway 2nd Division champions and then 1st Division challengers. Reluctance to spend big cost us the chance to compete for silverware beyond the Anglo-Scottish cup. Bruce Rioch – brought club back from relegation and liquidation to Division Two in one season then top flight in two seasons. Charismatic and still worshiped here. Bryan Robson – took Boro up to another level – made us into a world brand in football. Had us dreaming with superstar signings and cup finals. Sadly couldn't ever bring home the cup. Steve McClaren – much maligned but phenomenally successful – won Boro's first ever trophy in 128 years, highest league finish 7th in over 30 years then got us to a Uefa Cup final. Brilliant strategist." Robert Nichols.

◄ Juninho celebrates Carling Cup final victory over Bolton in 2004.

GETTY IMAGES

semi-final against Steaua Bucharest was miraculous. God bless Massimo Maccarone." Robert Nichols, Fly Me To The Moon, fmttmboro.com.

Lowest moments on this ground

"Funnily enough we always seem to get relegated away from home. Maybe it's better that most of the fans don't face the pain. Being soundly beaten 0-2 by Championship side Cardiff City in the FA Cup quarter final in 2008 was sickening because with all the big teams out the path was open to FA Cup glory, something we have never achieved. Some fans have still never returned to the Riverside after this depressing defeat." Robert Nichols.

Heroes of the turf

"Riverside Legends – Juninho because he lit up the place with his dazzling skills and took us into a dream land. All time legends – John Hickton, old fashioned number 9; never say die attitude and a real gentleman from the 60s and 70s when every kid would say he was Big John Hickton in the school playground. Tony Mowbray – courageous skipper also from the Ayresome Park era. Leader of the team of local lads that came back from liquidation. Bruce Rioch said about him that if he had to take a flight to the moon he would want Mowbray by his side – hence Fly Me

To The Moon – this fanzine's name. Bernie Slaven – sharp shooting Scot who became Irish and played in Big Jack's squad now a radio Legend. Wilf Mannion – the Golden Boy – 1930s-1950s named by many as the greatest player of all time – Sir Bobby Robson and Stan Matthews amongst his admirers. I never saw him play but met him many times, what a gent. He always signed his autograph in a flowing fountain pen script – Wilf Mannion Middlesbrough, England and Great Britain." Robert Nichols.

Zeroes of the turf

"Well Afonso Alves may well fall into this category – big money signing heralded by samba dancers and bands in front of thousands at the Riverside. Tipped to win the golden boot – misfired big style. Left Riverside for a knock down fee.

Mido – came with big reputation quickly became too big for his boots and shorts. Never short of words but had to lose nearly two stone in weight to get fit again after long lay off. Could have been a hero as a big crowd favourite – talked himself into being a zero." Robert Nichols.

That's quite interesting

"Middlesbrough FC was actually the second professional and football league club from the town. The fantastically named Middlesbrough Ironopolis actually turned pro first

"Embarrassing – our one and only FA Cup final appearance was plunged into doom after just 42 seconds when Roberto di Matteo shot over keeper Ben Roberts' alice band and into the net. We have had to put up with this stat and replays every year since. I think someone should erect a statue to Louis Saha for finally ending our torment with his new record strike on 25 seconds (for Everton vs Chelsea, 2009)." Robert Nichols.

and entered the Football League in Div 2 in 1893 – but the Nops sound got into debt and were forced to leave at the end of their one and only season. League paradise had been lost at their Paradise Ground." Robert Nichols

Villains

"Peter Beagrie enjoyed a long career but was never forgiven by Boro fans for leaving when the club went bust in 1986. Whenever this Teessider returned to Ayresome Park he was barracked as Judas. Maybe a little unkind because it was later revealed that some of the heroes of Rioch's side that had neither contracts or pay following administration had come precious close to leaving." Robert Nichols

Not a lot of people know that

"Pandemics are nothing new to Middlesbrough. We once were unable to play a FA Cup Amateur Cup semi final versus Thornaby at Darlington owing to an outbreak of smallpox. The people of Darlington were not willing to run the risk of smallpox being brought into their town by players and spectators from the two Teesside clubs. The FA had the game played in secret in a little village of Brotton in East Cleveland." Robert Nichols

The ground

Middlesbrough left Ayresome Park for The Riverside in 1995. This is a modern enclosed arena but with a 'stepped' design. The **West Stand** is the largest with two tiers of seating separated by a row of executive boxes. It runs the length of the field and wraps around the corners, there is then a step down to the **South** and **North** stands which are identical single tiers. They both join with the **East Stand**, meaning the rest of the stadium is an uninterrupted bank of covered seating. As with all modern stadia there are no pillars to obstruct views and the Riverside has managed to maintain quite a light and open feel, despite being enclosed. Away fans are given a large area in the South Stand with an allocation of just under three and half thousand. There are two electronic scoreboards, one at each end and outside the ground there are statues to the legendary Wilf Mannion and George Hardwick. They have also rescued the old gates from Ayresome Park – the ones that were once famously padlocked shut when the club nearly went bust.

Getting there

By Road/Parking On the banks of the River Tees and just off the A66 that leads through Middlesbrough, the

Riverside Stadium is fairly easy to access. Following signs for Teeside from the A1, the A19 meets the A66 from the north and south. Having passed through Middlesbrough town centre on the A66, following signs for Redcar, the stadium becomes visible on the left. Take slip road on the left signed for the stadium, the stadium will be on your right. No stadium parking. "There are plenty of car parks just off A66," says Robert Nichols, a number of the match day car parks are private and all charge the same price – around a fiver. A number of pay and displays can also be found just off this road.

By Train Middlesbrough train station, Zetland Road is less than a mile from the ground. Exit the station and head under the railway bridge, turning right onto Bridge Street East. Take the next right turn onto Windward Way which follows the railway line to the stadium which will be on your left.

> **HOME**
> **AWAY**

Pubs for home fans
Over the tracks from the Riverside, The Navigation on Marsh Rd is one of the closest pubs to the stadium. "Lord Byron on Bridge Street East between the railway station and the football ground," recommends Fly Me to the Moon's Robert Nichols. "One of the earliest pubs in Middlesbrough, reopened after being closed for many years."

Good food near ground
"There are many sandwich shops and takeaways that side of town," says Robert. "And restaurants like Nandos, Etsuko (Japanese and Chinese) Pizza Hut and even McDonalds in the complex near the Cineworld Cinema" (Middlesbrough Leisure Park)

Pubs for away fans
Set on the dockside and as a modern stadium, there's little surrounding the Riverside in the way of amenities. However the stadium is close enough to the town centre – a 20 minute walk or so meaning a detour can yield, "plenty of choice for food and watering holes," says Fly Me to the Moon's Robert Nichols. Doctor Browns, Corporation St, opposite the Middlesbrough Leisure Park is a popular spot offering real ales, sports TV and a decent mix of home and away fans so is consequently heaving pre-kick off.

Top tips
Aside from at the stadium itself, Doctor Brown's is the closest watering hole to the ground so make sure you get your prescription filled here if you're ailing!

THE LAST **WORD**

fmttmboro.com
smogchat.com
theborofc.info

- **Nicknames** The Lions
- **Founded** 1885
- **Ground** New Den (opened 1993)
- **Address** Zampa Road, Bermondsey, London SE16 3LN
- **Capacity** 20,146
- **Best attendance** 20,093 vs Arsenal, FA Cup 3rd round, 10 January, 1994
- **Contact** 0207-232122
- **Ticket Number** 0207-231 9999
- **Email** questions@millwallplc.com
- **Website** millwallfc.co.uk

MILLWALL

Most people's image of Teddy Sheringham is probably the dramatic last few seconds of the Champions League final of 1999 when a two goal deficit was overcome by a red blur and Bayern Munich players lay shocked around the Camp Nou turf, or of the striker peeling away in celebration after slotting home the fourth against Holland in Euro 96 at Wembley. What many probably don't realize is that England legend Edward Paul Sheringham is also a true Millwall legend – probably THE Millwall legend. After joining the club as a 16 year-old, this prolific striker played through the Third, Second and First Divisions with the Lions, notching up 244 appearances and 111 goals for the team from The Den. Here was a striker with an amazing record and the heart of a lion, who epitomized the Millwall spirit – a collective spirit that saw the team jostling in the top third of the top table throughout the 1988/89 season. The southeast London club had risen through the leagues building on the foundations provided by one George Graham (in his first managerial role south of the border) and completed by fellow scot John Docherty. This had something of a poetic symmetry considering the historical links between the clubs formation in the heartland of the East End Docks, and the Scottish dockers who made up a large balance of their early membership. Sheringham and Tony Cascarino were deadly that first season in Division One, but unfortunately the dream proved all too short lived. Since the move to the New Den in 1993, Millwall have visited Wembley for an FA Cup final, ventured into European football and seen more than their share of play-off heartbreak. The club is certainly trying to shed its off-field infamy while at the same time gaining a reputation as a team to be feared on it.

RIVALS

West Ham, Chelsea, Crystal Palace and Leeds United.

Greatest moments on this ground

"At the New Den, it would probably be the May 2001 win against Oldham Athletic, where we celebrated the Third Division title with a 5-0 romp. Harris scored a hat trick, the players celebrated on the podium, and when they were finished with it, sections of the same podium were spotted in a variety of South London hostelries that evening." Paul Casella, editor, *The Lion Roars*.

Lowest moments on this ground

"There have sadly been several. Perhaps the worst however was the last minute of extra-time against Birmingham City in May 2002. Over the two legs of the play-offs the Lions enjoyed little luck and Stern John popped up to grab an unlikely winner before penalties with seconds ticking away." Paul Casella.

Heroes of the sideline

"John Docherty – he led us to the promised land in 1988, then went on to take us to the top of the Football League three months later. He brought in the best players in the club's history and we had a great ride mixing with the best clubs in England. George Graham – with relegation to the bottom tier looming, the QPR coach came in and performed some sort of miracle to keep the club up, with a team built in just two months. He then built another of the great Lions sides before leaving for Arsenal. Billy Gray – he built a Millwall team in the sixties that went on a League record run of 59 matches without defeat. It is upon this legacy that The Den's reputation was built." Paul Casella.

Heroes of the turf

"Harry Cripps – he represents the image of Millwall FC to fans. He was not the best, but he was the most committed. Teddy Sheringham – the youth despise the fact that he wore a West Ham United shirt, but those old enough will remember a player that showed great loyalty when we needed him most, contributed unmatched goal-scoring feats, and was almost certainly the greatest-ever Lion. Jack Cock – few are still alive who remember, but he played for England, he won medals in the First World War and he captained one of the all-time great Lions sides. Terry Hurlock – to other club supporters, Our Tel is seen as a bit of a cartoon hard-man but we all saw one of the most under-rated midfielders of his generation. Barry Kitchener – our longest-serving player and a man that would represent all the best qualities of a seventies legend, the greatest time for English football." Paul Casella.

Zeroes of the turf

"Paul Goddard – we mortgaged our top-flight future on Goddard in 1989. He scored one goal. We went down. Paul Wilkinson – perhaps the first of the glaringly obvious wage thieves who we came across as football moved into the modern age. A player that we believed simply turned up for the money and put no effort in whatsoever. A disgrace who has been followed by a generation of similar players for all clubs. Bob Peeters – a move into the exotic world of free-scoring European strikers cost the Lions an absolute fortune for virtually no reward. Uwe Fuchs: See above." Paul Casella.

That's quite interesting

"Dennis Wise split the opinion of Millwall supporters precisely down the middle. For some he was the man that led us to a remarkable FA Cup final in 2004 (and Europe). For the other half, he persuaded the chairman to build a club beyond its means and put us on the path to relegation, and we haven't recovered since." Paul Casella.

Not a lot of people know that

"Millwall were the biggest non-league club south of the Midlands before the turn of the 20th century, and refused a place in the professional Football League. Arsenal benefited from this decision and joined the League instead, mostly to emerge from our club's shadow. In 1934 Manchester United and Millwall were locked in a relegation battle to the third Division. The Lions lost at home on the last day, to dubious officiating. If Manchester United had gone down instead it is widely believed they would have declared bankruptcy. Bitter? No, of course not." Paul Casella.

VILLAINS
"Any player that wears the colours of West Ham United after playing for Millwall and those that run their contracts out before leaving for nothing, those that spend a year injured and then slag the club off after leaving." Paul Casella.

The ground

The New Den is pretty much enclosed by railway lines, embankments and warehouses; you're kind of funnelled into the ground. There is a slightly uneasy feeling around the place for the visiting fan, due to the lingering reputation for hooliganism that still hangs in the air (alongside the CCTV cameras trained on the crowds). There's certainly a high intimidation factor. The ground is an all-seater stadium with almost identical, two-tiered stands. Visiting supporters are housed in the **North Stand** behind the far goal – usually in the upper tier, opposite the Cold Blow Lane **South Stand**. The **West Stand** houses an executive seating area as well as changing rooms.

Getting there

By Road/Parking For an easy toll-free route: exit the M25 at junction 2 onto the A2 and follow all the way in, through Greenwich Park passing Depford Bridge and New Cross Gate tubes. At 500m past New Cross Gate turn right onto Kender Street to stay on the A2 and left onto New Cross Road. Right onto Ilderton Road, Left onto Zampa Road and left at Bolina Road, the ground is on the right.

Parking can be a nightmare here but spaces can be found on residential roads. Watch for permit parking on the streets Around the Grounds.

Coach travel for away supporters is encouraged.

By Train South Bermondsey station is the best bet – a few minutes walk to the ground (on match days away fans are separated off via a fenced walkway). For most, the station is accessed via London Bridge – a four-minute train ride. Underground access also via New Cross Gate and Canada Water – around a 20 minute-walk.

▼ Huge crowds pack The Den, as Millwall take on Derby County in the 1927 FA Cup.

Pubs for home fans
A number of the traditional haunts near the ground have closed but pubs along 'The Blue' (Southwark Park Road), including the Queen Victoria, get packed out with home fans on match days and are about 15 minutes from The Den.

Good food near ground
See above.

Pubs for away fans
Drinking around The Den is definitely not an option and if you've arrived by coach you won't be allowed out to explore the local sights. As most arrive via London Bridge, that is the best place for a drink and something to eat. Nearby Borough's famous Saturday market has plenty of pubs, cafés and restaurants.

Top tips
Away fans never drink around the ground!

THE LAST WORD

thelionroars.co.uk
millwall.vitalfootball.co.uk
hof.org.uk
independentmillwall.com
noluthemag.blogspot.com

DON'T MENTION THE...

"Nudity. Mick McCarthy said he'd bare his arse in Burton's window if Jan Aage Fjortoft had meant his 30-yard goal in Swindon's League Cup quarter final win over us in 1995. Chairman Theo Paphitis threatened to run around Trafalgar Square starkers if we made the 2004 FA Cup final. Fortunately, neither saw their promises through." Paul Casella.

HOME COLOURS

- ❷ **Nicknames** MK Dons, The Dons
- ❷ **Founded** 2004
- ❷ **Ground** Stadium:mk (opened 2007)
- ❶ **Address** Stadium Way West, Milton Keynes MK1 1ST
- ❷ **Capacity** 22,000
- ✪ **Best attendance** 17,717 vs Leicester City, League One, 28 February, 2009
- ❶ **Contact** 01908-622922
- ❶ **Ticket Number** 01908-622900
- @ **Email** info@mkdons.com
- ⓦ **Website** mkdons.com

MILTON KEYNES DONS

Wimbledon were looking for a move, Milton Keynes were looking for a club. Few believed the FA would sanction a US-style 'franchise move', but they did. Suddenly the purpose-built new town had a purpose-built Football League team. There was no need to go to the trouble of forming their own club from scratch, with all those pesky promotions through the non-league system that everyone else has to endure. Wimbledon claimed they could no longer survive in London, but one has to wonder if the dice were somewhat loaded after the chairman sold the ground from under them. The move focused many minds on just what a football club consists of. Is it a name, its location or its supporters? Well, Wimbledon had lost all three. At least the new MK Dons did finally put their hand in the air and renounce all claim to the Wimbledon history and handed back the trophies. After all the denials, it was good just to come clean and admit this was a new club starting from fresh.

Since 2004 the Dons have simply got on with the task of establishing a club in an area with no real footballing heritage. They now have a 22,000-seater stadium, which fills up with more supporters every season, and they have the one thing no team can live without – a real, solid hardcore of fans. They love their team, follow it home and away and turn up on wet Tuesday nights for Johnstone's Paint Trophy games when many armchair Premier League fans are at home watching *Coronation Street*. They also put up with the taunts of 'Franchise FC' from the fans of every team they play. A pretty good team has been assembled too, which missed out on a promotion to the Championship by a hair's breadth in 2009. "We get a lot of stick as fans of 'the franchise'," says Brando, editor of The MooCamp, "but I've loved every single minute of my time with this club. I've discovered a love for lower league

football that has seen me visiting more than 50 clubs in the last few years, and I'm really very proud of what we've achieved in such a short space of time." In 10 years most people will have forgotten the turbulent relocation – but by then the rapidly climbing AFC Wimbledon may well have caught them up. Now that'll be an interesting game.

Greatest moments on this ground
"Beating Leeds 3-1 at home was quite awesome. I know we all love to claim that they're not famous any more, but they are. It was a big, big thing to beat them, and we did it with some style as well. Their fans were silent for most of the match, which in itself was quite an achievement (although when they did sing they sounded awesome). It's surprising how many grown men and women have photos of the scoreboard for that match as their desktop picture." Brando, The MooCamp.

Lowest moments on this ground
"Losing on penalties in the play-off semi-finals to Scunthorpe in the 2008/09 season. In a season where we didn't expect much at the start, we'd found ourselves playing some great football, and had been comfortably second for a large part of the season. At one point we were something like nine points ahead with three games in hand, and we really should be playing Championship football this season." Brando.

Heroes of the sideline
"Martin Allen – he turned this club around. We were going nowhere other than down, he came in and gave every single part of the club a kick up the backside and said that losing was not acceptable. Paul Ince – he gave us a truly incredible season. League Two champions and JPT winners at Wembley… and he's back! Paul Heald – currently a goalkeeping coach; he's been around since the Wimbledon days and is a genuinely nice guy. Due to the number of management changes we've had, he's been called on to start pre-season training an awful lot too. Ray Matthias – he brought the lower league knowledge that allowed Incey to be successful the first time around." Brando.

Heroes of the turf
"Dean Lewington – our ginger ninja. He's consistently been the best left-back in every division we've played in. He's an old Wimbledon boy and is pretty much universally adored by Dons fans. Izale McLeod – the best striker I've seen in the lower leagues. He never did himself any favours with the fans, as he never really acknowledged

us, which got on a lot of people's backs. Keith Andrews – he was the linchpin of our double-winning season in 2007/08. He runs like a girl, but as a creative midfielder he was fantastic. Also Gareth Edds and Jude Stirling – his passion and commitment is truly spectacular." Brando.

Zeroes of the turf
"Leon Knight, for wasting such an incredible talent." Brando, The MooCamp.

Don't mention the…
"Fact that the upstairs doesn't have seats in it yet. Or the chairman's hair." Brando.

Villains
Martin Allen, for promising he wouldn't leave should an offer from a higher club come in and then doing just that.

The ground
Stadium:mk is a bright and open modern arena. The glass roof panels and panels at the rear of the stand let plenty of light in. The stands are all a uniform shape and wrap around in two tiers, apart from the **West Stand** where the upper tier is home to the executive and directors' boxes. The lower tier has excellent seats with good views to everywhere in the ground – even the concourse area. The upper tier is without seats at the moment but they will follow and raise the capacity to 30,000. About 3,000 away fans can be seated in the **Northeast Corner**.

Getting there
By road/Parking From the M1, exit at junction 14 following the A509 to Milton Keynes/Newport Bagnell. At the second roundabout take the third exit onto the A509/Portway H5 and follow through nine roundabouts until the A5 junctions. At the roundabout take the first exit (the A5) and follow for just over two miles. Take the A421 exit (Buckingham/Milton Keynes). At the roundabout take the fourth exit onto Grafton Street. Turn left. There's limited parking (£5) at the stadium. Alternatively park in the industrial areas surrounding the stadium.

By train Milton Keynes Central is about three miles away with MK Metro and Centre buses operating services close to the ground – see transportdirect.info. Bletchley Station is the alternative – it's 30 minutes' walk from the ground (or get a connecting train onto Fenny Stratford, which is just a mile from the stadium and has a few decent pubs).

That's quite interesting
"We've got the highest number of under-16 season ticket holders in the country, which bodes well for the future." Brando.

Not a lot of people know that
"Our average home attendance has more than doubled in the past four seasons, and is now over 10,000." Brando.

∧ Top: Shaun O'Hanlon scores the second goal in the Johnstone's Paint Trophy final match against Grimsby Town at Wembley, 2008.
∧ Above: Stadium:mk .

Pubs for home fans
The Beacon, Mount Farm, isn't great, but is the closest pub to the ground – about a 10-minute walk away – and has a mix of fans.

Good food near ground
Close to the ground Asda and Ikea have cafés. In Fenny Stratford try The Napoli Fish Bar, Aylesbury Street.

Pubs for away fans
The Beacon is the closest. Not far from Milton Keynes Central station, Wetherspoons on Midsummer Boulevard is well run with a decent range of ales. In Fenny Stratford try The Chequers, Watling Street, which has Sky Sports and a couple of real ales or the CAMRA award-winning The Red Lion, on Lock View Lane, which has a decent range of guest ales. In Bletchley try the CAMRA award-winning Enigma Tavern, on Princes Way.

Top tips
There is very little nearby, so you may be best grabbing a bite to eat in town (or you'll have to make do with Ye Olde Asda for comfort).

THE LAST **WORD**

moocamp.com
thebucksfizz.com

MORECAMBE

- ⊖ **Nicknames** The Shrimps
- ⊕ **Founded** 1920
- ⊙ **Ground** Globe Arena (opened 2010)
- ⓘ **Address** Globe Arena, Westgate, Lancashire, LA4 4TL
- ⊛ **Capacity** 6,918
- ✪ **Best attendance** 9,234 vs Weymouth, FA Cup 3rd round, 6 January, 1962 (at Christie Park)
- ☎ **Contact** 01524-411797
- ☎ **Ticket Number** 01524-411797
- @ **Email** office@moreccambefc.com
- Ⓦ **Website** morecambefc.com

GETTY IMAGES

They say that moving house can be one of the most stressful experiences you can go though. Well, for Morecambe FC their 2010 relocation to the shiny, modern, purpose built Globe Arena on Westgate heralds the start of a new era of positivity for the club. The Shrimps have resided at their Christie Park address for some 90 years and the old ground has seen them through good times and bad, from the dark days of the eighties when crowds sometimes struggled to break three figures, through to the glories of the upper reaches of League Two. Souvenir programmes were printed for their final game of the season: Morecambe v Aldershot, the last game ever to be played at Christie Park. Or so they thought. The plucky Shrimps had spent the 2009/10 campaign slowly clawing points together to end the season in fourth, earning them a place in the play-off semi-finals and another 'final' day out at their old ground. Yes, the worry over their impending move had clearly affected the team.

They also say that going through a divorce can be one of the most stressful experiences you can go through. Morecambe manager Jim Harvey had guided the club for more than a decade in a successful marriage of minds, seeing them rise from the Northern Premier League in 1995 to just miss out on promotion from the Conference to the Football League. In 2005 Harvey suffered a heart attack just before the Shrimps game at home to Cambridge United. Jim's old friend Sammy McIlroy, who he had assisted in the Northern Ireland post, stood in for Harvey while he recuperated. There was to be a Shakespearean twist in the tale; on the day of Harvey's return to work the board dismissed him, ending his 12 year relationship with the club. His friend McIlroy was appointed to the post full-time. The following season McIlroy guided the team he inherited to the play-off final and promotion to League Two in front of a crowd of

40,000. Needless to say, Harvey and McIlroy are no longer good friends, a situation perhaps compounded by his ex-club's, continued rise under his successor. Yes, the trauma of the break up had clearly affected the team.

Morecambe is a town perhaps more famous for a person than the actual place. Eric Morecambe was born here and took his stage name from the town. His statue looks out over the seafront, a tribute to one of Britain's best-loved comedians. Shrimps fans are famous for the fact that they occasionally dress as the town's favourite son for away games, complete with macs, pipes and specs – perhaps this light-hearted approach is the secret of Morecambe FC's stress busting strategy. "What do you think of it so far?"

Greatest moments on this ground
The greatest Morecambe moment was probably the 2-1 play-off final at Wembley against Exeter in 2007 which brought League football. But the greatest moment at Christie Park was probably the 2-1 win over York City to earn a place in that play-off final.

Lowest moments on this ground
When, in November 2005, long-term manager Jim Harvey suffered a heart-attack during a game against Cambridge United. It was the last game he took charge of as he was controversially sacked on his first day back from recuperation.

Heroes of the sideline
Jim Harvey managed the team from 1994

VILLAINS
Sacking a manager of nearly 12 years on his first day back at work after he suffered a heart attack at a game? Ouch, some people might think that's a bit harsh, chairman Peter McGuigan.

That's quite interesting
Sol Campbell played his one and only game for Notts County at Christie Park, a 2-1 defeat to Morecambe, in September 2009.

Not a lot of people know that
According to a 1929 obituary in the *Lancaster Guardian*, club benefactor JB Christie gave Christie Park to the club "on condition it should be used by Morecambe F.C… and if the club was ever disbanded it should become a playground for the children of Morecambe." Nice guy. Hope the kids enjoy the new Sainsbury's Superstore.

DON'T MENTION THE...

During the eighties, crowds of nearly 200 would flock to Christie Park.

to 2005, leading them to promotion to the Conference in 1996. In 2003 he led the team to runners-up position before losing on penalties in the play-off semi-final.

Sammy McIlroy, former Northern Ireland manager, took over as caretaker, then full-time manager. Saw his team promoted to the Football League in 2007. In 2009/10 The Shrimps finished fourth in League Two, qualifying for the play-offs, but defeated in the semi-finals.

Heroes of the turf
Gary Thompson was a talented winger who came through the academy and spent nearly 10 years at Christie Park. He scored in the Conference play-off win in 2007 before leaving for Championship side Scunthorpe United. Dave Perkins, a midfielder with just under 200 appearances for the Shrimps over seven years. Chris Blackburn, a midfielder who moved into defence and formed a formidable duo with Jim Bentley that helped see the team promoted to League Two. Jim Bentley, captain and defensive rock, with over 300 appearances for the club. Michael Twiss, a former Manchester United apprentice who turned out a couple of times for Sir Alex before moving on. Found a home in the midfield at Christie Park and was in the promotion winning side before moving on to link up with former manager Harvey.

Zeroes of the turf
Dean Howell, Alan Morgan and Graham Gill.

The ground
The Shrimps new ground from the 2010/11 season is the purpose-built Globe Arena, a modern four-sided ground. The **South Stand** is the main stand and an all-seater covered tier with room for 2,173 fans. It is also home to the changing rooms and club shop as well as a bar and main reception. The **West Stand** behind the goal is the home stand and accommodates 2,234 standing fans with a bar and catering in an enclosed concourse to the rear.

The **East Stand** behind the far goal is for away fans with a capacity of 1,389 while the **North Stand** is an open terrace for 606 standing home fans.

Getting there
By Road/Parking Leave the M6 at junction 34 and follow A683 signed Lancaster/Morecambe, then the A589 for Morecambe over two roundabouts. At the next roundabout take the first left for West Promenade, passing the Toby Carvery on your right. Continue up Westgate, the ground will be on your right. Parking to be confirmed.

By Train Morecambe train station is around a mile from the ground through a residential area. Alternatively, take in the seafront, an ice cream and a couple of the alternative pub choices by heading up Central Drive passing the KFC and turning left along Marine Road West, the sea will be on your right. Turn left down Regent Road, ground will be on your left.

HOME AWAY

Pubs for home fans
In the Christie Park days, the club bar was always a firm fixture with the home support.

Good food near ground
Both north of the train station and just back from the seafront are a number of cafés. There is a KFC on Central Drive, a short walk from the train station on the seafront.

Pubs for away fans
Morecambe is not exactly overrun with fine alehouses, having said that, the Smugglers Den, Poulton Street, is worth hunting out. There are a number of watering holes on the seafront including strange little spots like the Ranch House, Marine West Road, on the cusp of being a bit of a theme pub, but it does stock an ale or two. The York Hotel, Lancaster Road, has sports TV, food and decent selection of beers – it used to be the gathering spot for the away contingent visiting Christie Park. Seeing as it is not too far from the new ground, no reason why it shouldn't remain a firm favourite.

Top tips
Head to the promenade and get your photo taken with the Eric Morecambe statue.

THE LAST WORD

morecambefc-shrimps-supporters.com
shrimpsvoices.co.uk

NEWCASTLE UNITED

- **Nicknames** The Magpies, Toon Army
- **Founded** 1881
- **Ground** St James' Park (opened 1892)
- **Address** St. James' Park, Newcastle-upon-Tyne NE1 4ST
- **Capacity** 52,387
- **Best attendance** 63,386 vs Chelsea, Division One, 3 September, 1930
- **Contact** 0844-372 1892
- **Ticket Number** 0844-372 1892
- **Email** custserv@nufc.co.uk
- **Website** nufc.co.uk

The Magpies have traditionally revolved around a cult hero, one who was nearly always a striker. In the pre-war era that talisman was an incredibly skilful Scotsman called Hughie Gallacher. He was a goal-scoring machine, a wizard with the ball at his feet and well known for having a Woodbine at half time. His crowning achievement was captaining Newcastle United to the League title, scoring 36 goals in the 38 League games. During and after the war, that hero was goal-scoring legend and local lad 'Wor Jackie' Milburn. As conflict swept through Europe, he would work down the mines during the week and come Saturday, don the black and white stripes for the Toon. His prolific goal scoring helped Newcastle to three Cup wins in five years in the fifties, and his total of 200 goals is second only to Alan Shearer in the all-time list. The early seventies saw the arrival of Malcolm Macdonald, or 'SuperMac' as he became known. Another prolific forward and favourite amongst the fans, Supermac's debut saw him score in a 3-2 win over highly rated Liverpool, and their rising star Kevin Keegan. The eighties brought a more turbulent time to the club, and relegation from the top flight, which was only reversed when Keegan himself arrived at the club and became the next great hero to pull on the black-and-white-jersey.

But Keegan the manager is probably what most fans think of today. When he took over the managerial reigns in 1992 with just two games to save them from relegation to the third tier, all previous dramas at the Newcastle United would soon be eclipsed. He pulled off the impossible and the next season they were promoted, and the following season they finished third in the Premiership. The man that they would later call the Messiah had well and truly arrive. An incredible three seasons followed, during which they finished runners up twice. Keegan and Sir

Alex famously jousted during a long psychological battle. Following Keegan's departure there were disappointing spells under Kenny Dalglish and Ruud Gullit until Bobby Robson entered centre stage. A County Durham lad, the ex-England manager was coming back to the club he supported as a boy, pulling them out of a relegation tussle and into Champions League contention again. He restored Newcastle's own Alan Shearer to the starting line up, seeing him become the next hero of St James' Park, and their greatest-ever goal-scorer. But the tale was not over – Robson was fired after a dip in form and Freddy Shepherd, then chairman, made a string of bad appointments before he sold the club to sportswear tycoon Mike Ashley. Another string of managerial appointments followed, including the second coming of the Messiah. This time the dream lasted just 232 days before King Kev departed citing boardroom meddling, leaving Ashley keen to sell up and Newcastle on the brink of relegation. Enter Alan Shearer. The United goal-scoring legend came to save the day, but the team had no fight left in them and The Magpies slipped back into the Championship. The bounce back was instant, St James' Park now awaits the next chapter and the dawn of the next hero.

Heroes of the sideline

"Frank Watt, from the club's most successful era in the Edwardian times pre-First World War, is shamefully neglected in the club's history. Stan Seymour (snr) played a big part in the club's post-Second World War recovery and in the three FA Cup wins of the fifties. Joe Harvey is the man fondly remembered for getting the club promoted in the sixties, winning the Fairs Cup and re-establishing the club in the top flight. Kevin Keegan saved the club from relegation to the Third Division, building a team which got promoted and then lit up the Premier League – finishing third, sixth, second and second in the four seasons he managed the club – though he resigned in his last season. Sir Bobby Robson put the club back

RIVALS

Sunderland, or the Mackems as they are known, are the main rivals. The Tyne 'n' Wear derby is a ferocious affair and with only 10 miles separating the clubs it's hardly surprising.

PUB QUIZ

That's quite interesting
Jackie Milburn's career began by replying to an advert in the local papers for trials at St James' Park, he turned up and started as a centre-back. At half-time his team were losing 3-0. In the second half he moved to centre-forward, scored six goals in a 9-3 win and was duly signed.

Not a lot of people know that
Newcastle have been runners up in the FA Cup seven times, a record that only Everton can beat.

↑ Alan Shearer takes a free-kick as Newcastle beat Arsenal at St James' Park 4-2.

together after the incompetence of Dalglish and Gullit; he took us into the Champions League second stage and gave us some great times as well as saving the career of Alan Shearer, a gentleman whose association with the club gave us a dignity we have been sadly lacking since he left." Michael Martin, *True Faith*, true-faith.co.uk.

Heroes of the turf

"In the early days Veitch, McCracken, Crombie, Appleyard, Fairbrother. Pre-Second World War – Hughie Gallacher, Seymour, Weaver; in the fifties – Milburn*, Robledo Brothers, Mitchell, Harvey, Keeble, Brennan; in the sixties – White, Allchurch, Davies,

VILLAINS

"All home-grown – all directors – Westwood, McKeag, Hall, Shepherd but eclipsed by Ashley, Llambias and Wise." Michael Martin.

Moncur, Pop Robson; in the seventies – Supermac, Tudor, McDermott, Green, Smith and Hibbitt; in the eighties – Withe, Shoulder, Varadi, Beardsley, Waddle, Gascoigne, Keegan, McDermott and Goddard; and in the nineties-to date – Beardsley, Ferdinand, Shearer*, Sellars, Ginola, Asprilla, Lee, Speed, Solano and Robert.

*"Tie between Shearer and Milburn for the title of NUFC's greatest player – though Beardsley pushes them both hard." Michael Martin.

Zeroes of the turf

"Jean-Alain Boumsong. Rangers had signed him on a free, we paid about £8 million – two costly errors against Manchester United and little else. I think there was an enquiry into his transfer under the Stevens report as the fee seemed so high, but it turned out we were just stupid. Titus Bramble at times was a calamity too." Stuart Green, fan. "Also Jon Dahl Tomasson, Silvio Maric and Stephane Guivarch."

Greatest moments on this ground
"Beating Barcelona 3-2 in the Champions League at SJP in 1997; they had players like Figo, Rivaldo etc in the team. The whole stadium gasped at what was happening before us. I've never celebrated a goal so much as David Kelly's winner against Portsmouth at SJP in the old Second Division when we were staring down the barrel of a relegation gun. Numerous hammerings dished out to Sunderland; beating Manchester United 5-0; beating Italian giants, the mighty Juventus 1-0 in the Champions League; Supermac's debut (beating Liverpool 3-2); Kevin Keegan's debut when we beat QPR 1-0 and KK scored at The Gallowgate." Michael Martin.

Lowest moments on this ground
"Too many to choose from. Losing to Manchester United back in 1996 when Cantona scored early in the second half after we'd battered them in the first half was probably the point at which we suspected the dream of winning the PL title was crumbling. Losing 1-0 to Fulham that season in our last home game of the season was pretty much the point where relegation became real." Michael Martin.

The ground
St James' Park is in the top five most impressive grounds in the country. From a distance, across the city, it dominates the skyline. It has been extensively redeveloped in recent years and is an enclosed modern stadium, which has a capacity of 52,000. This is likely to be extended to around 60,000 in the near future with the redevelopment of the Gallowgate End, which will make it the second largest stadium in the League, and the Geordies wont have any trouble filling it either.

Away fans are seated in the very top corners of the **Sir John Hall Stand**, although it feels like you're up in the gods; with up to 3,000 fellow fans and the whole of the Toon Army the atmosphere is electrifying. The view despite the distance is excellent, as long as you have a head for heights. The stand itself is comprised of two huge tiers and a massive opaque roof. Splitting the two tiers are executive boxes.

The Sir John Hall sweeps continually round into the **Milburn Stand** that runs along the length of the pitch

GETTY IMAGES

∧ Newcastle legend Sir Bobby Robson.

and, like the stand behind the goal, has two massive tiers divided by executive boxes. The two stands are huge and have to be seen to be truly appreciated. In the corner between the two stands is the players' tunnel.

The **Gallowgate End** is home to the hardcore Newcastle fans and is one massive single tier with a low-slung roof, which makes for an acoustically incredible stand. It has always been home to the vocal part of the crowd and generates much of the noise during a game. There are future plans to add a second tier.

The Gallowgate sweeps around to the **East Stand**, which is also a large, single tier, at any other ground in the country it would be an impressive structure, but facing the two larger stands it is somewhat dwarfed.

> ST JAMES' PARK IS IN THE TOP FIVE MOST IMPRESSIVE GROUNDS IN THE COUNTRY.

> St James' Park.

Getting there

By Road/Parking Follow the A1 until the junction with the A184 signposted Newcastle. The road then splits after about two miles, take a left onto the A189 (the ground is signposted) cross the Tyne and continue on the dual carriageway. You will now be able to see the ground. Parking is in any of the many town centre car parks, all of which are pay and display. Be aware that the city centre can get congested, so allow for plenty of time. An alternative is to park in Gateshead on the other side of the river and catch the metro into the city centre.

By Train Newcastle main station is only a 10- to 15-minute walk from the ground; there are plenty of pubs and restaurants on the way.

HOME
AWAY

Pubs for home fans
The Bigg Market area, Haymarket and newly developed Quayside all have numerous bars which will be packed with home fans, none are specifically designated, but if you are an away fan keep your colours covered.

Good food near ground
Being central, the choice of food outlets is great with all the usual fast food and quality restaurants a city centre has nearby. There is also an area known as China Town not far from the ground, which does excellent food.

Pubs for away fans
St James' Park is very central for a football ground and hence the choice of pubs within a few minutes is almost unrivalled. Whilst the choice is high, many will not admit fans if they are obviously in team colours, so dress wisely. If travelling by train there are a number of pubs around the station that are popular with away fans, The Head of Steam being one. If you have time though it's really worth going a little further as there are many fine establishments that serve great beer and food, and you're never that far from the ground.

Top tips
Newcastle is a pretty friendly city, but it is wise to hide colours on match days if you want to have a pint.

THE LAST
WORD

true-faith.co.uk
nufcblog.com
nufcblog.org

NORTHAMPTON TOWN

- **Nicknames** The Cobblers
- **Founded** 1897
- **Ground** Sixfields (opened 1994)
- **Address** Upton Way, Northampton NN5 5QA
- **Capacity** 7,653
- **Best attendance** 24,523 (at Sixfields) vs Manchester City, Division Two, 26 September, 1998
- **Contact** 01604-683700
- **Ticket Number** 01604-683777
- **@ Email** paula.kane@ntfc.tv
- **Website** ntfc.co.uk

PUB QUIZ

That's quite interesting
"Probably the most notable fact that the Cobblers will be remembered for is losing 8-2 to Manchester United in 1970 with George Best scoring six of the goals." Mark Kennedy.

Not a lot of people know that
"Graham Carr, father of comedian Alan Carr, used to manage the Cobblers. Also, TV presenter Des O'Connor used to play for the club briefly before pursuing his career in entertainment!" Danny Brothers.

RIVALS
Peterborough United, MK Dons, Rushden and Diamonds.

For some smaller clubs life in the Football League is a battle. Campaign victories need to be celebrated because the war rages on. While the rest of England basked in the 1966 World Cup win, the folk of Northampton had already been revelling after a dream year in Division One, taking on the likes of Manchester United, Liverpool and Arsenal. Three successive promotions had seen the Midlanders rise from the footballing basement to the penthouse suite. It was a real football fairytale, but alas the team was always punching above its weight. The decrepit County Ground and a lack of finance meant they couldn't attract the talent or funds needed to maintain life with the big fish and by the end of the sixties Town found themselves back where they had started in Division Four. The next two decades weren't great. Stands were condemned, crowds dropped, but the move to the new Sixfield Stadium has seen a fresh start for The Cobblers, a new raft of battlefield skirmishes to savour. "Picture this," says Mark Kennedy, author of *We All Follow The Cobblers*. "Your team is 3-1 down from the first leg of the play-off semi-finals. The opposition fans travel to your ground already wearing their Wembley T-shirts." This was the scenario facing Town as the 1998 Division Two campaign was drawing to a close. "The Bristol Rovers announcer had been singing 'Wembley, Wembley' at their place at the end of the game," says Danny Brothers of aloadofcobblers blog. "But that only helped to spur us on." It was time to bring in the cavalry. "When Ray Warburton's header hit the net for 3-0 the roar was immense. It set up a second successive trip to Wembley," says Mark. "Roy of the Rovers stuff!"

VILLAINS
Terry Fenwick, Giles Coke. "Billy Turley, a promising keeper given a chance under Ian Atkins but managed to go off the rails a little before signing for Rushden & Diamonds. He lost the respect of Cobblers fans when he came out patting his back pocket to the away following during a pre-season friendly at Nene Park." Mark Kennedy.

Greatest moments on this ground
"The 3-0 victory over Bristol Rovers in the 1998 Division Two (League One) play-off semi-final…" Danny Brothers, aloadofcobblers.blogspot.com.

Lowest moments on this ground
"As a Cobblers fan you have some pretty dire moments at Sixfields, the worst includes the 0-5 home defeat to Wycombe in 2003 which ended Kevan Broadhurst's spell in charge as manager (and started Terry Fenwick's, the biggest managerial mistake in recent history). Drawing 2-2 with Burnley and getting relegated in 1999 was pretty hard to take as well." Mark Kennedy, Editor HotelEnders and author of *We All Follow The Cobblers*.

Heroes of the sideline
"Number one has to be Graham Carr, who assembled a team of nobodies who ran away with the Division Four title in 1987. He was a real wheeler-dealer with a down-to-earth approach and the fans loved him. Ian Atkins arrived following a barren run for the club in the mid-nineties. He brought a no nonsense approach – ultra defensive and some real kick and rush football – which led the club to Wembley twice. Phil Chard deserves a special mention. He was a player but in 1992 the club plunged into administration. He took over the unenviable task of keeping the team going on the pitch. He mastered a last day relegation escape with a 3-2 win at Shrewsbury overturning a 0-2 half-time deficit." Mark Kennedy.

⌄ Scott McGleish, 2005 and 2006 Cobblers player of the year.

Pubs for home fans
The ground is part of a leisure park so the pubs nearby are a bit formulaic but do the job. Hungry Horse Sixfields Tavern does serve real ales plus beers and decent food with big sports screens. The Magic Tower comes complete with bouncers.

Good food near ground
In the leisure park there's everything from Pizza Hut to Red Hot World Buffet – all you can eat 'global cuisine' for £7.95.

Pubs for away fans
At Sixsmiths, the Sports Bar has bowling, sports screens, pool tables and a mix of home and away fans. Also in the complex is TGI Fridays and Franky and Benny's. Foundrymans Arms, St James's Road (before the rugby ground) is a good rest stop for those coming via train. For real ale try Malt Shovel Tavern, Bridge Street (east along Street Peter's Way and half a mile in wrong direction for the ground).

Top tips
Don't park elsewhere in the leisure park as it can result in clamping, fines or stupid charges.

Heroes of the turf
"Neil 'Larry' Grayson – he never stopped giving 100% and scored some great goals in his time. My all-time favourite Cobbler. Ian 'Sammo' Sampson – a defender who stayed loyal to the club for over 10 years, with 449 appearances and is now assistant manager at the club. Ray Warburton – the central defender who played and led the side alongside Sammo in the mid to late nineties. Andy 'Woody' Woodman – a goalkeeper who never seemed to lose his joy of playing the game. He saved a penalty at Wembley, and was a mainstay of the 1997 centenary season where we reached the twin towers for the first time. Roy Hunter – a solid midfielder who epitomized the Ian Atkins era… he was never one to go on winding runs or score wonder goals but he had a commitment to the cause that worked as a backbone to the team." Danny Brothers.

Zeroes of the turf
"Northampton is a breeding ground for non talent or destroying a perfectly good striker with a good goal-scoring record. We'll start with Leon Constantine – a nice guy off the pitch, but looked lazy and couldn't score for toffee on it. Paul Wilkinson – he came with top-flight credentials and scored once at Burnley from on the goal line (he almost missed as well). James Quinn – another

Terry Fenwick era… he came in to pick up from the sacked, somewhat unfairly, Kevan Broadhurst around January 2003. Still in a decent enough position, he started with five defeats and two draws in seven games and was promptly shown the door. We went down that season." Danny Brothers.

striker with international experience who didn't set the world on fire at Northampton. Chris O'Donnell lasted 45 minutes in 1987 – he arrived on loan from Ipswich on the Friday, was late for training, had a stinker on Saturday and was on his way by full time." Mark Kennedy.

The ground
The Sixfields Stadium is a good example of a modern, purpose-built small stadium. Although it currently has a small capacity there is always the option to expand. The **Main West Stand** can accommodate 4,000 seated and houses changing rooms and a supporters' bar. Behind the goal is the all-seater **Dave Bowen North Stand** that holds 1,000 home fans. The **Alwyn Hargrave East Stand** is a single tier of seats but it also has another side backing onto the athletics track. Visiting fans are accommodated in the all-seater **South Stand** behind the far goal.

Getting there
By Road/Parking From the M1 north exit at junction 16 and follow the A45/Weedon Road to Northampton. The ground is just off the A45 to the left. From the M1 south exit at junction 15a onto the A43 and go straight over the roundabout onto the A45. Turn right towards the ground. Parking at ground is £3 – get there early.

By Train The train station is just over a mile and a half away – 30 minutes walk but it is simple to find. Go right out of the station onto St James Road, pass the rugby ground on the left, continue on. Turn left towards the leisure park then turn right. The stadium is ahead.

aloadofcobblers.blogspot.com
thehotelend.co.uk
web.ukonline.co.uk/ntfc

HOME COLOURS

- ⚽ **Nicknames** The Canaries
- 📅 **Founded** 1902
- 📍 **Ground** Carrow Road (opened 1935)
- ℹ️ **Address** Carrow Road, Norwich NR1 1JE
- 🎫 **Capacity** 26,0018
- ⭐ **Best attendance** 43,984 vs Leicester City, FA Cup 6th round, 30 March, 1963
- 📞 **Contact** 01603-760 760
- 🎟️ **Ticket Number** 0844-826 1902
- @ **Email** ticket@ncfc-canaries.co.uk
- Ⓦ **Website** canaries.co.uk

NORWICH CITY

Norwich City are a club that it's difficult to dislike. The county city of Norfolk has a sizeable and passionate support for a team that has built a reputation over the years for playing attractive and entertaining football. Their periods of success, though short-lived, have burned bright. Under Mike Walker they built a formidable side in the early nineties and in the inaugural Premier League season they led the top flight for most of the campaign. Players like Chris Sutton and Jeremy Goss were at the forefront of exciting and well-crafted football, but ultimately they finished third behind Manchester United and Aston Villa. The following season they enjoyed a glorious adventure on their first run out into European football, with an incredible win away at Bayern Munich. Germany's most powerful side had never lost a game at home in Europe, but Norwich outplayed them and ran out convincing victors. Prior to this, Europe had eluded them due more to misfortune than league position. Having won their only piece of modern silverware, The League Cup in 1985, they were denied European entry due to the blanket ban on English clubs. They also qualified twice for Europe later in the decade but faced the same fate. After that first Premiership season though, the club failed to repeat the feat again. Then-chairman Robert Chase sold top talent to

'balance the books' (Chris Sutton went for a then record £5 million) and re-invested little back on the pitch, frustrating fans and managers alike with an apparent lack of ambition. Martin O'Neill resigned as manager after just six months, citing Chase as the main reason. Since those heady days, Norwich have steadily slipped, and despite the best efforts of popular TV cook and majority shareholder Delia Smith they recently found themselves in the third tier of English football – though they quickly bounced back to the second. Their support has never wavered through this and they consistently pull bigger crowds of loyal supporters than you would expect of a club of their size.

Greatest moments on this ground

"It would have to be the Munich game way back. One of the top sides in the world at the time, and 'little old Norwich' not only managed to beat them in their own backyard two weeks before, but also show the world that it was no fluke, by finishing the job at home. Jerry Goss was the hero of the day with what became a trademark volley to see us through, something, which I am sure, will live in the memory of everyone that was there, till their dying day. At the time it was thought that this was to be the start of something big, unfortunately it has not turned out that way." Ricky Bilverstone, canarycorner.net.

Lowest moments on this ground

"This doesn't really have any connection to a single match at Carrow Road, but the fate of the club as it is today. When we heard star striker Chris Sutton was being sold for £5 million, the fans were promised that the club would have a new signing within the next week or so. And so we did, a £1 million flourmill on the outskirts of the ground (Norwich invested money in land and property rather than players). It was the start of 'prudence over ambition.'" Ricky Bilverstone.

Heroes of the sideline

"Mike Walker guided the side into the top three of the Premiership and European football. Dave Stringer will, of course, jump to mind. He was the man that built our European team, although he had decided a year before that he had taken us as far as he could, leaving Mike Walker the task of finishing the job. A star during his playing days as well, Stringer lined up 499 times for the club and was manager of the youth side that won the FA Cup back in 1983." Ricky Bilverstone.

RIVALS

Ipswich Town by a country mile.

PUB QUIZ

That's quite interesting
Norwich were the first English team to beat Bayern Munich in European competition on their own ground.

Not a lot of people know that
Before moving to Carrow Road, Norwich played at a ground in a natural bowl giving it an incredible atmosphere, it was appropriately named 'The Nest.'

⌃ The goal by Jeremy Goss against Bayern Munich in October 1993 is considered by many Norwich fans the best ever. The Canaries went on to a famous 2-1 away win.

Villains

"Robert Chase and Kevin Muscat. In 1998, playing for Wolves, Muscat 'assaulted' Craig Bellamy with a terrible tackle, and with it, ended any chances of a top finish for The Canaries. Muscat was always in for a warm welcome whenever he returned to Carrow Road," Ricky Bilverstone.

Don't mention the…

Fact that in 1978 when Ipswich Town won the FA Cup, Delia Smith was pictured in the local Ipswich paper in a blue and white scarf and hat (she says the producer of a TV show she was in asked her to wear them)!

The ground

Carrow Road is a modern stadium on an old site, with the four sides of the ground having been replaced during the nineties. It is now situated in amongst a modern retail park on one side and older terraced houses on the other. The whole area used to be very much one of old industry, which has slowly been redeveloped, and the football ground stands in the middle as a fine stadium.

The **Barclay End** is the home to the core of City fans and holds 6,107. The two-tier all-seater is an impressive end stand; the two tiers are divided by a row of executive boxes. The lower tier is where all the noise comes from in a game.

The **Jarrold South Stand** is the newest of the four sides and the biggest of the two side stands. At the Barclay stand end is seating for between 2,500 and 3,000 away supporters, it offers an excellent view and an opportunity for good banter with the home faithful. Capacity 8,184.

The **River End** or Norwich and Peterborough, is the oldest of the four stands but is again an impressive two-tiered affair split by a row of executive boxes that can hold 5,799; there is also an electronic scoreboard.

The main stand is The **Geoffrey Watling Stand** and is home to the directors' box and press areas as well as dressing rooms. Three of the four corners of the ground are also filled in, giving an enclosed feel to it. Both of the side stands are designed so an extra tier could be added should the club regain its Premiership status.

Getting there

By Road/Parking From the A11 and A47 the ground is well signposted and is easy to find. Take the A146 towards the city, turning right at the first set of lights then left at the next roundabout. Turn right at the next lights and follow the inner ring road over the river and you are in Carrow Road.

There is some limited street parking a distance from the ground at the away fans end, but more and more of this is becoming permit-only. There are a number of car parks, the one near County Hall as you come into the city is a good bet.

By Train Norwich is on the mainline from Liverpool Street. The ground is an easy 10-minute walk and is clearly visible from the station.

Pubs for home fans
The proximity of the city centre means a lot of home fans have the option of drinking all over, but with the development along the riverside area many have relocated to these pubs. Squares, Brannigans and Lloyds No.1 are popular, and will often have bouncers on the doors for big matches.

Good food near ground
There are plenty of excellent places to eat in the city and in the surrounding pubs, as well as a Morrison's supermarket right next to the ground. But bear in mind that board member Delia Smith prides herself on her cooking and brings a new level of standard to the in-stadium cuisine.

Pubs for away fans
The Compleat Angler opposite the station has long been the away fans pub and is about a ten-minute walk from the ground. However, with the redevelopment of the riverside area there are a number of Wetherspoon-type pubs on the way, not all are welcoming, but some will let you in with colours covered. You can make the journey from station to ground a fun pub crawl.

Top tips
Don't try and park on any of the retail chain car parks unless they are operating a match-day car park, you will get clamped.

HOME COLOURS

NOTTINGHAM FOREST

- **Nicknames** Forest
- **Founded** 1865
- **Ground** City Ground (opened 1898)
- **Address** Nottingham NG2 5FJ
- **Capacity** 30,576
- **Best attendance** 49,946 vs Manchester United, Division One, 2 October, 1967
- **Contact** 0115-982 4455
- **Ticket Number** 0871-226 1980
- **Email** enquiries@nottinghamforest.co.uk
- **Website** nottinghamforest.co.uk

Sometimes it's hard to put into perspective the successes from decades long gone, especially when they are viewed from the lofty position of the comfortable 'executive box of hindsight'. To look back and truly appreciate the accomplishments of Brian Clough and Peter Taylor, one must first forget the League title, the European silverware, the Trevor Francis diving header in Munich and the awesome squad they assembled. "To have led Forest from near relegation in the second tier (where they are now in the 2010/11 season) to League and European champions would be the equivalent of, well, of Billy Davies doing the same thing now," says the editor of nffcblog.com. "Doesn't seem likely does it?" When the management team regrouped at the City Ground in the mid-seventies, Clough was best known for his 44 day failed tenure at Leeds United and Taylor for his stint at lowly Brighton. While at Derby, the duo had won the 1972 League title but many questioned whether they could do it again. Forest were still considered small by English League standards, but they were ambitious, and by the end of the following season Clough/Taylor had steered them to promotion to the top tier. The year after they were champions of all England. Not only that but the team they built took two consecutive European Cups and made household names of every player.

Since the reign of Clough ended in 1993, Forest have seen little in the way of success, struggling even to maintain a presence in the top flight. Fourteen managers have sat in the dugouts at the City Ground, trying to emulate the glory of that era. It's ironic that just as as Don Revie dominated Leeds, the club that proved to be Clough's 'White Whale', so Clough's record now stands supreme at the small club that, thanks to his reign with Taylor, we now describe as a sleeping giant.

> There are few keener fought derbies than that between Forest and County. Rob Earnshaw fires in the first goal of an FA Cup tie at Pride Park.

RIVALS

Notts County, Derby County and Leicester City.

GETTY IMAGES

⌃ HEROES OF THE TURF

"Stuart Pearce. He gave 100% every single game and didn't know the meaning of the word defeat. He played with his heart and had passion for the club and its supporters. Not a bad player either. Peter Shilton – probably the best goalkeeper in the world, during his spell with us. John Robertson – Brian Clough changed him from a mediocre player going nowhere fast, into one of the best wingers in the world back in his day. A ripple of excitement would go around the ground whenever the ball was passed to him and he always beat his man," Kevin Finnegan.

"Stan Collymore; could and should have been the greatest, an ill-conceived move to Liverpool saw him never recapture the form that scintillated the City Ground crowd for two seasons. Such a wasted talent. Brian Rice – he's still sung about to this day, now the Hibernian Assistant Manager, he is an enduring cult hero. A group of Forest fans from popular forum ltlf.co.uk, numbering around 30 or 40, all have the name Rice emblazoned on their current Forest shirts!" Editor, nffcblog.com.

GETTY IMAGES

That's quite interesting

"Sam Widdowson was a rather inventive chap who played for Forest (and even ended up chairman of the club). He can be credited with inventing shinpads and was the first to referee a match which featured goal nets!" Editor, nffcblog.com.

Not a lot of people know that

"In 1980 the City Ground was the first to use different coloured seats to create writing in the stand, spelling out FOREST. This is now a ubiquitous feature in modern-day stadia." Editor, nffcblog.com.

PUB QUIZ

∧ Different world – Trevor Francis on the flight deck, coming home with the European Cup.

PIERRE VAN HOOIJDONK WAS FAMED FOR GOING ON STRIKE. HE REFUSED TO PLAY, BECAUSE OF OUR APPARENT LACK OF AMBITION.

Greatest moments on this ground

"I curse my parents weekly for being too slow off the mark, because the greatest moments at the City Ground occurred before I was born or whilst just a baby. Upon the arrival of a certain Brian Clough and Peter Taylor, at a club that ironically occupied a similar position to the current team, Forest were promoted, League champions and then champions of Europe twice all within four seasons. My own personal highlight is a sad occasion, but the send-off we gave to Brian Clough despite being relegated was – in its own way – a wonderful moment that I cherish the memory of." Editor nffcblog.com.

Lowest moments on this ground

"The play-off semi-final defeat of 2007 against Yeovil still hurts to this day. 2-0 up after the first leg should have meant we were home and dry. We even went 3-1 up at one stage in the second leg, but we conspired to take the game into extra-time and lost 5-4 on aggregate. It ruined an entire summer and consigned us to a third year in League One. For me it was the realization of just how low this club had sunk." Kevin Finnegan, Vital Forest.

Heroes of the sideline

"This is an extraordinarily easy question for Forest fans. Brian Clough and Peter Taylor, as a team they were – and are – peerless. The important part is Peter Taylor as well; too often his contribution gets ignored or understated. A rare subject upon which Forest and Derby fans will agree." Editor, nffcblog.com.

Zeroes of the turf

"David Platt; I've cheated a bit here, but technically he was player-manager, and it's for his (mis)management he is still a deeply unpopular man in Nottingham. He wasted millions on substandard players, culminating in the financial difficulties Forest only just find themselves recovering from." Editor, nffcblog.com.

Villains

"Pierre Van Hooijdonk was famed for going on strike. He refused to play, because of our apparent lack of ambition. As wrong as he was to go on strike, he did have a point." Kevin Finnegan.

Don't mention the…

"Coffee cup. This incident happened at Pride Park in a game we eventually lost 4-2. Derby came back when a backpass to 'keeper Barry Roche struck a coffee cup on the pitch, making him miss-kick directly to Paul Peschisolido who scored into an open goal. The coffee cup game still gives me nightmares." Editor, nffcblog.com.

The ground

The City Ground has a large, mostly modern feel to it with excellent views. The **Brian Clough Stand** is the largest accommodating 10,000 fans, a two-tier structure running the length of the pitch. It was built in 1980 with the help of the proceeds from the successful European missions. Away behind the goal, the two-tier **Trent End Stand** is the most recent, built in time for Euro 96 with a capacity of 7,500. The 5,708-capacity **Main Stand** was rebuilt after a fire in 1968 and now looks dated in comparison to the rest of the ground. The changing rooms are located here. Behind the other goal stands the distinctive **Bridgford Stand** that drops from two tier to single tier left to right as you look at it. The lower tier can hold 5,131 and is usually allocated to away fans. The unusual shape was a planning requirement to allow sunlight to reach houses in nearby Colwick Road.

Getting there

By Road/Parking From the north, leave the M1 at junction 26, and take the A610 to Nottingham. Take the A6514 (Ring Road South) and go straight over the next roundabout onto Middleton Boulevard (becoming Clifton Boulevard). Turn left onto Loughborough Road (passing County Hall parking on your left) and right onto Radcliff Road.

From the south, exit the M1 at junction 24 following the A453 towards Nottingham. Take the A52 signed Grantham joining Gamston Lings Bar Road then left onto the A6011, Radcliffe Road. The ground will be off on the right and there are local signs for parking. Home fans can use the park and ride facility on Queen's Drive for £4. There are a number of reasonably priced car parks nearby including Meadow Lane (Notts County) and the Cattle Market (£3).

By Train Nottingham station is about a 15-minute walk from the ground. Turn left out of the station and then left again. Follow the road down to the dual carriageway and then turn right. Keep walking and cross the Trent Bridge, the City ground is on your right.

nffcblog.com
forest.vitalfootball.co.uk
u-reds.com
forestfans.net
ltlf.co.uk
nottinghamforest-mad.co.uk
eighteensixtyfive.co.uk

Peter Taylor and Brian Clough, 1979 European Cup final against Malmö in Munich. Forest won 1-0.

GETTY IMAGES

Pubs for home fans
The large Trent Bridge Inn is a home fans' favourite with big screen and pub grub (plus bouncers on match days pointing away supporters elsewhere). The Southbank, Trent Bridge has large sports screens, real ales plus a good selection of food – from baguettes to steaks. Larwood and Voce Tavern, Fox Road, next to the cricket ground, is a gastro pub with guest ales and big screens showing live sport.

Good food near ground
Larwood and Voce by the ground serves breakfast until 1200 with a good bar menu after. Hooters, Queen's Road near the station, serves all American-food with extras, resulting in a smile!

Pubs for away fans
Vat and Fiddle, Queensbridge Road is by the station with decent food and real ales. Ye Olde Trip To Jerusalem, Brewhouse Yard, five minutes from the station, claims to be the oldest inn in Britain. Good selection of ales in warren of cave-like snugs hewn from rock beneath the castle. On the other side of the river, Wheelers, Meadow Lane at Notts County is becoming a bit of an unofficial away supporters venue on Forest match days.

Top tips
Avoid parking in residential roads as many parking restrictions operate on match days.

NOTTS COUNTY

- 🏷 **Nicknames** The Magpies
- 📅 **Founded** 1862
- 🏟 **Ground** Meadow Lane (opened 1910)
- ℹ **Address** Nottingham NG2 3HJ
- ℹ **Capacity** 19,588
- 🏆 **Best attendance** 47,310 vs York City, FA Cup 6th round, 12 March, 1955
- 📞 **Contact** 0115-952 9000
- 🎟 **Ticket Number** 0115-955 7204
- @ **Email** office@nottscountyfc.co.uk
- 🌐 **Website** nottscountyfc.co.uk

Pubs for home fans
The Globe, London Road – excellent selection of hand-pulled real ales and an emphasis on local breweries. Filled rolls on match days. The Southbank, Trent Bridge has large sports screens, real ales plus a good selection of food. Popular with home and away fans. Cattle Market Tavern, Cattle Market Road is one of the closest pubs to Meadow Lane.

Good food near ground
Aside from the pubs, try Hooters, Queen's Road near the station. The food is all American and the service definitely comes with a smile.

Pubs for away fans
Vat and Fiddle, Queensbridge Road is by the station and next to Castle Rock Brewery whose wears they sell with other guest ales. Decent food. Ye Olde Trip To Jerusalem, Brewhouse Yard, five minutes from the station, claims to be the oldest inn in Britain. Good selection of ales in warren of cave-like snugs hewn from rock beneath the castle.

Top tips
Depending on who The Magpies are playing, the pubs nearest the ground may or may not be happy to let away fans in.

With an amazing 12 promotions and 15 relegations to their name, County are your archetypal yo-yo team. Not for them the monotony of mid-table anonymity; it's do or die at Meadow Lane. Plot a graph of the club's league positions over their nearly 150-year history and it has more peaks and troughs than the Himalayan mountain range; more highs and lows than a World War Two fighter ace. Through the seventies and into the eighties the team saw an Apollo 11-like rise from the basement of the fourth tier to the astronomical heights of the top division. But supporters also experienced the Columbia-like descent that started the year the Premier League was founded and saw County plummet from the top flight and freefall in a plume of debris back to bottom of the professional tree.

In today's world of football haves and have-nots, where some clubs fight off bankruptcy while others splash billionaires' cash, at the start of the 2009/2010 season it seemed that County's boat had come in. The club, having seen off its own financial troubles, attracted the attention of a high-rolling Middle Eastern consortium. County fans awoke a few mornings later to find their fourth-tier team had a new director of football in the form of ex-England manager Sven-Göran Erikson. It is unclear whether they were lured by the prospect of owning the world's oldest professional football team or whether it was the promise of an annual adrenaline-fuelled ride back to the big time. But whatever the motivation, the financial realities didn't live up to the hype and less than a year later Notts County found themselves being sold, for the princely sum of one pound to a saviour of more modest means and realistic ambition. Despite these distractions, the Magpies kept their eye on the real prize, the silverware, claiming the League Two title and guaranteeing their survival.

RIVALS
City rivals Nottingham Forest are the fiercest. Also Mansfield Town, Derby County, Leicester City and Lincoln City.

Greatest moments on this ground
"There have been a number of great moments at Meadow Lane, both the former ground and the rebuilt version which stands today. From the huge crowds that saw Tommy Lawton ply his trade in Division Three to 1994's 2-1 derby day victory over Nottingham Forest, dubbed 'Charlie Palmer Day' by fans." Jacob Daniel, editor, *Notts County Mad*.

Lowest moments on this ground
"Many of the worst moments of Meadow Lane have come in recent times. A 7-1 home defeat to Newcastle United in the League Cup and a 1-0 defeat to minnows Havant & Waterlooville in 2007's FA Cup are some of the more embarrassing. Notts also found themselves staring down the relegation barrel to the Conference when 2-0 down at home to Bury before coming back to draw 2-2, and a 1-1 draw with Luton Town was believed to be the club's last-ever match when the Magpies looked to be heading into liquidation." Jacob Daniel.

Heroes of the turf
"Tommy Lawton – the England centre forward stunned the footballing world when signed for Third Division Notts County for a world-record transfer fee. He attracted huge crowds and is one of the finest players seen at the club;

he later returned for a spell as manager. Don Masson – a Scotland international midfielder, with cultured passing and a footballing brain. Tales are often told by the club's older fans of Masson's genius. Brian Stubbs – an uncompromising defender who spent his whole career at Meadow Lane, from the bottom tier to the top flight; he played over 400 games. Mark Draper – talented midfielder Draper came through the youth system, he was comfortable on the ball, with an eye for a pass. Tommy Johnson – another youth product, with explosive pace and finishing; he scored one of the Wembley goals that saw Notts gain promotion to the top flight." Jacob Daniel.

Zeroes of the turf

"Tony Hackworth – he came with a pedigree having played in a Champions League semi-final for Leeds. He cost £125,000, scored three goals and rarely impressed, and left to play for Scarborough and Whitby Town. Guy Branston – centre-back played just 45 minutes against Stockport County, but will always be remembered. In that time he cost the side two goals, nearly got sent off, had an argument with his centre-back partner and kicked most of the opposition team before being hauled off at the break. Darren Caskey – he came from Tottenham Hotspur and Reading, and never lived up to his astronomical wages. He put on huge amounts of weight and was criticized for his lazy demeanor on the pitch. He's has gone on to non-league sides and America." Jacob Daniel.

Don't mention the…

"Time a squirrel ran onto the pitch during a home game against Milton Keynes Dons, leading to fans chanting 'there's only one Jimmy Squirrel.'" Jacob Daniel.

The ground

County moved to Meadow Lane in 1910 but today it is a modern, all-seater stadium with a 20,000 capacity and excellent views and facilities. The **Main Stand** or Derek Pavis Stand houses the offices and changing rooms. It is single-tier with no pillars and runs the length of the pitch. At the far end behind the goal is the two-tier **Kop**. For many years away fans were housed here, but as of the

2008/09 season away fans are now housed in a section of the **Jimmy Sirrel Stand**. Named after the legendary manager, this stand runs the length of the pitch and has a distinctive flag pole on the front of the roof on the half-way line. Excellent views and no pillars. Behind the other goal is the single-tier **Family Stand**. The ground lies only 300-m away from Nottingham Forest's City Ground, although on the other side of the River Trent.

Getting there

By Road/Parking From the north, leave the M1 at junction 26, and take the A610 to Nottingham. At the second roundabout take the second exit onto the A6008/Maid Marian Way and follow. At the roundabout take the third exit onto the A60/London Road. Turn left at the Cattle Market Road (the ground is on your right). From the south, exit the M1 at junction 24 following the the A453 and signs for Nottingham (south) to Trent Bridge. Cross the river and follow the one way system. Turn left then turn right at the traffic lights and head right onto Meadow Lane.

There are a couple of reasonably priced car parks nearby including one at the Cattle Market. Street parking is also available including the Embankment.

By Train Nottingham station is just a 10 minute walk from the ground. Turn left out of the station and then left again. Follow the road down to the dual carriageway and then turn right. Keep walking until you see the ground on your left (about a quarter of mile).

That's quite interesting
Notts County are the oldest Football League club in the world, having been formed in 1862, and are founder members of the Football League. They are set to celebrate their 150th anniversary in 2012.

Not a lot of people know that
Cray Wanderers of Bromley were founded in 1860 and currently play in the seventh tier of English football, the Isthmian League Premier Division. If they are ever promoted to the fourth flight they will take Notts County's record of oldest professional team.

PUB QUIZ

THE LAST **WORD**

nottscounty-mad.co.uk
youpies.co.uk
nottscountyfc.cjb.net
homepage.ntlworld.com/carousel/maggies00.html
nottscounty.vitalfootball.co.uk

VILLAINS
...am Allardyce – he left the club
...n acrimonious circumstances
after leading The Magpies to the
Third Division title. He joined
Bolton Wanderers days after
resigning at Meadow Lane citing
personal problems." Jacob Daniel.

⌃ **HEROES OF THE SIDELINE**
"Jimmy Sirrel – easily the club's greatest-ever manager, he masterminded The Magpies' rise from the bottom division to the top flight, building a side that played attractive football with home-grown players and shrewd signings. He hugely influenced Sir Alex Ferguson's career and his death in 2008 left the club in mourning. Jack Wheeler – Sirrel's right hand-man. Wheeler spent over 25 years at Meadow Lane in various roles including trainer, coach and caretaker manager. He was a true Magpies legend on the touchline for 1,152 consecutive games and his death shortly after Sirrel's meant the end of an era for the club. Neil Warnock – he joined the club from Scarborough as a young manager and oversaw the club's most recent rise to the top flight thanks to successive promotions. He unearthed a number of young gems at the club and is still extremely popular at Meadow Lane to this day." Jacob Daniel.

HOME COLOURS

- **Nicknames** The Latics
- **Founded** 1895
- **Ground** Boundary Park (opened 1904)
- **Address** Furtherwood Road, Oldham OL1 2PA
- **Capacity** 10,638
- **Best attendance** 47,671 vs Sheffield Wednesday, FA Cup 4th Round, 1930
- **Contact** 0871-226 2235
- **Ticket Number** 0871-226 1653
- **Email** enquiries@oldhamathletic.co.uk
- **Website** oldhamathletic.co.uk

We're in an era when football pundits are all to happy to tell us a certain team will be 'down by Christmas' or that another has 'lost their chance of the title in August', so it's refreshing to think back to the early summer of 1993. The World Wide Web was born at CERN, Whitney Houston tortured the planet as *I Will Always Love You* recorded its eighth consecutive year at number one and *Jurassic Park* tore up the carcass of *Free Willy* to become the top grossing film around the globe. Meanwhile, in a small town in Lancashire, Joe Royle's Oldham were all but down and out in the inaugural Premiership. With three games to go The Latics needed nine points to have any chance of survival. They had high-flying Aston Villa first, then Liverpool and finally Southampton to play, all in the space of a week. In a massive shock they turned over Villa away, then rolled into the game against The Reds and stormed a 3-2 win. It was all down to the last game. "We had to beat Southampton at Oldham and Arsenal had to beat Palace," says Royle. "We knew that Palace were losing 2-0 but it didn't matter because Southampton got back from 4-1 down to 4-3 and suddenly there was panic." Oldham's survival was hanging by a thread. "There's footage of me running up and down the stairs to try and get a better view of the game," says the ex-Oldham manager, "and the referee laughing at me as he played six minutes of injury-time." When the final whistle blew the crowd erupted. Palace were down on goal difference and Oldham had survived. This era is still celebrated by fans at Boundary Park; it wasn't just Royle – at times it was Regal.

VILLAINS

"New chairman Chris Moore arrived in 2001 and promised Premiership football within five years, but in 2003 the team lost out in the play-offs and the club went into administration. He left under a cloud." Dave Moore.

Greatest moments on this ground

"Athletic beat Hull City 3-0 in their final Second Division game on 30 April, 1910 to secure their first-ever promotion to the First Division. The Boundary Park gate of 29,083 at that match was a record. The first leg in the semi-final of the League Cup was played on 14 February, 1990 and Athletic all but booked their first Wembley trip with a 6-0 annihilation of West Ham." Dave Moore, Editor, Oldham Athletic Mad, author of *Oldham Athletic: On This Day* and *Oldham Athletic: Miscellany*.

Lowest moments on this ground

"On 17 May 1987 in the first-ever year of play-offs, Athletic played the second leg at Boundary Park but the 2-1 final scoreline for the Latics, watched by 19,216 supporters, meant that Leeds went through on the away goals rule." Dave Moore.

Heroes of the sideline

"Jack Rowley, best remembered for the inspirational signing of Bobby Johnstone, brought fans flocking to Boundary Park and resulted in Athletic winning promotion in 1962/63. His reward for promotion was the sack. Jimmy Frizzell, a player and manager for 22 years, took the side from a struggling Fourth Division team to a respected Second Division team after winning the Third Division Championship in 1973/74. He was sensationally sacked in 1982 and was the second longest serving manager in the league. Joe Royle, Athletic's most successful manager ever, took the club to Wembley for the first time ever in the Littlewoods Cup final in 1990, also to two FA Cup semi-finals and won the Second Division Championship to return Athletic to the First Division after a 68-year break." Dave Moore.

Heroes of the turf

"Bobby Johnstone, allegedly the best-ever player to grace Boundary Park. Crowds quadrupled when he signed and his time at Oldham became known as the Johnstone era. Roger Palmer, good with both feet and his head was the all-time goal-scorer with 141 goals in a career that lasted from 1980 until 1992. Andy Ritchie scored many brilliant goals and made a huge contribution to the 'pinch me' years. A loyal supporter of the Latics, he was well respected by all. Bert Lister, one of our greatest goal-scorers, banged in six of 11 against Southport on Boxing Day 1962. Ian Wood played a record 585 games for

Oldham between 1965 and 1980 and achieved an unbroken appearance record of 161 games." Dave Moore.

Zeroes of the turf

"Albert Quixall, former golden boy of Old Trafford, came with a big pedigree but his injured knee always flared up before away trips – he never fulfilled his expected potential. Tony Hateley was another big name who fell into the same mould. Ian Olney came as a record signing – he was 6ft-plus but never scored many goals with his head. Dean Windass thought that he was going to set the world alight but his scoring record was abysmal. Brian Kilcline, Phil Starbuck and Richard Butcher have all been described by Latics fans as the worst players ever to tread the turf at Boundary Park." Dave Moore.

The ground

The **Detect All Alarms (Chaddy) End** is the second largest in the stadium with 3,754 seats. The changing rooms and offices are currently housed in the main **Pentagon Vauxhall Stand**, much of which dates back to 1904. It has two tiers totalling 2,455 seats. The **Rochdale Road Leesfield Developments Stand** is a single tier of covered seating built in 1992. It has a capacity of 4,609 divided between just under 3,000 home and just over 1,600 visiting fans for the majority of games. The stadium is currently a three sided affair with the Broadway side in 'redevelopment'. However a move to a new stadium is being mooted.

Getting there

By Road/Parking Just north of the city centre and on the eastern side of greater Manchester, Oldham is easy to reach from the motorway. From the M62, exit junction 20 (signed Oldham) and follow the A627M. Take A627 exit and follow. Boundary Park will come into view on your left. From the M60, exit junction 21 following signs for Chadderton/A663 and follow (either all the way to the car park or for the club) to the roundabout taking fourth exit onto the A627. The ground will come into view on the left. The official car park cost £3 and is signed off the A663.

By Train Oldham Werneth (with connections via Manchester Victoria) is the closest station to the ground – around a 15-minute walk. Heading north, turn right out of the station onto Featherstall Road (with a number of pubs for the travel weary) and continue along, passing Tesco. Go left onto the dual carriageway – via the underpass – and follow. Go right onto the Boundary Park Road for the stadium.

THE FA VIA GETTY IMAGES

That's quite interesting
Former team Pine Villa took possession of the bankrupt Oldham County's old ground (Oldham Athletic Grounds), and changed their name to Oldham Athletic.

Not a lot of people know that
Athletic have taken part in three play-offs and three FA Cup semi-finals and have won none.

∧ The excitement of the FA Cup as Leeds are the visitors to Boundary Park on a November night in 2009.

HOME AWAY

Pubs for home fans
Old Grey Mare, Oldham Road is just around the corner from the stadium with large sports screens and food available. Visiting supporters are usually welcome. Clayton Arms, Furtherwood Road, is just behind the ground with Sky Sports, food, Lees Bitter and generally a good buzz on match days.

Good food near ground
In the nearby retail park there is a wide range of exotic fare including KFC and Pizza Hut.

Pubs for away fans
There are a good number of pubs in the locality of the ground. The White Heart, Oldham Road, is just down the road from the Old Grey Mare, a Courage pub that also serves food.

Top tips
As long as you don't support Manchester United, you should be fine! Also there always seems to be a cold wind blowing, so keep your scarf wrapped tight.

DON'T MENTION THE...

Mid-season punch-up at the dogs between Manager John Sheridan, bad-boy striker Lee Hughes and assorted others.

THE LAST WORD

oldhamathletic-mad.co.uk
oafc.co.uk

HOME COLOURS

- **Nicknames** The U's
- **Founded** 1893
- **Ground** Kassam Stadium (opened 2001)
- **Address** Grenoble Road, Oxford, OX4 4XP
- **Capacity** 12,500
- **Best attendance** 12,243 vs Leyton Orient, League Two, 6 May, 2006
- **Contact** 01865-337 500
- **Ticket Number** 01865-337 533
- **Email** admin@oufc.co.uk
- **Website** oufc.co.uk

OXFORD UNITED

There's nothing quite as dramatic as a play-off victory at Wembley, it could be argued it's better than actually winning the League title. After all, you get all the suspense of the knock-out semi-finals, plus a day out at the home of football that has a lot more at stake than a piece of silverware – the work of a whole season is riding on these ninety minutes. There's nothing as good as winning a play-off final because there's nothing as bad as losing one. Walking up Wembley Way, the expectation, the hopes and the dreams – yes play-off final day is a nerve shredder. In 2010 it was Oxford and York fans turn to bite their nails and put their heads in their hands within the embrace of the famous stadium, this season of symmetry ending with the tie that started it all off back in August. For Oxford it was a chance at redemption, a place back in the big time after the banishment to the realms of non-league football.

For some U's fans this trip would have brought back memories of the 1985/86 season when Oxford, then a top flight team, lifted the League Cup in the shadow of the twin towers. A three year stay in Division One, the yellow and blue rampant, John Aldridge banging in the goals for fun, Ray Houghton, Billy Hamilton, Trevor Hebberd and Malcolm Shotton. They even had a high profile owner in Robert Maxwell. At one point he proposed merging the team with rivals Reading to produce a Thames Valley super club – obviously the fans were buying none of it.

For supporters it's often easy to look back on an era and wonder whether it really happened at all. From the depths of the Football Conference, Oxford were looking a long way up the ladder. Yet, as the final-whistle blew on the 2010 play-off final, the U's fans finally had something to celebrate. Perhaps better than if they'd stormed the League title as looked likely early on in the season, now they'd had their day out at Wembley, three goals to cheer

and promotion back to League Two. As the Icelandic ash splashed the sunset with crimson brushstrokes, burning bright over the capital, it was a yellow and blue stream of fans that meandered last from within the hallowed ground, strangers hugging strangers, the end of an era, tomorrow's dawn promising a clean slate.

Greatest moments on this ground
"The 1-0 win over Swindon in the FA Cup second round in 2002 would be considered by most to be their best memory at the Kassam, especially when you consider that it was live on TV. However, the 2010, 2-0 play-off semi-final win over Rushden just edges it for me, because of the atmosphere, the prize, and the excellent goals Oxford scored." Martin Brodetsky, editor, rageonline.co.uk.

Lowest moments on this ground
"Without a doubt this would have to be the 3-2 defeat by Orient in 2006 on the last day of the season. Both because it meant relegation from the Football League to the Conference, and also because the result meant automatic promotion for Orient, leading to their fans' wild celebrations on the pitch in front of us. To cap it all, the goal that sent us down was scored by United old-boy Lee Steele, in the final minute too." Martin Brodetsky.

Heroes of the sideline
"Jim Smith took United from the Third Division to the First Division in successive seasons. Arthur Turner took United from the Southern League to Division Two in just six seasons. Chris Wilder, the current incumbent, turned a team of no-hopers into a Football League side in less than two seasons." Martin Brodetsky.

Villains
"Wayne Biggins was signed by Denis Smith to be the goal-scorer to lead United to promotion. After just two goals in his first 15 games, and a number of uncommitted performances, Smith admitted he'd made a mistake and "Bertie" was allowed to move to Wigan. Courtney Pitt was given a nickname that rhymed with his surname after the former Portsmouth winger gave a number of inept displays. Emiliano Diaz was then-manager Ramon Diaz's son, but he failed to inherit any of his father's footballing ability, being instead a liability. His brother Michael failed to even make the first team, but he allegedly crocked the recuperating Jamie Brooks during training, setting back Brooks' recovery several months." Martin Brodetsky

⩘ **HEROES OF THE TURF**
"Joey Beauchamp. A local boy and a supporter who had the talent to go all the way, but preferred to play for United. Matt Elliott was a giant centre-half who could also play with the ball at his feet – a rock. John Aldridge just couldn't stop scoring! Scored the goals that took United into the top flight. Ray Houghton was an inspirational midfielder and part of the 'Glory Team' that won the League Cup. Roy Burton was a superb goalkeeper who played for over 10 years, making a number of impossible saves despite being relatively short." Martin Brodetsky.

⩗ **ZEROES OF THE TURF**
"Peter Fear. A former Premiership midfielder who just couldn't be bothered to lower himself to play for the U's. Ray Gaston was a a Northern Ireland international and fearsome striker with Coleraine who looked totally out of his depth in the Second Division. Mike Salmon signed on loan from Charlton with a decent reputation; conceded seven goals in his first game and never played for United again!" Martin Brodetsky.

Not a lot of people know that
"The club was formed as Headington FC in 1893. They changed their name again, to Headington United, and finally became Oxford United in 1956." Martin Brodetsky.

Don't mention the…
"FA Cup in 1951, when United were thrown out for fielding an ineligible player. Goalkeeper Colin McDonald, later to win eight England caps, was doing his National Service at Moreton-in-Marsh and was given permission by Burnley to play for Headington United. However, they refused to allow him to play against Wycombe Wanderers in the FA Cup. United registered McDonald as an amateur with the Oxfordshire FA and played him anyway and won 3-2. Burnley complained and an FA commission found that United should be eliminated from the competition, with Wycombe going through to the next round instead." Martin Brodetsky.

That's quite interesting
"Joey Beauchamp, who later became an Oxford legend, was a ballboy at the 1986 League Cup final when Oxford beat QPR 3-0. He was sold to West Ham for £1 million in 1994 but played just once, in a friendly against Oxford City, before confessing that he'd made a mistake, leading West Ham to sell him to Swindon. Then 14 months later Oxford signed him back for just £75,000 and he went on to become a hero again." Martin Brodetsky.

The ground
The ground sits near the Oxford Science Park. It is a three-sided ground with a space for expansion with the addition of a west stand behind the goal, currently a car park. The **South Stand** is a two tier structure that runs the length of the pitch with a high cantilever roof. The stand holds 4495 and has 28 executive boxes. There is the Quadrangle bar downstairs for home fans. The dugouts are on the half way line as is the tunnel and the changing rooms. The **East Stand** Oxford Mall is a single tier high roof cantilever structure behind the goal. It holds 2879 home fans, and is home to the most vocal support. The **North Stand** is another single tier structure with cantilever roof, that runs the length of the pitch opposite the south stand. This stand has a capacity for 5,026, split between home and away fans, with away fans allocated the western end.

Getting there
By Road/Parking South of the ring road that corrals Oxford city centre, the stadium is well signed. From the M4 exit junction 13 and follow the A34 for Oxford, exiting left for Ring Road Oxford (A4144). At roundabout take third exit for A4074 and follow through two roundabouts. Exit left signed to Kassam Stadium and Oxford Science Park and left at the roundabout onto Grenoble Road, the stadium will be in your left.

Free parking is available at the club (capacity for 2,000 cars with over flow) as well as street parking. Parking available in the pub car park (see above).

By Train Oxford station is a real trek to the ground so it is best to hop on a bus. The regular number 5 runs to Blackbird Leys, taking about 25 minutes, and it is around a five-minute's walk to the ground from there. An alternate Saturday bus service operates between the train station and Kassam Stadium – jump on Thames Travel's 106 bus route.

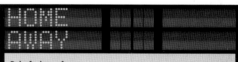

Pubs for home fans
"There's a pub almost next to the ground, just behind the Bowlplex, called the The Priory. It's a listed building but it has a large bar which is complemented by overflow bars in a marquee set-up in the car park. It sells all the usual lagers, plus has a wide selection of bottled ales and ciders. They also do food, although mainly burgers and hot-dogs – it is extremely vegetarian unfriendly. You can park in the pub's car park for £3, but you get that back when you buy at the bar. It's away-fan friendly and also popular with home supporters. Further from the ground the Blackbird, Blackbird Leys Road, is pretty much for home fans only." Martin Brodetsky, editor, rageonline.co.uk

Good food near ground
"Places to eat in the Ozone (the complex adjacent to the ground) are the Oxy, an excellent Chinese eat-as-much-as-you-like venue, Frankie and Bennie's pizzeria, and a new fish and chip shop," recommends Martin.

Pubs for away fans
"The Bowlplex itself also has a bar inside (no real ales though) and does fast food (including vegeburgers). Further from the ground there are half-decent pubs in Littlemore (the George) and Sandford (the Catherine Wheel and the King's Arms)," says Martin.

Top tips
Don't make a traffic warden's day: be aware that 'residents only' parking schemes operate on some streets close to the stadium and that double yellow lines do extend to cover the grass verges of the roads!

rageonline.co.uk

HOME COLOURS

PETERBOROUGH UNITED

- ⊘ **Nicknames** The Posh
- ⊙ **Founded** 1934
- ⊕ **Ground** London Road Stadium (opened 1934)
- ⊙ **Address** London Road, Peterborough PE2 8AL
- ⊙ **Capacity** 15,152
- ⊙ **Best attendance** 14,110 vs Leicester City, League One, 2009
- ⊙ **Contact** 01733-563 947
- ⊙ **Ticket Number** 01733-865 674
- @ **Email** info@theposh.com
- Ⓦ **Website** theposh.com

In the conventional business world, trouble-shooters are called in to lend advice, experience, and help steady a somewhat leaky ship. But football exists in a universe where the laws of business no longer apply – a kind of event horizon of logic and sense. In the world of football management where bluff, bravado and swagger reign supreme, and only the almighty ego is turned to in rare moments of doubt, this does not happen. If you can't stand the heat, you're out of the kitchen – Gordon Ramsey style. One exception is Bryan Robson utilizing El Tel's sun bed of experience at Middlesbrough. If the offer had come from, say, Ron Atkinson, and he came with a Sky TV crew in tow to film a fly-on-the-wall documentary – you can only guess what Robbo's response would have been. But that's the position Steve Bleasdale found himself in at Peterborough. What chairman Barry Fry thought was going to happen, who knows? It made for cringe-worthy TV – which must ultimately have been Sky's goal – but naturally didn't do Fry, Bleasdale or the players any favours. It culminated in Bleasdale resigning, minutes before a game kicked off, in front of the team, Fry and the rolling cameras. All anyone watching could think was, 'how did you stand it for so long?'

However, like the butterfly effect, it led indirectly to a saviour arriving at the club. In 2006 Darragh MacAnthony replaced Fry as chairman. He must have seen something in a certain ex-Manchester United bit player and handed the reigns to Darren Ferguson, a complete managerial novice; the club has never looked back. In 2008 The Posh were promoted to League One where they faced a tough

RIVALS

Cambridge United, Northampton Town, Leicester City, Ipswich Town, MK Dons and Nottingham Forest.

HOME AWAY

Pubs for home fans
The Cherry Tree, Oundle Road welcomes both home and away supporters and gets packed out on match days.

Good food near ground
If you don't fancy a bite to eat in the pubs, there's a KFC just opposite the ground as well as a range of eateries along the London Road.

Pubs for away fans
There is no shortage of pubs. By the station, The Brewery Tap, Westgate, houses the Oakham Ales micro-brewery. It's a large, open space with a range of award-winning real ales and well-priced Thai food. It's under threat of redevelopment – have a pint, show your support! Palmerston Arms, Oundle Road, excellent range of real cask ales. Charters Barge on the river by Town Bridge has a huge beer garden and a great selection of Belgian Beers and real ales including local brewery Oakham Ales. Plus well priced Thai food.

Top tips
There are a number of excellent real-ale pubs in the vicinity besides the ones mentioned so take your time and enjoy.

fight. They were in with the likes of Leeds United, Leicester City, MK Dons, Millwall and Oldham, all of whom were scrapping for their lives. Ferguson's team, however, maintained their momentum from the previous year and, with the season entering the home straight, ghosted through the pack into an automatic promotion place leaving Mk Dons pinching themselves as they saw promotion slip away. The essence of the season was distilled into a resounding 2-0 home win against champions Leicester City. Now, if you wanted drama, excitement and a Hollywood ending, that would have been a great year for a fly-on-the-wall documentary – only minus Big Ron Manager.

VILLAINS

"Stuart Brace missed an open goal in an important game. Dennis Pearce could not play football. Lee Phillpott allegedly stole a handbag from a local nightclub and was sacked by the club." Brian Seaton.

Greatest moments on this ground
"Versus Wrexham, our first-ever Football League game on 20 August 1960; we won, 3-0. We beat Arsenal 2-1 in the FA Cup in 1965, and against Liverpool in the League Cup in December 1991, when we won 1-0." Brian Seaton, fan.

Lowest moments on this ground
"Any game where the team as a whole players did not put in the required effort, and there have been a few." Brian Seaton.

Heroes of the sideline

"Chris Turner – son of God, an extraordinary man, apprentice player, player, coach, manager, owner, chairman… you name it. Heart like a lion. Noel Cantwell – the team would play through fire for him. Jimmy Hagan was the best 'reader' of the game I ever met. He was also hard but results were incredible." Brian Seaton. Also Darren Ferguson, two promotions before moving on.

Heroes of the turf

"Denis Emery, the best Posh footballer of all time, not disputed by anyone. Ian Ross, an incredible wing half. Bobby Doyle – stylish, neat, beautiful to watch. Terry Bly – 52 league goals in one season will never be bettered. Freddie Hill – old school inside forward, so clever, so neat, a lethal shot and a joy to watch. George Boyd – a modern-day Emery and so, so skilful and fluid. Chances from his feet by the dozen, you could cry with joy when he is on full song." Brian Seaton.

Zeroes of the turf

"Ashley Neal, Dennis Pearce, Eddie Clamp, Bill Green and Derek Kevan – none were real footballers whilst at Posh. Steve Morrow, who we loaned from QPR. He was famous for breaking his arm when Tony Adams dropped him during celebrations after the final whistle of 1993 League Cup final. A bit of a donkey, in fact useless and played only 11 games." Brian Seaton.

Don't mention the…

"Demotion from the old Division Three into the Fourth Division for illegal payments to players in the 1967/68 season." Brian Seaton.

The ground

London Road has a warm, small club feel with a great atmosphere. The **Thomas Cook South Stand** is a two-tier modern structure that runs the length of the pitch and was completed for the end of the 1995/96 season. It has seating for 5,000 home fans. Behind the goal is the **Moyes Terrace**, a covered terrace of standing only for 3,475 away supporters (also an additional 850 seats in A block of the Main Stand). The **Main Stand** is a single-tier older structure of under 4,000 capacity with some pillars. (Some seats have come second-hand from Leicester's Filbert Street and Millwall's old Den). **London Road Terrace**, behind the goal, has little changed since the fifties and has room for 3,000 home fans.

Getting there

By Road/Parking From A1 north, take the A47 exit (signed Peterborough N/Leicester) and follow. Exit junction 15 towards Peterborough and follow the A1260. Turn left onto Oundle Road towards Woodston. The stadium is at the end of the road (on opposite side of London Road). From the south, exit the A1(M) at junction 16 and follow the A15/London Road, after around six miles the ground will be on your right. There are a couple of reasonable car parks just off the London Road, close to the stadium.

By Train Peterborough station is less than a mile away – around a 15-minute walk. Go right out of the station and onto the main road. Turn right (passing Asda) and right into the pedestrianized Bridge Street. Go straight on crossing River Nene Bridge. The ground will be on your left.

THE LAST WORD   londonroad.net

˅ Craig Mackail-Smith beats the blue and white defensive curtain to score against West Brom at The Hawthorns.

GETTY IMAGES

That's quite interesting
"We had a player called Ray Hankin who was sent off five times in 46 appearances for the club and finally sacked by manager John Wile." Brian Seaton.

Not a lot of people know that
"Dick Beattie was found guilty of match-fixing by the FA, including a game I remember against QPR in September 1962, when he threw the ball straight to a QPR player, who duly scored." Brian Seaton.

PUB QUIZ

HOME COLOURS

- ☤ **Nicknames** The Pilgrims
- ⊕ **Founded** 1886
- ⚑ **Ground** Home Park (opened 1901)
- ℹ **Address** Plymouth PL2 3DQ
- ⊕ **Capacity** 19,500
- ✪ **Best attendance** 43,596 vs Aston Villa, Division Two, 10 October, 1936
- ☏ **Contact** 01752-562561
- ⊕ **Ticket Number** 0845-338 7232
- @ **Email** argyle@pafc.co.uk
- Ⓦ **Website** pafc.co.uk

PLYMOUTH ARGYLE

RIVALS

Exeter City are by far the biggest rivals, the Devon derbies are fought with as much passion as any other derby game in the country. There is also the dockyard derby with Portsmouth and the second Devon derby with Torquay United.

Plymouth Argyle, a bit like their opposite number Newcastle United up in the northeast, strike fear into away fans' hearts, not because of the ferocious atmosphere of Home Park, but for the sheer distance it is for many visiting supporters to actually get there. When Plymouth welcome Newcastle, the Toon Army has to cover 410 miles to get to football's southwest outpost, a hike for even the most passionate of fans. Perhaps this remoteness in football terms may go some way to explain Plymouth's most unfortunate claim to fame in football: they are the biggest city in England never to have played in the top flight. With a population of 250,000 it ranks 15th in the list of English cities. If you then factor in the surrounding football void on its doorstep, such as the county of Cornwall, it easily has the supporter base to fill a Premiership ground. Their other striking feature is their name. Why would a club based in the southwest of England include the name of an area of western Scotland? Well, as with many teams names, it is a simple coincidence. The two founders of the club lived on Argyll Street in Mutley, a road named after the Argyll and Sutherland regiment, which was based in Plymouth in the 1880s. Not only were the Argyll and Sutherland regiment based there, but they also had a rather fine football team, well known throughout the country and very successful. Hence the name Argyle was used from the outset, and Plymouth's green-and-black strip were the same colour as the regiment's tartan.

That's quite interesting
At the height of the Cold War in the sixties, Argyle went on a tour of Eastern Europe, which included losing 2-1 to Legia Warsaw in front of 100,000 fans.

Not a lot of people know that
In 2006 *Viz* magazine ran a one-off comic strip *The Pirates of Plymouth Argyle* based on the team.

PUB QUIZ

Greatest moments on this ground
"24 April, 2004 when Argyle beat QPR 2-0 to get promotion to the Championship. The place was jumping! We went up as champions." Gerald Taylor, rubofthegreens.com.

Lowest moments on this ground
"18 May, 1994 when we lost at home 3-1 to Burnley in the Second Division play-off semi-finals. The feeling could not have been any flatter." Gerald Taylor.

Heroes of the sideline
"Argyle are one of the few clubs who appreciate Neil Warnock. Paul Sturrock is also a manager respected by many." Gerald Taylor.

Villains
"Ian Holloway, who abandoned the club as manager days after professing undying love! Also George Reilly, his ear was bitten off by a man who simply whispered the word 'Plymouth'. Reilly had scored Watford's winning goal against Argyle in the 1984 FA Cup semi-final." Gerald Taylor.

The ground
Home Park has been extensively redeveloped and on three sides is a modern well-proportioned and comfortable stadium. The three sides were opened in 2001 and 2002, with the remaining side due for redevelopment. This redevelopment got a boost when in 2006 the club purchased the ground from Plymouth City council for £2.7 million, releasing it from its previous 125-year lease.

The **Grandstand** is the only side of the ground that is undeveloped. The lower tier, which stretches the length of the pitch, is open, a legacy of the open terrace that used to be there and is uncomfortable in wet weather. The upper tier is covered but only stretches three-quarters of the pitch. It is an ageing stand, which looks out of place compared to the rest of the ground. The dressing rooms are located below the stand and there is a scoreboard between it and The Devonport End.

The **Devonport End** was the first of the new stands to open and is home support only, including a family enclosure. Like the other two sides it forms one continuous sweep around the ground in a single tier. The corners are filled in, allowing for a real atmosphere to be generated.

The **Lyndhurst Stand** is a large single tier, which continues the sweep Around the Grounds, joining the

DAVE ROWNTREE

two ends. The louder Plymouth fans sit in the Barn End corner which generates an excellent atmosphere between opposing support.

The **Barn Park End** houses away support that take up a varying amount of the stand, depending on the match. The views and facilities are top-notch.

Getting there

By Road/Parking All fans will travel down the M5, which turns into the A38 Devon expressway just outside Exeter. Keep on this road until Plymouth and then follow signs for Plymouth along the A386 (also signposted Home Park). Follow this road for about half a mile and, when the road splits, follow the left lane signposted Plymouth and Home Park. Continue for around about a mile until you can see the ground and start looking for parking here.

There is a large free, car park operating on a first-come, first-served basis right next to the ground. It will be full by 30 minutes prior to kick off. Other than that, there is limited street parking near the ground, but beware that some streets operate a permit system. There are also plenty of city centre car parks that are about 25 minutes from the ground.

By Train The mainline station is about a 20-minute walk from the ground. On leaving the station turn right under the railway line and continue on this road, which goes around to the ground, or you can cut across the adjacent park.

HOME / AWAY

Pubs for home fans
The Embassy Club is a home favourite and to be avoided by away support. The Britannia Pub is welcoming of both sets of fans as is The Pennycomequick, closer to the station, a little further away towards the city centre. Other than this there are no other pubs close to the ground.

Good food near ground
Great fish and chip restaurant called Windy Ridge, 33 Market Avenue. Even after a poor game you will remember the fish. An area known as Mutely Plain is about 10-minutes' walk away, which has takeaway and fast-food outlets on it.

Pubs for away fans
The Britannia Pub, which is 10 minutes from the ground, is a large Wetherspoon pub and popular with home and away support; away colours and rowdy supporters will be dealt with by the bouncers though. Other than this go to the city centre where there is good variety. Beer is available in the ground.

Top tips
Like Portsmouth, Plymouth is a naval town and things can get rowdy, especially around the popular pubs and nightspots on Union Street, which are best avoided – especially in team colours.

THE LAST WORD

rubofthegreens.com
plymouthargyle-mad.co.uk
plymouth.vitalfootball.co.uk
pasoti.co.uk

○ **Nicknames** Pompey
○ **Founded** 1898
○ **Ground** Fratton Park (opened 1898)
○ **Address** Frogmore Road, Portsmouth PO4 8RA
○ **Capacity** 20,700
○ **Best attendance** 51,385 v Derby County FA Cup 6th round, 26 February, 1949
○ **Contact** 02392-731204
○ **Ticket Number** 0844-847 1898
@ **Email** info@pompeyfc.co.uk
W **Website** portsmouthfc.co.uk

PORTSMOUTH

RIVALS

Southampton are the only real rival, plus naval town Plymouth Argyle.

**HOME
AWAY**

Pubs for home fans
Close to the ground on Goldsmith Road is the Shepherd's Crook, a real football pub that's a home-fan-only haunt. The Milton Arms on Milton Road is also a popular hangout with hardcore Pompey fans; away support should definitely avoid.

Good food near ground
Most of the aforementioned pubs serve food, from good bar grub to pasties and sandwiches. There is also McDonalds and KFC close to the ground.

Pubs for away fans
If you're visiting Portsmouth and it's a nice day early or late in the season, then it's worth heading down to Southsea for a pre-match pint. Around the common are a number of good pubs, which also serve food. The Good Companion pub on Eastern Road is a good option for visitors, it's within walking distance, large and serves decent food; it will have a mix of support but is friendly. Other pubs close to the ground will generally be packed with home support.

Top tips
Remember that Portsmouth is the country's main naval town so things can and do get rowdy in the public houses at times, regardless of what team you support.

The Pompey Chimes have become synonymous with the south coast's powerhouse of the modern game. The shrill ring of a large bell by a tattooed man, draped in Pompey gear, named John Portsmouth Football Club Westwood (yes, he did change his name), is perhaps one of the first things non-Portsmouth fans think of when the club is mentioned. He has become instigator of the chimes and often initiates the battle cry of "Play Up Pompey, Pompey Play Up". The chimes have a long history, which in fact starts prior to the football club. Back in the 1890s when Royal Artillery Portsmouth Club played at The United Services Ground in Burnaby Road (overlooked by the Guildhall clock) referees used to use the chimes at four o'clock to signify the end of a game. The fans would sing along to the chimes to encourage the ref to blow his whistle.

Portsmouth have risen to become the most successful team from the south coast, a title that they revel in, especially where close rivals Southampton are concerned. Their golden years were post war; two titles in 1949 and 1950 and a semi-final appearance in the FA Cup in 1949 made them one of the teams to beat at the time. But it's the club's recent exploits that have really caused a stir. On the brink of administration, a Serbian business tycoon and former owner of French side Nice, Milan Mandaric stepped forward and purchased the club. He soon installed Harry Redknapp as manager, and one of the most enthralling managerial sagas in Premiership history began when Redknapp and assistant Jim Smith got Portsmouth back into the Premiership. After stabilizing the club in the first season, Harry left in December of the second season after a disagreement with Mandaric. Incredibly, just a matter of weeks afterwards he was manager of archrivals Southampton, enraging Pompey fans. He couldn't keep

the Saints in the Premiership though, and after a season in the Championship he returned to Portsmouth, this time tasked with keeping them in the Premiership. He did, and then went on to build a quality side and win the FA Cup, Portsmouth's greatest success in modern football. Just when things were starting to look very good for the south coasters, Redknapp left again, this time for Tottenham, which ended the Harry Redknapp era at Fratton Park, though there's still a strange love/hate relationship between the club and the larger-than-life manager.

2010 was terrible year for the club – the horrors of administration and relegation could not be offset by a day out at Wembley and the cold comfort of FA Cup runners-up medals. Financial ruin nearly saw the final bell toll for the club, who now face a long road back to recovery. One consolation, they've rung out the changes before, they can do it again.

Greatest moments on this ground
"The first 30 minutes of 24 April 2005 take some beating. Turncoat Harry Redknapp skulked back to Fratton in charge of bitter rivals Saints for a vital relegation battle and within half an hour his side had been blown away. Lua Lua's spectacular strike to make it 4-1, before

hobbling off with a hamstring injury, is as close as many fans will have got to self actualization." Colin Farmery, pompey-fans.com.

Lowest moments on this ground
"Steve Moran scoring a last-minute winner for Saints in an FA Cup 4th round tie in 1984 left three-quarters of Fratton Park stunned and sick in equal measure." Colin Farmery.

Heroes of the sideline
"Harry Redknapp has a Division One championship title and the FA Cup for Portsmouth and Saints' relegation on his CV. Legendary." Colin Farmery.

Villains
"Even though he built a solid team, won the FA Cup and helped keep us in the Premiership, for walking out on us twice, Harry Redknapp fits the villain profile for me." Tom Clayton, fan. Terry Venebles' tenure as chairman was seen by most fans as a waste of time.

Don't mention the…
Harry Redknapp saga or administration.

The ground
Fratton Park is ageing by Premier League standards. Their city location means expansion on site is restricted. It is dominated by the **Fratton End** stand, a new-ish, single-tier, all-seated area for 3,000 home supporters. It is the engine room for noise during games.

Opposite is the **Milton End**; this, thankfully for the away supporters who are seated here, has been covered at last. The roof has helped created a base for an excellent atmosphere. It is also home to some of the home support, which generates a good bit of banter, typically away support get between 1,200 and 2,000 seats. Legroom is limited and there are also some supporting pillars that can impede the view.

The **South Stand** dates back to the 1920s and shows its age. The two-tiered stand is also home to the dressing rooms, which have recently been renovated. There are some supporting beams in the upper level, which can disrupt viewing.

Opposite is a slightly more modern stand. Again two-tiered, the **North Stand** is nothing if unremarkable. There are supporting beams and the front of the lower tier can get wet still when the conditions are right, or wrong depending on how you look at it.

GETTY IMAGES

∧ Paul Merson, 2003, the year Pompey won promotion to the Premiership as champions.
◁ Play-up Pompey.

Getting there
By Road/Parking From east or west on the M27 take junction 11 onto the A27. Continue on the A27 until you reach the junction with the A2030 and then follow signs for Southsea and Fratton; continue along the A2030 and you will soon see the ground. From the north/M25 take the A3 (M), which becomes the A27 and then follow as above.

Parking is a bit of nightmare, the area around Fratton is tight and there are only a few match-day car parks, which fill early. The best bet for away fans is to park in one of the residential streets, the further from the ground the better, most don't have parking restrictions or permits but it's worth checking first. The roads off the A2030 before you get to the ground are good options. Alternatively car parks in the city centre are about a 20-minute walk from the ground.

By Train Fratton Station is under a mile from the ground. Exit over footbridge and turn left into Goldsmith Avenue. Continue for half a mile past the Pompey Centre, Frogmore Road is on your left and Fratton Park is at the bottom.

PUB QUIZ

That's quite interesting
On 22 February, 1956 Pompey played Newcastle United in the first floodlit game.

Not a lot of people know that
There are about eight theories as to why Portsmouth is referred to as Pompey. The most plausible is that a group of Portsmouth sailors scaled Pompey's Pillar in Egypt in the 1781, they became known as the Pompey boys and it stuck.

THE LAST WORD

pompey-fans.com
portsmouth.vitalfootball.co.uk

HEROES OR ZEROES?

⩘ HEROES OF THE TURF
"Jimmy Dickinson, Alan Knight and Linvoy Primus are true club men. Paul Walsh, Robert Prosinecki and Paul Merson gave us some fabulous memories and a touch of class during a period in our history when we didn't take it for granted." Colin Farmery.

⩗ ZEROES OF THE TURF
Laurent Robert who, after a bizarre loan/transfer from Newcastle, did little except storm out of a vital relegation battle with Sunderland when he was relegated to the bench. Also Konstantinos Chalkias, Trevor Robertsand Carl Tiler.

HOME COLOURS

- **Nicknames** Vale, Valiants
- **Founded** 1876
- **Ground** Vale Park (opened 1950)
- **Address** Vale Park, Hamil Road, Burslem, Stoke-on-Trent, ST6 1AW
- **Capacity** 18,947
- **Best attendance** 49,768 vs Aston Villa, FA Cup 5th round, 20 February, 1960
- **Contact** 01782-655800
- **Ticket Number** 01782-811707
- **Email** enquiries@port-vale.co.uk
- **Website** port-vale.co.uk

PORT VALE

Why do fans pick a team? Is it because they are successful or glamorous? Is it because they play in the Champions League or have exotic, foreign stars? Or is it about passion and belief? It's like voting for a political party: you don't just tick the box of the biggest, the one with the most money behind it, or the one you know will come out on top – that would be pointless. You vote for who you can believe in. If they win, great. If they lose, at least you acted with your heart and conscience.

It's like that at Vale Park. The Valiants may never have played in the top flight, but they have some of the most passionate supporters in the Football League and have certainly enjoyed some great victories over the years. At the end of a long campaign in 1989, fans of Port Vale were rewarded when their side beat Bristol Rovers 2-1 in a tense play-off final to secure a place in the second flight of English football. In 1993, 20,000 Vale fans enjoyed their first ever day out at Wembley, beating Stockport County 2-1 in the Autoglass Trophy final. More recently they have enjoyed a couple of spells in the second tier and won the LDV Vans Trophy at the Millennium Stadium. Of course, it hasn't all been plain sailing. The choppy waters of administration took their toll, but under new ownership the club is now back on a more even keel. A loss of form at the

Pile on! Tony Naylor scores against Leeds in the FA Cup 5th round replay match at Vale Park, 1996.

GETTY IMAGES

end of their 2009/10 campaign saw The Vale narrowly miss out on the League Two play-offs. But they'll be back.

It's a sad day when a kid in Burslem picks a Chelsea or Arsenal shirt and says, "That's my team." They might not realise it, but they're condemning themselves to a life of aseptic Sky Sports and a remote football experience of flat screen games, when they could be enjoying the passion, the sound and the smells of the terraces at Vale Park, a team of real players, players that represent them, their town, their community, their interests. People of Burslem, vote for your team – Vote Port Vale!

Greatest moments on this ground
In 1996 we played Everton in the 4th round of the FA Cup. After a 2-2 draw at Goodison Park we brought them back to Vale Park and although the 2-1 scoreline suggests it was a close game, we ripped the Scousers apart." David Griffiths, editor, Vital Port Vale.

Lowest moments on this ground
"Administration. Fan protests against the appointment of Dean Glover in 2008. Quite a few more too painful to think about." Robert Fielding, onevalefan.co.uk.

Heroes of the sideline
"John Rudge was manager of Port Vale FC for 15 years from 1984 to 1999. The man is God. Under 'Rudgie' we played exhilarating, classy attacking football that brought promotions, FA Cup heroics and two Wembley appearances. The talent he either nurtured himself, or persuaded to come to Vale Park, is incomparable outside of the very top tier. A true genius. Freddie Steele was manager between 1951-57. Freddy created the legendary 'Iron Curtain' team that reached the FA Cup semi-finals in 1954." David Griffiths.

RIVALS

Stoke City, Crewe Alexandra, Burton Albion, Macclesfield Town and Shrewsbury.

PUB QUIZ

That's quite interesting
"Simon Webbe of pop band Blue fame was on Vale's books as a junior. He failed to make the grade." Robert Fielding.

Not a lot of people know that
"Brothers Mark and Neville Chamberlain both played for Vale (not to be confused with the Prime Minister who got duped by Adolf Hitler). Mark meanwhile went on to represent England." David Griffiths.

Villains

"Leon Constantine. Despite scoring 38 goals in 85 appearances Leon incurred the wrath of the Vale faithful with his 'laid-back' work ethic. Leon criticised the fans and cited the abuse he received from the stands as the reason why he would not be accepting a new contract. Bill Bell, former chairman and second-hand car salesman who took the club worryingly close to extinction." David Griffiths.

"Barry Siddall, one of the few to play for Vale and Stoke. He failed to endear himself when, returning to Vale Park (as a Blackpool player), he removed his goalkeeping jersey to reveal a Stoke City shirt!" Robert Fielding.

The ground

Vale Park was dubbed the 'Wembley of the North' with a planned 70,000 capacity when first proposed, but opened with a somewhat smaller capacity of 50,000 in 1950. Today the capacity is almost 19,000. It is still a great ground to visit, with large covered stands, all seating and largely unobscured views. Behind the goal the eastern **Hamil End** has always been the away end. Once an open terrace it is now a single tier of covered seating for about 4,500 fans. The **Railway Stand**, running the length of the field, is an old school grass terrace banking from behind, but inside is a more modern, large, single tier of seating with a row of pillars about half way up. In the corner is The **Family Stand** which sits at an angle, rather than curving, and so looks a little strange. The **Bycars Road End**, behind the far goal, was re-opened in 1992 after a rebuild into a single tier of seats. The main **Lorne Street Stand** has taken a while to finish. Work began in the late nineties and as of the end of the 2010 season the stand only has half the seating open. Its high roof covers a large tier of seats, with two rows of executive boxes above, each with their own mini tier of seats outside.

Getting there

By Road/Parking Vale Park is in Burselm, one of the northern most towns that make up Stoke-on-Trent. The ground is easily accessed via the M6, leaving at junction 15 or 16 and following the A500 towards Stoke-on-Trent. Take the A527 exit signed to Tunstall and follow. At roundabout take second exit onto Newcastle Street/B5051 and follow through town. Turn left opposite the church onto Hamil Rd, and the ground will be on left.

Street parking. Match day parking also at carpark next door (£4).

By Train Stoke-on-Trent station is four miles from the ground. Take the hourly connection to Longport Station, a 25-minute walk from Vale Park. Head past the Pack Horse, Station Street, and follow as it becomes Newcastle Street and Market Place (passing though the town centre). Left onto Hamil Road, ground on the left.

"Lorne Street stand. Widely regarded as Vale Park's white elephant, the stand remained uncompleted nearly 10 years after work began. On the pitch, embarrassing cup defeats to Canvey Island and Chasetown are best forgotten." Robert Fielding.

HOME AWAY

Pubs for home fans
The majority of pubs in town are for home fans only. The Post Office Vaults, Market Place, is a tiny bar with plenty of character in the centre of Burslem serving a good selection of well kept real ales. Ye Old Smithy, Moorland Road, is a no frills kind of joint close to the ground with some decent ales available. Red Lion, Moorland Road, is another popular spot close to the ground.

Good food near ground
The Strawberries Café, Hamil Road, is a traditional café round the corner from the ground, serving up the usual delights. There's a KFC on Market Place for those in need of a fried chicken fix.

Pubs for away fans
"The Vine, Hamil Road, (approximately 500 yards from the ground) is your best bet if you want a drink or two before the game," recommends Vital Port Vale's David Griffiths. It's a small pub with a couple of decent ales that tends to get packed out. "The Bull's Head, St Johns Square in the town centre is away friendly but you'll find quite a number of pubs will carry 'home fans only' signs on the door." Popular with the home and away contingent, The Bull's Head is tied to the Titanic Brewery so a cracking choice if you want to sample the finest of Burslem's local wares. Pork pies available.

Top tips
Connections between Stoke-on-Trent and Longport stations are few and far between. If you miss your connection take the 21 First Potteries bus on into Burslem.

THE LAST WORD

onevalefan.co.uk
northlondonvaliants.co.uk
thewonderofyou.co.uk
portvaleonline.com/forum

PRESTON NORTH END

- **Nicknames** Lilywhites
- **Founded** 1881
- **Ground** Deepdale (opened 1881)
- **Address** Sir Tom Finney Way, Preston PR1 6RU
- **Capacity** 23,408
- **Best attendance** 42,684 vs Arsenal, First Division, 23 April, 1938
- **Contact** 0870-442 1964
- **Ticket Number** 0844-856 1966
- **Email** enquiries@pne.com
- **Website** pne.com

RIVALS

Primary rivals are Blackpool, but also Burnley and Blackburn Rovers.

That's quite interesting
"Our ground holds the National Football Museum, which is situated on the corner of the ground – well worth a visit for any fan." Simon Ostiadel.

Not a lot of people know that
"We still play on the same ground that we played on when the 'Invincibles' were crowned first-ever League Champions back in 1888/89 – also winning the first double." Stephen Cowell.

GETTY IMAGES

∧ Deepdale.

The terms 'hero' or 'legend' have become almost workaday in footballing circles. 'He played for us for a whole season – he was a legend.' But when the great Bill Shankly described someone as "… the best I've seen and I'd bracket Pele, Eusebio, Cruyff, Di Stefano and Puskas up there with him," you know the term legend most certainly applies. Not 'he was as good as Pele', no, 'Pele was as good as him' – there's a subtle difference. Sir Tom Finney was born in Preston on 5 April, 1922 and came up through an embryonic youth system that the club was pioneering. Finney's early career was interrupted by the outbreak of the Second World War and he served in the torrid arena of North Africa under Montgomery, before returning to make his post-war debut for the club as a 24 year-old. He could play down the middle or on either wing and the young forward quickly established a reputation as an excellent two-footed striker. Finney soon drew comparisons with another forward from the northwest, Blackpool's Stanley Matthews, but many saw Finney as a more complete package. "Much of his footwork resembles that of Matthews," said Tommy Lawton, "but Finney cuts in more than Matthews does, and is also a goal-scorer, whereas Matthews is content to let others do the scoring." Sir Matt Busby added: "Stan Matthews was basically a right-footed player, Tom Finney a left-footed player, though Tom's right was as good as most players' better foot. Finney was more of a team player. He would beat a man with a pass or with wonderful, individual runs that left the opposition in disarray. And Finney would also finish the whole thing off by scoring, which Stan seldom did."

What makes Finney a true legend is the remarkable loyalty he showed to his home town club. He turned out for the Lillywhites 473 times scoring 210 goals. Although he never won a championship or cup medal with the club, he spent his entire professional career at Deepdale, even though lucrative offers came in from other teams. When Tom Finney finally retired in 1960, he was a two-time Player of the Year, had 76 England caps and had scored 30 times for his country. A player of this quality, loyalty and modesty is almost unique in the game – Sir Tom Finney is not just a Preston North End hero, he's a true football legend. As Bill Shankly said, "Tom would have been a great in any team, in any match and in any age …even if he'd been wearing an overcoat."

Greatest moments on this ground
"In recent times we have had quite a few good memories. Play-off semi-final victories against Torquay and Birmingham stick in the mind, along with a title-winning season with the trophy being lifted at Deepdale to a full crowd." Simon Ostiadel, Preston North End Mad.

Lowest moments on this ground
"What can be worse than your local rivals (Blackpool) winning on your patch 3-0 and, even worse for us, that was enough to send us down and saw them gain promotion. It still have nightmares about it and it was over 30 years ago!" Stephen Cowell, Manager of Preston North End Supporters Team.

PUB QUIZ

Heroes of the sideline

"All who have been involved with the recent revival of the club. Gary Peters got us promotion from the basement division and then David Moyes took us to within 90 minutes of the Championship." Simon Ostiadel.

Don't mention the…

"Our mascot, the Deepdale Duck. He distracted the linesman in a derby game against Blackpool – the official missed a clear offside and we went on to score and win the game." Simon Ostiadel.

The ground

Deepdale is an attractive, modern stadium with an angular, uniform construction. The **Sir Tom Finney Stand** is a single tier built in 1995 that runs the length of the pitch and can house 8,100 home fans. Finney's face is designed into the stand using coloured seating. Behind the goal is the **Bill Shankly Kop**, celebrating the former Preston player. Built in 1998, this stand can house 6,000 fans and the away contingent is housed in part or all of this area. **The Invincibles Pavillion** is the newest part of the ground development, it's an unusual stand with a small single tier of seats for just over 3,000 fans, a large area of executive boxes and the potential for more terracing to be built here should Preston North End make the Premiership. The **Lana Kelly Town End** behind the other goal is a single tier of 6,000 and houses the changing rooms.

Getting there

By Road/Parking Take the M6 to junction 31 and follow signs for Preston/A59. At the mini roundabout by Hesketh Arms take the second exit onto Blackpool Road. Follow for just over one mile until the stadium comes into view. Take a left turn before the lights (signed Football Ground/Town Centre) onto Sir Tom Finney Way. The ground is on the left. Moor Park High School offers parking for £5 per game. Some street parking also available.

By Train Preston Station is around 1½ miles from the ground. Out of the station turn left in front of Fishergate Centre and turn right at the T-junction. Walk down the main high street (Fishergate Street) and continue for around a mile until you reach junction with the A6/Ring Road. Cross the road with the prison on the right and then turn left along Deepdale Road. Continue, the ground will be on your right.

HEROES OR ZEROES?

HEROES OF THE TURF
"Perhaps heroes of the plastic is more appropriate with Gary Brazil and Brian Mooney. More recently, on the grass, Sean Gregan has been the fans' favourite as we have established ourselves in the Championship." Simon Ostiadel.

ZEROES OF THE TURF
"Any player who doesn't bust a gut for the cause. Only two to my knowledge share that accolade, Johnny Macken and David Healy, who both knew they were offski to somewhere else so decided to take the piss before they went!" Stephen Cowell.

GETTY IMAGES

> The legendary Tom Finney, 1950.

VILLAINS
"Billy Davies, our former manager, who touted himself for every job that came up when he was manager of Preston North End and then tried to blame the chairman for not trying hard enough to keep him when he finally left!" Stephen Cowell.

Pubs for home fans
Finney's Sports Bar, East View, has big screens showing sports action, football memorabilia and a couple of real ales. Most of the pubs in the city are the preserve of home fans on match days with away supporters encouraged to drink elsewhere.

Good food near ground
There's a Domino's Pizza on Deepdale Road, south of the ground. At the top end of Fishergate by the station, there are a couple of good coffee shops selling sandwiches, including Nero's.

Pubs for away fans
Stephen Cowell recommends Sumners Arms, Watling Street Road, five minutes from the ground, which welcomes home and away fans. Sky Sports, beer garden, car park with good home-cooked food. The Garrison opposite is another good choice for home and away fans with a good atmosphere. The Hesketh Arms is another decent spot for those coming in via the M6.

Top tips
Those wearing away colours, are encouraged to avoid the city centre.

THE LAST WORD

prestonnorthend-mad.co.uk
pnembt.co.uk
lilywhitemagic.co.uk
pne-online.net

HOME COLOURS

- **⊘ Nicknames** The Hoops, The Rs, or simply QPR
- **⊘ Founded** 1882
- **⊘ Ground** Loftus Road (opened 1917)
- **ⓘ Address** South Africa Road, London W12 7PA
- **⊘ Capacity** 19,100
- **⊘ Best attendance** 35,353 vs Leeds United, Division One, 27 April, 1974
- **ⓒ Contact** 020-8743 0262
- **ⓘ Ticket Number** 020-8740 2505
- **@ Email** boxoffice@qpr.co.uk
- **Ⓦ Website** qpr.co.uk

QUEENS PARK RANGERS

RIVALS

Chelsea, Brentford and Fulham are their main adversaries, although any London club will get a 'warm' welcome at Loftus Road.

Queens Park Rangers are the second richest club in the land (Manchester City pipping them to the post by a mere £20 billion), well sort of anyway. You certainly would not know it looking at either their recent form or the state of their compact Loftus Road ground. But their owners, Lakshmi Mittal, Flavio Briatore and Bernie Ecclestone have a combined wealth of somewhere in the region of £12 billion, accumulated from steel and motor racing. This wealth has sparked incredible speculation in the press over the past few seasons, rumours of the best players in the world strutting their stuff on the Loftus Road turf have sadly been exaggerated, though the club's financial side is on a much firmer footing. If millions of pounds, the press would like to believe, *are* going to be unleashed on building QPR into the latest super team full of internationals, it would be by no means the first time such talent would have graced the Loftus Road pitch.

In 1974 Dave Sexton took over as manager and in the 1975/76 season Queens Park Rangers had a team full of internationals from the home nations and abroad. Not only that, but when they finished their last game of the season they were sitting at the pinnacle of the League. Unfortunately, Liverpool still had a game to play, needing to win against an already relegated Wolves side; they did, thus pipping QPR to the title. It was Rangers' highest ever finish and at the time they were certainly a force to be reckoned with. Prior to this, their greatest achievement was a rather unique double. Under legendary manager Alec Stock they won the Third Division title and the League Cup, beating then holders West Brom 3-2 in the final. The final was special for two reasons, firstly QPR had to come from two goals behind and, secondly, it was the first-ever final of the competition to be held at Wembley.

Greatest moments on this ground

"Our 1-0 win over Oldham in the 2003 play-off semi-final will be etched in the minds of every single QPR fan not just as we won but because of the atmosphere. Loftus Road is a unique little ground and if the crowd get going the place is simply deafening. The whole ground sang from start to finish. When Clark Carlisle put a fantastic through ball from the half way line to Paul Furlong to finish amazingly and score our winner in the 81st minute, well… I think the whole of London heard the eruption from Loftus Road. It wouldn't have surprised me if we had literally have taken the roof off." Scott Jones, wearetherangersboys.com

Lowest moments on this ground

"Relegation from the Premiership in 1996. At the end of the season we needed to beat West Ham, and we did, but were relying on results from elsewhere. It was the end of the game and we were eagerly awaiting the scores and no-one near me had a radio. Then the tannoy kicked in and announced excitedly 'here are the scores…' He went silent, then swore, and then started playing *Hi Ho Silver Lining*. We knew we were down." Scott Jones.

Heroes of the sideline

"Alec Stock – took QPR from Third Division to First. Dave Sexton – took on the team from the equally excellent Gordon Jago and blended experienced men like Frank McClintock with players in their prime like Gerry Francis and mercurial mavericks like Stan Bowles to almost win the Championship. Terry Venables – took us to the 1982 FA Cup Final as a Second Division side, then promoted us into the First Division, then left for Barcelona." Clive Wittingham, *Loft for Words*.

That's quite interesting
"QPR hold the record for having more home grounds that any other team with at least 16 different homes." Adam Boxer.

PUB QUIZ

Not a lot of people know that
"Les Ferdinand was never called "Sir". Our chant for him was 'SAY' as in, 'Say, Les-ley Ferdiand, say, Lesley Ferdinand'. The media thought we were saying 'sir', it stuck and who was he to correct them!" Scott Jones.

Heroes of the turf

Stan Bowles was voted as the greatest-ever player in a recent poll, he was well-loved by the fans and was at the heart of the side that finished runners-up in the 1975/76 season, he also liked a pint and the odd flutter on the horses. Also, Rodney Marsh, Tony Currie, Phil Parkes, Tony Ingham, Les Ferdinand, David Bardsley, Clive Allen, Gerry Francis, Ray Wilkins, Terry Venebles (as a manager too), Roy Wegerle, Brian Bedford and David Seaman.

Zeroes of the turf

"Ned Zelic – the only Australian who couldn't settle in West London. 'English grass is too hard for me' was one of his greatest excuses." Scott Jones.

"The £6 million accrued by the sale of Les Ferdinand was frittered away on signings such as Simon Osborn, brought in around the same era with Mark Hateley, also joining with a hefty £1 million plus price tag. Other names such as loanee Gus Caeser go down in Rangers folklore." Adam Boxer, editor, *Vital QPR*.

Don't mention the…

"Mascot 'Spark' the Tiger. As far as we can tell this imposter has no connection with our club and looks suspiciously like the Hull City Tiger. He replaced popular mascot Jude the Cat, named after St Jude's Institute which was the first name of the club, who was ousted by the new owners because, we're told, Italians think black cats are terribly bad luck." Clive Wittingham.

∧ "Sir" Les Ferdinand.

∧ Ian Dawes crosses the ball on the Loftus Road carpet, England's first all-weather ground.

The ground

The ground feels a little old-fashioned but its total enclosure gives it more of a modern stadium feel and excellent atmosphere.

The away **School End** has many posts and is so close to the pitch that you may have to stand and lean forward to see the goal. Away fans get the whole upper deck and for big games can also be allocated the lower level. The opposite **Loftus Road** end is similarly double-decked and is home to the more vociferous home support. Great views but a little cramped.

VILLAINS

"Vinnie Jones. He came, he did nothing, he got paid a massive amount, he quit as he thought he was going to be Manager (randomly) he went off and made some films. There's a few that would like to give him lock stock and two smoking barrels. He bans anyone from mentioning QPR during interviews."
Scott Jones

'
STAN BOWLES WAS VOTED AS THE GREATEST-EVER PLAYER IN A RECENT POLL, HE WAS WELL LOVED BY THE FANS…

The **Ellerslie Road Stand** is plain, single-tiered and compact. It has a few supporting pillars but views are generally good.

The **South Africa Road** stand is two-tiered, with a larger upper tier and a smaller lower tier split by a row of executive boxes. It also home to the dressing rooms and dugoutss.

Getting there

By Road/Parking Driving to the ground is pretty straightforward, parking however is not. Simply take the M40 and then the A40 and follow signs for Shepherds Bush, this will eventually turn into Wood Lane and you will soon see the ground. There are a couple of match-day car parks signposted on local industrial estates and there is some street parking. This is mostly metered, but some areas are residents-only.

By Train By far the easiest way to get to the ground is by train. The closest two tube stations are White City, on the Central line, and Wood Lane Station, on the Hammersmith and City line. A good idea is to park at a railway station on the edge of the city and catch a tube in.

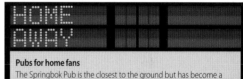

HOME AWAY

Pubs for home fans
The Springbok Pub is the closest to the ground but has become a home-fans-only pub. Other than this most are welcoming of all fans.

Good food near ground
The Shepherds Bush Green area is the place to head for food, there is such a wide variety here that you're sure to find what you want.

Pubs for away fans
With alcohol not served in the away end it's best to head to the Shepherds Bush Green area where there are numerous pubs, which will be busy on a match day. Walkabout and O'Neill's will be busy but welcome home and away fans, there are plenty more establishments in the area as well.

Top tips
It really is a good idea to take a train in; traffic and parking is a nightmare around the ground.

THE LAST WORD

qpr.vitalfootball.co.uk
loftforwords.co.uk
wearetherangersboys.com

HOME COLOURS

- 😊 **Nicknames** The Royals
- 📅 **Founded** 1871
- 🏟 **Ground** Madejski Stadium (opened 1998)
- 📍 **Address** Reading, Berkshire RG2 OFL
- 👥 **Capacity** 24,161
- 🏆 **Best attendance** 24,134 vs Manchester United, Premier League, 19 January, 2008
- 📞 **Contact** 0118-968 1100
- 🎟 **Ticket Number** 0844-249 1871
- @ **Email** customerservice@readingfc.co.uk
- W **Website** readingfc.co.uk

Ah, the ancient art of nomenclature, the skill of classification, identification, identity. Take The Biscuitmen; it's a name dripping with history, like a generous layering of chocolate. It has a touch of intrigue and mystery, like the moment your teeth sink unknowingly into a plump raisin or crunch through a toasted hazelnut. What are they, where have they come from? Just who are these shadowy Biscuitmen? They could almost be a dastardly 'one dunk' master race releasing mind-controlling crumbs into brews across the land in the style of a *Doctor Who* super villain. OK, so it has a less otherworldly origin – a nickname for a certain team of footballers from Reading, but still the name has a certain ring to it. And also bear in mind they had Death on their side – Steve Death that is, the legendary goalkeeper who made over 530 appearances for the club. Then came the seventies and the brave new world. Local biscuit giants Huntley and Palmers, on whom the name was based, were no more. The club wanted a new moniker, so the local Chronicle ran a competition and a new name was chosen – The Royals (Berkshire is a Royal County, don't you know). Granted, it is more interesting than being called The Blues, but it was a shame that the links with the biscuity past had to crumble away.

After years of batting the middle order, hovering between tier two and three the club's fortunes were about to change. In 1998 they moved to a state-of-the-art stadium and soon a squad was assembled to do it justice. In 2006, under the guidance of Steve Coppell, and defying the odds, Reading ascended to the Premier League.

This startling turnaround was precipitated by the arrival of a multimillionaire as chairman, one who'd made his fortune through selling his *Autotrader* titles. The name of the saviour? We'll it's written around the stadium in giant letters for all to see. Ah yes, the ancient art of branding.

Greatest moments on this ground
"Most of the first season in the Premiership was special, but beating West Ham 6-0 at home is perhaps only beaten by the 3-1 win against Liverpool in the Premiership in 2007. Most Reading fans would never have expected us to beat Liverpool in the League. Not ever." Graham Loader, Hob Nob Anyone?, royals.org.

Lowest moments on this ground
"Reading fans have been spoilt and relegation is a rare thing indeed at the Madejski Stadium, so the 0-2 home defeat to Fulham in April 2008 was hard to take as it dawned on fans we really were going down. The game summed up the season, as Reading limply gave up in a crunch fixture." Graham Loader.

Heroes of the sideline
"Steve Coppell will always be an absolute legend for transforming the side into the best team the Championship had ever seen. He guided us to a record-breaking Championship win playing some great football and then immediately to a remarkable eighth place in our first-ever season in the top flight. Happy days." Graham Loader.

That's quite interesting
"The ground is built on an old rubbish tip. Vents strategically placed around the car park release the gas being generated underground by the mutating junk." Graham Loader.

Not a lot of people know that
"If you exclude the Championship trophy, our main silverware triumph was the Simod Cup in 1988. The trophy, for the top two divisions, saw Reading victorious despite one of the lowest league places in the competition. Our relegation at the end of the season meant we were unable to defend the cup despite being holders." Graham Loader.

VILLAINS

"Stephen Hunt went from hero to villain after making it clear he wanted to leave the club. He was a hugely popular player and everyone leapt to his defence after the infamous Cech accident against Chelsea. However all that popularity faded on relegation." Graham Loader.

RIVALS

Aldershot is the big local rival, plus Swindon and Oxford.

GETTY IMAGES

> Reading's James Harper celebrates scoring the Royal's third goal against Liverpool in the Premier League, 2007.

Don't mention the…

"Number 13. A few seasons ago Reading fans, via the Hob Nob Anyone? website, thought it would be a good idea to wear number 13 on their shirts. The number was spare and it was a bit of fun. Unfortunately, the club got hold of the idea and destroyed it in a commercial frenzy. Before the fans knew it the club had applied to the Football League to officially get the number (and fans) in the squad list. Before every home game we'd get it shouted out over the tannoy. Fun for a while, but then horribly, embarrassingly cringe-worthy." Graham Loader.

The ground

This is a modern, purpose-built all-enclosed arena. The **West Stand** is the main stand and includes the family enclosure and changing rooms. This is a two-tier structure with corporate boxes between the levels. The **North Stand** behind the goal is a single-tier structure for home fans, as is the **East Stand** which it wraps around to meet. The **South Stand** can accommodate up to 4,350 away fans behind the far goal. There is a four-star hotel behind the west stand and a Jazz Café in the east stand. Niiiice!

Getting there

By Road/Parking Traffic and parking can be a problem. Exit the M4 at junction 11 and follow the A33 which leads to the stadium complex. Very limited stadium parking costs £8. Also worth Grange (off the A33) costs £8 and has 1000 spaces. The Foster Wheeler park and ride, Shinfield Park (exit B3270), costs £3.50 return/adult. Street parking is also available.

By Train Reading Station is around three miles from the ground so the No 79 Football Special bus is the best bet. It runs from the station (opposite the Three Guineas) every 15 minutes and takes 15 minutes (although as kick-off approaches the traffic increases as does journey time).

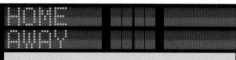
HOME AWAY

Pubs for home fans
The Nags Head, Russell Street, is a CAMRA award winning with Sweeney's pies, sports TVs and a fans' coach to Reading FC. The Spread Eagle, next to Elm Park has memorabilia with a fans' bus to the ground. (call to secure a place).

Good food near ground
"Walk across town to Sweeney & Todd (Castle Street) for the ultimate pie and pint experience," recommends Graham Loader. McDonalds, KFC, Pizza Hut are all near the ground.

Pubs for away fans
Three Guineas at the station is handy with a wide range of real ales and beer. Pubs near the ground are limited. However, there's a shuttle from the station between the town centre and the stadium – all the usual chains on Friar Street, including a couple of Wetherspoons – keep colours covered to get in some of these. Thanks to Graham for 'the knowledge'.

Top tips
The bus is used by all supporters so a relaxed attitude should ensure away fans are welcomed back on board post-match.

THE LAST WORD

royals.org
reading-mad.org.uk
hobnob.royals.org/forum

⌃ HEROES OF THE TURF
"Robin Friday was the greatest player I never saw, while Trevor Senior was a big club favourite scoring goals all over the place. Phil Parkinson will always be a legend; a blue-and-white blooded midfield machine. Graeme Murty had a tough job following some tough acts as club captain, but will be remembered a true gentleman and Reading through and through. Kevin Doyle will be remembered fondly – cheap as chips but pure class." Graham Loader.

⌄ ZEROES OF THE TURF
"Half a million pounds is a massive amount for Madejski's Reading to spend, back in 1999 it was even more massive so big things were expected from Sean Evers. He was anonymous for a few games, dropped to the bench, then from the squad before being shipped out on loan, eventually disappearing to non-league football. Leroy Lita kept on promising to do something for Reading but never quite came up with the goods. He did the necessary to get back in the starting line-up only to blow his chances. He went out on loan to Norwich, hit the net, got a recall, and then… failed again." Graham Loader.

HOME COLOURS

ROCHDALE

- **Nicknames** The Dale
- **Founded** 1907
- **Ground** Spotland Stadium (opened 1920)
- **Address** Willbutts Lane, Rochdale OL11 5DR
- **Capacity** 10,249
- **Best attendance** 24,231 v Notts County, FA Cup 2nd round, 10 December, 1949
- **Contact** 08448-261907
- **Ticket Number** 08448-261907
- **Email** admin@rochdaleafc.co.uk
- **Website** rochdaleafc.co.uk

Mercurial is hardly an adjective one might attach to Rochdale Football Club. Even their own fans would be forced to admit that following the team from Spotland has been anything but a rollercoaster ride over the years. In fact, the only way you might relate the team from Greater Manchester with this mesmerising fluid is the fact that both seem to be relatively heavy, finding the earthly bonds and the pull of gravity difficult to overcome. The Dale had occupied the bottom tier of English football for so long that opposition fans had begun to call it 'the Rochdale Division'. They had, in fact, been in the basement longer than any other team. The last and only time they'd managed to break the gravitational pull and celebrate a promotion was the year that Man first walked on the moon – an equally amazing feat, some might say.

However 2010 was a land mark season for the Lancashire club, a season when the 'Spruce Goose' of Spotland finally took to the skies and flew, when the earthly constraints of the bottom tier were left behind and the dressing room flowed with laughter and singing and the heady aroma of champagne soaked kits. Keith Hill, the 41-year-old manager, was not even born the last time this dressing room had a promotion to celebrate. Rochdale chairman Chris Dunphy waited a long time for this moment. "I was here the last time we got promoted and everyone had a pitch invasion then – but I was only 18." Rochdale have always had to run a tight ship. There was a slightly surreal period in the mid eighties when multi-millionaire Tommy Cannon of 'Cannon and Ball' fame took over the club, but he didn't exactly turn out to be a Lancastrian Roman Abramovich and things didn't end well. Since then it's been a case of slowly building, improving the ground dramatically and keeping the club on an even keel. Dunphy used to stand on the terraces at Spotland, but

RIVALS
Bury, Oldham and Burnley.

Pubs for home fans
"For a pre-match drink fans of both sides are more than welcome at the Cemetery Hotel, Bury Road, which does snacks as well as the Dale Bar which is to the left of the ticket office," recommends Ryan Tomlinson, editor, RochdaleAFC. "It has a relaxed atmosphere and a good range of ales, making it a popular spot. Another option is Studds Bar which fans will find to the left of the club shop."

Good food near ground
"The Wilbutts Lane Chippy has been popular with fans for as long as I can remember", says Ryan Tomlinson. "Whether you're after fish 'n' chips or a traditional rag pudding, this place delivers."

Pubs for away fans
The most convenient pub for away fans is the Church Inn, Wilbutts Lane, two minutes up the road from the away turnstiles.

Top tips
This is a cracking ground to visit with a number or friendly watering holes surrounding it. Take a sound attitude with you and, despite it being a bit of a trek from the station you won't go far wrong.

THE FA VIA GETTY IMAGES

the expedition into the third tier will be a new experience for him; for the whole club. The Dale have broken through the doors of perception into a brave new world and now they've shaken off the shackles of the 'Rochdale Division', who knows where their trajectory might take them?

Greatest moments on this ground
"The greatest moment I have ever enjoyed at Spotland would have been the semi-final second leg of the play-offs against Darlington at the end of the 2007/08 season. Dale went into that game 2-1 down and pulled through a controversial penalty given against us as well as a red card for David Perkins which never should have been given, Dale eventually won 5-4 on penalties." Ryan Tomlinson, editor, RochdaleAFC.com.

Lowest moments on this ground

"My lowest moment at Spotland would have probably been one of my earliest memories of Rochdale. Bury trounced us 3-0 and we couldn't get anywhere near them with Dave Nugent showing what a talent he was that day." Ryan Tomlinson.

Heroes of the turf

"Gary Jones, the captain of Rochdale, has been the driving force of our midfield for as long as I can remember. Rickie Lambert was part of the best strikeforce we've ever seen at Rochdale, with Grant Holt as his partner. Unlike Holt he stayed to fire the goals that kept us up that season. Glenn Murray was an absolute class act, who we signed from next to nothing and sold for £300,000 – not bad business eh? Tommy Lee came in on loan from Macclesfield to be our number one after injuries left us without any goalkeepers. I'll never forget his penalty save in the shoot out against Darlington. Adam Le Fondre was our popular top-scorer for two seasons recently, before he left." Ryan Tomlinson.

Zeroes of the turf

"We apparently beat a selection of clubs to sign Paul Tait from Bristol Rovers, but he was awful and was last seen at Barrow. Keith Barker signed on loan from Blackburn as a replacement for Lambert. He was awful too and has since given up football for cricket!" Ryan Tomlinson.

That's quite interesting

Port Vale remained in the bottom division from 1974 until 2010.

Villains

"Paul Simpson. More for the mess he made as player-manager rather than a player. Reuben Reid was sent back to Plymouth after an unsuccessful loan spell where he was suspended for his conduct. Somehow earned himself a move back to the Championship with West Brom." Ryan Tomlinson.

Not a lot of people know that

Tommy Cannon had a short spell as chairman.

The ground

Spotland Stadium is much improved over the last 10 years, and is considered to be one of the best lower league grounds to visit. The **Twaites Beers Stand**, or Sandy Road, is the only standing terrace in the ground.

It is behind the goal and this covered terrace can accommodate 1898 home fans. The **Westrose Leisure Stand** or Willbutts Lane is the newest. This is where away fans are housed and there are excellent views from here. It has a capacity of 3,644 but the stand can be divided between home and away if needed. There are no pillars to obstruct and good facilities. The Pearl Street **T.D.S. Stand** was opened by Sir Nat Lofthouse in 1997 and has the capacity for 2,584 home fans. It is a single tier of seats covered by a high roof and sits behind the far goal. The older **Main Stand** has room for 1774 home fans with a row of executive boxes along the middle of the back of the stand. The dug outs and tunnel are on the half way line here. Studds Bar is found under the T.D.S. Stand.

Getting there

By Road/Parking The stadium is west of the town centre. Take the M62 to junction 20 and follow the A627 (M) signed to Rochdale. Turn left onto A664/Edinburgh Way passing B&Q and Aldi. Go straight over a roundabout onto the B6425 and follow it. The road eventually becomes Sandy Lane, with the stadium on the right. Street parking. (Residents parking schemes operate on some of the roads close to the ground).

By Train The train station is a couple of miles southeast of the ground – around a 35-minute walk. From the station head up Maclure Road, turning left onto Drake Street. At the end of Drake Street, turn right onto Manchester Road, crossing the road in order to turn left at the next junction onto Dane Street (where you will pass a big ASDA). Continue to follow as road becomes Mellor Street. At top of road turn left onto Spotland Road and left onto Wilbutts Lane, where you can revive your self with ale and chips!

▽ Rochdale fans wait on the touchline for the final whistle to celebrate Rochdale's first promotion in 41 years at the end of the Coca Cola League Two Match against Northampton Town at Spotland, April 2010

clubfanzine.com/rochdale

- **Nicknames** The Millers
- **Founded** 1868
- **Ground** Don Valley Stadium (opened 1990)
- **Address** Stadium: Worksop Road, Sheffield S9 3TL;
  Club: Mangham House, Mangham Road, Barbot Hall Industrial Estate,
  Rotherham S61 4RJ
- **Capacity** 25,000 (limited to 10,000)
- **Best attendance** 25,170 vs Sheffield United, Division Two
  (Millmoor Stadium), 13 December, 1952
- **Contact** 0844-414 0733
- **Ticket Number** 0844-414 0737
- **Email** office@rotherhamunited.net
- **Website** themillers.co.uk

ROTHERHAM UNITED

RIVALS

Sheffield United,
Sheffield
Wednesday,
Barnsley and
Doncaster.

GETTY IMAGES

Rotherham sits at the heart of the South Yorkshire football landscape. There's a seam of passion for the beautiful game that runs deep through this land. For generations it's been mined by the reds of Barnsley and has run molten through the Sheffield twins of United and Wednesday. Now it's been rediscovered on the ex-brown field arena of Doncaster Rovers. In Rotherham the love of the club is seemingly the only currency they've been trading on for the last few years. The recession came early for the Millers. As a team they could now be playing Championship football, but as a club they seem to have become mired in a financial bog that has threatened their very existence. During the 2002/03 season United were sitting in the middle of the second tier of English football, but in the last three years they have been penalized a whopping 37 points and entered administration twice. Not only that but they're now homeless, playing their games at Don Valley Stadium in Sheffield and training at facilities in Doncaster. One has to wonder sometimes whether the football authorities are wielding their big stick a little too gleefully when some teams are fighting for their survival in this way.

Through all this, the glue that's holding this club together is the fans. They've followed the club to the Valley, and hopefully they'll emerge from it to see the promised land of a new stadium and some financial security. For it's the financial backing that seems to be holding the team back, a side that has haemorrhaged players and staff at an alarming rate, but still seems to

VILLAINS

"Deon Burton – he couldn't play for us in a game because he had 'flu', but miraculously signed for rivals Sheffield Wednesday and managed to shake off his 'flu' and play for them a couple of days later." Caz Neale.

take to the pitch and produce performances that see them forge their way back up the league. Maybe now, without the handicap brought on by the footballing powers, the team can be left to get on with winning games, and the fans can go about their business of making the Valley feel like a fortress – albeit a temporary one.

Greatest moments on this ground
"Well, we're into another season at Don Valley and despite what can only be described as a good first season the highlight at DVS has to be the 4-2 wins over Leeds and Leicester in the JP Trophy, and Wolves and Southampton in the League Cup. Back at Millmoor, there's been a few great moments, many that a lot of Millers fans would like to go back to. Wins over a mardy West Ham (who got changed at a local hotel rather than the porta-changing rooms) and other billy big-head former Premier League teams stick in the memory banks." Richard Gaynor, editor, millersMAD.

◄ Adam Le Fondre celebrates scoring the only goal of the League Two playoff semi-final 1st Leg against Aldershot Town, 2010.

"Administrations. Over the last two, we've lost 37 points in three years… We're now playing in Sheffield and that's just not good." Richard Gaynor.

Lowest moments on this ground

"Don Valley – it's pretty low after the novelty has worn off, for a start it's an athletics ground and it's in Sheffield. Things can't get much lower than that, but at least we still have a club to support." Richard Gaynor.

"Our 1-0 win over Barnet on the last day of the 2007/08 season. I think we knew in our hearts that would be our last game at Millmoor. And when we lost on penalties in the League Two play-off semi-finals against Leyton Orient in 1999." Caz Neale, editor, Vital Rotherham.

Heroes of the sideline

"Ronnie Moore – he did the unthinkable with us by taking us into the Championship and kept us there for four years." Richard Gaynor

"I've got to mention John Breckin who has been 'number two' at Millmoor with both Ronnie Moore and Mark Robins. Danny Williams – he became manager in 1962, but resigned after his young players were sold from under his feet." Caz Neale.

Heroes of the turf

"Ronnie Moore – he's just a total Rotherham legend. Tony Towner – up there with Ronnie, a fast winger who beat men for fun and chipped in with goals. Gerry Gow – a hard man who was good." Richard Gaynor.

"Alan Lee – it took him a while to get his first goal for The Millers, but once he started scoring he never looked back. Dave Watson – he was plucked from Notts County reserves by Tommy Docherty and put at centre-half." Caz Neale.

The ground

Rotherham enjoyed 101 years at Millmoor, but will spend the foreseeable future at the Don Valley Stadium in neighbouring Sheffield. While the ground can hold 25,000, it has been limited to 10,000 for league games. Primarily an athletics arena, the pitch is below ground level with banked stands. Only the main stand is covered and usually this is the only part of the ground open, with away fans seated in the corner stand (also covered), an extension of the main. The stands are set back from the pitch due to the track and long jump.

Getting there

By road/Parking The ground is northeast of the city, just a couple of miles from the M1, junction 34. From the north, follow the A6109/Meadowhall Road, signed Sheffield Centre. Pass the retail park on the left, turn left into Hawke Street and right into Atercliffe Common. Go left into Worksop Road and the ground is on the left. From the south follow the A6178/Sheffield Road, becoming Atercliffe Common. Turn left onto Worksop Road. Match-day parking at Pic Toys, Worksop Road, for £3.

By train From Sheffield station take the Supertram out to the stadium (over two miles). Take the tram one stop to Fitzalan Square/Ponds Forge, cross the platform to board the Yellow route tram towards Meadowhall. Darnall Road station is closest, situated one mile from the ground. Go out of station and follow Main Road (becoming Darnall Road then Worksop Road). The ground is on the right.

Pubs for home fans
The Cocked Hat, on Worksop Road, is right outside the stadium with decent beer (Marstons) and well-priced food.

Good food near ground
Don Valley Fisheries, Atercliffe Road, is handy for the ground. If coming in off the M1 try Meadowhall retail park, Atercliffe Road. It has a world of fast food from sushi to pizza and everything in between.

Pubs for away fans
Faras, opposite The Cocked Hat, is a decent enough spot with food also available. The (pretty average) Britannia is also on Worksop Road. There are plenty of good pubs in the centre, including the real-ale gem Kelham Island Tavern, on Russell Street; it's a trek north of the city centre but a worthwhile diversion.

Top tips
Remember to head to Sheffield not Rotherham for away games!

PUB QUIZ

That's quite interesting
"Apparently someone forgot to inform the Football League we were moving our home from Millmoor to Don Valley! They were well chuffed!" Sy.

Not a lot of people know that
"The first black professional footballer to play in Britain, Arthur Wharton played for Rotherham Town (1889-1894)." Caz Neale.

THE LAST WORD

rotherhamunited-mad.co.uk
rotherham.vitalfootball.co.uk

⊕ **Nicknames** The Iron
⊕ **Founded** 1899
⊕ **Ground** Glanford Park (opened 1988)
ⓘ **Address** Doncaster Road, Scunthorpe
⊕ **Capacity** 9,088
✪ **Best attendance** 23,935 vs Portsmouth, FA Cup 3rd round, 30 January, 1954
ⓒ **Contact** 0877-221 1899
ⓒ **Ticket Number** 0877-221 1899
@ **Email** admin@scunthorpe-united.co.uk
Ⓦ **Website** scunthorpe-united.co.uk

SCUNTHORPE UNITED

RIVALS

Hull City, Grimsby, Doncaster Rovers and Lincoln City.

A Cliff Byrne header two minutes from time – that was the difference between promotion and failure. Looking back on the season it's amazing how 46 games can hinge on one move, one strike of the ball, the merest fraction of a degree. Play-offs elicit myriad feelings from football fans no matter which team they support, apart from maybe the big four. They make all the difference between celebrating a truly righteous victory as your team rises from the ashes of a lesser division, and seeing your hopes and dreams dragged into a black hole of despair while your club is tossed back in the can for another season.

But try telling a Scunthorpe fan that they're a bad idea. With 10 minutes to go in the 2008/09 season, the team was a goal down to fellow promotion hopefuls Tranmere Rovers, and effectively seventh place in the table. A mere draw would mean that the team would scramble above Rovers and scrape across that magical line drawn on League tables separating dreams from nightmares. Byrne delivered that hammer blow for the Iron and Tranmere had no time to recover – Scunny were play-off bound. In this pressure-cooker environment reputation means nothing, form means nothing, history is forgotten. Scunthorpe would be in with MK Dons, who seemed to throw away an automatic place; Millwall, always a tough team to beat; and the overwhelming favourites Leeds United. Three weeks later it was the Scunthorpe players doing the Wembley lap of honour, holding the cup high as fireworks lit up the sky, the Iron fans celebrating life in a new division. New teams to play, new grounds to visit. The sixth place team was going up!

Greatest moments on this ground

"Playing wise, beating Chelsea 4-1 in the old League Cup in 1988. At the time they were flying high in the second tier and full of expectation, and we were Fourth Division. Atmosphere-wise, the 1999 play-off semi-final victory against Swansea. The ground was absolutely buzzing an hour before kick-off. It continued through the entire match, which ebbed and flowed and was in the balance right until the last kick of the entire 120 minutes." Jim Balderson.

Lowest moments on this ground

"Watching Cardiff City fans celebrating winning promotion having been given the home end. Embarrassing effort from the club who showed no loyalty to the fans." Trevor Hannan, fan.

Heroes of the sideline

"Mick Buxton – some of the best football I have ever seen by a Scunthorpe United team was in the late 1980s and early 1990s played under his management. Brian Laws – any manager who has 10 years at one club and leaves them in a much better position than when he arrived and is courted by a bigger club has done a tremendous job. Nigel Adkins – he's taken the club to the second tier twice now on a shoestring budget and got the club punching above their weight on a regular basis." Jim Balderson.

Zeroes of the turf

"A bit harsh to call them zeroes as they came at the end of good careers, but unfortunately it never worked out for them here – Ian Ormondroyd, Tommy Johnson and Geoff Horsfield." Jim Balderson. "Jim Goodwin's passing game in midfield was appalling at times." Trevor Hannan.

Don't mention the…

"Not too much to be embarrassed about for a small club, but the red away strip from the mid-nineties has to be a low point." Jim Balderson.

Villains

"The only one that springs to mind is Jim Goodwin who left us for Huddersfield Town. He made some unsavoury

PUB QUIZ

That's quite interesting
Ian Botham turned out 11 times for the club. Yes, Beefy!

Not a lot of people know that
"We were the first football league club to lose an FA Cup tie on penalties when we lost at Rotherham in November 1991 following a 3-3 draw after extra-time." Jim Balderson.

and disparaging remarks when he left and always gets roundly booed whenever he plays against us now. Unfortunately, it seems to lift his game and he always performs well against us now – perhaps we should just ignore him!" Jim Balderson.

"Dave Hill for leaving us to join Lincoln City, Jamie Forrester for slagging us off as a town when he left to go to Belgium for better things (apparently)." Trevor Hannan.

The ground

A pleasingly symmetrical ground that holds about a coachload over 9,000 fans. The stadium has excellent access and was opened in August 1988, replacing the Old Show Ground.

The **East** or **Grove Wharf Stand** runs down the side of the pitch and is a single-tier seating area. This is the largest stand.

The **North** or **Arcelor Mittal Stand** behind the goal is home to vocal core supporters and is the only remaining standing area at the ground. Like the rest of the stadium, there are some pillars to contend with. The Iron Bar is situated behind here for home supporters only.

The **West** or **Telegraph Stand** runs the opposite length of the pitch and houses the executive area and has fewer pillars to restrict views. The changing rooms and players' tunnel are here.

The away support usually occupies the **South** or **Caparo Stand**, a seating area of about 1,600, although extra seats can be made available in the south corner of the Scunthorpe Telegraph stand. There are a few pillars again so some restricted view seats.

Getting there

By Road/Parking Just off the motorway and at the edge of Scunthorpe, Glanford Park is an easy stadium to reach by car. Follow the M180 to junction 3 and take the M181 to Scunthorpe, following it to the end. Turn right at the first roundabout onto the A18 and right again into the ground car park. Parking available for 600 cars at £2. Limited street parking also available.

By Train Scunthorpe's station is a couple of miles from the ground. Heading left out of the station walk toward the crossroads and turn right onto Oswald Road. Continue along the road passing The Honest Lawyer and Blue Bell pubs before turning left at the lights onto Doncaster Road. Continue along here and Glanford Park will eventually be on your left.

∧ Play-off final 2009 – sheer joy!
➤ Martyn Woolford scores the winning goal for Scunthorpe in the League One play-off final against Millwall at Wembley 2009.

HEROES OR ZEROES?

≪ HEROES OF THE TURF
"Steve Cammack and Andy Flounders – top goal-scorers. Joe Murphy – best goalkeeper for many years who commands his defence and gives them bags of confidence. Peter Beagrie – although getting on in years when he came to us, he played more games for us than any other club. An absolute pleasure to watch when turning defenders inside out. He raised the profile of the club tremendously in his time here. Billy Sharp – smashed all sorts of goal-scoring records in his two seasons here, which got us into the second tier of English football for the first time in over 40 years." Jim Balderson.

Pubs for home fans
The Iron Bar in the grounds behind the North Stand is one for home supporters only while, The Old Farmhouse is at the entrance to the ground and a popular spot with both home and away fans – no team colours allowed. Guest ales.

Good food near ground
There are a number of unmemorable fast-food joints on Doncaster Road and in the retail park just off it which you'll pass if heading from the train station.

Pubs for away fans
Around the corner from the ground, the art deco-inspired Berkley on Doncaster Road has a good atmosphere and well-priced beer. If walking from the train station you'll pass the popular Honest Lawyer with good food and a beer/real ale selection plus the local CAMRA award-winning Blue Bell Wetherspoon pub, which also does a good line in cask ales, both on Oswald Road and decent spots for a swift pint or two.

Top tips
Be aware that due to the pillars there are restricted view seats in the south stand (and the rest of the stadium).

THE LAST **WORD**

iron-bru.net and suosc.co.uk
scunthorpeunited-mad.co.uk
scunnyfan.co.uk

- **Nicknames** The Blades
- **Founded** 1889
- **Ground** Bramall Lane (opened 1862, first football match)
- **Address** Sheffield S2 4SU
- **Capacity** 32,609
- **Best attendance** 68,287 vs Leeds United, FA Cup 5th round, 15 February, 1936
- **Contact** 0871-995 1899
- **Ticket Number** 0871-995 1889
- **Email** info@sufc.co.uk
- **Website** sufc.co.uk

SHEFFIELD UNITED

GETTY IMAGES

∧ David Cotterill scores against Cardiff City.

"I remember taking my daughter to her first Blades game, thus ensuring another generation gets to suffer as I have," is a fan's admission that says as much about the United fan base as it does about the team. It takes a certain kind of stoicism to support a giant club that hasn't really brought home any silverware since 1925. But then this is South Yorkshire and in the Steel City you had to decide early whether you were either Wednesday or United. There are many football rivalries, but this one is as fierce as any. Through the steel mills and across the South Yorkshire coalfields you were either blue or red. The Blades have a reputation for building workmanlike teams, solid and aggressive with mountains as centre-backs and giants as centre-forwards. Add to that plain-speaking managers like Neil Warnock, no-nonsense strikers like Brian Deane and staunch celebrity supporters like Sean Bean, none of whom would ever make a shortlist to conduct sensitive UN negotiations. Then there was Sir Dave of Bassett. The highlight of pre-season preparation was, as one Blades fan puts it, "taking the players to the steel works to remind the overpaid prima donnas what the real world is like and who it is they're playing for." Basset was a renowned motivator, as Tony Agana says, "you might have won 4-0 and he'd still come in and give you a roasting." Asked what he looks for in a player, Bassett said, "I look for talent, whether he's got something about him. It's a gut feeling. Then I ask myself, does he understand the game? Is he athletic? Is he brave? Is his character sound?"

But it would be an over simplification to paint a picture of life at Bramall Lane as trench warfare. The United faithful appreciates smooth, full-bodied red with its field rations. One only has to look at the sublime skills served up by Tony Currie to see that. Currie was one of the most talented players of his generation; with a deft touch and an eye for openings he would float the ball around the field or beat defenders to create attacking opportunities from nothing. The Blades' number 10 could also find the top corner with a Beckham-esque curl from outside the box with apparent ease – the Currie 'banana shots' are imprinted on a generation of fans' memories from both sides of the terraces. Currie went on to make 376 appearances for the Bramall Lane club and, despite committing the crime of being lured north to close rivals Leeds, still ranks as the all-time Blades legend. Currie ensured the fans would always have a taste for football with a bit spice.

Greatest moments on this ground

"Ask any fan of Sheffield United and undoubtedly they would suggest that the best match ever seen at the Lane would be the play-off semi-final victory over Forest (2002/03). Trailing 2-0 just after half-time the Blades steamed back into life and eventually won the game 4-3 in extra-time. Paul Peschisolido was a hero that day and will not be forgotten." Paul Holland, editor, blades-mad.co.uk.

Lowest moments on this ground

"Relegation against Wigan – with all the context of the Tevez Affair and Sir Alex playing his U16 girls' side against

RIVALS

Sheffield Wednesday – fierce local rivalry in the Steel City derbies. Leeds United, Rotherham United, Barnsley, Nottingham Forest and Doncaster Rovers.

PUB QUIZ

That's quite interesting
"Bramall Lane is the only venue to have hosted a cricket test match, the FA Cup final, a full football international – the only venue to be home of the County Championship champions, and the home of the Football League champions." Happyhippy.

Not a lot of people know that
"We weren't always Blades. We used to be Cutlers." Shorehamview.

GETTY IMAGES

HEROES OR ZEROES?

⌃ HEROES OF THE TURF

"Alan Kelly (keeper) – the Irish shot-stopper was a great representative for United in a spell which lasted seven years; best remembered for his penalty shoot-out saves in 1993 and 1998. David Holdsworth (defender) – he was magnificent at the back, a pleasure to watch. Michael Brown (midfielder) – dynamic in the middle, he scored 22 goals during the 2002/03 season. Brian Deane (forward) – he knew how to find the back of the net, he had three spells with the Blades and is one player who is always welcome back at the Lane. James Beattie (forward) – he scored over 20 goals in his first season and in the next into double figures before being sold to Stoke City."
Paul Holland.

"Tony Currie, nuff said (though his goal against Liverpool is still the finest goal I will ever see)." Sheepdip Blade.

❮ James Beattie shows United commitment.

DON'T MENTION THE...

"We had a three-sided ground in the nineties, because we knocked down one stand and were too skint to replace it for a while, so we had a nice strip of wasteland to look at." Shorehamview.

◄ Tony Currie lines up a shot whilst holding off Coventry defender Alan Dugdale.

The Cheating Bubbles on the last day of the season. Worst I'd felt since my dad died – and Brooking refused to dock West Ham points as it might upset their fans. What, southern bias?" Sheepdip Blade, from sheff-utd.co.uk.

Heroes of the sideline

"'Sir' Neil Warnock, for managing the Blades as we all wanted to, with the passion that only a Blade can. Yes, we may have done things differently, but he genuinely cared. Sir Dave of Bassett. What he achieved on a budget smaller than most pub sides was nothing short of miraculous. Loaves and fishes? Next to Deane and Agana, a mere gesture." Shorehamview from sheff-utd.co.uk.

Zeroes of the turf

"Vassilis Borbokis… it was just a shame he was a defender who knew nothing about defending. Michael Twiss – we were told he was the new Ryan Giggs. Thanks, Sir Alex. Lee Baxter – he was so spectacularly poor in the 45 minutes he played in the net for us away at Burnley, I was tempted to make him a legend. Peter Withe – signed just over three years after scoring the winner in the European Cup final for Villa. We should have stayed Withe-out.

Ian Rush (loan) – are we the only side he never scored for? He may have been getting on, but he was still crap." Happyhippy, from sheff-utd.co.uk.

"Axel Smeets (defender) – Belgian national who was a signing of Adrian Heath; Smeets was sent off on his debut at Portsmouth. Heath didn't last long and neither did the Belgian; he made just five appearances in total. John Ebbrell (midfielder) – he cost the Blades £1 million from Everton in January 1997, he played just 45 minutes of football against Reading, was substituted after picking up an injury and never recovered." Paul Holland.

The ground

In an era of new builds and modern arenas, Bramall Lane has a certain appeal. The stands lack uniformity and are mostly single-tiered, with an unusual corner office block. Away fans used to occupy the higher tier in the Bramall Lane End, and so enjoyed excellent views. This has recently changed.

Halliwells Stand behind the goal at the Bramall Lane End is a two-tier stand that was opened in 1966. The lower tier now houses the away fans, while the upper tier is for home supporters. Its capacity is 5,680. Looking at the stand, the Blades Business Centre is situated to the right, a white block of offices.

The single-tier **Malta Family Stand** has a row of 31 executive boxes at the back of the stand. This is the family stand and has a capacity of just under 7,000. It was built in 1996.

Frasers Property Kop behind the far goal is where the core support sits. It is a large single-storey stand that is half-built into a hillside, unfortunately it has three supporting pillars that may obscure views.

Valad Stand has a capacity of 7,500 and is also known as the Main Stand or Laver Stand. It houses the press box and television gantry.

Getting there

By Road/Parking The ground is easily accessed from the M1. From the north, take the M1 to junction 36 and follow the A61 heading to Sheffield (north). Continue on through two roundabouts before joining the ring road A61/Hoyle Street. At the junction with A621, take the third exit at the roundabout onto the A621/Bramall Lane. Ground is on left. From the south, exit the M1 at junction 33 and follow the A630. Continue along as road becomes the A57. Join the inner ring road and follow the A61 along Sheaf Street and St Mary's Road before turning off onto the A621/Bramall Lane. Alternatively exit the motorway sooner at junction 29 and take the A617 (Chesterfield/ Matlock). On approaching Chesterfield, take the fourth exit at the roundabout onto A61. Follow the A61 almost to the ground and, while on London Road, turn right onto Queen's Road before turning left onto Bramall Lane.

Parking on the streets near the ground is difficult and unsurprisingly busy (unless you get there very early). There are a couple of NCP car parks nearby including Sidney Street and Furnival Gate.

By Train From Sheffield's station it is only a 15-minute walk to the ground. From Sheaf Street take the right fork onto Shoreham Street. Cross over St Mary's Road, continue along Shoreham Street, you will see the ground on your right.

⌃ High passions in the Steel City Derby – you're either blue or red!

IN AN ERA OF NEW BUILDS AND MODERN ARENAS, BRAMALL LANE HAS A CERTAIN APPEAL.

Pubs for home fans
There are several decent pubs around the ground on Bramall Lane that are popular with home fans, including the Sheaf House and The Railway. Just off Bramall on Alderson Road The Golden Lion is another for home fans only with multiple screens that show the games, an outside terrace, as well as decent pub grub such as burgers.

Good food near ground
There are plenty of places to grab a bite to eat – particularly on the London Road where there's everything from Vietnamese to Chinese restaurants, including the quality Pho 68. If you feel the need to visit the golden arches, there is one on St Mary's Road.

Pubs for away fans
The city centre is only a 10-minute walk from the ground with a number of decent pubs, including the usual generic Wetherspoon just off the main drag, a number of which are open to away supporters who don't promote their colours. Royal Standard, St Mary's Road, A61, is a popular spot for home and generally away fans too. Beer garden and food also available. The Bridge Inn is a nice little pub, food also. For those in the market for a real ale, The Sheaf View, Gleadless Road is an ideal spot with beer garden and a great atmosphere, as such it gets busy on match days so get there early.

Top tips
If you are thinking of parking at Meadowhall and taking the tram into the city centre be aware the free parking is up to three hours, after which a heavy fine kicks in. With a 20-minute tram journey there and back if there's any extra-time added, you might be cutting it fine.

THE LAST **WORD**

s24su.com
sheff-utd.co.uk
sheffieldunited-mad.co.uk
redandwhite-wizards.co.uk

- **Nicknames** Wednesday, The Owls
- **Founded** 1867
- **Ground** Hillsborough Stadium (opened 1899)
- **Address** Penisone Road, Hillsborough, Sheffield S6 1SW
- **Capacity** 39,812
- **Best attendance** 72,841 vs Man City, FA Cup 5th round, 17 February, 1934
- **Contact** 0871-995 1867
- **Ticket Number** 0871-900 1867
- **Email** enquiries@swfc.co.uk
- **Website** swfc.co.uk

SHEFFIELD WEDNESDAY

The date is 21 April, 1991, the time is 5pm. A champagne-soaked John Sheridan is holding aloft the League Cup trophy in front of 30,000 Wednesday fans, at Wembley. Peter Shirtliff, Danny Wilson and David Hirst salute the sea of blue and white as the Manchester United section of the ground drains with unfeasible speed. Sheridan's lone strike was enough to secure the trophy for the South Yorkshire club and ITV regions around the country joined in the celebrations, broadcasting the victory. Meanwhile in Sheffield, the tanned face of Jan Gabriel and chisel-jawed Claude Akins were staring out into living rooms across Yorkshire from a very different stadium. Rather than screening the post-match jubilation at Wembley like the rest of the country, YTV in their wisdom decided that watching the steroidal pick-ups 'First Blood' and 'Big Foot', crushing and smashing their way through an arena full of scrap cars in *War of the Monster Trucks* would be more interesting for their viewers. The switchboards lit up and the blue half of the city of Sheffield has never forgiven the Leeds-based local channel – in fact the incident spawned one of The Owls' most famous fanzines, also titled *War of the Monster Trucks*. Grudges are not easily forgotten in these parts. They've never forgiven Leeds for signing Eric Cantona from under their noses, or the fact that Leeds always got more room on YTV's teletext. Some fans even believe Gordon Strachan was going to The Owls before he went to West Yorkshire outfit instead.

RIVALS

Sheffield United, Leeds United, Barnsley, Doncaster and Rotherham United.

However, the rivalry with the Whites pales into insignificance when compared with the red-hot hatred of the 'other' Sheffield team. Workforces and sometimes even families are split along red and blue lines. Players who cross the divide are certainly never forgiven. There is even a perceived ethical difference in playing styles

for Wednesday fans. While United battled, the blues boasted that their team served up a more cultured fare. The likes of Paulo Di Canio, Chris Waddle, David Hirst and John Sheridan meant that the Owls were always a team that played attractive football – even though they weren't afraid to throw in the long ball for the likes of Lee Chapman to latch onto the end of. But ask any fan about highlights, or lowest ebbs and they usually revolve around the Steel City derbies. As Terry Hibberd, editor of Owls Online says, "Probably the worst thing is that we only managed our first double over our neighbours last season, after a wait of just 95 years!"

Greatest moments on this ground

"The greatest moments unfortunately seem to be in the past, but the stadium has a decent heritage so I suppose it's quite fitting. Promotion back into the top flight in 1984; we beat Crystal Palace 1-0, sealing promotion to Division One through a Mel Sterland penalty, and were only denied the championship on goal difference. In 1991, promotion again in front of over 30,000, with a 3-1 win over Bristol City took us up to Division One." Terry Hibberd, editor, owlsonline.com.

Lowest moments on this ground

"Without doubt one of the lowest moments in English football was the Hillsborough disaster. For 96 people to have lost their lives on what would have started out as one of their most exciting days of the season is incomprehensible. It is shocking that it took a tragedy of this magnitude to make the authorities take the safety of supporters at football grounds seriously." Chris Morris, editor, owls-mad.

Heroes of the sideline

Robert Brown, Jack Charlton, Ron Atkinson and Howard Wilkinson.

Heroes of the turf

"David Hirst is most people's Owls hero of the modern era. The last man to score 100 goals for the club, Hirsty was spoken of in the same vein as Alan Shearer in the early nineties before injury took its toll. Paolo Di Canio – his Owls career ended in infamous fashion but prior to that he was regarded as one of the most skillful players ever to play in the blue and white stripes. Chris Waddle – the Football Writers' Player of the Year in 1993 was at times mesmeric. Not blessed with pace, he used trickery to turn full-backs inside out. They often knew what was coming but still couldn't stop him. Only Graham Taylor can answer why he wasn't picked for any of the 1994 World Cup qualifiers and we all know how that turned out!" Chris Morris.

"Terry Curran. Our neighbours had Tony Currie, we had our own TC. A bit of a footballing journeyman but arguably he played his best football whilst with us. John Sheridan; Brian Clough didn't take to him at Forest, heaven knows why! The best passer of a football ever seen at Hillsborough and he just happened to win us the League Cup against Man United at Wembley in 1991." Terry Hibberd.

Zeroes of the turf

"We have had a few of these, so it's hard to choose. Gilles De Bilde came with a decent reputation as a goal-scorer at

international level for Belgium and cost a lot of money. He just never seemed to care – your typical 'take the money and run' type. Wim Jonk was known throughout the game as a pass-master and renowned throughout Europe, but he just didn't fit in – another big-money buy that just went very wrong. Klas Ingesson – on the evidence we saw I cannot understand what Trevor Francis ever saw in him. He

⌄ "You'll never beat Des Walker".

PUB QUIZ

That's quite interesting
"The Owls were formed when a cricket club who played on Wednesdays came up with the idea to keep the players together and in shape during the non-cricket playing season." Chris Morris.

Not a lot of people know that
"We were once known as the 'Blades', the nickname which our neighbours now use. Our current nickname comes from the area of Sheffield that we moved to, Owlerton." Terry Hibberd.

GETTY IMAGES

BOB THOMAS/GETTY IMAGES

did one good thing whilst at the club, scoring one goal away at Everton. He was sold to Italian side, Bari, and won defender of the year in Serie A. How he managed that I will never know!" Terry Hibberd.

Don't mention the…

"Arsenal! The Gunners became Wednesday's nemesis in the nineties, particularly in 1993 when Wednesday became the first team to lose the two major domestic cup finals in the same season. The Owls were seconds away from the first-

ever FA Cup final penalty shoot-out when Andy Linighan scored in extra-time in the replay to break Wednesday fans' hearts, and other than a couple of brief highs it's been pretty much downhill ever since." Chris Morris.

The ground

The stadium has been much improved since the Hillsborough disaster in April 1989 and hosted several games during the Euro 96 tournament. This is a great stadium to visit, not clinically modern, but with great balance and atmosphere. It carries with it a certain weight of history as some of the game's most memorable moments have occurred here during its tenure as an FA Cup semi-final venue. There are plans underway to modernize the stadium, including removing the pillars in the Kop and West Stand and adding a corner between the North Stand and Kop.

⌃ Clash of giants! Pele takes on the Sheffield Wednesday defenders during a game between Santos and Wednesday at Hillsborough, February 1972.

The **South Stand** opened in 1914, replacing an original stand that had been moved from the old Olive Grove ground in 1899. It is Hillsborough's most recognizable, running the length of the field and with the clock sitting above the halfway line on a large triangular face on the stand's roof. It became an all-seater ahead of Euro 96 and has a capacity of 11,354.

The **Spion Kop** behind the goal is home to the core Wednesday fans and when a roof was added in 1986 it could hold a massive 22,000 fans – making it the largest covered standing area in Europe. Today the all-seater single tier has a capacity of 11,210.

The **North Stand** was the first cantilever stand in Britain to run the full length of the pitch when it opened in 1961. It is a single tier that can hold 9,255.

The old Leppings Lane End is now known as the **Carlsberg West Stand**. This two-tier structure is all seating and can accommodate up to 7,995 fans. There are pillars here that can restrict views. Away fans are sited here. Usually up to 3,700 in the upper tier, but can be extended into the lower tier and northwest corner.

Getting there

By Road/Parking Whichever direction you are headed from, the ground is most easily accessed from the M1, junction 36. Follow the A61 heading to Sheffield (north) for just over seven miles and the stadium will be on your right. There is limited street parking. Try the Wednesdayite match-day car park, just opposite the stadium. It is run by the supporters' society and charges £5 for non-members and is open to home and away fans (season tickets available). Also try Owlerton Greyhound Stadium just a little further along Penistone Road (A61) on the left.

By Train Sheffield Station is about three miles from the ground but you can easily get a bus from the Interchange on Pond Street – a five-minute walk. No 78 First South Yorkshire drops you to Owlerton on Pennistone Road – a two-minute walk to Hilllsborough. Door to door from the station to the stadium takes 25 minutes. Alternatively take a blue tram to the city centre and change for a yellow tram out to the stadium. See supertram.com.

BOB THOMAS/GETTY IMAGES

THIS IS A GREAT STADIUM TO VISIT, NOT CLINICALLY MODERN, BUT WITH GREAT BALANCE AND ATMOSPHERE.

HOME AWAY

Pubs for home fans
Close to the ground, The Park, The Gate and The Travellers Rest have a strict door policy on match days and are the domain of home fans only.

Good food near ground
Penistone Road has a good range of places to eat from all the usual fast-food joints – McDonalds, KFC and Pizza Hut, to plenty of pubs serving decent old-school pub lunches. The Corner Café and Chinese takeaways including Hoong Too, serves up decent potions. On Trafalgar Road (near The Pheasant) Trafalgar Fisheries is a decent chippy.

Pubs for away fans
Horse and Jockey, Wadsley Lane (right off A61 before the ground onto Leppings Lane, right onto Wadsley Lane) does hot pies and a good pint. Just off Halifax Road (A61) The Pheasant on Trafalgar Road has big screens showing sport and generally has a decent vibe. For a cracking real ale, try the New Barrack Tavern, Penistone Road just past the stadium heading towards town. Good food. Also on A61 try Norfolk Arms and The Red Lion.

Top tips
Unofficial car parks spring up along Penistone Road on match days for around £3 a pop.

THE LAST **WORD**

owlsonline.com
sheffieldwednesday-mad.co.uk
londonowls.co.uk
owlstalk.co.uk
owlsalive.com
wednesdayite.com

SHEFFIELD WEDNESDAY
Hillsborough

HOME COLOURS

- **Nicknames** The Shrews
- **Founded** 1886
- **Ground** New Meadow/Prostar Stadium (opened 2007)
- **Address** Oteley Road, Shrewsbury SY2 6ST
- **Capacity** 9,875
- **Best attendance** 8,429 vs Bury, League Two play-off semi-final, 7 May, 2009
- **Contact** 0871-8118800
- **Ticket Number** 01743-273943
- **Email** info@shrewsburytown.co.uk
- **Website** shrewsburytown.com

Pubs for home fans

With the stadium located on the outskirts of the town, in what feels a little like a vacant lot, there's very little nearby in the way of facilities. Maybe as a result of this, home and away fans mix pretty happily in the nearby Brooklands Hotel, just off Meole Brace Roundabout on Mill Road. Parking also available – £5.

Good food near ground

Very limited except for the Meole Brace retail park with the usual fast-food options plus a Sainsbury's. For a better choice, head into town.

Pubs for away fans

Brooklands Hotel, Mill Road is the closest to the ground. Shrewsbury is an old-fashioned market town with a number of decent real-ale houses in the centre for those looking for a different experience.

Top tips

On match days, parking is prohibited at the Meole Brace park-and-ride. For those who feel particularly fit and want to ride in there are cycle racks at each corner of the stadium!

H e was off and running before the ball hit the back of the net. As the 30-yard strike sailed past the Leeds keeper, the crowd in three of the four stands rose as one, saluting the lone figure who peeled away below, springing into a celebratory somersault. It was 2 April, 1988 and The Shrews went on to beat the mighty Leeds United 1-0. This was a winning goal that epitomized the quicksilver talents and flamboyant flare of Victor Kasule (pronounced Kasulay) but he was soon stretchered from the field, though not, Kasule stressed, for having injured his toe during his gymnastic exuberance.

Born in Glasgow to a Scottish mother and Ugandan father, he moved south to sign for the Shrews in January 1988 and was soon teamed up with fellow Scots Dougie Bell, Steve Pittman and Alan Irvine. The hard-partying Scottish contingent became well known in the pubs and clubs of downtown Shrewsbury and saw fanzine *A Large Scotch* named in honour of their infamous exploits. 'Vodka Vic' had a god-given talent for two things – football and partying – and his silky skills made him not only a hero on the field at Gay Meadow, but legendary off it. Famous Kasule stories include the time he overturned team mate John McGimlay's car on the way to the corner shop. "We wanted a few beers so I went out to get them," explains Vic. "I didn't realize the car was so powerful and when I came back I attempted to do a hand-brake turn and bang, the car was over. It was a write-off. John wasn't too keen on the car anyway. Everyone was happy except me." All who saw Kasule play agreed he had the talent to go to the very top, however, his on-pitch prowess was overshadowed by his off-field antics and soon he was on his way down through a succession of smaller clubs. "He came back for the 'Heroes and Legends' celebration following the last-ever League game at Gay Meadow," says Adrian Plimmer who used to write for ALS. "He was greeted with great affections by those that

attended, and ran up a huge bar bill, but who cares!" Kasule also holds the record of playing for four different teams, in four different countries in one season – no mean feat!

Greatest moments on this ground

"2009/10 is Town's third season at the Prostar, so not too many yet. Beating Gillingham 7-0 has to be up there. However, coming back from 3-0 down to draw with the MK Dons back in 2008 was a joy. And, of course, beating Wrexham 3-0 to almost confirm their relegation to the Conference in 2008. At the old lady that was Gay Meadow: beating Everton in the FA Cup 3rd round in 2003 was very special, as was putting Man City to the sword in 1979. The last league game at Gay Meadow was very emotional and special." Adrian Plimmer, media director, shrewsTRUST.

VILLAINS

"It would have to be Victor Kasule. Probably the most talented player I've seen pull on a Shrewsbury shirt. Liked the odd tipple, and the rest is a trail of destruction." Adrian Plimmer.

Lowest moments on this ground

"Would have to be losing to Carlisle to confirm our relegation to the Conference back in 2003. It was inevitable but to be fair it still hurt like hell. What made it even worse was that

Carlisle beat us in the Area Final of the 'Daffy Duck Cup' a couple of months before." Adrian Plimmer.

Heroes of the sideline
"Graham Turner. The team was tipped for relegation and Turner took over as player coach, (from Richie Barker who left for Wolves in October of 1978). Town beat Manchester City on the way to an FA Cup quarter-final with Wolves, which they lost in a replay. In front of 14,000 fans at Gay Meadow Town beat Exeter to secure the 1979 Third Division title. After a shaky start Town started to cause ripples, and so-called big teams – Chelsea, Newcastle and West Ham – were put to the sword. He took Shrewsbury to the promised land of what is now Championship Football – forever a 'god' at Shrewsbury." Adrian Plimmer.

Don't mention the…
"Don't mention we're Welsh. We're not and it's boring. Get your atlases out people. Also we don't have a coracle any more and our new ground doesn't flood." Adrian Plimmer.

The ground
New Meadow is a uniform single-tier ground of four stands with open corners. All the stands are cantilevered so have excellent views. Away fans are housed in the **North Stand**, which has a Police Command Bow in the top corner. The stands have glass backs to allow light into the ground. The new build seems to polarize some fans' views.

Getting there
By Road/Parking On the southern perimeter of the town, just off the A5 ring road, the ground is easy to reach. The simplest approach is from the M6 junction 10A, following the M54 as it becomes the A5 (sign A5/Shrewsbury). At the second roundabout, take the third exit onto Thieves Lane (signed Cross Houses/A458). Continue straight on as way becomes Oteley Road, the stadium is on the left.

Brookland Hotel, Mill Road, has parking for 100 cars, £5. The Club operates a park-and-ride scheme. Also Shirehall car park, Abbey Foregate – from the A5 follow the A5064 to Column roundabout, take the third exit and turn right into car park. Shirehall Overflow is before the roundabout (bus leaves from main car park). Free parking, £2.50 return bus fare. Harlescott park-and-ride also.

By Train Shrewsbury train station is about a 30 minutes' walk from the ground – around two miles – or catch a bus from the station in the town centre. Details on arrivabus.co.uk.

That's quite interesting
As an English border club Shrewsbury used to enter the Welsh Cup, first winning the trophy in 1891 beating Wrexham 5-2. They won a further five times but were not allowed to progress into the European Cup Winners Cup competition as they were from the wrong side of the border.

Not a lot of people know that
"Arthur Rowley was the holder of the all-time aggregate goal-scoring record for League goals. Totalled 434, of which 151 came for Shrewsbury. It is a record unlikely ever to be broken (Alan Shearer, John Aldridge, Andy Cole don't even come close!), and why some have called for a posthumous knighthood. He made Shrewsbury a team to be feared in 10 great years during the sixties." Adrian Plimmer.

THE LAST WORD

shrewschat.com
blueandamber.proboards.com
shrewstrust.co.uk
themightyshrew.proboards.com

HEROES OR ZEROES?

⋗ HEROES OF THE TURF
"George Arthur Rowley – because he is. Graham Turner is a legend in his own lifetime. Alf Wood is one of Town's all-time leading goal-scorers. Michael Brown – Town's leading appearance holder, and single-handedly kept us in the Great Escape of 2000. (Exeter away anyone!) Joe Hart is a Shrewsbury product and local lad who, following his transfer to Man City, gained a full England cap." Adrian Plimmer.

⋙ ZEROES OF THE TURF
"The majority of the 2002/03 team that basically just didn't give a toss and saw us relegated. Stories abound that we can't print here. But let's just say, how can players one minute lose to Boston 6-0, beat Bury 4-1, lose to Rushden 5-0 and then beat Everton? Says it all really." Adrian Plimmer.

GETTY IMAGES

⌃ Shrewsbury fan at Wembley for the 2009 League 2 play-off final.

HOME COLOURS

- **Nicknames** The Saints
- **Founded** 1885
- **Ground opened** St Mary's Stadium (opened 2001)
- **Address** Britannia Road, Southampton SO14 5FP
- **Capacity** 32,689
- **Best attendance** 32,151 vs Arsenal, Premier League, 29 December, 2003
- **Contact** 0845-688 9448
- **Ticket Number** 0845-688 9288
- **Email** tickets@saintsfc.co.uk
- **Website** saintsfc.co.uk

SOUTHAMPTON

PUB QUIZ

That's quite interesting
The name The Saints comes from their original incarnation as Southampton St Mary's FC.

Not a lot of people know that
Southampton's only major piece of silverware, the 1976 FA Cup, was one of the biggest shocks of the competition. As a Second Division side they beat fancied Manchester United 1-0 at Wembley.

HOME AWAY

Pubs for home fans
The closest pub to the ground is the King Alfred and as such is home fans only; tickets are sometimes checked on the door to make sure. There are not that many pubs around the ground so many fans drink in the town centre.

Good food near ground
Around the ground there is nothing of note, so it is better to eat in the city centre where there is a good choice of restaurants, fast-food outlets and greasy spoon cafés.

Pubs for away fans
Near the ground isn't great, but the town centre has a plethora of good drinking establishments and most allow for a mix of fans, except on derby days. A few that come recommended are The Giddy Bridge, a Wetherspoons pub and probably the closest away-friendly pub, plus The Eagle, about halfway from the town centre. The facilities in the stadium are excellent for food and drink with plenty of TVs showing Sky.

Top tips
Traffic on leaving Southampton, especially on a Saturday afternoon is a nightmare, either park and ride or be patient.

O n 10 February 1980 the press gathered at the Potters Heron Hotel in Ampfield, a small town in Hampshire. The Saints had an announcement to make. Their manager Lawrie McMenemy had already steered an unfashionable Southampton side out of the Second Division and into the top flight, winning an FA Cup on the way, but his ambitions for the club were about to surprise everyone. Out strode McMenemy to calmly announce to the assembled media that one of England's greatest footballers and a man who had just been named the European Player of the Year for the second consecutive year would be wearing the red and white of Southampton the following season – McMenemy had sensationally signed Kevin Keegan. It's no exaggeration to say that this was one of the most unexpected signings of all time. Here was Southampton giving notice that they were deadly serious about becoming a Division One force to be reckoned with.

The following season Southampton topped the table looking for all the world like Championship contenders, but a dip in post-Christmas form saw them finish sixth – their highest ever place at the time. Over the following years, Southampton built on these foundations to become a firm fixture in the top flight. Their original home, the Dell, became a fortress – a tight ground with an idiosyncratic sloping terrace behind one goal and stands that loomed so close to the pitch they generated a truly intimidating environment. This atmosphere and proximity of the crowd unsettled many a big side, and undoubtedly played a part in their excellent home record. Over the next 27 years many heroes came and went, most notable among them the legendary Matt Le Tissier, who many would argue was one of the main contributory factors to the club remaining in the top flight for so long. In 2001 Southampton moved to a new ground, St Mary's,

a switch meant to generate more income for the club and allow a sustained challenge for the title. Gordon Strachan then guided The Saints to eighth place in the Premiership, but by 2005 a sliding team had finally slumped to relegation. Mismanagement of the club's finances and a series of poor managerial appointments has left Southampton in the third tier of English football. While the Saints may currently be down on their luck, this small club with a lion's heart still has big ambitions, to bring the fight and spirit of the Dell back to the top flight.

Greatest moments on this ground
"Personally, the great days were at the Dell, the last game was especially emotional with Matt Le Tissier scoring the winner to beat Arsenal 3-2. There was a 6-3 win over Manchester United in 1996 too." Peter Gibson, fan.

Lowest moments on this ground

"There were a lot in the relegation season. Charlton at home for me was the end of the road, some will say the exit from the Premiership, but losing at home to Charlton when we still had a chance to stay in the Championship was bad; the following home draw with Burnley which sealed the deal was close." Peter Gibson.

Heroes of the turf

Matt Le Tissier is considered almost a god in Southampton. He terrorized many a defence and is one of the main reasons for the long Premiership stint. Also Kevin Keegan, Mick Channon, Terry Paine, Jason Dodd, Alan Ball, Peter Shilton, Steve Moran, Danny Wallace, Kevin Phillips and Kenwyn Jones.

Zeroes of the turf

"There have been a few, but they are all eclipsed by Ali Dia," says Peter Gibson. Ali Dia's agent posed as Liberian international George Weah and convinced Graham Souness he should take Ali on trial. In reality he wasn't even of non-league ability, but somehow he managed to come on for legend Matt Le Tissier in a league match against Leeds. It was soon obvious he was out of his depth; he was substituted after 21 minutes.

Don't mention the…

Harry Redknapp fiasco.

Villains

"In the last decade it's all about the board of directors and chairman; in my opinion profiteering and mismanagement of the club's affairs have been the main reason for our demise." Peter Gibson, fan.

The ground

St Mary's Stadium is one of the finest grounds in the country, a true arena; all the sides are the same height, all one large single tier. The atmosphere is excellent when the ground gets close to full, and whilst it hasn't been as much as a fortress as the Dell used to be, it is intimidating nonetheless.

The two ends are identical, away fans are situated in the **Northam Stand** and the capacity varies from 3,000 to 4,700 depending on the game. The view and facilities are excellent, making it a fine place to visit.

The **Chapel Stand** is the same in every way as the Northam but is home fans only. Both have large electronic scoreboards on the roof incorporating video screens.

The **Kingsland Stand** runs the full length of the pitch and sweeps round both corners to join seamlessly with the two ends. The view is excellent and the facilities and legroom are first rate.

The **Itchen Stand** differs from its opposite number only in the fact that the players' tunnel and dug-outs are in the front, and at the back there is a row of executive boxes, filling the gap between stand and roof.

Getting there

By Road/Parking The club and police are trying to encourage visiting fans to use the park-and-ride service at junction 8 of the M27 motorway. It is free for ticket holders and the journey takes 15 minutes by bus, it is clearly signposted. Where you really win on time is on the way out, as Southampton gets easily gridlocked. If you do head into the city then it is advisable that you follow signs for the city centre and that you do not head towards the ground itself. There are plenty of car parks around the centre and it is only a 10- to 15-minute walk back to the stadium.

By Train Southampton's main station is about a 20-30-minute walk from the ground, it is possible to get a shuttle bus on match days, although the walk does involve going past plenty of pubs and food outlets.

THE LAST **WORD**

thesaintsfc.proboards.com
upthesaints.com

⌄ First Team Squad, 1981/82, including the likes of Mike Channon, David Armstrong, Kevin Keegan, Lawrie McMenemy (manager), Alan Ball, Steve Moran, Trevor Hebberd, Dave Watson and Chris Nicholl.

BOB THOMAS/GETTY IMAGES

HOME COLOURS

- **Nicknames** The Shrimpers
- **Founded** 1906
- **Ground opened** Roots Hall (opened 1955)
- **Address** Roots Hall, Victoria Avenue, Southend-On-Sea SS2 6NQ
- **Capacity** 12,306
- **Best attendance** 31,090 vs Liverpool, FA Cup 3rd round, 10 January, 1979
- **Contact** 01702-304050
- **Ticket Number** 0844-477 0077
- **Email** info@southend-united.co.uk
- **Website** southendunited.co.uk

SOUTHEND UNITED

RIVALS

Colchester United by far; the Essex derby is a hard-fought affair with Southend holding the better record.

A
ny aspiring manager wanting to up their percentage performance against the might of Manchester United need look no further than the estuarine coast of Essex for advice. Here dwells the only league club in the country that can boast a 100% record against the most dominant force in English football for the last 20 years.

Okay, so they've only played them once, but you can only play the games as they come, and the Shrimpers have dispatched the Reds whenever they've taken to the field. Plus they weren't taking on an injury depleted side, or one of Fergie's youth-filled League Cup B teams either. That evening a team of household names were involved in a thrilling match. Ronaldo and Rooney pummelled the Southend goal only to be thwarted by on-form keeper Darryl Flahaven. Then, up stepped one Freddy Eastward, already a firm favourite amongst the Roots Hall faithful, to thunder home a 30-yard free kick, and the rest, as they say, is history.

Although that was one of their greatest nights, Southend have not been without success. Spells in the second tier of English football have been brief but regular in the last two decades and they constantly flirt with a return. One of their main problems has been holding on to their home-developed stars. Great players like Stan Collymore and Freddy Eastward made their names at Southend but then got tempted away either out of necessity to balance the club books or just to move on to further their own careers. It has left Southend in a position not unfamiliar with lower league sides – they regularly create teams with promise and potential

but if success does not come quickly they run the risk of losing players and having to rebuild. They are hoping to avert this in the future by moving to an out-of-town stadium, which will allow for bigger crowds and push up revenues. Never an easy team to beat, Southend are hoping to make the regular humbling of larger teams an expectation, rather than a bonus.

Greatest moments on this ground
"There have been two in recent years, the first was beating Bristol City 1-0 to clinch the League One title in 2006, we were already promoted at this point. The second was beating Man United 1-0 in the League Cup." Dom Clarke, fan.

Lowest moments on this ground
"The end of the 2006/07 season was dire, we lost form badly and got soundly beaten by Colchester as we faced relegation." Stuart Ridge, fan.

Heroes of the sideline
"Steve Tilson in recent years has got us on the right track, it's been a rollercoaster ride, though it hopefully still has an up left in it. David Webb in his three spells as manager." Stuart Ridge.

Don't mention the...
Financial problems of the eighties, which led to arrests and almost the end of Southend. The club was lent money by Robert Maxwell and Ken Bates.

VILLAINS
"Personally it was Barry Fry jumping ship and leaving us high and dry for Birmingham, although there have been plenty of others in and outside of the club. Former owner Anton Johnson left us in a right mess." Stuart Ridge, fan.

The ground
Roots Hall is a compact ground with a mixture of ageing and quite modern stands. There has been much talk of the club moving out of town to a purpose-built stadium and at the moment that is due to happen at the beginning of the 2011/2012 season, although nothing is set in stone.

The **East Stand** is what you'd call the main stand at Roots Hall; originally it only ran for part of the length of the pitch but was later extended. It's a decent if a little old-fashioned single-tiered stand with executive boxes at the back and the players' entrance and dug-outs at the front.

> Southend players celebrate after Junior Stanislas' 94th-minute winner against Northampton Town, Boxing Day 2008.

GETTY IMAGES

The **South Stand** used to be a bigger terrace but when the club was in financial trouble the land behind was sold and the terrace compressed. To get over the depth of the stand when seating came in, it was made into an unusual double-decker structure, which resulted in the top deck being right on top of the pitch offering excellent views.

The **North Stand** is another area of ex-terrace, so now has cramped seating, and is host to the away support. This used to be the home end during the standing days and the view of the playing area is average at best. There is also a scoreboard on the roof.

The **West Stand** has a very unusual roof, three-quarters of it being barrel shaped; the stand is single-tiered and remarkable only for the number of supporting pillars impeding the views.

Getting there

By Road/Parking Roots Hall is easy to find. If you're approaching from the M25 take junction 29 signposted Southend on the A127, keep on this road all of the way until you see the ground. Then it's a case of either going for a match-day car park, of which there are few, or battling it out for street parking; watch out for the residents' schemes in the area.

By Train Prittlewell Station is only a five-minute walk from the ground; it is served by trains from Liverpool Street in London.

PUB QUIZ

That's quite interesting
Southend are called The Shrimpers because of the historically important shrimp fishery that existed in the town when the club was formed.

Not a lot of people know that
Although Colchester are their fiercest rivals, the closest club to Southend as the crow flies is Gillingham, straight across the Thames Estuary.

HOME AWAY

Pubs for home fans
The closest pub to the ground is the Golden Lion. It is home fans only, as are the other pubs close to the ground, including the club bar at the ground.

Good food near ground
Most of the pubs serve food. A short walk into town and there is a good choice of fast food and café food as well as pizza and Chinese and Indian takeaways. It is not known for its excellent cuisine though.

Pubs for away fans
Away fans are best either stopping outside of the town for a pub and something to eat, or heading into the town centre itself. If you have the time there are better establishments along the seafront, the Borough Arms coming recommended, as is Nelson Hotel.

Top tips
Stop and eat in a nice country pub on the way to the town.

THE LAST WORD

shrimperstrust.co.uk
shrimperzone.com

HOME COLOURS

- 🏷 **Nicknames** The Boro
- 🗓 **Founded** 1976
- 🏟 **Ground opened** Lamex Stadium (opened 1980)
- ℹ **Address** Broadhall Way, Stevenage, Hertfordshire, SC2 8RH
- 👥 **Capacity** 7,100
- 🎫 **Best attendance** 8,040 vs Newcastle United, FA Cup 4th round, 25 January, 1998
- ☎ **Contact** 01438-223 223
- 🎟 **Ticket Number** 0871-855 1696 (credit card ticket line)
- ✉ **Email** see website
- 🌐 **Website** stevenageboroughfc.com

STEVENAGE

Since their formation out of the ashes of Stevenage Athletic, this club has risen through the league system from a roped-off field in the Chiltern Youth League in 1976 to League Two and a place in the Football League's upper echelons. Along the way they have even enjoyed the thrill of winning a couple of FA Trophies to add to the silverware cabinet. In 2007, The Boro came back from 2-0 down against Kidderminster Harriers to win the first final to be held at the newly opened Wembley Stadium. A whopping 53,262 fans watched them lift the trophy in a thrilling 3-2 victory. Two years later the club repeated the feat, this time beating York City. But as far as cup exploits go, perhaps the most famous tie involving Stevenage was the FA Cup fourth round game at home to the mighty Newcastle United.

In January 1998 The Boro hosted the Premier League outfit, who had finished runners-up in the title race the previous season. However the Tyneside club were not that keen on a visit to the Hertfordshire ground. Concerns about Broadhall Way were voiced and the Magpies dispatched a team of safety inspectors to the ground. Many clubs would have buckled under the pressure and agreed to move the contest, content to earn a big away game pay-day. But not The Boro. As the frosty wranglings escalated, the media descended like carrion crows and it was Newcastle who were forced to back down. A temporary stand was erected for the visiting Toon Army, bringing the ground capacity to over 8,000 and the teams took to the pitch. Alan Shearer, just back from injury, put the favourites one up with a looping header into the far corner of the net. But then, in a moment that will live long in the memory of many a Boro fans, Giuliano Grazioli rose at a corner and directed the ball down past the Magpies keeper and over the line. The crowd went ballistic. The

RIVALS

Woking, Barnet, Kettering, Cambridge United.

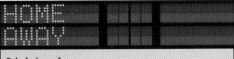

HOME AWAY

Pubs for home fans
The Broadhall Suite clubhouse. "I can't say with any certainty whether the clubhouse will be available to away fans as Boro go into the Football League. If a large away following is expected, sometimes the clubhouse is made 'home fans only'," advises Pete Hayman.

Good food near ground
In the retail park opposite the stadium are a couple of fast food joints, including Pizza Hut, McDonald's and Burger King while opposite the station in the Stevenage Leisure Park is a KFC.

Pubs for away fans
"The Roebuck Inn, London Road, to the south of the ground offers a cosy atmosphere, while Our Mutual Friend, Broadwater Crescent, to the east of the ground is also welcoming. If away fans are coming from the train station, there is also a Wetherspoons within a five-minute walk into the town centre," recommends Pete Hayman.

Top tips
Stevenage has good, regular and fairly fast train connections via London's King's Cross with the East Coast train company offering the best bet.

Boro held out for an improbable draw and celebrated as if they had won the cup – which in a way they had, earning a big money return to St James' Park. Newcastle were needled, irritated that the part-timers had proved such stubborn opposition. In the replay it took a goal by Shearer that clearly didn't cross the line to settle the tie in the Premier League team's favour. Despite being edged out 2-1, Stevenage came away with their heads held high and their reputation enhanced.

In the 2009/10 season Boro stormed to the Conference title. They had flirted with promotion a few times over the years but in a gruelling season of 44 games, on all kinds of playing surfaces, in all kinds of weather conditions, they kept their eye on the goal. They lost only five fixtures, including a solitary defeat at fortress Broadhall Way. Just 30 years after their formation, Stevenage have flown the non-league nest. No longer fledglings, they have spread their wings in search of loftier pursuits.

VILLAINS

"Numerous players have not got a good reputation at Broadhall Way. Here are just some; Billy Turley, Chris Lane, Rory Prendergast, Daryl Clare, Richard Brodie, Jefferson Louis and even Alan Shearer." Matthew Kett.

Greatest moments on this ground

"Hosting Newcastle United in the FA Cup is arguably the club's finest hour, not least because Boro earned a draw and a replay at St James' Park. After all the furore (from them) about whether our ground was up to scratch, Broadhall Way put on a fine show and guaranteed a memorable day." Pete Hayman, editor, BoroGuide.co.uk.

"I think winning the Conference back in 1995/96 has to be one of the greatest moments on this ground too." Matthew Kett, FC Boro.

Lowest moments on this ground

"There have been a few low moments down the years, but I think losing 4-1 at home to Woking in 2002 is the lowest." Matthew Kett.

Heroes of the sideline

"Paul Fairclough will always be held in the highest esteem at Broadhall Way after a hugely successful period during the 1990s, which arguably culminated with the Conference title season of 1995/96. However, even though he was unable to repeat the title-winning feat, he also gave us the FA Cup tie against Newcastle to remember. It's Graham Westley who secured his place in Boro folklore as the man who took us into the Football League." Pete Hayman.

Zeroes of the sideline

"Peter Taylor came in with a big reputation and ruined our play-off hopes. Mark Stimson, for not finishing what he started when he left for Gillingham." Matthew Kett.

Don't mention the...

"Jason Soloman and his tracksuit bottoms. Having been forced to fill-in between the sticks against Woking in 1997, midfielder Soloman was half-way through putting on some tracksuit bottoms, as the ball came his way. Not one to shirk his makeshift duties, he rushed out with the offending garment swinging around his ankles... Somehow the game finished 0-0. I'm led to believe it may have appeared on *Question of Sport* as a 'What Happened Next...'" Pete Hayman.

The ground

Broadhall Way has a capacity of 7,100 housed in four fairly uniform stands. The **South Stand** or Buildbase is a single tier of seating that holds 1,400 away fans behind the goal. The scoreboard on the roof came from Southampton's old ground The Dell. The **Main Stand** has the same roofline and runs the full length of the pitch. The changing rooms

are here, as are the tunnel and dug-outs. The **East Stand** is a covered terrace for home fans that runs the length of the field. It has a capacity for 3,000 and is the home of the Barmy Army. The **North Stand** or Broadhall Way End is a small terrace behind the far goal for 700 fans, though the roof only covers about two thirds. There are plans to replace this stand sometime in the future.

Getting there

By Road/Parking North of London's sprawl and barely a mile off the motorway, this is another easy to reach, out of town clubs. Exit the A1 (M) at junction 7 and follow the A602 for Stevenage. Straight over the first roundabout, and having spied the floodlights, straight over the second roundabout, turning left into the stadium's car park opposite the ground. Free parking. (For the ground itself, turn right at second roundabout)

By Train Stevenage Railway Station is about a 20-minute walk to the ground. Head up Lytton Way towards the Six Hills Roundabout, heading under the underpass and onto Six Hills Way. Go right at next roundabout onto Monkswood Way and follow passing Asda on your right and then McDonald's. At the end of the road, the stadium is dead ahead. Alternatively, walk over the footbridge and into town to pick up the bus.

◀ Graham Westley leaves the pitch before restart of the FA Trophy Cup semi-final second leg match at Broadhall Way, March 2010. The Boro won 5-1 over the two legs.
▼ 1998 FA Cup tie propaganda.

THE LAST **WORD**

boroguide.co.uk
fcboro.co.uk
The Broadhall Way fanzine

PUB QUIZ

That's quite interesting
"Stevenage won promotion to the Football League in 1996, but were denied entry as their ground wasn't up to scratch, even though it was ready in time for the following season." Matthew Kett.

Not a lot of people know that
"Former Olympic gold medallist Daley Thompson played for Stevenage reserves in the early nineties – and scored two goals." Pete Hayman.

HEROES OR ZEROES?

⌃ **HEROES OF THE TURF**
"Up there with the very best are Barry Hayles, Efetobore Sodje, George Boyd, Ronnie Henry and Mark Roberts. The first three were always destined to move onto greater things. Henry has been one of our longest-serving players of recent years. Roberts arrived in January 2009, instantly took command of the defence before captaining the team to the league title. Some fans will recall others but none would begrudge these." Pete Hayman.

⌄ **ZEROES OF THE TURF**
"Former Liverpool star Ray Houghton came in towards the end of his career and was woeful in his short spell at the club." Matthew Kett.

HOME COLOURS

⊗ **Nicknames** The Hatters, County

⊗ **Founded** 1883

⊗ **Ground opened** Edgeley Park (moved here in 1902)

ⓘ **Address** Hardcastle Road, Edgeley, Stockport SK3 9DD

⊗ **Capacity** 10,832

✪ **Best attendance** 27,833 vs Liverpool, FA Cup 5th round, 11 February, 1950

ⓒ **Contact** 0161-286 8888

ⓒ **Ticket Number** 0871-222 0120

@ **Email** fans@stockportcounty.com

ⓦ **Website** stockportcounty.com

STOCKPORT COUNTY

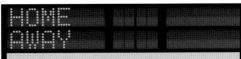

HOME
AWAY

Pubs for home fans
Try the Royal Oak on Castle Street. Good pre-game atmosphere.

Good food near ground
Fast-food outlets near the station and a chip shop on Castle Street called the Friary.

Pubs for away fans
The Armoury is just five minutes walk from the ground on Shaw Heath. Has a selection of bar food and some good ale.

Top tips
"Don't miss the Friary restaurant on Edgeley, always packed, good food and good prices (something you won't find in the stadium)," says Sam Byrne.

Stockport County is a team born of in an era when football was in its fiery infancy, forged in the furnace of the northwest, the industrial foundry where many of the great teams were cast. This was the breeding ground for hard teams and harder players whose iron-clad wills stoked the fires of intense rivalries. It was with this spirit that County took to the field on 30 March 1946 in a Division Three (North) Cup replay against visiting Yorkshire rivals Doncaster Rovers. In this closely fought match County took the early lead before Rovers hit back with two goals to still the Edgeley Park faithful. On 72 minutes, after a sustained attack, Shaw equalized for the home team and horns were locked until the referee blew for full time. A nil-nil draw was not an option, but through the 30 minutes of extra-time the two teams couldn't be separated. While the term 'Golden Goal' might be a modern, cuddly FIFA-ism, the concept of 'sudden death' certainly wasn't, and as the two teams kicked off for the second period of extra-time they knew the first to score would advance into the next round.

At this point, after more than two hours of play, some of the crowd left to have their teas before returning to the ground to carry on watching. County player Arthur Burrows remembers, "A pal of mine went to my house in Vernon Park to tell my wife that I was still playing. He then came back to watch the rest of the match!" Then, just shy of three hours into the game, Les Cocker fired home for County; the Rovers players sagged to their knees as the Stockport team mobbed the hero of the hour (or three). Fans invaded the pitch, half in revelry, half in relief, but their celebrations were cut short – an infringement had been spotted by the referee and a free kick awarded to Donny. County were upset, the crowd was stunned and by this stage even members of the Rovers team were disappointed! Considering some of them had been working the night before, it must have been like kicking around a medicine

ball in jack boots. Moments later, the referee collapsed with cramp and it looked like the end was in sight but, eventually soildering on, it seemed nothing could halt this game. By 7pm and 203 minutes of hard slog, the encroaching darkness mercifully forced the curtain to fall on the longest game ever held. The record is upheld by *The Guinness Book of Records* and is undoubtedly one that will never be broken. Who can imagine a modern game stretching to three and half hours? It is the strength of spirit and fire in the belly that has seen County through the good times and the bad – no matter how big their neighbours may get, the will to succeed and ingrained determination means that this is a team that will soldier on till the final whistle.

Greatest moments on this ground
"A 1-0 play-off semi-final win over Wycombe at Edgeley Park in 2008 to send us into the final. We scored so early on, the nerves were unbearable! But it made it feel so much better when the final whistle eventually blew and we knew we were on our way to the new Wembley in a final that we went on to win 3-2." Sam Byrne, editor, VitalStockport.

Lowest moments on this ground
"Shortly before Christmas in 2005, we were battered 3-0 at home by Darlington. Absolutely torn apart. We were bottom of the league under Chris Turner and this game, even so early in the season, just made us all feel that we were as good as relegated. Shortly after, on Boxing Day, we were defeated 6-0 by local rivals Macclesfield. Miraculously, Jim Gannon was installed as manager and we stayed up on the final day." Sam Byrne.

RIVALS
Manchester City, Burnley and Stoke City.

"Boxing Day 2006. Bottom of the Football League away to fellow strugglers and rivals Macclesfield Town, the 2,000 strong blue 'n' white army witnessed us reduced to 10 men and concede six goals, as well as getting rained on."
Chris Larkin.

Heroes of the sideline

"Jim Gannon – after playing for us for 10 years, 'Jimbo' returned as manager in 2005 when we looked doomed and led us to promotion two years later. Danny Bergara – the little man from Uruguay became the first manager to get us promoted since the sixties." Chris Larkin, county4life.com.

Heroes of the turf

"Jack Connor – one of the best-ever marksmen, scored 132 goals in just 206 appearances. Mike Flynn – joined in 1993 and went on to stay until 2002, he became a legend due to his exploits in the 1996/97 League Cup live on TV, winking at the Southampton fans when he cleared a shot off the line. Kevin Francis – 'Big Kev' was a hero, he scored over 100 goals in total for us between 1989 and 1995." Chris Larkin.

"Luke Beckett – a personal favourite. One of those strikers who knocks goals in for fun and becomes your idol, the one you pretend to be while playing football with your mates. Liam Dickinson – he burst into the team in 2005 shortly after the 6-0 Boxing Day defeat, his seven goals in the second half of the season invariably kept us up. He then played as a lone striker with 21 goals, including the winner at Wembley to send us up to League One." Sam Byrne.

VILLAINS

"Paul Lambert, then Wycombe manager. Also Carlton Palmer and Danny Williams. Williams was out injured, but turned up in the Cheadle End in a Manchester City coat. He was soon shipped out on loan."
Sam Byrne.

Zeroes of the turf

"Ludo Dje – resembled Patrick Vieira as a big midfield unit, but played like Carlton Palmer. Absolutely shocking. One half of our dynamic midfield duo of Dje and Tomlinson. Zeke Tomlinson – the other half. A poor man's Ludovic Dje." Sam Byrne.

"Carlton Palmer – the most hated man ever to wear a Stockport County shirt, exceptionally poor player-manager, responsible for a relegation. Tim Flowers – with his fantastic Premiership career over, he conceded 13 goals in four games. Harpal Singh – came to us on loan from Leeds United, a fantastic debut, then a complete and utter waste of time, space and effort." Chris Larkin.

The ground

The stadium was first used by County back in 1902 and is an all-seater ground shared with Sale Sharks rugby union team. The modern Cheadle End dominates, while the Railway End may go unused on wet match days. There are plans to redevelop the ground but no timetable has been set.

The **Main Stand** is an old-school structure that can seat 2,013. There are a couple of supporting pillars. The stand is also home to the changing rooms, boardroom and executive seats.

The **Railway End** is a small stand that once housed 6,000 Liverpool fans for a 1965 FA Cup tie. Today it is an open bank of blue seats with a capacity of 1,365 allocated to away fans.

In reality most away fans will probably find themselves in the **Popular Side**, an area of undercover seating running opposite the Main Stand. It is reached by a separate entrance around the back of the Railway End. There are pillars which can create a restricted view.

The **Cheadle End** was home to the Cheadle Enders of the sixties. The all-seater redevelopment was opened for the 1995/96 season with a capacity of just over 5,000. This modern two-tier stand offers excellent, unrestricted views with the upper tier generating great noise and being the new home to the hardcore Cheadle Enders.

Getting there

By Road/Parking Edgeley Park is easily accessible off the M60 and the A6. Exit the M60 at junction 1 (Stockport Town Centre). At the roundabout follow signs to Cheadle A560 and Stockport County FC into Hollywood Way. Go straight through first set of traffic lights, turn right at the next (signposted Stockport County FC) onto A560. After a mile, turn left (no signpost, by the Farmers Arms) onto the B5465 Edgeley Road. After another mile turn right at the traffic lights into Dale Street then take second left into Hardcastle Road. There is a car park off the Castle Street precinct or else it's the off-street parking lottery.

By Trains Stockport's station is next to the ground. Don't exit through the ticket hall side. Walk left up Station Road, cross at the Blue Bell then up towards the roundabout. Head along Mercian Way and left into Arnold Street.

THE LAST WORD

county4life.com
stockport.vitalfootball.co.uk

STOCKPORTCOUNTY.COM

STOKE CITY

HOME COLOURS

- **Nicknames** The Potters
- **Founded** 1863
- **Ground** Britannia Stadium (opened 1997)
- **Address** Stanley Matthews Way, Stoke-on-Trent ST4 4EG
- **Capacity** 27,500
- **Best attendance** 28,384 vs Everton, FA Cup 3rd round, 5 January, 2002
- **Contact** 0871-663 2008
- **Ticket Number** 0871-663 2007
- **Email** info@stokecityfc.com
- **Website** stokecityfc.com

You could forgive Stoke fans for thinking things didn't quite turn out as well for them as it did for others. That maybe they haven't always had the rub of the green. Remember 1976? The heatwave, water shortages, hosepipe bans, sun, sun, sun. While other teams remember it as the year the grass was a bit brown around the pitch, for Potters fans it was the year Mother Nature conspired to dismantle the best Stoke team of a generation and relegate them back to the second tier. By the start of the seventies, Stoke manager Tony Waddington felt he was only a few pieces away from assembling a Championship-winning team. The Potters reached the FA Cup semi-final in 1971 and again in 1972 when they made up for the disappointment by defeating the mighty Chelsea 2-1 to lift the League Cup. In 1974 Waddington lured the great Peter Shilton to keep goal and a young Alan Hudson was tempted away from Chelsea. The team was ready for a push on the title. Then, in a cruel 'twister' of fate, a whirlwind blew through Victoria Ground ripping the roof off the Butler Street Stand as well as the club's chances, leaving the splintered remains of both scattered across the ground. The financial crisis that followed crippled the club. Among those sold off to rebuild the stadium were Jimmy Greenhoff to Manchester United for £120,000 and Alan Hudson to Arsenal for £200,000. Stoke could not survive the exodus of talent. The season may have started in glorious sunshine, but not even the new roof could shelter the fans from the dark cloud of relegation.

But for the melancholy Stoke fan there is always the legend that is Sir Stanley Matthews. Matthews started and finished his long and illustrious career for his hometown club. "He first played for Stoke aged 17, and pulled on the red and white striped shirt for a final time 33 years

RIVALS

Wolves, West Brom and Port Vale.

> Players walk out at a snowy Britannia Stadium, January 2010.

THE BOOTHEN END

HEROES OR ZEROES?

≈ ZEROES OF THE TURF

"Staring relegation in the face we shelled out £500,000 for Kyle Lightbourne in the hope he would keep us up. He didn't. The name Gordon Marshall still sends a shiver down the spine. Considered a decent keeper up in Scotland, we brought him in on loan in 1993. He endured a nightmare time for Stoke, but did get really good at picking the ball out of the net. Striker Keith Scott – nicknamed 'Lethal' – he got just three goals in a year. We didn't quite get our £300,000 worth." Dave Knapper.

later, aged 50," says Alec Vještica of One Stoke Fan. "He is rightly remembered as one of the most talented, skilled and elegant footballers ever." Few records are set that will never be broken, but Matthews certainly broke the mould when he took to the field for the Potters for the last time in February 1965. His illustrious career saw him become the first player ever to be knighted while still in top class football. Matthews was also voted Footballer of the Year twice and the 1956 European Footballer of the Year. "It's just a shame he's more widely remembered for his time at Blackpool," says Alec. It appears that every silver lining has its cloud.

Greatest moments on this ground

"At the current ground there is only one moment that few fans will forget – 4 May 2008. A rather drab 0-0 against Leicester City got us back into the top flight. On the final whistle, supporters flooded the pitch, with many not sure what to do. Some hugged friends and relatives while other just slumped to the grass and kissed the turf. For the majority of our time there previously it was mainly disappointment and heartache!" Dave Knapper, Why Delilah, Stoke City reporter.

Lowest moments on this ground

"The 10th January 1998, let's just call it a day to forget. Mid-way through our relegation season of 1997/98,

Birmingham came to Stoke. A local derby of sorts, there was pride at stake, but what we saw that day from Stoke was a display so desperate that it made you question the pride of anybody connected to Stoke City Football Club. We leaked goal after goal, seven in all, without so much as troubling Birmingham keeper Ian Bennett. No surprise, we went down." Alec Vještica, One Stoke Fan.

Heroes of the sideline

Tony Waddington, Lou Macari, Tony Pulis.

Heroes of the turf

"Denis Smith. Any Stoke player from the halcyon days of the early seventies is going to be remembered fondly, but Smith is admired more than most. A local born centre-back, he was one of the game's true hard men, racking up more than 400 Stoke appearances and is now a pundit on Radio Stoke, his frank commentary earning him plaudits in this role as well. Abdoulaye Faye – strong in the tackle yet so very cool on the ball, immensely passionate but humble with fans, the Senegalese centre-back is the full package. When Superman goes to sleep he puts on a pair of Abdoulaye Faye pyjamas. Peter Hoekstra – it was a major coup to attract the Dutch international winger. For the next three years he dazzled fans with astonishing pace and skill, and was the sort of player whose contribution pays for the ticket price to matches alone.

◄ Stoke fans silhouetted in the stands at the Britannia Stadium.

Gordon Banks – without doubt the greatest goalkeeper ever to have played the game, Banks graced the Victoria Ground pitch for five glorious years and remains a significant part of the club in his current role as President. Stanley Matthews 1932-47 and 1961-66. There could really be only one winner in this category." Alec Vještica.

Villains

"The biggest villain in recent years is most certainly Steve Cotterill. After getting promoted back into the Championship in 2002 our Icelandic owners sacked their fellow countryman Gudjon Thordarson. They turned to up-and-coming manager Steve Cotterill who had performed miracles for Cheltenham Town. He managed 13 games and hot-footed it, overnight allegedly, to Sunderland to become newly appointed manager Howard Wilkinson's assistant. He'll always be booed at Stoke." Dave Knapper.

Don't mention the…

"BLYTH SPARTANS. Aaaaaaargh! Back in the 1977/78 season FA Cup, Blyth took the lead in the 10th minute and stunned the crowd at the Victoria Ground. Stoke banged in two after the break and that seemed to be that. No, Spartans equalized and then hit an injury time winner." Dave Knapper.

The ground

This £15-million stadium opened in 1997. The **Boothen Stand**, or North Stand, holds just over 6,000 fans. This is home to some of the most passionate and vocal fans in the country – in 2008 Stoke fans they were officially monitored as the loudest in the league. The L-shaped structure swings round and connects with the **East Stand**, another single tier stand, in a single sweep. The East Stand has a capacity of 8,789 and runs along the side of the pitch. At the far end behind the goal. The **South Stand** is where the away support sits. Just under 5,000 visitors can be accommodated here. The main **West Stand** is a two-tier structure with seating for 7,357. Dressing rooms are in the southwest corner where the club superstore is.

Getting there

By Road/Parking Exit the M6 at junction 15 onto the A500 towards Stoke-on-Trent. Keep right at the fork and follow signs for Fenton/Derby/A50/Uttoxeter). At the roundabout, turn right onto the A50 and move into the left-hand lane. Follow slip road and turn right over the bridge. Follow the Gordon Banks Drive onto Stanley Matthews Way to the stadium. Pre-book parking at the stadium £5 and must be booked in advance though your club. Limited pay parking at Powerleague and the Harvester also.

By Train Stoke-on-Trent station is a fair walk to the ground but match day buses run from Glebe Street. Turn right from the station and then the next right under the bridge and stay to the left as the road curves around to reach Glebe Street.

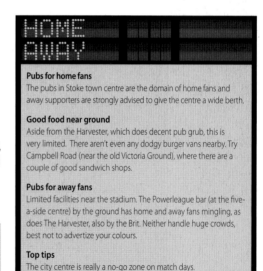

Pubs for home fans
The pubs in Stoke town centre are the domain of home fans and away supporters are strongly advised to give the centre a wide berth.

Good food near ground
Aside from the Harvester, which does decent pub grub, this is very limited. There aren't even any dodgy burger vans nearby. Try Campbell Road (near the old Victoria Ground), where there are a couple of good sandwich shops.

Pubs for away fans
Limited facilities near the stadium. The Powerleague bar (at the five-a-side centre) by the ground has home and away fans mingling, as does The Harvester, also by the Brit. Neither handle huge crowds, best not to advertize your colours.

Top tips
The city centre is really a no-go zone on match days.

THE LAST WORD

whydelilah.co.uk
onestokefan.co.uk
oatcakefanzine.proboards.com
The Oatcake Fanzine
delilahs.co.uk

PUB QUIZ

That's quite interesting
"Sir Stanley Matthew's ashes are buried under the centre circle of the pitch." Dave Knapper.

Not a lot of people know that
"In 1891, stoppage time was first introduced as a result of an incident in a game between Stoke and Aston Villa. 1-0 down, Stoke were awarded a late penalty, but the Villa keeper booted the only ball out of the ground. By the time it had been retrieved, the 90 minutes were up and the game had ended. So next time you find yourself moaning at Manchester United's mandatory six minutes of injury time, blame Stoke." Alec Vještica.

⊖ **Nicknames** The Black Cats
⊗ **Founded** 1879
⊘ **Ground** Stadium of Light (opened 1997)
ⓘ **Address** Sunderland SR5 1SU
⊘ **Capacity** 49,000
⊗ **Best attendance** 48,353 vs Liverpool, Premier League, 12 April, 2002
ⓒ **Contact** 0871-911 1200
ⓒ **Ticket Number** 0871-911 1973
@ **Email** enquiries@safc.com
ⓦ **Website** safc.com

SUNDERLAND

For decades Sunderland seemed to have the advantage of a twelfth man when playing in front of their faithful followers on Wearside, such was the size of the crowd, the passion and the incredible volume it generated. This so-called 'Roker Roar' could strike fear into the hearts of many a visiting team. Some opposition players would talk nervously of playing in front of the crowd at Roker and how it would pile on extra pressure. So when the club decided in the 1990s that the ageing ground had had its day, many wondered whether it would be possible to re-create that atmosphere in a modern arena. The answer turned out to be an unequivocal yes. Unlike many bland, purpose-built stadiums that have sprouted around the land in recent years, The Stadium of Light is a beacon; a ferocious fortress of passion, atmosphere and noise, capable of intimidating any visiting team. When it was built it could initially hold just over 42,000, but within a couple of years it had been upgraded to 49,000, and plans are afoot to increase the stadium's size in two more increments to as much as 69,000, thus guaranteeing the future roar will more than match the original.

When the club left their former home The Rokermen, as they were widely known, decided a new nickname was needed. After much deliberation and voting The Black Cats were born. This was not a name that came entirely out of the blue, and it has several sources. During the Napoleonic wars 'The Black Cat Battery' was a gun emplacement on the banks of the River Wear. Legend also has it that in the 1937 cup final one supporter took a black cat with him for good luck and that in the 1960s a black moggy called the terraces of Roker Park home, with the club feeding and caring for it. This all resulted in the official supporters' club having a Black Cat as their emblem, so the new nickname was a logical progression.

RIVALS

Newcastle United, there is a great rivalry between the northeast cities. also The Boro, to a lesser extent, and Leeds United since the famous cup win in the early 1970s.

HOME
AWAY

Pubs for home fans
Being close to the city centre, pretty much every pub will be packed with home fans prior to a game.

Good food near ground
The food in the ground isn't bad, on the seafront there are numerous chippies and the town centre, which is only a 10-minute stroll away, has every sort of food you could want or need.

Pubs for away fans
There are no real away pubs as such, but from the seafront, which is about 20 minutes' walk through the city centre to the ground, there are loads of options. Most will be busy on a match day but the local hospitality is legendary and usually friendly banter is forthcoming. Of coarse, on a derby day this all changes, so Newcastle and Middlesbrough fans are advised to go straight to the ground or have a pint on the way.

Top tips
Getting out of Sunderland on a busy Saturday afternoon after a big game can be a nightmare and so the park and ride scheme is a pretty good idea for a faster getaway.

On the pitch Sunderland's greatest period began at the end of the 1800s and ran until 1958. During this time they won six First Division titles, were runners up five times and won an FA Cup. They were a powerful side and when they finally dropped out of the top flight at the end of the 1950s they had spent 68 consecutive seasons plying their trade in the First Division, a record that only Arsenal can better. Since then the highlights have been a famous FA Cup win over Leeds in 1973, when they were a Second Division team, and their recent resurgence. When Peter Reid took over they were a yo-yo side in the Championship – he pulled the team together, got them playing decent football and returned them to the top flight. Since then the road has been a little rocky, but now, under the management of Steve Bruce and chairman Niall Quinn, Sunderland fans have enjoyed the taste of success and once again feel like the cat that got the cream.

Greatest moments on this ground
"Losing at home to Chelsea on the last day of the season – not the game but hearing after the final whistle that Newcastle had been relegated!" Graham Saunders, fan.

HEROES OR ZEROES?

⩘ HEROES OF THE TURF

"I'm a bit of youngster compared to many, so it's got to be Kevin Phillips in my era," says Graham Saunders. Also Bobby Gurney, Ned Doig, Charlie Buchan, Ned Carter, Charlie Hurley (voted Black Cats player of the century), Len Shackleton, Ian Porterfield, Niall Quinn, Brian Clough, Bobby Kerr, Kevin Ball and Raich Carter (captain of the 1936 championship-winning team).

⩗ ZEROES OF THE TURF

"I could fill teams with crap from the eighties – we sure did! Probably the most amusing though was Honduran striker Milton Núñez. He played one game. I think Peter Reid thought he was signing his strike partner or something when he arrived, he was soon sent back. He's a cult hero now!" Graham Saunders.

> Niall Quinn prepares to unleash against Liverpool at the Stadium of Light, 2002.

◀ 1973 FA Cup final.
▼ Stadium of Light.

Lowest moments on this ground

"Not a moment but two seasons – 2002/03 and 2005/06. We got the lowest-ever points total of 19 in the first period then managed to beat it with 15 three seasons later, it was just painful." Graham Saunders.

Heroes of the sideline

"Recently, Peter Reid. He dragged us out of a pretty dire spell in our history and got us into the top flight and our highest finish in the Premiership. Our post-war and possible all-time hero has got to be Bob Stokoe. Then our two most successful managers ever – Tom Watson and Alex Mackie (late 1800s)." Graham Saunders.

The ground

VILLAINS
anybody who has anything to do with Newcastle United.

The Stadium of Light stands like a cathedral on the skyline of Wearside. Its size, design and atmosphere is a beacon for the local community and is without a shadow of a doubt one of the greatest grounds in the country. Unlike many new builds it has managed to retain some of the character that is so lacking in many modern arenas. An amazing ground to visit.

The stadium can roughly be divided in half by the size of the stands. The **West Stand** and **North**

Stand are both two tiered to the same height with a row of executive boxes splitting the tiers. They are both massive and the corners sweep round to give the stadium a fully enclosed look. The stands are for home fans only and the players tunnel and dressing room are situated under the West Stand.

The East Stand and **South Stand** are both large single tiers; again the corners are filled as the seats sweep around the ground. The away support is housed in the South Stand closest to the main West Stand; up to 3,000 tickets are allocated depending on the game, and the facilities are first class. The atmosphere in the ground when full has to be experienced and it's not surprising that it is considered one of *the* grounds to visit if you're an away supporter.

Getting there
By road/Parking

Standing like a citadel above the river Wear, The Stadium of Light is not hard to find. To avoid going through the city centre continue up the A1 (M) to junction 65 and take the A1231. Once into Sunderland and running parallel to the river, the road splits – the A1231 crosses the river but the B1289 continues to the ground. There is a clearly signposted park and ride on this road and it is free for home and away fans; the bus stop is located behind the North Stand. Alternatively you can take the A690 at junction 62 into Sunderland.

By train Sunderland's main station is a 15- to 20-minute walk to the stadium, which is signposted. You could also take a metro to the Stadium of Light; the closest stations are Stadium of Light and St Peters.

That's quite interesting
Sunderland were known as 'The Bank of England' just after the war as they broke the British transfer record on numerous occasions.

Not a lot of people know that
Kevin Phillips, Sunderland goal-scoring legend, became the first Englishman to win the coveted Premiership Golden Boot and European Golden Boot in one season –1999/00.

PUB QUIZ

THE LAST **WORD**
a-love-supreme.com

HOME COLOURS

SWANSEA CITY

- **Nicknames** The Swans, The Jacks
- **Founded** 1912
- **Ground** The Liberty Stadium (opened 2005)
- **Address** Morfa, Swansea SA1 2FA
- **Capacity** 20,500
- **Best attendance** 19,288 vs Yeovil Town, Football League One, 11 November, 2005
- **Contact** 01792-616600
- **Ticket Number** 08700-400004
- **Email** info@swanseacityfc.co.uk
- **Website** swansea city.net

There have been many great rises and falls in British football, but all others pale into insignificance compared to the Swansea City rollercoaster of the late seventies and early eighties. In 1977 they were a team in the Fourth Division going nowhere fast, but by the 1981/82 season they were battling for the title in the top division. Then, by 1986, they were almost bankrupt and back in the Fourth Division again. This meteoric rise was down to the League's then youngest-ever player-manager, the ex-Liverpool star John Toshack, who was aided by his assistant Harry Griffiths. Griffiths had started the season as manager, and a lot of the credit for the initial team building should be his. However, feeling he was unable to take the team further, he moved aside for Toshack. Unfortunately Harry did not see the fruits of his hard work as a heart attack claimed him before the rise.

Three promotions in four seasons followed, with legends like Leighton James, Alan Curtis and Jeremy Charles all key players. Reaching the First Division was one thing, but when they got there they served notice by thrashing Leeds United at the Vetch 5-1, including a hat trick from new signing Bob Latchford. The following few months saw them occupy the top slot in the division on and off, only slipping to finishing sixth after injuries ravaged the squad. The fall was just as spectacular – two straight relegations and then the final drop into the Fourth in 1986 with the club on the verge of bankruptcy capped off an incredible nine years. Since that meteoric rise and fall there has been little to shout about; financial irregularities, takeovers, players being sacked to save money have all been part of the rollercoaster. Now, though, Swansea are on the way back – with a new ground and a place in the Championship, they can dare to dream of being at the summit of the top division again.

RIVALS

Cardiff City by miles, the rivalry between the two cities is intense on every level. There is also a strong rivalry with the two Bristol clubs, and the general Welsh/ English rivalry.

> Above: The Liberty Stadium.
> Below: Andy Robinson, stand-out in promotion winning team of 2007/08.

That's quite interesting
The nickname 'The Jacks' derives from sailing history. With the reputation of the city's sailors being so high, ships would accept them on reputation alone with the phrase, "any Swansea Jack is welcome to sail with us".

PUB QUIZ

Not a lot of people know that
Prisoners from the neighbouring jail used to be able to see into the Vetch Field and watch games.

Greatest moments on this ground

"We won promotion to the First Division away from home. The 5-1 demolition of Leeds in 1981 was mesmerizing, no one could believe what we'd just done, there were many more moments like that in that season too. There's been some good times in the last couple of seasons at the new ground too, as the team has vastly improved."
Alan Wessel, fan.

Lowest moments on this ground

"The period around Aussie owner Tom Petty's reign, where players were threatened with the sack, the team were losing due to the low morale, the future of the club looked bleak, and there were no positive vibes around the ground. It was horrible." Adam Griffiths, fan.

Heroes of the sideline

"John Toshack – he was responsible for the meteoric rise into the top flight of English football in the early eighties. He's the most successful manager by far." Adam Griffiths.

Don't mention the…

Fall from the First Division back to the Fourth in just five seasons.

The ground

The Liberty Stadium is such a huge improvement on the old Vetch Field ground that few fans complained when the move was decided, in fact attendances have risen. The ground is compact, holding just over 20,000, but there is room for expansion should the club make it into the Premiership. They share the ground with the Ospreys rugby union team.

The **West Stand** is slightly bigger than the rest of the stadium; it is two-tiered with a row of executive boxes at the back of the top tier. Being modern, views are excellent. All the corners of the ground are filled to give it a real stadium feel.

The **South Stand** is for home fans only; an electronic scoreboard is suspended from the roof. Perhaps the most interesting part of the ground is the roof – the south end has an almost transparent roof to aid pitch growth whilst the north is solid with a gradual blend in between. This may not seem like much, but it gives the stadium a distinctive look.

The **East Stand** sweeps around and is a modern two-tiered stand like the rest of the stadium, with few other distinguishing features.

The **North Stand** is home to the away support, and the view is excellent around the whole stadium. The facilities in the away end are amongst the best in the country, with a concourse level with bars and televisions for pre-match entertainment.

Getting there

By road/Parking The easiest thing to do if you're driving to the match is to turn off at junction 45 of the M4 and park up at the park and ride; it will cost £5, but is the most hassle-free way of getting to the ground. Alternatively, leave at junction 45 and take the A4067 towards the city centre, this road passes the stadium after about 2½ miles. Parking around the ground is very limited.

By train Swansea High Street station is just a 20-minute walk from the ground and is on the mainline from Paddington.

Pubs for home fans

All of the pubs near the ground, like Morfa Parc, are home pubs and do not admit away support.

Good food near ground

Close to the ground is a retail park with several fast-food outlets, including a KFC and a Pizza Hut. There's also Rossi's Chip Shop very close to the ground. Other than that the food in the ground is okay, but for a decent meal the city centre is the place to go.

Pubs for away fans

As an away supporter the options for a pre-match pint are limited; as stated above all the local pubs are home only and this is enforced. There are some decent chain-style pubs in the middle of the city, but avoid the Railway Pub. The best advice is to have a pint in the ground. The new concourse area serves decent beer and has TVs showing sky.

Top tips

Best to avoid the local pubs, they are strictly home fans only. Parking is also tricky near the ground, so either head for the city centre or the park and ride. Also buy tickets in advance; there's no cash on the turnstiles.

THE LAST WORD

swanseacity-mad.co.uk
scgc.co.uk

SWINDON TOWN

- ☺ **Nicknames** The Robins
- ☺ **Founded** 1879
- ☺ **Ground** The County Ground (opened 1896)
- ☺ **Address** The County Ground, County Road, Swindon, SN1 2ED
- ☺ **Capacity** 14,700
- ☺ **Best attendance** 32,000 v Arsenal, FA Cup 3rd round, 15 January, 1972
- ☺ **Contact** 0871-4236433
- ☺ **Ticket Number** 0871-2232300
- @ **Email** enquiries@swindontownfc.co.uk
- ☺ **Website** swindontownfc.co.uk

RIVALS

Oxford United, Cheltenham Town, Bristol City, Bristol Rovers and Reading.

Midway through the first half, Alan McLoughlin, ball at his feet, middle of the Wembley pitch. He pushes the ball forward into acres of space and unleashes an ambitious low shot. This is one of those moments that footballers dream of the night before a big game, one of the images that plays through their minds in Super 8 as they enter the surreal landscape of half sleep. In McLoughlin's dreamscape the ball rifles into the top corner; in the reality of a tight Division One play-off the outstretched leg of Sunderland defender Gary Bennett gets to it. But wait – the ball loops high and drifts over the stranded keeper and into the back of the net. The crowd goes wild. Swindon are on their way to the top flight for the first time in their history. Colin Calderwood steps up to receive the play-off trophy and raises it aloft to a surge of noise from the Swindon end of the stadium. However, 10 days later a dramatic statement was issued. Swindon would not be rising into the top tier of English football for the 1990/91 Season. Manager Ossie Ardiles would not see his side visiting Old Trafford and Anfield, they were in fact threatened with trips to Brentford and Exeter instead. Financial irregularities meant not only were they denied promotion, but were hit with relegation to the third tier. The Robins appealed and were eventually reinstated to the Second Division, but the scandal had cost the team from Wiltshire a place in the big time and their chairman his freedom. Many expected the team to buckle and the following season did indeed see them struggle, but under Glenn Hoddle they won the 1992/93 play-off final against Leicester and finally moved into the shiny new Premier League.

Swindon Town was formed in 1879 and still play at the County Ground, a much modernized stadium that has experienced football in all flights of the English league. During the Second World War it was home to POW's, housed on the pitch in huts that covered the playing surface. In 1969 it saw the League Cup paraded to the faithful, silverware plundered from under the noses of the mighty Arsenal who the Robins had beaten 3-1 at Wembley – an unprecedented feat for a team from the third tier. Despite periods of financial difficulty, the Town have also strived to produce exciting, attacking football, and have a history of taking down bigger, more fashionable opponents, no matter which league they inhabit.

Greatest moments on this ground

"1963 versus Shrewsbury Town when Roger Smart scored the only goal and we won promotion to the Second Division for the very first in our history time with the team of 'Bert's Babes'. For those of you not around then, Swindon Town were regarded as just another average Third Division club who had never won anything, had lost two FA Cup semi-finals sometime before the Great War and were content to tick along season after season. Bert Head came in and started building a team centred on young local players and for the first time there was a real pride, not to say passion, in the town and surrounding countryside about OUR football club." The Professor, thetownend.com.

Lowest moments on this ground

"The 5-0 defeat against Leeds in Town's only season in the Premier League, which meant we had conceded 100 league goals." Mark Merriman.

Heroes of the turf

"Don Rogers. If you saw him play you'd understand. If you didn't, then it would take me the rest of this book to tell you how good he was. There have been others like Maurice Owen, Ernie Hunt, Mike Summerbee, Rod Thomas, Peter Noble, Peter Downsborough, Shaun Taylor, Colin Calderwood, Jan Åge Fjørtoft, Mark Walters and more. But for me the Don was the best." The Professor.

"Steve 'Chalkie' White was best free transfer ever. The only Town player to receive a standing ovation from Swindon fans for scoring a goal for the opposition. Leigh Barnard, for

VILLAINS

"Who now remembers Graham French, the left-winger and would-be murderer and a guest of her Majesty? Or Jimmy Gauld who liked a bet or two, especially on games he was playing in?" The Professor.

That's quite interesting
"The Town had to move from a previous ground, Bradford's Field, when a kid who was watching the game fell into an adjoining quarry. Yes, health and safety were around keeping us safe even in those days!" The Professor and Reg Smeeton.

Not a lot of people know that
"The Shrivenham Road stand (now long since gone) was purchased from the Aldershot Military Tattoo site." The Professor.

HEROES OR ZEROES?

⌄ HEROES OF THE SIDELINE
"Hoddle and Ossie Ardiles – because of the football their teams played. Lou Macari for bringing the club back from the dead and for giving us that amazing season when we won the Fourth Division, and the subsequent seasons of achievement. Bert Head who started the ball rolling and Danny Williams for that game at Wembley." The Professor.

running all day and for epitomizing a Lou Macari Swindon side who never gave up. And Chris Kamara – don't mess with Kammy." Mark Merriman.

Zeroes of the turf
"Probably David Peach. My gran was still a better full-back than him when she died aged 103." The Professor.

"Kim Heiselberg. The 'rapid' full-back signed by Colin Todd, but roasted by Paul Hall and never seen again. David Geddes ran like he was running through treacle. And Joey Beauchamp – need I say more?" Mark Merriman.

Don't mention the…
"We celebrated our centenary in 1981 but then discovered we were actually formed in 1879, a couple of years earlier. But that didn't stop the club having a 125th anniversary dinner in 2006 – two years too late." Summerof69.

The ground
The stadium sits in quite a green location, with playing fields and the cricket ground adjoining. The South Stand or **Don Rogers Stand** is the newest at the County Ground and boasts a high cantilever roof and quite a steep single tier of seats, which combine to offer great views. The **Adkins Family Stand (and Stratton Bank)** is where away fans are seated, an open bank that is a single tier of seating but with quite a shallow rake. No roof here so bring your waterproofs. It has a capacity for 2,200 fans and the scoreboard and clock – a Rolex no less – are found at the back. The **Arkell's Stand** is the main stand behind the dug-outs. It has a high roof that only covers the rear half of the seats, but only has two supporting pillars, so views are good. There is a segment of seating here for 1,200 away fans toward the Stratton Bank end separated from the home fans by a zone where the seats have been removed. There's a groovy little fence around the directors area. The **C&D Town End** behind the far goal is an old school terrace converted to seating with a

◄ Above: The 2010 League One Playoff semi-final 1st leg against Charlton Athletic.
◄ Below: Glenn Hoddle, Swindon Town Player Manager, 1992.

low roof and a row of pillars running along the front. This is where the more vocal fans congregate.

Getting there
By Road/Parking Take the M4 to junction 15, following the A419 dual carriageway. Exit left (roundabout) onto A4259 signed for Swindon and follow over next roundabout signed for the County Ground (onto Queens Drive). Straight over next roundabout then steel yourself as you're about to take a journey on 'The Magic Roundabout' and hopefully come out on the other side of the A4259, County Road, unscathed! First right and the ground will be dead ahead. Street parking and independent match day car parks nearby.

From the north, exit the M40 at junction 9 and follow the A34 then A420 to Swindon. Straight over the White Heart roundabout onto the A4312, continuing to follow signs for Swindon/County Ground.

By Train Swindon train station is a 10-minute walk to the ground. Head up Station Road, turning right onto Corporation Street. Turn left into Manchester Road and follow to the end. Turn right onto County Road, the ground will be on your left.

Pubs for home fans
The County Ground Hotel, County Road, by the ground, is an Arkell's Brewery pub so has a selection of their ales on hand pumps as well as a range of seasonal beers. Beer garden also.

Good food near ground
There are a couple of dubious looking takeaways peppering Manchester Road from Pizza King to a kebab shop. Behind the Cricket Ground is a Tesco Extra where you can pick up a quick sarnie.

Pubs for away fans
The Merlin, Drove Road, is fine, with sports TV and around a 10-minute walk from the ground. The Cricket Club behind the Arkell's Stand extends the hand of hospitality to visiting fans looking for a place to revive themselves and enjoy a pre-match beer or two.

Top tips
Check out the Magic Roundabout next to the ground, voted 'Britain's scariest junction' and the 4th worst in the world, ahead of Paris's Arc de Triomphe, according to *Auto Express* magazine.

THE LAST WORD
swindontownsupportersclub.com
swindon-town-fc.co.uk

HOME COLOURS

- **Nicknames** The Gulls
- **Founded** 1899
- **Ground opened** Plainmoor (opened 1921)
- **Address** Torquay TQ1 3PS
- **Capacity** 6,104
- **Best attendance** 21,908 vs Huddersfield Town, FA Cup 4th round, 29 January, 1955
- **Contact** 01803-328666
- **Ticket Number** 01803-328666
- **Email** reception@torquayunited.com
- **Website** torquayunited.com

The day of 9 May 1987 saw a match that has gone down in Torquay folklore. "It was the last game of the season, at home to Crewe Alexandra," explains Chris Cox of Gloucester Gulls. "This was the first season of automatic relegation into the Conference. At the start of the match Torquay United were second from bottom on 47 points, below us were Burnley on 46 points. Lincoln City had 48 points and seemed in the least danger." At half-time Crewe were leading 2-0. Two minutes into the second-half Torquay's centre-half Jim McNichol scored from a free kick but, despite an all-out attack, Torquay seemed unable to get the equalizer. But with seven minutes to go, running across to clear a ball from the touchline, McNichol was to have a starring role once again. "A police dog by the name of Bryn thought that Jim McNichol was running to attack his handler, so he sank his teeth into the centre-half's thigh," says Chris. McNichol went down for treatment and, in the resulting pause in play, news started to filter around the ground that Lincoln City were losing; now a draw would be enough to keep Torquay up. The Gulls continued to press. Chris explains, "Four minutes of injury time were added. Then, when we thought it was all over, Paul Dobson scored possibly the most important goal in the club's history to keep us in the Football League. The scenes of jubilation and celebration at the end of the match were unbelievable." There have been some footballing great escapes over the years, but only one that involved a player being mauled by a police dog. Rumours of a stuffed and mounted 'Bryn' residing in pride of place in the Torquay United boardroom have abounded ever since!

RIVALS
Exeter City,
Plymouth Argyle,
Weymouth, Yeovil
and Bristol Rovers.

Greatest moments on this ground
"9 May 1987 – see above." Chris Cox, Gloucester Gulls.

That's quite interesting
"Pat Kruse, the centre-half broke a world record by scoring an own goal after just six seconds in the League match against Cambridge United at Plainmoor." Chris Cox.

PUB QUIZ

Not a lot of people know that
Torquay United goalkeeper Gareth Howells became the first goalkeeper to both save and score a penalty at Wembley in the May 1991 Fourth Division play-off final victory against Blackpool.

HOME
AWAY

Pubs for home fans
The club has its own pub under the Family Stand serving food and drinks. "Away fans are generally welcomed unless the match is classified as a 'high' category game," says Chris Cox. The Union Inn, St Marychurch Road, has sports screens and is closest to the ground.

Good food near ground
Hanbury's, Princes Street, is around the corner from The George Inn, selling award-winning fish and chips cooked to order that are worth the wait! Takeaway is cheaper than the licensed restaurant.

Pubs for away fans
A number of pubs are open to fans on St Marychurch Road and in the Babbacombe area. "Most visiting supporters tend to go The George Inn, Babbacombe Road, about 10 minutes' walk from the ground," says Chris Cox.

Top tips
Waitrose supermarket in Plainmoor on St Marychurch Road can be handy for grabbing a pre-match bite or a can of something refreshing.

Lowest moments on this ground
"When Craig Mackail Smith scored the penalty to send us down to the Football Conference. It was coming for a while, but the silence at the end of the game was unbelievable." YellowMurphy, Torquay United dotNET.

Heroes of the sideline
"Cyril Knowles, his first season in charge started with a 6-1 victory over Wrexham and ended with Torquay just missing out on automatic promotion and losing in the play-off final. The following season he guided the club to their first Wembley appearance in the final of the Sherpa Van Trophy. Leroy Rosenior – in first stint at the club he guided The Gulls to automatic promotion from League Two in the 2003/04 season. Paul Buckle – when he took over the club was at its lowest ebb, newly relegated from the Football League there were just four players on the

club's books. Yet at the end of his first season in charge Buckle had guided The Gulls to a play-off place in the League and an appearance at Wembley in the final of the FA Trophy. Last season (2008/09) he led The Gulls back into the Football League. An amazing turnaround." Chris Cox.

Heroes of the turf
"Derek Dawkins – The 'Dude'. A fans' favourite who enhanced his reputation by scoring the goal that gave the Gulls a 1-0 victory over Tottenham Hotspur. Mark Loram – a local player whose skills saw him break into the Torquay United first team and later transferred to QPR. Wes Saunders – a no-nonsense defender who was captain of Torquay United when they were promoted in the 1990/91 season and later returned as manager. Rodney Jack – a speedy and skilful winger, spotted playing for a Caribbean select side in a pre-season friendly. Three years after joining the Gulls Jack was sold for a club record transfer fee of £650,000. Kevin Hill signed from the local football league in 1997 and made a record-breaking 474 league appearances for The Gulls. Principally a midfielder, Hill played in virtually every outfield position for The Gulls and scored some crucial goals. Bryn – for the tackle that resulted in Torquay United's survival in the Football League." Chris Cox.

Villains
"Chris Roberts – in October 2006, he took over as the new owner. It soon became apparent that Roberts did not have the money to invest in the club. By the time his position became untenable it was too late for the club, which by then was in disarray and ended the season relegated from the Football League." Chris Cox.

Don't mention the…
Leroy Rosenior's 10 minute reign as manager: "I'm not promising overnight success," he said. Little did he know how prophetic those words would prove to be. "I did the press conference on Thursday, all the interviews, and within 10 minutes, Mike (Bateson) called me to let me know he had actually sold the club," says the now ex-Torquay manager. The shortest tenure in English football, beating Bassett's four days at Palace and making Clough's time at Leeds seem an epic.

The ground
Plainmoor is a small, compact ground with plenty of character. All the stands are covered. Behind the goal is the all-seater **Yelverton Properties Family Stand**. The Popular

△ Tim Sills congratulated by Elliot Benyon after scoring in the Carling Cup match against Crystal Palace at Selhurst Park in 2009.

Terrace runs down the side of the pitch and is a home-only stand with a TV gantry perched on the roof. Behind the goal the **Sparkworld Stand** is a covered terrace with a low roof that houses away fans and generates a great atmosphere. The **Main Stand** is made up of a couple of old-school pavilion-like stands that don't run the full length of the pitch. It has a small terrace area next to it.

Getting there
By road/Parking Follow the M5 to the end (Exeter) and onto the A38. Exit onto the A380 towards Torquay and follow. At the roundabout turn left onto the A3022/Riviera Way and follow through one roundabout before turning left onto Hele Road. Turn left onto Teignmouth Road and immediately right onto Westhill Road (becoming Warborough Road). The club is on the right. There is street parking available.

By train Torquay train station is a couple of miles from the ground – equating to around a 40-minute walk, so a taxi is a good bet.

THE LAST
WORD

gloucestergulls.co.uk
torquayunited.net
torquay.vitalfootball.co.uk

HEROES OR ZEROES?

≋ ZEROES OF THE TURF
"Jean Pierre Simb – a French midfielder who epitomized Torquay United's title as 'frustratingly entertaining'. A mercurial player who could go on an 80-yard dribble and yet seemed amazed that he still had the ball. Andy Rowlands: during the dark years of the mid-1980s, he was recruited as a centre-forward from the local football league. Although over 6 ft tall, when he jumped he would be no higher than 5 ft 6 in!" Chris Cox.

HOME COLOURS

TOTTENHAM HOTSPUR

- ● **Nicknames** Spurs
- ● **Founded** 1882
- ● **Ground** White Hart Lane (opened 1899)
- ● **Address** Bill Nicholson Way, 748 High Road, Tottenham, London N17 0AP
- ● **Capacity** 36,257
- ● **Best attendance** 75,038 vs Sunderland, FA Cup 5th round, 5 March, 1938
- ● **Contact** 0844-499 5000
- ● **Ticket Number** 0844-844 0102
- @ **Email** onehotspur@tottenhamhotspur.com
- W **Website** tottenhamhotspur.com

What sets this particular north London team apart from every other great team in the country? Is it their eight FA Cups? Their desire to play attractive, attacking football at all costs? Hoddle and Waddle's superior fashion trends and classic mullets? Although all are commendable in their own ways, what immediately sets Tottenham apart is their swashbuckling name. Like most other major football clubs in the country, they were formed by a group of 'sporting young chaps' around the turn of the century. But rather than plump for a name like rovers, city or town, these fellows delved deep into chivalrous history and created one of the most distinctive monikers not only in English football but right across the football world.

The name Hotspur was inspired by one Harry Hotspur, real name Harry Percy, a roguish nobleman of the late 1300s; famed for his hot-headedness and the enthusiastic use of his spurs when riding into battle. This spirit inspired the formation of the team in 1882 and it has been their ethos ever since. They're certainly not a club renowned for their methodical, defensive approach and have at times played some of the most exciting football seen in the English game. At Spurs, fans have revelled in the

Darwinian divide between the approach of the two great north London rivals, lessened under the Arsène Wenger years, but at almost Cold War levels during George Graham's time at the Gunners.

This cavalier attitude demanded cup success, but may also explain why Spurs could never quite secure a long enough drive for a modern title challenge. Their double-winning side of 1960/61 is the stuff of legend, led by managerial genius Bill Nicholson. Here was a man whose ethos was forged by the club he had joined as an apprentice in 1936. He built a team of class and guile who played thrilling football with a flowing approach. The resulting winning streak of 31 games secured the first League and cup double of the 20th century.

In the early eighties Tottenham again had an electrifying team, with the likes of Ossie Ardiles and Ricky Villa from Argentina linking up with Glenn Hoddle to win two FA Cups and a Uefa Cup. For Spurs fans, a lack of titles is an irritation and a frustration, but ask any and we're sure they'd settle for stylish play, consistent north London derby wins and regular Champions League cup runs. Maybe titles demand trench-hardened foot soldiers, while White Heart Lane seems to prefer the excitement of the cavalry charge.

Heroes of the sideline

"There's only one real legend and that is Bill Nicholson, the first man to lead a side to a post-war double, he is simply the greatest manager we've had. Keith Burkinshaw also deserves a mention – two FA Cups and a Uefa Cup make him the best since Bill." Richard Banks, fan.

Villains

Christian Gross – much-hyped, much-hated manager.

GETTY IMAGES

RIVALS

Arsenal, The North London derby is one of the fiercest rivalries in the English game. There is a significant rivalry with Chelsea, but on a different scale to Arsenal.

That's quite interesting

PUB QUIZ

Spurs manager Bill Nicholson signed Jimmy Greaves for £99,999 because he didn't want Greaves to have the pressure of being the first £100,000 footballer.

Not a lot of people know that

Arsenal and Tottenham's rivalry stems from Arsenal moving to north London, then being given a place in the First Division while Spurs were improperly relegated to the Second. Thus, Arsenal never technically won promotion to top-flight football.

GETTY IMAGES

⌃ **HEROES OF THE TURF**

"Of all time, probably Jimmy Greaves. He was not only Tottenham's most exciting and highest ever goal-scorer but one of England's. He'd have been the World Cup-winning centre forward had it not been for injury," says Richard Banks. Also Danny Blanchflower, Dave McKay, Pat Jennings, Alan Gilzean, Alan Mullery, Steve Perryman, Martin Chivers, Glenn Hoddle, Ossie Ardiles, Chris Waddle, Paul Gascoigne, Gary Lineker, Jurgen Klinsmann, Teddy Sheringham and David Ginola.

⌄ **ZEROES OF THE TURF**

"There have been disappointments. Biggest for me is probably Bobby Zamora. Jason Dozzell was a disaster at Spurs too," says Gareth Anderson. Gary Doherty (Ginger Pele!), Ramon Vega, Clive Wilson and Benoît Assou-Ekotto.

> Polishing the cock at White Hart Lane, 1934.
< August 1967: The Spurs team with the FA Cup (back row, left to right) Kinnear, Cyril Knowles, Mike England, Pat Jennings, Alan Gilzean, Alan Mullery, (front row) Robertson, Jimmy Greaves, Mackay, Terry Venables, Frank Saul.

GETTY IMAGES

Greatest moments on this ground

"It's hard to define a single moment. For fans as old as I am (and I was only 15 at the time), the whole of the double-winning season was one long great moment – 31 wins in one season, incredible." Richard Banks.

Lowest moments on this ground

"There have been a few, the (2009) 5-2 defeat away to Manchester United was hard to swallow, especially as we had been by far the best team in the first half and led 2-0. But the defeat was largely down to a dubious penalty that got Man United back in it." Gareth Anderson, fan.

The ground

White Hart Lane is one of the most well-proportioned and attractive football stadiums in England. Extensively redeveloped over the last two decades, the ground is completely enclosed by four, two-tiered stands, which sweep round to lock together almost seamlessly, creating an incredible atmosphere. Perhaps the most distinctive feature of the ground, and one that is totally unique, is

the two giant video screens built into the roofs of the stands, behind the goals. There are plans afoot to build a larger stadium next to the current one, it would be 60,000 capacity and would keep the club in Tottenham.

The **West Stand** is perhaps the most impressive of the four sides, simply because it has a row of double-decker executive boxes. Unusual in England, hospitality boxes were introduced at White Heart Lane early in the stadium redevelopment process. Both tiers offer uninterrupted views of play. In the southwest corner, between the west and south stands, is a rather futuristic-looking police control tower; this hangs from the roof like something out of a sci-fi movie. Below this is the area for away support, which can fit up to 2,900 of them dependent on the game (big cup games can mean more room is allocated). The view is excellent even from up in the back of the top tier, and the proximity to the home fans in the South Stand makes for an excellent atmosphere.

The **South Stand** is home to the core Spurs fans, and the proximity to the aforementioned away support makes for good banter. It is two-tiered, but without

⌃ Peter Crouch slots home for Spurs at the City of Manchester Stadium at the end of the 2010 season to clinch 4th spot and a Champions League slot for Spurs.

DON'T MENTION THE…

Fact that Arsenal have been a dominant force in English football over the last decade, and that at times they have played some football that actually isn't that boring.

> WHITE HART LANE IS ONE OF THE MOST WELL PROPORTIONED AND ATTRACTIVE FOOTBALL STADIUMS IN ENGLAND.

HOME AWAY

Pubs for home fans

The Phoenix is traditionally one of the main home pubs around White Hart Lane. The Cockerel is also one which away fans would be wise to avoid. A number of the others have either closed or, in extreme cases, have been demolished.

Good food near ground

Being London you pretty much have the choice of any cuisine you fancy. Tottenham High Road has everything from greasy spoons to Mediterranean restaurants; most of the pubs in the area also serve food as do vans around the ground.

Pubs for away fans

As mentioned above, pubs around the ground are getting scarcer. If you're coming to London by train it's not a bad idea to have a pint around the mainline station you arrive in or nearer the centre. But if you're arriving in Tottenham then most of the pubs will allow low-key away fans in. The Antwerp Arms on Church Road is a decent boozer; it gets packed on match days but is fine for a pint as long as you're not overtly sporting colours or an Arsenal fan. Gilpins Bell is a large Wetherspoons pub, which admits both sets of fans near Silver Street station and serves food. Alcohol is also served in the ground.

Top tips

Avoid the very partisan pubs, especially on big games or those involving London clubs.

Street parking within a mile of the ground is not possible due to restrictions and your best bet is to look to the north, both for an easy getaway and for finding a space.

By train The closest tube is Seven Sisters (Victoria line); this is at the other end of Tottenham High Road and a solid 20-minute walk. If you've got time though, you pass some good places to get some grub and a couple of pubs. Alternatively you can catch an overland train from Liverpool Street to White Hart Lane, which is only five minutes from the ground.

THE LAST WORD

planetspurs.com
spursnetwork.com

GETTY IMAGES

executive boxes. It has one of the two towering video screens built into the roof.

The **East Stand** continues the sweep around and is, again, two-tiered. Like the opposite West Stand, the tiers are split by executive boxes, although only on a single deck. There are two supporting pillars in the structure, which do cause minor obstruction issues.

The **North Stand** is also home to the family enclosure and roughly mirrors the opposite end.

Getting there

By road/Parking From outside of London it is best to stay on the M25 from all directions. Leave at junction 25 and take the A10 towards the city, signposted Enfield. Continue through Enfield until you hit the North Circular (A406), then turn left onto the North Circular and continue to the junction of the A1010. Continue down this road as it turns into Tottenham High Road.

There are plenty of match-day and other car parks, charges range from £5 to £15, so they can be pricey.

> Harry Redknapp

HOME COLOURS

TRANMERE ROVERS

RIVALS

Liverpool, Everton, Oldham, Wrexham and Bolton.

- **Nicknames** The Rovers, Super Whites
- **Founded** 1884
- **Ground** Prenton Park (moved here in 1912)
- **Address** Prenton Road West, Birkenhead, Wirral CH42 9PY
- **Capacity** 16,567
- **Best attendance** 24,424 vs Stoke City, FA Cup 4th round, 5 February, 1972
- **Contact** 0871-221 2001
- **Ticket Number** 0871-221 2001
- **Email** info@tranmererovers.co.uk
- **Website** tranmererovers.co.uk

There was a time when football meant every team around the country lining up at three o'clock every Saturday afternoon to do battle, come rain or shine. If it snowed, a bright orange ball was produced from a magic cupboard somewhere and the game went on. It would take a weather event of the magnitude of *The Day After Tomorrow* to stop Saturday football. It was a religion, an institution. But there was one small corner of Merseyside where the laws of time could be suspended for one glorious evening, for Tranmere Rovers had somehow made Friday night, fight night. Long before the money of Sky Sports moulded and distorted playing schedules, Tranmere pioneered the Friday night game. It became a domain that the 'third club' from the Wirral took as their own. Whether on 'police advice' to avoid overstretching resources on a busy Saturday, or a clever ploy to increase gates, Tranmere made these games an occasion to remember. Since the seventies Friday football has taken on a cup-tie atmosphere, and the team hasn't been slow to capitalize on it. During the 1975/76 season Tranmere legend Ronnie Moore scored the majority of his 37 league and cup goals under the Friday floodlights. "You can't beat a Friday night at Prenton Park," says Moore. "The atmosphere is different to any other day or night game here. And when you win your Friday night game, the rest of the weekend is especially good. All the pressure is on the other teams playing on a Saturday afternoon."

But Tranmere is no 'Friday night special' team. There were periods under Moore and Aldridge when they were knocking on the door of the top league. They've seen many memorable cup runs and big scalps taken along the way. A League Cup final loss to top Premiership side Leicester came in a close-fought game, but then there have been glory days that almost equalled lifting the

PUB QUIZ

That's quite interesting
"The BBC Sport presenter Ray Stubbs is a Tranmere fan (and also used to play for the club), often bringing recognition Tranmere's way on a Saturday afternoon as the scores roll in." Mike Jackson.

Not a lot of people know that
Tranmere are the only English team to hold a 100% record at Highbury. Played one, won one.

League Cup itself. On 27 January 2001, on a date that has now become known as St Yates Day, Tranmere travelled to great local rival Everton's home at Goodison Park and thrashed their illustrious neighbours 3-0. Tranmere still remain a club that on their day can turn over any team in the country – whether that day is a Friday or a Saturday.

Greatest moments on this ground
"Tranmere 3, Bolton 0, to send us through to the League Cup final in 2000. We were bitter rivals and a full house under the lights at Prenton Park is fantastic, but it was a great victory and wonderful atmosphere in the ground. It reminded me of the old 'Friday night football' when we also had some great nights, like beating Exeter to stay in the Football League in 1987." Paul Harper, contributor, WhiteReview.

Lowest moments on this ground
"Failing to make the play-off final in 2005 against Hartlepool despite coming back from 2-0 down after the first leg – eventually losing on penalties. The season we were relegated from the Championship to League One was also low moment (on several occasions)." Mike Jackson, editor, Total Tranmere.

Heroes of the sideline
"Johnny King – he was more of a hero as a manager to most fans, but he also played for Rovers. The time under his management was the best we've had as a club." Mike Jackson.

Don't mention the…
"Towels! When we had then world-record throw-in holder Dave Challinor, referees and Sam Allardyce didn't like our

VILLAINS

"Sean Thornton thought he was so much bigger than the club that he manufactured his transfer to Sunderland behind the club's back. And where is he now? Said 'superb prospect' plies his trade at Leyton Orient. Gone on to really great things eh Sean?" Paul Harper

"John Aldridge was simply the greatest goal-scorer in the club's history. A superb striker and as manager he took us to the League Cup final in 2000, arguably the club's greatest achievement to date. Pat Nevin, a genius with a football. The most skilful player to grace Prenton Park for sure. Dave Higgins, an unsung hero but a cult hero for Rovers fans. A committed defender who was a good player but also a great goalkeeper when needed, keeping two clean sheets! Bunny Bell, a legend of the club with a bar named after him in the Main Stand, he scored nine goals in a record 13-4 win over Oldham and missed a penalty in that game too." Paul Harper.

⩗ **ZEROES OF THE TURF**
"Godwin Antwi, a loan signing from Liverpool who came with a great reputation but wouldn't get in our Sunday league side. Ivano Bonetti – he's Italian so he must be good; he used to play for Juventus so he must be good… Erm, he wasn't great. Kevin Gray, quite simply the worst player to play for the club." Paul Harper.

tactic of letting the ball boys carry towels to allow Dave to dry the ball before launching it into the penalty area." Paul Harper.

The ground

The **Kop Stand** is the tallest stand with a single tier of seating offering excellent unobstructed views. Sitting opposite the Cowshed behind the goal it seats 5,696.

The **Main Stand** runs the length of the pitch and houses the changing rooms and tunnel. The front section has the Town Paddock and Bebington Paddock, and the rear area has the Town End separated from the Bebington End by the executive area.

The **Cowshed Stand** behind the goal is a single tier of seating with a distinct right to left sloping at the back as the number of rows decrease. This is because the stadium actually backs onto the Prenton Road West at a slight angle, effectively cutting part of the stand off. This is home to up to 2,500 away supporters.

The **Johnny King Stand** is a smaller stand that holds 2,414 and runs the length of the pitch.

Getting there

By road/Parking On the south side of the Mersey, Prenton Park is easy to reach from the M53 (fed by the M56). Exit the M53 at junction 4 (A5137/Heswall/Bebington). Take the fourth exit at the roundabout onto the B5151/Mount Road. Continue for around 2.5 miles along Mount Road, which then becomes Storeton Road. Turn right at the traffic lights onto Prenton Road West and the ground is on the right. Alternatively, from the city centre take the Queensway Mersey Tunnel (Birkenhead), which has a £1.40 toll for cars. Then bear right onto the flyover/Borough Road. The ground is signed from here.

Car parking at the ground costs £4 per game but get there early to get a space, or book in advance – T0871-221 2001. Be aware that residents parking schemes operate on roads close to grounds.

By train You have a choice of three stations. Via Liverpool Lime Street: Conway Park – 100 yards from Birkenhead bus station with links to Preston Park. Via Chester: Birkenhead Central – cross Argyle Street and it's a 30-minute walk along Borough Road (parallel to the flyover). Also via Chester: Rock Ferry – a 15-minute walk – turn right onto Bedford Road, continue along Bedford Avenue, Bedford Drive and Mount Road before turning right onto Borough Road.

Pubs for home fans
There are two pubs right on the doorstep, which naturally heave on match days and are popular with home and away fans – Prenton Park Hotel close to the away end and the smarter Mersey Clipper behind the main stand, which does a decent carvery.

Good food near ground
There are a number of cafés and takeaways on Borough Road including Eastern Delight, which serves up decent Chinese food, and Sayers Bakery for pies and sausage rolls.

Pubs for away fans
Both of pubs listed above are also popular with visiting fans – and because of this, there is a police presence. The Swan, Woodchurch Road, Prenton, is another pub that welcomes away fans and while it may be a bit of a trek to the grounds – around 20 minutes – it serves decent food and has handy parking for around 100 cars.

Top tips
Don't drink on the streets around Birkenhead. A local by-law makes it a criminal offence for which you (or home fans for that matter) could be arrested.

THE LAST WORD

whitereview.co.uk
total-tranmere.co.uk

GETTY IMAGES

THE FA VIA GETTY IMAGES

⌃ Top: Steve Yates celebrates one of his two goals in the FA Cup 4th Round match against Everton at Goodison Park in 2001. Tranmere won 3-0.
⌃ Above: Prenton Park before the covers come off for a Friday night game.

HOME COLOURS

- ☻ **Nicknames** The Saddlers
- ☻ **Founded** 1888
- ☻ **Ground** Banks's Stadium (opened 1990)
- ☻ **Address** Banks Stadium, Bescot Crescent, Walsall, WS1 4SA
- ☻ **Capacity** 11,300
- ☻ **Best attendance** 11,049 vs Rotherham United, First Division, 9 May, 2004
- ☻ **Contact** 01922-622791
- ☻ **Ticket Number** 01922-651414
- ☻ **Email** info@walsallfc.co.uk
- ☻ **Website** saddlers.co.uk

They may be from the Black Country, but the recent history of the Saddlers has certainly been colourful at times. In 2003 they signed a self-confessed drinker and inveterate gambler who then had to take an important chunk of the season off to go into rehab. While he was away the club went into a tail-spin and were finally relegated. His punishment? Well, he was made player-manager of course. Former Arsenal and England player Paul Merson has always been something of an enigma, but this chain of events left many in the game more than a little puzzled.

When the former England and Arsenal star chose to join the team from the Banks's Stadium, hopes were high. He'd completed a storming spell at Pompey and had been instrumental in the south coast team's promotion to the Premier League. So when the Saddlers kicked-off their 2003 First Division programme with a win over West Brom – not only local rivals but a team who had vied for Merson's services – the signs were good. However, by February the wheels had fallen off the cart. The talented midfielder had been revisited by old demons and was recovering in a clinic in Arizona. By the end of the season the club had dropped to the third tier of English football and manager Colin Lee, the one who had brought the talismanic midfielder in, was sacked. Under Merson's reign the team struggled, but a stable of new signings saw Walsall mount a charge to stay in the third flight (or League One as it was now known). From this point it could have gone either way: rehabilitation for Merson and the club, fight back and promotion, Walsall back in the Championship, cue the slow motion knee slides across the turf and punching of air. Unfortunately there were no Hollywood scriptwriters on hand: Merson was sacked, replaced as manager by Kevan Broadhurst and the Saddlers faced final day agony as results turned

against them and they found themselves in the bottom tier. Broadhurst was then given the boot. The post-Merson era had begun.

Since climbing back into the saddle in League One in 2007 Walsall have consolidated and 2010 saw them record a top 10 finish with some impressive results. In the competitive environment of Midlands football, the team from the Banks's Stadium are keen to return to the era at the dawn of the new millennium which saw them jockeying for position in closely fought local derbies against the likes of Wolves, Birmingham and West Brom. But the fans aren't blinkered, they know they're up against bigger spending clubs. They're just hoping that a line will open up on the inside rail and the team will have the legs to see them through.

Greatest moments on this ground

"Beating Stoke 4-2 in the play-off semi-final in 2001,

RIVALS

Wolves, West Brom, Brimingham, Aston Villa, Shrewsbury Town and Port Vale.

HOME AWAY

Pubs for home fans
Just off the ring road, The New Fullbrook, West Bromwich Road, is one of the closest pubs to the ground.

Good food near ground
There's a McDonald's in a retail park next to Walsall FC and very little else close by. Those choosing to walk the mile and a half from Walsall's main rail station can seek out more exotic delights such as a sandwich from the nearby Asda or Tesco.

Pubs for away fans
The King George V, Wallows Lane, is the closest pub to the ground (generally its best selling point) so gets packed out pre-match. The Saddlers Club generally allows admission to away fans (for a small 'donation') but given the sparsity of pubs in the vicinity, gets packed out pretty quickly. And when it's full, it's full! For those arriving via Walsall's main station, The Black Country Arms, High Street, is a good bet, stocking a cracking range of real ales.

Top tips
The motorway traffic around Birmingham always seems to be bad (read; at a stand still) so this needs to be factored into any journey planning.

VILLAINS

"Paul Merson, for reasons that everybody already knows."
Jeff Bonser, our chairman.
Steve Roy.

and Gavin Ward dropping two of them into his own net. The Roger Boli hat trick which included an overhead kick. Playing like Premier League champions and beating West Brom 4-1 to go top of Division One on the first day of the season in 2001/02. The Tuesday night when the floodlights kept going out every time Jorge Leitão scored." Steve Roy, editor, upthesaddlers.com.

Lowest moments on this ground
"Andy Petterson letting in six goals on his debut. Four months later, the goalkeeper had been released." Steve Roy.

Heroes of the sideline
Ray Graydon – controversially sacked.

The ground
Floors-2-Go Stand is the biggest in the stadium, a large two tier structure with a cantilever roof. It sits behind the goal and is home to the most vocal Saddlers fans. The rest of the stadium is pretty uniform with the stands at a lower height and very similar layout. The Main Stand, or snazzily named **Txt 64446 Health Stand**, is a single tier of seating with four supporting pillars at the front and executive boxes at the back. The players tunnel and dug-outs are on the half way line here. Behind the far goal the **Homeserve Stand** has room for about 2,000 away fans in an all seater, covered structure, again with a row of pillars along the front. Running along the side of the ground is the **West Bromwich Building Society Stand**, almost a mirror image of the stand opposite. Floodlights are mounted on four posts on top of the stands on each side that are extensions of supporting pillars.

Getting there
By Road/Parking North of the city of Birmingham, the Banks's Stadium is close to the M6, so close you can catch glimpses of it as you sit in the steady stream of log-jammed motorway traffic on your way to the game. Exit the M6 at junction 9 and follow the A461 signed Walsall. Turn right onto the A4148 and right again at the lights onto Bescot Crescent. Parking available at the ground (£3).

By Train On the opposite side of the M6, Bescot train station is a couple of minutes walk from the ground and has decent connections via both Birmingham New Street and Walsall train stations.

That's quite interesting
Portuguese striker Jorge Leitão spent nearly six years at the club. During the 2002/03 season he formed an all Portuguese-speaking strike-force with Brazilian José Júnior, which returned 30 goals.

Not a lot of people know that
"The most Walsall have ever paid for a player was £175,000 for Alan Buckley, 31 years ago." Steve Roy.

upthesaddlers.com
walsall.vitalfootball.co.uk

HEROES OR ZEROES?

⌃ HEROES OF THE TURF
"Alan Buckley. Jimmy Walker was the best goalkeeper I've ever seen play for Walsall, and stuck with us for 10 years. Jorge Leitão was the best striker at the club for a long time; worked hard and was loyal. Chris Marsh was the step-over king, and emergency goalkeeper extraordinaire." Steve Roy.

⌄ ZEROES OF THE TURF
"Paul Merson. Started brilliantly, then went downhill. Then took over the club, and almost ruined it completely." Steve Roy.

WATFORD

- **⊘ Nicknames** The Hornets
- **⊕ Founded** 1881
- **⊕ Ground** Vicarage Road (opened 1922)
- **ⓘ Address** Watford WD18 0ER
- **⊕ Capacity** 19,900
- **⊕ Best attendance** 34,099 vs Manchester United, FA Cup 4th round replay, 3 February, 1969
- **⊕ Contact** 0845-442 1881
- **⊕ Ticket Number** 0870-111 1881
- **@ Email** yourvoice@watfordfc.com
- **Ⓦ Website** watfordfc.co.uk

That's quite interesting
Elton John purchasing Watford was no coincidence, it had been his childhood ambition to one day own the club and see them into the top division.

Not a lot of people know that
Despite being known as The Hornets, Watford has a hart (male deer) on their badge, representing the Hart in Hertfordshire.

RIVALS

Luton Town, their closest and longest rivalry goes way back to the days of the Southern League.

These days football takeovers are ten-a-penny – a Russian billionaire here, a Middle Eastern conglomerate there – it's got so common that we barely bat an eyelid, but these high-profile takeovers are not just a modern phenomenon. Back in the early seventies Elton John was well on his way down the 'Yellow Brick Road' to pop superstardom. He was fashionable, he was famous, but perhaps more importantly he loved Watford Football Club. His public association with the club started in an ambassadorial role as president, but by 1976 his ambitions for the club led him to the all-important chairman's seat. He made his intentions quite clear – he wanted to see Watford in the First Division and he decided a young manager by the name of Graham Taylor was the man to do it.

The first thing Taylor did was to shed the ground's all-purpose sports stadium skin by ripping up the greyhound track that edged the pitch. This was a football ground, dammit! He then set about building a formidable team, and by the 1982/83 season they had achieved their goal, transforming from a totally unfashionable fourth tier side to a serious First Division outfit. Taylor brought on young stars like John Barnes and Luther Blissett and in that first season they finished runners-up to Liverpool – an almost unbelievable feat. Elton saw his team rocket skyward – from languishing in the Fourth Division they made it to an FA Cup final and Europe, all in under six years. Now honorary life president, he's remained with the club through thick and thin as it's yo-yoed between divisions (resignation from his role and falling out with the management at the end of 2008 excepted). A surprise play-off

VILLAINS
Gianluca Vialli – he sacked Watford legends, blew a lot of money and took the club absolutely nowhere.

win under manager Aidy Boothroyd saw an unexpected return to the top flight in 2006. It was short lived, but did give the club a vital financial shot in the arm. The Hornets have succeeded in establishing themselves as a good Championship team and certainly not one the sun is about to go down on without a fight.

Greatest moments on this ground
"There were some great games in the eighties, and one that sticks in my mind was the 8-0 destruction of Sunderland in 1982. We had suddenly become a force to be reckoned with and for someone like me, who had watched them from the Fourth Division, it was amazing." Andrew Worthington, fan.

Lowest moments on this ground
"In recent years, it has to be almost every game we played in the last outing in the Premiership. We were a bit under gunned when we went up." Andrew Worthington.

Heroes of the sideline
"Graham Taylor is without doubt the greatest manager – from Fourth Division obscurity to runners-up in the First Division and Europe – a true legend." Andrew Worthington.

Don't mention the…
Assistant referee Nigel Bannister, who awarded a ghost goal to visitors Reading in September 2008. The ball didn't go within a yard of the goal and even Reading were surprised! (Watford scored twice to take a 2-1 lead before the referee gave an 87th-minute penalty to Reading.)

The ground

Vicarage Road is a real mix of old and new, and a stadium that's restricted by its environment, something that any away fan can relate to if they've walked around the allotments to get in. Three of the sides have been redeveloped, either totally or just by adding a roof and seats; 2009 saw the fourth going through the process.

The **East Stand** has, for over a season now, been unused, except by directors and guests and players changing underneath it. The ageing structure has finally come to the end of its safe life and is earmarked for development into a fine two-tier structure, which will be a larger, modern version of its opposite number. On completion it will make the ground into a compact and well-proportioned stadium.

The **Vicarage Road** stand used to be a large open terrace, but like most stands in the early nineties, it was made all-seated and a roof was put on. It now houses a split between home and away fans, with a capacity of just under 5,800. The allocation to visiting supporters varies depending on the competition and club.

The **Rookery Stand** is at present the newest of the four sides, rebuilt in the mid-nineties it holds over 6,000 of the most vocal Watford fans. It also houses the administrative area of the club and the club shop.

The **Rous Stand** was built during Watford's heyday in the mid-eighties, with the help of club benefactor Elton John. It's a decent two-tier structure with an unusual wavy roof. There is a row of executive boxes at the back. In the corner between the Rous Stand and the Vicarage Road end is a large electronic scoreboard.

Getting there

By road/Parking Most fans will arrive along the M1 and should leave at junction 5 onto the A4008, signposted Watford. Coming in from this direction the ground is clearly visible, and by joining the inner ring road you will soon find yourself in close proximity. Parking-wise there is some street parking near the ground but it is limited. The best bet is to follow signs to one of the match-day car parks that charge £5-£6, or park in the town centre and walk the short distance.

By train Most will arrive at Watford Junction. The ground is about a 20-minute walk from here, or you can catch a second train to Watford High Street, which is only a 5- to 10-minute walk. There is also a tube station, which is on the Metropolitan line, but this is a little further away.

HEROES OR ZEROES?

⌃ HEROES OF THE TURF
Luther Blissett (415 games, 158 goals). He played in every division and is considered Mr Watford. John Barnes cut his teeth in Watford's best team before moving on to even greater things with England and Liverpool. Also Tommy Smith, Tommy Mooney, Ashley Young, Nigel Gibbs, Tony Coton, Steve Sherwood, Ben Foster, Marlon King, Kenny Jackett, Ian Bolton and Taffy Davies.

⌄ ZEROES OF THE TURF
"Ramon Vega – he was known for being dangerous at both ends of the pitch. Steve Talboys, Trevor Senior, Trevor Putney and Devon White."
Sam Franklin, fan.

HOME COLOURS

WEST BROMWICH ALBION

☻ **Nicknames** The Baggies
☻ **Founded** 1878
☻ **Ground** The Hawthorns (opened 1900)
➊ **Address** The Hawthorns, Halfords Lane, West Bromwich, B71 4LF
☻ **Capacity** 26,500
☻ **Best attendance** 64,815 v Arsenal, FA Cup 6th round, 6 March, 1937
☻ **Contact** 0871-271 1100
☻ **Ticket Number** 0871-271 9780
@ **Email** enquiries@wbafc.co.uk
Ⓦ **Website** wba.co.uk

E very so often there is a surging groundswell of opinion that rises and washes over the public conscience, a wave of nostalgia that tells us the seventies was a great time to be around, a 'Golden Era'. *Life on Mars* with its metallic bronze Mk3 Cortina brings back warm feelings about those corduroy flares, leather jackets and overlong scarves. Old footage of Billy Bremner in the all white of Leeds United going head to head with Franny Lee in the powder blue of Man City tend to have a somewhat rose tinted hue when viewed through the mists of time. Terraces crowded with real fans; real men watching real football. And yet it wasn't really such a perfect era, a footballing Eden where it was all about 'the game'. Stands were death traps, terraces were crumbling, fans were penned in like dogs while racists handed out NF leaflets by the turnstiles and hurled abuse onto the pitch. And that's without even touching on the fights, the lack of facilities and pitches that looked like cows grazed on them through the week.

However, change was afoot at the Hawthorns. The pies were still terrible and the toilets still stank but a revolution was happening on the pitch. West Brom entered the second half of the decade with Johnny Giles at the helm, assembling a team that would not only climb out of the second tier of English football, it would go on to challenge for the League title, challenge perceptions and in doing so, help break the mould of the English game forever. In 1977 Giles resigned, with The Baggies seventh in the League and Big Ron picked up the reigns. The stage was set. In their centenary year Albion stormed the table playing dream football and Laurie Cunningham, Cyrille Regis, Brendon Batson and Remi Moses were the engine room. Sure there had been black and Afro-Caribbean players in English

RIVALS
Wolves, Aston Villa, Birmingham.

➤ Fans at the home game against Middlesbrough 2010.

⌃ HEROES OF THE SIDELINES

"Alan Ashman took Albion to an FA Cup triumph in 1968 and managed Albion in the top division for four years (1967 to 1971). Although he inherited a very good squad, Ron Atkinson got them playing exciting football, with the 'Three Degrees' – Batson, Cunningham and Regis – playing prominent roles that marked a major breakthrough for black players in the British game. This was perhaps best epitomised in an Old Trafford game in December 1978, when Albion triumphed 5-3 over Man United in a thrilling encounter. Gary Megson managed Albion from March 2000 to October 2004. He famously took Albion back to the top division in 2002 for the first time in 16 years. A manager who attracted mixed opinions amongst supporters because of his somewhat abrasive style, he nevertheless fully deserves legend status because, along with then chairman Paul Thompson, he takes full credit for shaking the club out of its slumbers to once again compete at the top level of English football." Paul, WBAFansonline.

football before, going back decades. But this backbone of talent assembled by Giles and Atkinson not only saw Albion storm their way to third in the League, but also helped to begin the reshaping of social attitudes on the terraces and on the turf. Think John Terry had a hard time? Well these players had to endure a torrent of bile and bigoted abuse from rival terraces week in week out, but this merely spurred Cunningham and co. on, and makes their achievements all the more remarkable.

West Brom's 1978/79 Uefa Cup run cemented the team's place in English football history and announced to the world what a talented team was plying its trade in the blue and white of the Baggies. Cunningham made such an impression on the European stage he was targeted by Real Madrid, becoming the first English player to make the move to the Bernabeu. He also went on to represent England, as did Cyrille Regis, while Brendon Batson and Remi Moses wore the three lions at B and U21 levels. The doors had been broken down, and while the catering may still have been terrible, this really was a golden era at West Brom, one that illuminated the rest of the game.

The Baggies fans have had to endure a somewhat volatile existence over the last decade. Their endorphin levels must be all over the place. Promotion, great escape, relegation, play-off defeats, promotion, relegation and promotion again. It's been a busy time. But I'm sure most Albion fans would now agree with the wise words of Ronan Keating when he sings "Life is a rollercoaster, just got to ride it. Life is a rollercoaster, just got to consolidate our position in the Premier League and build from there!"

Greatest Moments on this ground

"In recent times, 21 April 2002, when Albion beat Crystal Palace 2-0 to clinch promotion to the Premier League to put Albion back in the top division after 16 years absence. Albion had clawed back an 11 points deficit to overhaul their bitter rivals Wolves to gain automatic promotion." Paul, WBAFansonline.

Lowest moments on this ground

"FA Cup, January 1991, Albion 2 Woking 4. Humiliating defeat at home to the non-league club, who fully deserved their victory on the day." Paul.

Heroes of the turf

"Ronnie Allen. The popular Albion and England centre-forward in the fifties, went on to manage the club and was also a chief scout. 'The King' Jeff Astle, was hugely popular Albion centre-forward in the sixties and early seventies, famous for his heading ability (tragically, the affects of heading heavy footballs for many years lead to his death in January 2002). In later years, Jeff followed Albion as a fan and made regular appearances on the Frank Skinner and David Baddiels' *Fantasy Football League* television show. Tony Brown was an Albion inside-forward and record goal-scorer (279 goals in 720 games) who earned the nickname 'Bomber' because of his ferocious shooting ability – he still commentates on Albion games on local radio. Cyrille Regis was spotted by Ronnie Allen and bought by the club for £5,000 (plus another £5,000 after 20 attendances), from non-league Hayes in 1977. He became a cult hero to Albion fans. His goal of the season against Norwich in the FA Cup at the Hawthorns in 1982 was typical of his speed, athleticism and raw power. 'Super' Bob Taylor was an Albion striker, from 1992 to 1998 and again from 2000 to 2003, who took the club and its fans to heart. Although scored outside the top flight, Bob's 113 goals for the club secured his legendary status – perhaps the most pleasurable being a diving header scored against Wolves at the Hawthorns." Paul.

Zeroes of the turf

"David Mills was a £500,000 British record signing from Middlesbrough in 1979, but scored only six goals in 59 appearances. Mike Phelan made 21 appearances for the club in 1994/95 after signing from Manchester United. His Albion career never got off the ground –when he did play, he was poor." Paul.

That's quite interesting

"If sea levels rise due to global warming, the Albion ground staff shouldn't be concerned. At 551-ft (168m) above sea level, The Hawthorns is the highest league ground in England." Paul.

Villains

"Steve Bull played for the club very early in his career, in 1985/86, scoring lots of reserve goals and two goals in four first team appearances. Infamously, he was then sold by Albion manager Ron Saunders to arch rivals Wolves for peanuts. His 250 goals in 474 games for Wolves bears testimony to the folly of that sale. Albion fans have booed Bull's name ever since, which probably says much about how much we know we missed out on a goal machine, to be honest. The late Ron Saunders (who was also an ex Villa manager) is still vilified for it." Paul.

Not a lot of people know that

"Bobby Gould was Albion manager from 1991/92. He took the club down to the old Third Division for the first time in its history (albeit he was only in charge for the latter part of that season). Gould was known for his 'off the wall' Wimbledon style training and motivational approaches and his methods had become somewhat of a joke amongst the playing squad. On one occasion, he brought two pairs of boxing gloves to training and offered to take on any player who fancied his chances. Colin West, a big strapping striker, took on the challenge… and promptly flattened Gould." Paul.

The ground

Has the big, open feel of many Premier League grounds, with an uneven roof line that stops it feeling like another uniform arena. No pillars and good views all round.

The **East Stand** is the biggest with one large bank of seating and the highest roofline. It has a capacity of 8,791 for home fans and a row of executive boxes at the rear. Away behind the goal is the **Smethwick End**, slightly smaller bank of seating for 5,816. Away supporters sit on the side nearest the East Stand, with a demarcation down the middle and home fans occupying the side nearest the West Stand. The **West Stand** or Halfords Lane runs the full length and is the smallest, with a single tier of seats for 5,110 home fans. It is the main stand with dug-outs on the half-way line and a more gentle rake to the seats.

Behind the near goal is the **Birmingham Road End**, a large single tier which holds 8,286 home fans. Outside the ground are the Jeff Astle memorial gates in memory of the Baggies legend who died in 2002.

Getting there

By Road/Parking The stadium is easily reached. Take junction 1 of the M5 and follow the A41 east to Birmingham – the Hawthorns is about half a mile along. Street parking plus independent match day car parks spring up and are usually well signed.

By Train The Hawthorns train and metro station (with connections from Birmingham Snow Hill, a 10-minute walk from the main Birmingham New Street) is about five minutes from the ground. Alternatively Smethwick Rolfe Street station is a 15-minute walk from the ground but is serviced by trains leaving from Birmingham New Street – so which ever way you look at it, it's still a 15 minute walk!

BOB THOMAS/GETTY IMAGES

⌃ Cyrille Regis celebrates after scoring the third goal of his hat trick against Birmingham October 1981.

Pubs for home fans

The Vine, Roebuck Street, is a cracking rabbit warren of a spot combining a pub with an indoor Tandoori barbeque restaurant. Decent beers as well as a guest ale on rotation and around a 15-minute walk from the ground. Heading away from the ground and under the M5 on the A41, The Horse and Jockey, Stoney Lane, has a great selection of cask ales, sports TV and a good match day vibe, whipped up by the Baggies flags outside.

Good food near ground

The Vine, Roebuck Street, serves up some of the best pre match fare. This pub-cum-tandoori barbeque restaurant serves up quality, well priced dishes to be washed down with a beer or two. McDonald's, just east of the stadium, on the A41 Holyhead Road is another choice.

Pubs for away fans

Being a classic out-of-town stadium, choice is fairly limited. The Royal Oak, Holyhead Road, is about 10 minutes' walk from the stadium on the right-hand side usually attracts a happy mix of away supporters.

Top tips

Best to give the pubs in West Bromwich town centre and those around the bus station a miss, especially if you're wearing team colours.

DON'T MENTION THE...

"Fabian de Freitas, Albion striker (1998 to 2000), once turned up hours late for a bank holiday afternoon home game. He thought it was an evening kick-off." Paul, WBAFansonline.

THE LAST WORD

fansonline.net/westbromwichalbion
westbrom.com
baggies.com
albiontillwedie.co.uk
oldbaggies.com

- **Nicknames** The Irons, The Hammers
- **Founded** 1895
- **Ground** Boleyn Ground, known as Upton Park (opened 1904)
- **Address** Green Street, London E13 9AZ
- **Capacity** 35,303
- **Best attendance** 42,322 v Tottenham Hotspur, Division One, 17 October, 1970
- **Contact** 0844-375 8200
- **Ticket Number** 0870-112 2700
- **Email** yourcomments@westhamunited.co.uk
- **Website** whufc.com

WEST HAM UNITED

The sixties were a golden time, not only for West Ham United, but for English football. The club from Upton Park has always prided itself on nurturing home-grown talent, and during those heady years it not only developed some of its greatest talent for the club, it delivered for the national cause too. Bobby Moore, Geoff Hurst and Martin Peters were all sons of West Ham and each played a pivotal role in bringing home the World Cup. Moore the inspirational captain and defensive pillar, Peters firing home one of the decisive goals against Germany and Hurst with a World Cup final hat trick. These were national as well as local heroes.

But for West Ham United the sixties wasn't just about that day in 1966, it was also the club's most successful period. During the late fifties manager Ted Fenton assembled a team full of home-grown youth and when Ron Greenwood took over in 1961 he built on this successful formula, with The Hammers first gaining promotion and then winning the FA Cup in 1964. The following year he led the side to the European Cup Winners' Cup final where they beat 1860 Munich at Wembley by two goals to nil. Many consider this to be one of the club's most glorious moments and, coming just a year before the World Cup, one that helped to provide members of the national squad with some vital winning experience.

RIVALS

All London clubs are treated to a warm reception at Upton Park, most notably Millwall, who have a long-standing rivalry with The Irons. Tottenham and Chelsea come in close behind.

PUB QUIZ

That's quite interesting
The club crest and nickname come from their origins as the Thames Ironworks team.

Not a lot of people know that
West Ham has only had 12 managers in its history, a record low in English football.

> Wealth of talent, Martin Peters, Trevor Brooking and Geoff Hurst in a 1969 game against Southampton.

Hooliganism. West Ham had one of the most feared hooligan elements in the land, The Inter City Firm.

< Tevez curls one over the wall against Bolton, one of the goals that helped keep West Ham up in 2007.

These cup successes helped West Ham establish a reputation as a team to fear in knockout football and further success has followed. They lifted the FA Cup in the mid-seventies and then again in 1980 – the last time a club from outside the top flight won the competition. Managed by the legendary John Lyall they lined up against old London rivals Arsenal, favourites by far, and beat them by a single but significant Trevor Brooking goal.

Since then The Hammers' attempts at major trophies may have been met with less success, but they've been exciting. Having risen to a highest-ever fifth place finish under Harry Redknapp in the 1998/99 season, they slumped back into the second tier, before bouncing back with a play-off victory to the top flight where they now reside.

While West Ham have always been renowned for bringing on young talent – as the likes of Frank Lampard, Joe Cole, Rio Ferdinand, Glen Johnson and Jermaine Defoe will attest – one 'discovery', Steve Davies, has gone down in West Ham folklore. "Lee Chapman was playing for us at the time," recounts Redknapp of the 1994 pre-season friendly against Oxford. "All through the first half some tattooed skinhead behind me was giving Lee terrible stick. At half-time I turned to this bloke who

had West Ham etched on his neck and asked 'Can you play as good as you talk?' He looked totally confused. So I told him he was going to get his dream to play for West Ham. We sent him down the tunnel and he reappeared 10 minutes later all done out in the strip. He ran on to the pitch and a journalist from the local Oxford paper sidled up and asked 'Who's that Harry?' I said 'What? Haven't you been watching the World Cup? That's the great Bulgarian Tittyshev!' The fella wasn't bad – actually, he scored!"

Greatest moments on this ground

"West Ham 5 Bradford 4 – one of the most memorable games in recent times (February 2000). We were 4-2 down with 25 minutes left. Shaka Hislop had gone off with a broken leg and was replaced by teenager Stephen Bywater, who proceeded to let in three soft goals. Lampard and Di Canio almost fought with each other over who should take a penalty, and at one stage Di Canio staged a one-man sit-in, in a vain bid to be substituted after being denied another penalty. What a game." Iain Dale, West Ham Till I Die.

"April 1976 – West Ham 3, Eintracht Frankfurt 1 (Cup Winners' Cup semi-final second leg)." Graeme Howlett, following a poll on KUMB.com.

VILLAINS

Paul Ince, Frank Lampard and Jermaine Defoe all get a very 'warm' welcome when they skulk back to play or manage at West Ham.

Lowest moments on this ground
"I remember a very dull 0-0 draw with Dave Bassett's Sheffield United in the mid-1990s, but there's a lot of competition for this accolade. Any number of cup defeats to lower league sides come to mind, along with many dire performances under the uninspiring Alan Curbishley." Iain Dale. "The Bond Scheme protests of 1992." Graeme Howlett.

Heroes of the sideline
"John Lyall, purely by dint of his record of winning the cup in 1980, getting to a League Cup final in 1981 and then coming third in the League in 1986. It could so easily have been first. Many of us thought Gianfranco Zola had it in him to be even better." Iain Dale.

The ground
The Boleyn Ground, probably better known to everyone in the football world as Upton Park, is a fine stadium that's undergone several phases of modernization. Three sides look as good as any other in the League and have the corners filled, with just one older stand still remaining.

The West Stand (formerly known as the Dr Marten's Stand) is by far the most impressive –two-tiered and separated by executive boxes, it holds a whopping 15,000 fans and dominates the ground. It is also the newest having been completed in time for the start of the 2001 season. The stand also holds all of the club offices and dressing rooms. The corners at either end are filled, giving half of the ground an enclosed feel.

The Sir Trevor Brooking Stand (formerly known as the Centenary Stand) is behind the goal and opened in 1995, for the club's 100th year. The upper tier houses the family area, whilst the lower is split between home and away fans. Away clubs get an allocation of between 2,000-3,000 tickets, the atmosphere is excellent as is the view.

At the opposite goal end The Bobby Moore Stand is two-tiered, divided by executive boxes. The lower tier is home to the engine room of Hammers fans that generate a lot of noise throughout matches. Between it and the West Stand there is a large screen.

The final side is the East Stand. Looking somewhat out of place, the distinctly tired-looking two-tiers of seating have been slated for replacement. The plan was to put a new two-tiered structure in its place to raise the capacity to over 40,000, but lack of money and planning opposition has meant it has so far been left undeveloped.

Getting there
By road/Parking Getting to West Ham can be difficult by car – congestion and lack of parking can add up to a miserable day out. The best advice is to park at an outlying tube station and catch a train into the area. If you must drive, then from the north and the west take the M25 to the M11 and head into the city until you hit the North Circular. Take the North Circular south until you hit Barking Road, the A124 (this gets very busy). Turn right along this and start looking for street parking where you can. From the south or east use the A13, following signs for East Ham, then come in on Barking Road, as above. It's all street parking, and the traffic can be terrible pre- and post-match.

By train By far the easiest way to get to a West Ham match is by train/tube, even if it means leaving your car at an outlying station. Upton Park, on the Hammersmith & City and District lines, is closest. From here it's just a five-minute walk to the ground, although it's heaving post-match. The best bet is to walk to one of the other nearby stations – Plaistow or East Ham.

HOME
AWAY

Pubs for home fans
All the pubs within 10-20 minutes of the ground are home fans only.

Good food near ground
There are some good cafés near Upton Park tube station; traditional East End food is excellent and plentiful. Duncan's Pie, Mash and Eels, in the heart of Green Street, just two minutes' walk from Upton Park tube is busy for good reason – the pies are top quality and the price is fair. Eat in or takeaway.

Pubs for away fans
Finding a pub close to the ground is not really a good idea – London clubs' fans should have a pint before travelling to the area, and most others would be advised to do the same. If you do want a pint, though, pubs more than 20 minutes away in East Ham usually accept well-behaved away fans.

Top tips
Get a train to the game – driving into West Ham and trying to park is not a great deal of fun.

THE LAST WORD

westhamonline.net
westhamfans.org
kumb.com
westhamtillidie.com

WIGAN ATHLETIC

RIVALS

Wigan Warriors,
Manchester City,
Manchester
United, Preston
North End
and Bolton.

- **Nicknames** Latics
- **Founded** 1932
- **Ground** DW Stadium (opened 1999)
- **Address** Robin Park, Newtown, Wigan WN5 0UZ
- **Capacity** 25,168
- **Best attendance** 25,133 vs Manchester United, Premier League, 11 May, 2008
- **Contact** 01942-774000
- **Ticket Number** 0871-6633552
- **Email** s.hayton@jjbstadium.co.uk
- **Website** wiganlatics.co.uk

On numerous occasions the green shoots of this football club have slowly reached towards the light only to be extinguished before they truly established themselves. Wigan County, Wigan United, Wigan Town and Wigan Borough all fell by the wayside before Wigan Athletic, in 1932, made a strong enough growth spurt to establish the roots needed to keep it alive. The club had to fight long and hard, like a sapling living constantly in the shadow of a huge shady tree, and for Athletic that tree was rugby-ball shaped. While soccer may have ruled the roost as far as the national game goes, in many towns and cities across the north of England, rugby league was king. Teams such as St Helens, Widnes, Warrington, Castleford, Bradford and Hull captured local interest with the efficiency of French pair trawlers, while rugby league giants Wigan were the Japanese whalers of the day – the streets would run red on match days as fans in replica shirts were drawn into the Central Ground.

By 1987 the fight back had begun and Athletic were finally elected to the Football League; by 2005 they had completed a fairytale climb all the way to the bright clear skies of the Premier League. Today the club has built on its firm foundations and, encouraging a growth in the young fanbase, is seeking to ensure a long-term tenure in the top flight. In terms of local popularity it's probably just about sneaked ahead of its long-term rival, and while some have no trouble supporting both the Warriors and Athletic, others can't forgive the days when the purveyors of the oval ball seemed to be boss of the football club. Today they make slightly uneasy bedfellows, sharing the DW Stadium and a section of the fans, but in the ancient game of survival of the fittest, Athletic have already proved they have what it takes.

Greatest moments on this ground

"Reading at home to get into the Premiership, May 2005. Although we finished second that year, there was something even more exhilarating about winning promotion on the very last day of the season. Many didn't believe it until the third went in, which produced scenes of grown men on their knees openly crying with joy." Martin Tarbuck, editor of *The Mudhutter*, author of *Pies & Prejudice* and *Let's Hang On*.

Lowest moments on this ground

"Almost every time we play the Big Four. We match them, often outplay them, the crowd roars, we love every minute as our lads take on one of the giants of the modern game… then the man with the whistle sees his arse, gives a dodgy decision their way or denies us a clear penalty. We lose in the last minute; and with our hearts saddened, wonder why we ever bothered turning up in the first place!" Martin Tarbuck.

Heroes of the sideline

"Paul Jewell – the man who took us from the lowest tier to the Premier League. No other manager is ever likely to do that again." Bernard Ramsdale, landlord, Ye Olde Tree and Crown. "Roberto Martinez – although it's very early days in his managerial career, 'Bob' is symbolic of the journey we've been on and there's mutual love and respect from both fans and manager." Martin Tarbuck.

Zeroes of the turf

"Andy Webster – many still feel he used us to escape his Hearts contract to play for Rangers. He arrived at the DW Stadium, was a complete flop, spent a season on loan to Rangers and then signed for them permanently. He only ever played twice for The Gers. Emerson Thome – there were high hopes following his signing but he played only League Cup games as his fitness was always in doubt. Olivier Kapo – he played like a superstar for Bruce at Birmingham City, but from almost day one the Frenchman wanted a move from Wigan and begged clubs to sign him during every single transfer window." Bernard Ramsdale, landlord, Ye Olde Tree and Crown.

Also Stefan Bidstrup, Jeff Peron and Alan 'The Invisible Man' McLoughlin.

Don't mention the…

"Press conferences. It's become traditional for new managers not to turn up for the press conference announcing their arrival. Both Steve Bruce and Roberto Martinez appointments hit last-minute hitches, leaving an empty chair both times. The waiting press do, however, speak very highly of chief executive Brenda Spencer's pots of tea." Martin Tarbuck.

Villains
"Pascal Chimbonda – the club rescued him from a 'race-hate' hell in France and he went on to become something of a cult hero, that is until the final game of the season against Arsenal (the last League game played at Highbury). He handed in a written transfer request before his team mates had even begun to get changed. He is now a pale shadow of the player that Paul Jewell signed, one who arrived at the club without even a pair of boots to his name." Bernard Ramsdale.

Also, Simon Haworth, Amr Zaki and Steve Bruce.

That's quite interesting
"Former Wigan Athletic midfielder Jimmy Bullard never missed a single league game after signing for the club from Peterborough United until his move to Fulham. He was also once selected for England international duty (unused substitute), putting an end to prospects of an international career with Germany!" Bernard Ramsdale.

Not a lot of people know that
"The DW Stadium was built on a plot of land once known as 'The Gant', the colloquial name for a sewage tip. Often in the summer months a foul stench can be found drifting through the ground, although it's not known whether this is down to the former utilization of the premises or merely the occupancy of several thousand rotund rugby league fans in the vicinity." Martin Tarbuck.

The ground
The DW stadium was initially called the JJB Stadium and was opened in May 1999 by Sir Alex Ferguson of all people. All the roofing is cantilevered, resulting in unobstructed views from around the ground, but the corners are not filled. The **East Stand** (Boston Stand) is the largest; it runs along the pitch and is a single tier of seating accommodating 8,238 fans. Behind the goal, the **South Stand** is also single tier and has a capacity of 5,412. The main **West Stand** (Springfield Stand) accommodates executive suites, changing rooms, commentary boxes, the players lounge and 6,100 fans, while the **North Stand** behind the far goal seats 5,418 and is usually used to house away support.

> Above: Wigan working the ball through midfield.
> Below: Wigan fans celebrate win over Arsenal, April 2010.

⤢ HEROES OF THE TURF
"Roberto Martinez spent six years at Wigan Athletic and only left because a certain Steve Bruce made the decision to release him. A sharp footballing mind and his range of passing skills were totally unsurpassable. He's returned along with another hero, Graeme Jones. 'Sir' Andy Liddell – a brilliant player who scored brilliant goals and was instrumental in our climb up through the divisions. Arjan de Zeeuw had two spells at the club and was the best centre half we've ever had. A true leader and hard as nails." Martin Tarbuck.

MANCHESTER UNITED VIA GETTY IMAGES

GETTY IMAGES

Getting there
By road/Parking From the north exit the M6 at junction 27 towards Shevington and go right onto Shevington Lane at the T-junction. Follow for a mile and turn left onto Church Lane (Standish Lower Ground) and right onto Wigan Road (B375). Continue for around two miles, then go right onto Scot Lane and left onto Stadium Way. From the south, exit the M6 onto the A49 to Wigan. Follow for 1½ miles and at the Saddle junction turn left onto Robin Park Road following signs for DW stadium. There's a free car park accessed via Frith Street (at Saddle junction) but it fills up quickly. There's also a car park and parking behind the East Stand (£4).

By train Wigan North Western Rail and Wigan Wallgate Rail are a 20-minute walk away. Head under the railway bridge and follow the right-hand side of Wallgate Road/ A49. Pass under the rail line again and the stadium will come into view. Negotiate the roundabout before turning down into Robin Park Road.

Pubs for home fans
The Swan & Railway on Wallgate, opposite Wigan North Western railway station, is a great-looking establishment serving up real ale and is a home fan favourite.

Good food near ground
Pop into the 24-hour Asda in Robin Park for supplies. Another option is the Brocket Arms Wetherspoon just off King Street and around the corner from the train station.

Pubs for away fans
Next to the 24-hour Asda superstore, The Red Robin, Anjou Boulevard, is a big, modern pub in the retail park near the DW. Pub food is also available in a two-for-one offer. Just around the corner from the train station, The Anvil, Dorning Street, is a popular spot with home fans watching the game, but away fans usually get a good reception too. It's a CAMRA award-winner with well kept real ales.

Top tips
Don't be tempted to park in the retail park. There's a strict two-hour limit (especially on match days) and hefty fines.

THE LAST **WORD**

mudhutsmedia.co.uk
yeoldetreeandcrown.co.uk
cockneylatic.co.uk
wiganathletic-mad.co.uk

- **Nicknames** Wolves, Wanderers
- **Founded** 1877
- **Ground opened** Molineux (opened 1889)
- **Address** Waterloo Road, Wolverhampton WV1 4QR
- **Capacity** 29,384
- **Best attendance** 28,525 vs Liverpool, FA Cup 5th round, 11 February, 1939
- **Contact** 0871-222 2220
- **Ticket Number** 0871-222 1877
- **Email** info@wolves.co.uk
- **Website** wolves.co.uk

WOLVERHAMPTON WANDERERS

WOLVERHAMPTON WANDERERS

RIVALS

Birmingham, West Brom, Aston Villa.

The eighties were a grey time across the UK. The blue rinse brigade occupied Number 10, there were three million unemployed and violence roamed the grounds. It was as though the colour spectrum had actually warped and twisted away from the bright optimism of the sixties towards a palette of drab, beige melancholy. Not even the golden shirts of the Wolves could fight off the oppressive nature of the period as Wolverhampton Wanderers were shunted from the top tier of English football. Between 1984 and 1987 the once great champions slipped through successive relegations before bottoming out in the old Fourth Division. Mighty Molineux was crumbling around a team that was self-destructing. With both the Main Stand and the North Bank closed, the ground made for a forlorn sight. The club was bankrupt.

Things could easily have faded to black. However, the arrival of two new faces at the ground offered some hope; Graham Turner took over the managerial reigns and one Steve Bull pulled on the gold shirt for the first time. The Tipton Skin, as he was affectionately known, scored 102 goals in two successive seasons as the team climbed back into the second tier and began to challenge for promotion. Wolves fan Jack Hayward took control of the club, the grey eighties were over and there seemed to be a glimmer of golden light at the end of the tunnel for Wolves fans.

May 2006 saw a Welsh day of destiny that many Wolves fans thought might never come. The play-off final trophy was held aloft at the Millennium Stadium – promotion had finally been secured along with a return to the big time. Wanderers had struggled for more than 20 years; perennial promotion favourites, the team had often come close, but not close enough, and a string of promising managers and players had been and gone. Hemmed in by deadly local rivals who were enjoying

greater success, the Wolves story had been as much about the hard times as the good, but throughout it all there was a spirit and determination epitomized by one man.

Bully resisted all proposals when the best clubs in the world came courting him. In an era when talent jumps ship at 16, Steve Bull showed what real loyalty means – the big money offers and promises of European football from the likes of Real Madrid, Barcelona, Juventus, Inter Milan, Liverpool and Manchester United could not tempt him away from the Midlands. It was the equivalent of Rooney staying at Everton, Joe Cole at West Ham or Alan Smith with Leeds. Steve Bull may not have quite made the promised land with his team, but he certainly gave the club the platform to get there. There isn't a fan around the country who doesn't wish they could have had a

^ Molineux through a fish-eye.

Steve Bull at their own club. With a new start in the top league, Wolves has a Premier League support, Premier League ground and finally the chance to secure a long-term future in the top flight.

Greatest moments on this ground

"We clinched three League Championships, but players point to the friendlies of the 1950s, and gates bear that out. These were seen as almost international fixtures. National pride was at stake. Visiting foreign teams attracted crowds of over 50,000 and gripped the support. They played the mighty Honved of Hungary in 1954: 2-0 down at half-time, they came back to beat them 3-2. That team contained many of the members of the Hungarian national team that had just beaten England and reached the 1954 World Cup final." David Instone, wolvesheroes.com.

Lowest moments on this ground

"I would say the mid-eighties. The closure of the two sides of the ground – the North Bank and Main Stand – following on from the safety implementations that followed Bradford and Hysel, plus the run of three relegations when crowds were regularly around 3,000 turning out to watch us play the likes of Lincoln, Halifax or losing to Wrexham." David Instone.

Heroes of the sideline

"Joe Gardiner, Mr Wolves, served the team for 50 years as player, trainer and scout. Married to the club and loved by all. He died in the 1990s." David Instone.

Villains

Henri Camara thought he was too good for a Championship-based Wolves and the fans don't hesitate to remind him of the fact. John McGinley, the Bolton striker who should have been sent off before condemning Wolves to defeat in the 1994/95 play-off semi-final.

Don't mention the…
A Birmingham-supporting bricky paved the words BLUES into a tiled floor just outside the turnstiles of Molineux. The word went unnoticed for four years. It has since been replaced.

The ground
Molineux Stadium is located just north of the city centre, close to the university, and is hard to miss. Although its current capacity is just over 29,000, there are plans to expand this to nearer 40,000. The stands were extensively rebuilt during the 1990s.

The **Stan Cullis Stand** way behind the goal was built on the site of the old North Bank in 1992. This large single-tier structure also houses the Terrace Bar and has a capacity of 5,174.

The **Billy Wright Stand** holds 8,350 and was built to replace the demolished Waterloo Road Stand in August 1993. This curving, two-tier stand offers great views but due to the curve, sits back from the pitch. It also houses the club offices and changing rooms. The team benches are out on the pitch-side away from the stand, making the pitch seem huge.

The **Jack Harris Stand** opened in 1993 to replace the South Bank. It's a single-tiered structure behind the goal to the right, looking from the tunnel. It can accommodate up to 5,345.

Seating 9,145, the **Steve Bull Stand** is the largest and was named after the Wolves legend in 2003. Again, a two-tiered curved seating area offers great views but is set back from the pitch. It's also home to 42 executive boxes running along the middle. The away fans have traditionally been seated here, in a block for up to 3,200 fans, at the end of the stand.

Getting there
By road/Parking Wolverhampton is easily accessed by the M6. From the north, leave at junction 12 (A5). At the roundabout take the third exit for the A5 west (Wolverhampton). At the next roundabout turn left onto the A449. Continue straight on the A449, passing under the M54. At Five Ways Roundabout, take the third exit onto Waterloo Road, the ground will be on your right. From the south, exit at junction 10 onto the A454 (Willenhall/Wolverhampton/

Wednesfield) and follow to the ring road. At Bilston Street Island take the fourth exit onto the A4150/ring road St David's and follow. Turn right onto Waterloo Road.

By train Wolverhampton's train station is less than a mile from the ground. Head left out of the station, left along Wednesfield Road and follow the ring road around to the left. The stadium will be on your right.

> Steve Bull, the Tipton Skin, Wolves all-time legend. Played for England including during Italia '90 World Cup.

HOME AWAY

Pubs for home fans
The city looks after its own, so most pubs cater toward the home crowd only, including The Wanderer right next to the ground. Decked out in Wolves colours, it heaves with home fans on match days – bouncers often operate a one in, one out policy. For a more mellow atmosphere and a cracking real ale, The Combermere Arms on Chapel Ash is good bet and not averse to small numbers of away fans.

Good food near ground
All the usual fast-food vans and takeaways are here, but the ground is close enough to the city centre to take your pick. The Staveley Fish Bar on nearby Staveley Road comes recommended.

Pubs for away fans
Not exactly an easy find – most pubs around the ground do not admit away fans, the same goes for a number of city centre pubs on match days. The wearing of colours is a definite no-no, as is turning up as part of a large group. The Litten Tree on Victoria Street in the city centre is pretty bog standard, but fairly friendly towards away fans.

Top tips
It's best not to advertise your 'away' status in the city centre or around the ground for that matter – keep your colours under wraps.

THE LAST WORD
wolvesheroes.com
wolves-mad.co.uk
the-wolf.co.uk
molineuxmix.co.uk

HEROES OR ZEROES?

⩘ HEROES OF THE TURF
Billy Wright, who earned 105 caps for England. Steve Bull's 306 goals helped Wolves to promotion almost single-handedly. Stan Culliss, player and manager of 25 years. Ron Flowers, with 49 England caps. Peter Broadbent was regarded by many as the most gifted Wolves player ever.

⩗ ZEROES OF THE TURF
Cédric Roussel, who cut the mustard briefly at Coventry but not at Wolves. Robert Taylor was a lot of money for someone who lived on the physio's couch. Havard Flo – another Bully-wannabee who fell miles short.

PUB QUIZ

That's quite interesting
"Wolves signing Nenad Milijaš was the only player at his old club Red Star Belgrade not to have his car trashed by the fans, as he was deemed the only one to be worthy." Shaun M, editor, Wolves MAD.

Not a lot of people know that
"Wolves' famous stadium clock is almost 75 years old. For almost a decade and a half from the late 1970s, it lay in rubble following the demolition of the old Molineux Street Stand before being spruced up and given a new home on the roof of the Stan Cullis Stand." David Instone.

- **Nicknames** The Chairboys
- **Founded** 1887
- **Ground** Adams Park (opened 1991)
- **Address** Hillbottom Road, High Wycombe HP12 4HJ
- **Capacity** 10,000
- **Best attendance** 10,000 vs Chelsea, friendly, July 13, 2005
- **Contact** 01494-472100
- **Ticket Number** 01494-441118
- **Email** wwfc@wwfc.com
- **Website** wycombewanderers.co.uk

PUB QUIZ

That's quite interesting
The unusual nickname,'The Chairboys' stems from the club's formation by a group of furniture makers.

Not a lot of people know that
Wycombe are the only League side in Buckinghamshire.

Superstitions and football sometimes go hand in hand, and anything that might give a club a psychological head start is likely to find a place in a team's routine, but a 5-ft wooden statue of a Native American? 'The Comanche' as it became known, was the club's lucky charm during a successful couple of seasons under Lawrie Sanchez. Its origins are very humble – the team were on their way to play Lincoln City on the final game of the 1999/2000 season, a game The Chairboys had to win to avoid relegation. On the way, they passed a second-hand shop with an American Indian in the window and it was decided that should they win, they would buy it for a mascot.

Wanderers scored in the 83rd minute to remain in the third tier of English football, so coach Terry Gibson found the statue and brought it to the club, much to the amusement of the players. It then became the lucky charm for the next couple of seasons; it was painted in the colours, given the squad number 31 and had pride of place in team photos and in the centre of the pitch before every home game. The following season was one of the most successful in club history with them reaching an FA Cup semi-final against the mighty Liverpool. However, when Sanchez and Gibson were eventually relieved of duties The Comanche disappeared with them. There have been rumours of it being in Scotland and appearing on eBay, and fans have even set up a Facebook group to help find it and return it to the ground. But the Comanche is still at large. The club is also famous for its surge out of non-league football and immediate promotion to the First Division under an inexperienced manager called Martin O'Neill. The club benefited from and helped launch one of the best home-grown managers of the last two decades, even without the help of the chief.

RIVALS

Colchester United, nothing to do with proximity but two very bad FA cup ties in the eighties and then an intense promotion campaign in 1991/1992 where they both vied for promotion to the Football League.

Greatest moments on this ground

"Although we've had many great moments over the years, strangely most of them have come away from home. For entertainment, a 5-3 victory over Brentford in the League in December 2001 and I also remember coming back from 2-0 down to draw 2-2 with West Brom in the FA Cup 2nd round in 1992. But the greatest moment, in the greatest game, was in January 2007 when José Mourinho's Chelsea came to town for the League Cup semi-final first leg; 1-0 down, a long ball from Martin was flicked on by Mooney to Easter who slotted home. It was magic." Phil Slatter, *The Wanderer*.

Lowest moments on this ground

"Losing 5-2 at home to Oldham in 2003 was horrific. One of Lawrie Sanchez's last games in charge saw us 1-0 down after 17 seconds and 3-0 down after about 20 minutes. The 'tactics' were so bad we made a double substitution just 25 minutes in." Phil Slatter.

Heroes of the sideline

"Nobody comes close to Martin O'Neil. Three successful Wembley finals, the Conference title and successive promotions in the early nineties." Phil Slatter.

Heroes of the turf

"Midfielder Dave Carroll earned the nickname 'Jesus' and, along with Keith Ryan, played in the non-League glory days as well as the FA Cup semi-final of 2001. Carroll scored 100 goals for Wanderers, and Rhino scored 50, with both players spending nearly all of their playing careers with the Blues. Steve Brown was also a fans' favourite. More recently, Roger Johnson was a promising youngster who has gone on to captain Cardiff in the 2008 FA Cup final and joined Birmingham for £5 million." Phil Slatter.

Mark West (scored the winner in the 1991 FA Trophy final), Steve Guppy, Mickey Bell, Terry Evans, Noel Ashford, Len Worley (known as the Stanley Matthews of non-league football), John Dellany, John Maskell and Jason Cousins.

The **Greene King IPA Terrace** (West) is the only standing area and is home to the core Wanderer's fans. Its low roof provides cover, focuses noise out onto the pitch and creates a great atmosphere.

The **The Dreams Stand** (East) is home to the away support and is all-seating. It is thankfully covered and the low roof provides a good atmosphere for visiting fans.

Getting there

By road/Parking Most fans arriving by car will be travelling along the M40 and should turn off at junction 4, following signs for Aylesbury along the A4010. Continue along this road and, at the fourth roundabout, turn left into Lane End Road. The ground is signposted, occasionally just labelled 'London Wasps'. Continue along this road into Hillbottom Road. There's a large car park that's well signposted near the ground and there are several other car parks within the industrial estate all within easy walking distance.

By train Wycombe station is a fair distance away; travelling fans either need to take a taxi or a match-day bus (times vary so check the club's website for times).

∧ Wycombe vs Leyton Orient at Brisbane Road, May 2010.

Zeroes of the turf

"Chris Sutton's younger brother John signed for us in 2007 and we were promised bagfuls of goals from him. He managed just six in his only full season and was released from his contract where he want back to the SPL." Phil Slatter.

Villains

"Colchester manager Roy McDonough and Colchester in general!" Charles Holnes.

The ground

Adams Park was opened in 1996 and is located on the edge of the town of High Wycombe, in the Sands Industrial Estate. It is named after Frank Adams, the man who donated the club its original ground, Loakes Park. The ground has a restricted capacity of 10,000 due to council regulations, which means it is never full, and is shared with Premier League rugby team Wasps. There are plans afoot for both teams to move to a purpose-built 15,000 stadium in the future, but nothing is finalized.

The **Frank Adams Stand** is an impressive two-tier stand with executive boxes between. It dominates the rest of the stadium and wouldn't look out of place in a higher division.

Opposite is a much less impressive single-tier stand, the **Bucks New University Stand**. The seating area is raised above pitch level and the view is excellent for the home fans seated there. The stand also has a row of boxes along the back.

Last-minute, wind-assisted winner by Colchester United goalkeeper Scott Barrett in injury time during the hotly contested promotion campaign in the 1991/1992 season.

Pubs for home fans
The ground is situated on an industrial estate on the edge of town, which means there are few pubs close by. Home fans tend to stay in town to drink or head to the supporters' club bar at the ground. There is a pub 15 minutes away in Sands called The Hourglass.

Good food near ground
Being on an industrial estate, food near the ground is limited to burger vans; if you want a decent feed pre-match, stop before you reach the area or go into town.

Pubs for away fans
The Hourglass, mentioned above, will allow away fans in as long as it isn't a derby, and there is a bouncer on the door who will refuse entry if he sees fit.

Top tips
If you want a bite to eat before the game, get it on the way and don't wait until you've parked – options are very limited.

THE LAST WORD

chairboys.co.uk
gasroom.co.uk

HOME COLOURS

YEOVIL TOWN

- ☺ **Nicknames** The Glovers
- ☺ **Founded** 1895
- ☺ **Ground** Huish Park (opened 1990)
- ☺ **Address** Lufton Way, Yeovil, Somerset BA22 8YF
- ☺ **Capacity** 9,665
- ☺ **Best attendance** 9,527 vs Leeds United, League One, April 25, 2005
- ☺ **Contact** 01935-423 662
- ☺ **Ticket Number** 01935-847 888
- ☺ **Email** ticketoffice@ytfc.net
- ☺ **Website** ytfc.net

Yeovil Town FC have struck fear into top-flight football clubs for years. Every time the balls go into the bag for the FA Cup 3rd round draw the top League sides have their fingers crossed that they will not be boarding a coach bound for the West Country. The notorious sloping pitch and the famous giant-killing reputation were, for years, the hallmark of this Somerset team. Since 1949 The Glovers have been punching well above their weight in the world's greatest domestic cup competition. The first giant killing was probably the greatest. Sunderland were the visitors – at the time they were known as the 'Bank of England' side due to the expense and outlay spent assembling their squad. However, in front of 16,000 of Somerset's finest they were well and truly dumped out of the 1949 FA Cup. It's still considered one of the greatest giant-killing achievements of all time. From then on Yeovil's reputation was set, and the distinctive sloping pitch was part of football folklore.

The club has, however, started to make strides away from the label of mere giant killers, and since the mid-seventies the aim has been to become part of the football elite themselves. The Glovers grew in stature over the next two decades and began challenging for a place in the Football League with resilient and consistent performances on the pitch. It took until the new millennium for the non-league outfit to achieve this dream of league status. A victory over Stevenage in the FA Trophy in 2001 was followed a year later by promotion to League Two, and then onto League One. This progress necessitated a move away from the original Huish – with its slope and history of David versus Goliath struggles – to the Groundstone site and an all-new stadium named Huish Park. The slope may have gone, but there is still an air of romance around the little Somerset club that puts fear into all – especially Premier League teams come the FA Cup 3rd round draw.

RIVALS

Weymouth are the biggest rivals from non-League days, but meetings now are rare so Yeovil look towards the Bristol teams, although this is a recent rivalry and not that fierce.

HOME AWAY

Pubs for home fans
The Archers is one of only a few pubs within a 10- to 20-minute radius of the ground, it's more of a home fan pub, although away fans are not excluded.

Good food near ground
The pubs all serve food, either bar snacks or full meals. There's also an Asda close by with a café. Around the ground and within it there are also the usual fast-food joints.

Pubs for away fans
There are few pubs close to the ground, The Arrow is large and has a mix of fans and serves some food, The Bell is a short drive away, or a 20-minute walk on Preston Road (turn right at the second roundabout on Bunford Lane); it too serves food. Towards town the Fleur-De-Lis and Half Moon are both decent pubs, which also serve food. However, as most away fans do before arriving in Yeovil, it's often best to stop in a neighbouring village for a pint and some grub and enjoy the Somerset hospitality.

Top tips
If you're travelling by car, it may be worth stopping off in one of the surrounding villages for a pint and something to eat, as the options in the suburbs close to the ground are not great.

Greatest moments on this ground
"The win over Sunderland in 1949 is probably the greatest-ever moment at home, although I don't know anyone who was there. In my time, more recently, there were many great games in the promotion season out of the Conference, although we won by 17 points, finally making it into the League was amazing, lifting the League Two Championship caps it all though." Simon Hodge.

Lowest moments on this ground
"The year prior to our promotion to the Football League we missed out on promotion to Rushden and Diamonds, losing or drawing a number of silly games. The home draw against Rushden when we could have gone top was a massive let down." Simon Hodge.

Heroes of the sideline
Gary Johnson was the man who finally saw the dream of Yeovil becoming a Football League team realized, he also won the FA Trophy in his first season and then went on to take them into League One. In the mists of time, player-manager Alec Stock is well remembered for his famous victory over Sunderland.

Don't mention the…

Mid-seventies; Yeovil were the best non-league side by far and just missed out on election to the Football League by only a handful of votes.

The ground

Huish Park is a compact, modern ground, unremarkable in appearance but with an excellent atmosphere. Although its capacity is on the small side, the ground has been developed so it could be expanded to around 20,000 should the club rise through the divisions further.

The Augusta West Stand is all seated and has a single tier with a row of a dozen executive boxes at the back straddling the halfway line. A modern stand, there are no obstructions; it's for home fans only.

Opposite is another covered, single-tier, all-seated stand of roughly the same proportions. **The Cowlin Stand** does not have any executive boxes and incorporates some away seating. These away fans sit towards the Copse Road Terrace End.

The Copse Road Terrace is an open area of traditional terrace that houses the core of the away support. It offers a rare chance for visiting fans, especially those from the upper divisions, to take a trip down memory lane and stand up! It offers a great view, but is open to the elements, so bring protection in the winter.

At the opposite end is **The Blackthorn Terrace**. It's another area of standing-only, which is home to the core Yeovil supporters. It benefits from a roof and is where most of the noise comes from during a game.

Getting there

By road/Parking Arriving in the area along the A303, visiting fans should turn off at the Cartgate roundabout (signposted Yeovil, Dorchester and Weymouth) and take the A3088 towards Yeovil (Huish Park is also signposted). Follow this road until you reach a roundabout with an airfield directly in front. Turn left into Bunford Lane (again signposted for Huish Park), and continue along this road across several roundabouts

until you pass Asda. Take the next left, again signposted. From the south, approach the town on the A37. At the junction with the A30 turn left and continue along this road until the roundabout with the A3088. Take the A3088 to the first roundabout and continue on this road. At the next roundabout go straight onto Bunford Lane, and at the next roundabout continue straight up Western Avenue. After about a mile you will see the ground on the left; start looking for parking. There's some street parking in the area, but there's also a large match-day car park, which costs £2.

By train There are two railway stations in Yeovil – Yeovil Junction and Pen Mill Junction. They're both some distance away, so either get a taxi, or catch a bus into the town centre and then a bus out to the ground from the bus station.

That's quite interesting
When Portuguese player Hugo Rodriguez played for Yeovil in the 2003/2004 season he was the tallest player in the League at 6 ft 8 in.

Not a lot of people know that
Cricketer Ian Botham had a brief spell with the club in 1985.

prideofsomerset.co.uk
ciderspace.co.uk

▼ Paul Terry, Kevin Gall and Phil Jevons celebrate the winning goal at Southend United, April 30, 2005

GETTY IMAGES

HEROES OR ZEROES?

⌃ HEROES OF THE TURF
Terry Skiverton scored 44 goals on the way to Yeovil's promotion to the Football League. Also Len Harris, Dave Taylor, Gavin Williams, Adam Lockwood, Chris Weale, Darren Way, Terrell Forbes, Lee Peltier, Warren Patmore and Dave Halliday.

⌄ ZEROES OF THE TURF
"Having been a non-league side for years, we certainly weren't watching Premiership-standard players every week, but they all came out and most of the time gave everything for Yeovil, so calling any of them Zeroes would be unfair. We've never been in the position to spend £10 million on a player who's rubbish unfortunately, unlike half the Premiership, who seem to do so every season!" Simon Hodge.

VILLAINS
The Football League between the fifties and seventies voted to keep Yeovil from entering the professional ranks on numerous occasions, despite the fact that they had all the credentials needed to do so.

Credits

Footprint credits

Project Editor: Alan Murphy
Design and production: Angus Dawson
Picture Editor: Demi Taylor
Editors: Jen Haddington, Damian Hall

Managing Director: Andy Riddle
Commercial Director: Patrick Dawson
Publisher: Alan Murphy
Publishing Managers: Felicity Laughton,
Jo Williams, Jen Haddington
Digital Editor: Alice Jell
Design: Rob Lunn
Marketing: Liz Harper, Hannah Bonnell
Sales: Jeremy Parr
Advertising: Renu Sibal
Finance & administration: Elizabeth Taylor

Print

Manufactured in India by Nutech
Pulp from sustainable forests

The views expressed in this book are the views of the
contributors and do not necessarily reflect the views of
the author or the publisher. While every effort has been
made to ensure that the facts in this book are accurate,
the author and publisher cannot accept responsibility
for any loss, injury or inconvenience however caused.

Publishing information

Around the Grounds
1st edition
© Footprint Handbooks Ltd
August 2010

ISBN 978-1-906098-77-3
CIP DATA: A catalogue record for this book is available
from the British Library

® Footprint Handbooks and the Footprint mark are a
registered trademark of Footprint Handbooks Ltd

Published by Footprint

6 Riverside Court
Lower Bristol Road
Bath BA2 3DZ, UK
T +44 (0)1225 469141
F +44 (0)1225 469461
footprinttravelguides.com

Distributed in North America by
Globe Pequot Press

Additional image credits:
Front cover: Getty Images; back cover: Getty Images.
Pages 1, 6, 118, 120, 124, 128, 130, 131: Getty Images;
page 117: Popperfoto/Getty Images; page 122: Andrew
Holt; page 136: Man Utd via Getty Images.